SHRM ◆ **BNA Series**

Employee
and
Labor Relations

Employee and Labor Relations

John A. Fossum
Editor

Jerauld Mattson
Consulting Editor

The Bureau of National Affairs, Inc., Washington, D.C.

Copyright © 1990
The Bureau of National Affairs, Inc.

Library of Congress Cataloging-in-Publication Data

Employee and labor relations / John A. Fossum, editor ; Jerauld
Mattson, consulting editor.
    p. cm. — (SHRM/BNA series ; 4)
    Includes indexes.
    ISBN 0-87179-604-X
    1. Industrial relations—United States. I. Fossum, John A.
II. Mattson, Jerauld. III. Bureau of National Affairs (Washington,
D.C.)   IV. Series: ASPA/BNA series; 4.
HF5549.A9574   1988 vol. 4
[HD8072.5]
658.3 s—dc20
[658.3'15]

                                              90-41668
                                                 CIP

Published by BNA Books, 1231 25th St., N.W., Washington, D.C. 20037

Printed in the United States of America
International Standard Book Number: 0-87179-604-X

Preface

It has been 15 years since the first volume of the original ASPA Handbook of Personnel and Industrial Relations was published. A great deal has changed in our profession since then. No longer is PAIR (personnel and industrial relations) the accepted acronym for the management of human resources, primarily because our roles and our accountabilities are so different. And just as the acronyms have changed to reflect the evolving role of the human resource professional, so too has the society which represents them.

In late 1989, the members of ASPA, which stood for the American Society for Personnel Administration, adopted a new name: the Society for Human Resource Management, or SHRM. There were three basic reasons for this change: Members were no longer merely administrators, but important players in the corporate hierarchy; member representation had expanded throughout the world; and more and more frequently their titles said human resource management.

Human resource executives have been broadening their horizons and learning new ways to make a bigger contribution to their organizations. So, too, does the focus of this new HRM (human resource management) series indicate the extent to which the field has changed and how pace-setting human resource executives have been reshaping management practice. We have tried to reflect those changes in this new series.

The original series was eight volumes with a heavy emphasis on "how-to-do-it." This new series, comprised of six volumes, focuses more heavily on the why than the how, on strategy and integration rather than the specifics of execution.

The very process we used to develop this series indicates the shift in orientation. Each of the six volumes had a different well-known academician as its editor. These individuals were supported by at least one consulting editor, a senior practitioner in the HRM field whose role was to provide the "real world" perspective so necessary to this kind of project. And the overall series was guided by an editorial advisory board made up of practitioners, academicians, and representatives of BNA and SHRM. Members of the editorial advisory board are listed opposite the title page of this Volume.

Collectively, we struggled through the development of each volume and its chapters, striving to achieve the proper balance between a macro perspective of the profession and an evolutionary approach to the material presented. Our target audience—middle to upper level practitioners and those who aspire to such positions—was a constant presence during all of our discussions.

The six volumes in this series and their key players are:

1. *Human Resource Management: Evolving Roles and Responsibilities* edited by Lee Dyer, professor at Cornell University with Jerry Holder, retired vice president of human resources for Marion Laboratories, as consulting editor. Additional consulting editors included Robert Berra of Monsanto, Leo Contois of Consolidated Foods (retired) and Garth Dimon of Bristol-Meyers.

2. *Human Resource Planning, Employment and Placement* edited by Wayne Cascio, professor at the University of Colorado with Donald Sweet of Hawkins Associates, Inc. as consulting editor.

3. *Compensation and Benefits* edited by Luis R. Gomez-Mejia, professor at the University of Colorado with consulting editors Ray Olsen of TRW and George Milkovich of Cornell University.

4. *Employee and Labor Relations* edited by John Fossum, professor, University of Minnesota, with Jerauld Mattson of International Multifoods as consulting editor.

5. *Developing Human Resources* edited by Kenneth N. Wexley, professor, Michigan State University with John Hinrichs of Management Decision Systems as consulting editor.

6. *Managing Human Resources in the Information Age* with Randall S. Schuler of New York University as editor and James Walker of Walker and Associates as consulting editor.

This new management series reflects the coming of age of human resource management. SHRM is grateful to the individuals whose work is reflected in its pages and proud to mark this professional transition with such an outstanding series.

Ronald C. Pilenzo
Alexandria, VA
June 1990

Introduction

The ASPA Handbook of Personnel and Industrial Relations was published in 1979. During the intervening decade, ASPA has become SHRM (Society for Human Resource Management) and personnel and industrial relations has been replaced for this volume by human resource management. Concurrently, the service economy has grown at a robust rate, union membership has fallen, and the stability of the employment relationship has been severely disrupted.

Authors of the 1979 volume's portion on employee and labor relations offered chapters on unions and worker participation, the role of industrial relations associations in personnel and industrial relations, employee relations in nonunion environments, labor relations in the public sector, collective bargaining, contract administration, and the role of third parties in labor relations.

This current volume reflects some of the changes in emphasis that have occurred during the intervening period. The current volume's chapters focus on the new structure of collective bargaining, the emphasis on and effects of industrial relations on firm performance, the increasingly combative arena surrounding union organizing activities, developments in due process in employee relations, cooperation and participation programs, and employee health and safety.

The chapters in this volume have been written by some of the top authorities in their specialties within the employee relations field. Peter Cappelli is widely seen as the first scholar to recognize the emerging pattern of union concessions that dominated the early and middle parts of the 1980s. Morris Kleiner has written extensively on the effects of industrial relations practices and programs on various organizational performance measures. John Lawler produced some of the earliest and best analytical work on the effects of employer campaign activities on the outcomes of union organizing efforts. Judy Olian has written numerous publications on the effects of employment environments on individual health and the interaction of environmental and genetic factors. Michael Schuster conducted the most thorough early research on gainsharing programs and has made these results accessible to managers and union officials through a number of practical articles drawing from the results of his research. Finally, Elizabeth Wesman is known for her work on equal employment opportunity and Dana Eischen has extensive experience in rights arbitration.

The editors and authors of the ASPA Handbook were trenchant participants and observers of employee relations during the period in which they wrote their chapters—the late 1970s. We would fail both to honor them and to benefit from their expertise if we did not recall what they saw as important points to emphasize to handbook readers of that earlier volume.

A Retrospective Look at Employee Relations

In looking at union and worker participation, John J. Flagler and William A. Schroeder noted, at Chapter 7.1 in the ASPA Handbook, the involvement of unions in the training and retraining of their members. Unfortunately, most of the examples from that period reflected primarily union efforts. It was not until unions were able to obtain retraining for displaced workers as a quid pro quo for concessions during the 1980s that this issue began to be important to management as well.

Health care facilities, pensions, financial services, and housing were all offered by some unions during the 1970s. Unions and employers are cooperatively addressing issues related to health care benefits due to their increasing cost and complexity. Health benefits appear to be the most critical issue for employees during the present time since concessions in this area are the most strongly resisted. Pensions is an issue requiring more frequent participation and bargaining since the assets of a pension plan can potentially be used to the disadvantage of present employees in financing takeovers. Many of the services that unions provided to their members in the 1970s may be used more often in the 1990s to encourage nonrepresented employees to become associate members of unions. Access to services such as credit unions, group health care plans, and prepaid advocate services would be potential lures for unorganized workers.

Joint labor-management responsibility for health and safety, productivity, and substance abuse treatment programs has grown as these have been related increasingly to both firm performance and individual employee welfare. Joint management, however, has not moved appreciably closer than existed in the 1970s. In fact, the

United States has probably less employee involvement in decision-making than any of the industrialized nations. This lack of use of employee intelligence, when compared with other industrialized nations, may account for the relatively low productivity growth we have recently experienced and the relatively low cognitive skills possessed by U.S. production employees—since employers are unlikely to create or foster work environments in which they would be used.

Employee relations in unorganized firms have developed rapidly during the 1980s with many firms enhancing communications programs and expanding their use of attitude surveys. Over the period, employers have been much more active and successful in union avoidance programs.

Public sector bargaining was completing its decade of adolescence in the 1970s with major experimentation with the "drug" of choice—interest arbitration. Legislators, managements, and unions tried each new version and clamored for modifications to the rules anytime the other side won. The 1980s have been a decade of increased maturity with decreasing numbers of public sector impasses but with more organization of public sector employees.

Reed C. Richardson argued, in "Positive Collective Bargaining" at p. 7-105 in the last volume, that collective bargaining should become much more goal oriented. Work done by Audrey Freedman[1] and Tom Kochan[2] suggested that employers were largely responsive to union demands in the 1970s. But Freedman's[3] later research in the early 1980s found management taking a more proactive stance in negotiations; that is, establishing goals and bargaining successfully toward them. Granted, the economic climate was substantially in its favor, but the thrust of bargaining reflected much more management initiative than earlier periods.

In the present volume, contract administration has been expanded to deal with a host of due process issues. With increased employer and governmental regulation of employee behavior through drug and chemical substance abuse laws, and employees more frequently using tort remedies for perceived unfair employer

---

[1]Freedman, A. *Managing Labor Relations*. (New York: Conference Board, 1979).

[2]Freedman, A. *The New Look in Wage Policy and Employee Relations*. (New York: Conference Board, 1985).

[3]Kochan, T.A. *Collective Bargaining and Industrial Relations*. (Homewood, IL: Richard D. Irwin, 1980).

conduct, due process becomes an increasingly important issue for management.

Third parties are somewhat less frequently used than they were during the 1970s—probably due to the low level of strikes and the use of other mechanisms by employers and unions to pressure each other. Unknown or little used at the beginning of the 1970s were corporate campaigns, the wholesale replacement of striking employees with scab laborers, and the use of bankruptcy law to abrogate contracts.

An Overview

Employees of the 1990s are members of a far more diverse group than their compatriots of the late 1970s. Substantially greater variance exists in almost every measurement. There is greater education and achievement among higher level employees and lower skills and literacy among the lower levels. Real income has not risen appreciably over the past decade, but the inequality of income distribution has increased greatly.

Much of what was written in the 1979 volume should have been taken to heart—and some was. If we do not more fully utilize and develop our human resources in the 1990s, we may not be asked to write a volume for the 2000 decade—rather we will import our knowledge to manage employment just as we import much of our energy and durable goods now.

John A. Fossum
Minneapolis, MN
May 1990

About the Authors

Chapter 4.1

Employee and Labor Relations in an Evolving Environment

John A. Fossum (Ph.D., Michigan State University) is a professor of industrial relations, chairman of the Graduate Faculty in Industrial Relations, and Director of the Industrial Relations Center at the University of Minnesota. Prior to his position at Minnesota, he was on the business faculty at the University of Michigan, and earlier was manager of personnel research for Control Data Corporation. He is currently the chair of the University Council of Industrial Relations and Human Resource Programs, a consortium of universities offering IR/HRM degrees. He is the author of over 40 articles and book chapters and 13 books and monographs, one of which is *Labor Relations: Development, Structure, Process,* a widely adopted college and university text; and between 1988 and 1990 was consulting editor for the *Academy of Management Journal.*

The author wishes to thank Kim Scow for her assistance in obtaining sources used in the preparation of this chapter.

Chapter 4.2

The Role of Industrial Relations in Industrial Performance

Morris M. Kleiner (Ph.D., University of Illinois) is a chaired professor of labor policy at the Humphrey Institute of Public Affairs and a member of the Graduate Faculty in Industrial Relations at the University of Minnesota. Professor Kleiner is Director of the Humphrey Institute's Center for Labor Policy. Prior to assuming his position at Minnesota, Kleiner was a faculty member in the School of Business at the University of Kansas. Professor Kleiner has also served as an associate in employment policy at the Brookings Institution, was a visiting scholar in the Department of Economics at Harvard University, and since 1983 has been a research economist with the National Bureau of Economic Research. He has published many articles and is the co-author of *Labor Markets and Human Resource Management* and a co-editor of the 1987 IRRA research volume, *Human Resources and the Performance of the Firm.*

Chapter 4.3

Union-Management Cooperation

Michael Schuster (Ph.D.) is a professor of management and human resources at Syracuse University and is a former Fulbright Scholar from the London School of Economics. Dr. Schuster publishes and consults in the areas of strategic human resource planning, gainsharing and competitive compensation strategies, and cooperation and change in union environments. More than 100 American and 20 British companies have participated in his research and consulting. Dr. Schuster has published more than fifty articles and has authored two books. In 1984, Dr. Schuster founded his consulting company *Competitive Human Resources Strategies* with the mission of developing human resource strategies that more effectively facilitate the achievement of strategic business and operating objectives.

Chapter 4.4

Due Process

Elizabeth C. Wesman (Ph.D., New York State School of Industrial and Labor Relations, Cornell University) is an associate professor of personnel and labor relations at the Syracuse University School of Management. In addition to her teaching she is a part-time labor arbitrator. Dr. Wesman has published several articles on employment discrimination, particularly in the area of comparable worth. Her current research interests include problems faced by hospitals as care givers to, and employers of, persons with AIDS, and international comparisons of pay equity legislation and implementation. She is also co-author, with Mr. Eischen, of a forthcoming text on labor contract administration.

Dana Edward Eischen (M.S., New York State School of Industrial and Labor Relations, Cornell University; J.D., Georgetown University Law Center) has more than 15 years experience as a full-time labor arbitrator in both the private and the public sectors. In addition, he has served as Special Assistant to the National Mediation Board, and as a member of two Presidential Emergency Boards. His publications include "Representation Disputes and Their Resolution in the Railroad and Airline Industries" in *The Railway Labor Act at Fifty*, and "The Arbitration Hearing: Administration, Conduct and Procedures" in *Labor and Employment Arbitration*.

Chapter 4.5

Union Organizing and Representation

John J. Lawler (Ph.D., University of California-Berkeley) is an associate professor at the Institute of Labor and Industrial Relations, University of Illinois (Urbana-Champaign). Prior to his current appointment, he was a faculty member at the Industrial Relations Center, University of Minnesota. Professor Lawler's interests include union organizing and employer opposition, information technology and expert systems applications in the human resource management field, and human resource strategies and management practices in multinational firms. He has published articles in such journals as *Industrial Relations, Industrial and Labor Relations Review, Administrative Science Quarterly,* and the *Journal of Applied Psychology.* His recently completed book, *Unionization and Deunionization: Strategy, Tactics, and Outcomes,* examines union and employer strategy formulation and implementation in connection with organizing and counter-organizing activity.

Chapter 4.6

Collective Bargaining

Peter Cappelli (D., Phil Oxford University) is the Joseph Wharton Associate Professor of Management at the Wharton School of the University of Pennsylvania and is Co-Director of the Center for Human Resources at Wharton. Professor Cappelli has degrees in industrial relations from Cornell University and Labor Economics from Oxford University where he was a Fulbright Scholar. He was also a Guest Scholar at the Brookings Institution and a 1987 German Marshall Fellow. Professor Cappelli served on the staff of the Secretary of Labor's Commission on Workforce Quality and Labor Market Efficiency in 1988 and 1989. He has served on the faculties at MIT, the University of Illinois, and the University of California-Berkeley and has published widely on issues of union-management relations and human resources.

Chapter 4.7

Workplace Safety and Employee Health

Judy D. Olian (Ph.D., University of Wisconsin) is associate professor of management and organization at the Maryland Business School, University of Maryland. In addition to her interests in the health and safety management area, her published research has focused on organizational staffing processes, mentoring relationships, and strategically oriented human resource management systems. Dr. Olian consults in these areas for public and private sector clients in the U.S. and internationally.

The author wishes to thank John Fossum for his support and helpful comments throughout the drafting of this chapter.

Contents

Preface   v

Introduction   vii

4.1   Employee and Labor Relations in an Evolving Environment   4-1
John A. Fossum

The Historical Evolution of Employment   4-1
Definitions of Employment, Labor Relations, and Employee
    Relations   4-5
Alternative Approaches to Understanding the Employment
    Relationship   4-12
Societal Issues and Employee Relations   4-14
Possible Scenarios for the Future   4-19

4.2   The Role of Industrial Relations in Industrial Performance   4-23
Morris M. Kleiner

Linkages Between HRM and Organizational
    Performance   4-24
Impact of Unionization on Industrial Performance   4-26
Union Policies Related to Industrial Performance   4-29
Impact of HR Policies on Organizational Performance   4-32
Future Research Requirements   4-38
Conclusions   4-39

4.3   Union-Management Cooperation   4-44
Michael Schuster

Evolution of Union-Management Cooperation   4-44
Present Stimulus for Union-Management
    Cooperation   4-46

The Process of Cooperation and Change in Union
        Environments   4-49
Forms of Union-Management Cooperation   4-56
The Success and Failure of American Cooperation   4-72
Conclusions   4-76

4.4   Due Process   4-82

Elizabeth C. Wesman
Dana Edward Eischen

Legal Basis of Due Process   4-82
Collective Bargaining Agreement Procedures vs. Unilateral
        Appeals Mechanisms   4-84
Statutory Entitlement to Due Process   4-89
Employees' Rights to Privacy   4-94
Employees' Rights and Access to Personnel Records   4-111
Discipline and Discharge   4-115
Conclusion   4-118

4.5   Union Organizing and Representation   4-134

John J. Lawler

Union Growth and Decline   4-135
Government Regulations of the Organizing Process   4-141
Management and Union Strategy   4-157
Unionization and Deunionization Strategies in
        Practice   4-161
Research Findings   4-167
Conclusion   4-172

4.6   Collective Bargaining   4-180

Peter Cappelli

Changes in the Environment for Bargaining   4-180
Collective Bargaining   4-186
Outcomes in Collective Bargaining   4-193
The Union Response   4-205
Conclusions   4-209

4.7   Workplace Safety and Employee Health   4-218

Judy D. Olian

Present Trends   4-218
Impetus for Workplace Health and Safety Programs   4-221
Present Issues in Wellness and Safety   4-241
Managerial Interventions   4-253
Conclusions   4-276

Author Index   4-287

Subject Index   4-295

4.1

Employee and Labor Relations in an Evolving Environment

John A. Fossum

The manner in which employee and labor relations take place has changed markedly during the 1980s and can be expected to continue evolving through the 1990s. The past decade brought significant turbulence to labor relations as a result of a major political reorientation, the actual emergence of the long-predicted global economy, and the final additions of the baby boom to the labor supply. On the economic side, employers extracted considerable deceleration, if not an actual stoppage or decline, in wage growth. At the same time, major restructurings within and between units of organizations dramatically altered promotional opportunities and job design. The explosion of information technology innovations enabled trimming layers of management while advancing the skill requirements of lower-level jobs. All of these changes have altered expectations of employees regarding employment and employee relations policies. The changes have also required that organizations approach the design and implementation of these policies much more carefully than they have in the past. To help examine the evolving role of employee relations, this chapter defines employee and labor relations, explores various perspectives on the employment relationship, and suggests a set of issues that will occupy practitioners in the 1990s.

The Historical Evolution of Employment

Employment is pervasive. This ubiquity has not always existed and during periods in which it has, employment has not necessarily taken the form found at present. Prior to the Industrial Revolution, most individuals were involved in agriculture or household production. On occasion, one had need to purchase goods or services from a craftsman, but large employment establishments did not exist. Families with sufficient members to keep the household going often apprenticed or indentured children to an employing craftsman to learn a trade in exchange for food and shelter.

The Industrial Revolution and the Rise of Employment

With the coming of the Industrial Revolution, technological developments allowed substantial returns to investment in capital and simplified production techniques for many products. Division of labor reduced skill needs. The creation of plants to house large machines required employing large numbers of workers in one location. Continuing division of labor made workers readily replaceable since learning time was short and several employees performed similar types of tasks.

These changes in the world of work had inevitable short- and long-term consequences. In the early 19th century, Luddites destroyed a number of British factories in an attempt to eliminate the machinery that they felt had laid waste to their lives.[1] Ever since, resistance to the introduction or sabotage of production equipment has evoked memories of the Luddite extremists.

Other reactions also took place during the 19th century. The advocacy of socialism and communism was, in part, a protest against the concentration of capital and the workplace conditions that helped to create and support it. Employers' hiring of security forces, calls for militia, and uses of injunctions and other legal maneuvers[2] helped to hone a working-class consciousness in industrialized countries. Trade unions began to develop, seeking to counterbalance the power of employers. Through collectivizing employees, unions empowered the withholding of labor and prevented hiring through strikes and picketing. Triggers for these collective actions included long hours, arbitrary employer discipline procedures, foremen with too much decision-making power, unsafe working conditions, and employer initiatives to cut wages whenever economic problems occurred.

While this type of environment characterized many plants throughout the 18th and 19th centuries, some new initiatives in employee relations also developed. Robert Owen, a Utopian

Socialist, established a factory in New Lanark, Scotland together with a company town. Unlike other employers who established factory towns, Owen offered a clean environment, did not employ significant numbers of children, provided a public school for children of the workers, established a primitive performance measurement and feedback system, and initiated an early version of an "open door" policy.[3]

During the early part of the 19th century, relatively little of the turmoil that was engulfing Europe occurred in the United States. Factory employment formed a relatively smaller factor in the economy and westward expansion was still continuing. Immigration was beginning to pick up as many Europeans fled factory environments, oppressive governments, and hereditary class systems. It was not until the later parts of the 19th century, after the railroads had laid track from coast to coast, slavery had been abolished, and the steel and coal mining industries had been established, that employee relations and labor organizations began to increase in importance. A number of major strikes took place, labor rallies were held, and new unions were organized during the 1870s through the 1890s. Employers, together with governments and often urged on by the newspapers, resisted strongly. Union activists were imprisoned, union activities were enjoined, and strikers were summarily fired. Employment at will was legally recognized. Employees frequently worked long hours, were hired and fired arbitrarily and capriciously, and children were employed in dangerous and unhealthy jobs. While unions made some progress in gaining a say in the workplace, this advance largely occurred among skilled craft workers. Industrial employees, on the other hand, had little advocacy or representation outside of the Wobblies (Industrial Workers of the World).

The 20th Century and Emergence of Employee Relations

In the beginning of the 1900s and following the first World War, employment patterns in the U.S. underwent some substantial changes. First, Henry Ford began offering $5 a day for assembly workers in his Detroit operations. Mass production had become a reality. Machinery had become capable of producing parts with tolerances close enough that mechanical gear no longer required custom fabrication and assembly. The assembly line had arrived. Ford's $5 per day allowed potential gains from motivated workers. Essentially unskilled employees could perform well on the assembly line with relatively little training. At the offered wage, workers found no attractive alternatives. Thus, employees needed to work hard and follow directions in order to retain their positions and continue earning the premium daily wage.

Second, through the scientific management movement, Frederick Taylor and other industrial engineers created new ways of looking at work. Division of labor had already led to production efficiencies, but how people performed tasks and methods to enhance productivity within present job designs received greater attention.

Third, while some industries remained highly concentrated, antitrust laws enabled competition in all industries. How managers organized plants, designed jobs, and directed their work forces could make a difference in the profitability of an enterprise. Job progression, job training, and employee development within the organization began to evolve among some employers. The internal labor market arose as a result. How employers decided eligibility for training and promotion became very important to employees. Lack of access condemned an individual to little economic optimism throughout one's working life. Organizations with advancement opportunities sowed the seed of employee commitment toward accomplishing organizational goals.

Some organizations began the early practice of personnel management with the creation of positions such as social secretary.[4] These employees held the responsibility of creating internal welfare systems to look to the recreational needs of employees and deal with catastrophic events in employees' lives. To an extent, these activities served as precursors of employee assistance programs (EAPs).

In the 1920s, the success of the American Federation of Labor (AFL) in organizing employees during World War I prompted many employers to establish company unions or employee associations. Using the American Plan or the Mohawk Valley Formula, employers sought employee and local area support to prevent union organizing.[5] However, as the 1920s gave way to the Depression of the 1930s and unemployment became rampant, employees and unions became more militant. They began to bargain collectively not only for wages, but also to overcome what they viewed as employers' excessive power in making employment decisions such as promotions, job assignments, layoffs, discipline for rules infractions, firings, and the like.

The 1930s saw several significant laws and regulations enacted. For the first time, employees were guaranteed the right to organize and to bargain collectively. The National Labor Relations Board was established to investigate charges of unfair labor practices. The law required employers whose employees had become represented to bargain with unions over wages, hours, and terms and conditions of employment. To bargain collectively meant negotiating to attempt not only to achieve a contract, but also to administer jointly the contract during its effective period. Collective bargaining guaranteed employees a voice in the design and implementation of the employment relationship. As collective bargaining began to enhance employees' input on how the workplace should be organized and operated, some nonunion employers began to incorporate aspects of unionized employee relations into their personnel policies and practices.

Additional legislation passed during the 1940s and 1950s placed further regulations on the collective bargaining relationship. Civil rights laws and regulations in the 1960s and 1970s and health and safety legislation in the 1970s also structured the governance of the workplace and the practice of employee relations. Tables 1, 2, and 3 summarize the major provisions of labor relations, civil rights, and health and safety laws and regulations.

Definitions of Employment, Labor Relations, and Employee Relations

In its most essential form, employment is the exchange of labor for pay. Employees do not normally own their places of employment. Employees come to the organization with certain levels of knowledge, skills, and abilities (KSAs) which employers expect to use together with capital and raw materials to produce products and services. An employer normally determines the tasks, duties, and responsibilities (TDRs) of a job and hires employees with KSAs necessary to perform them. As a result, an employer has a good idea about what a job entails, how it's going to be done, and what employee qualities are necessary to do it.

The TDRs of some jobs, however, particularly those of executives and some professional employees, are not entirely clear to employers. Owners of organizations may hire executives and professionals to accomplish certain results and depend on the expertise of

Table 1

Labor Relations Laws and Regulations

Law	Coverage	Major Provisions	Federal Agencies
Railway Labor Act (1926)	Nonmanagerial rail and airline employees and employers in private sector.	Employees may choose bargaining representative for collective bargaining, no yellow-dog contracts, dispute settlement procedures including mediation, arbitration, and emergency boards.	National Mediation Board, National Board of Adjustment.
Norris-LaGuardia Act (1932)	All private sector employers and labor organizations.	Outlaws injunctions for nonviolent union activities. Outlaws yellow-dog contracts.	
Labor-Management Relations Act (originally passed as Wagner Act, amended by Taft-Hartley Act and Landrum-Griffin Act) (1935, amended in 1947 and 1959)	Nonmanagerial employees in nonagricultural private sector not covered by Railway Labor Act, postal workers.	Employees may choose bargaining representative for collective bargaining. Both labor and management must bargain in good faith. Unfair labor practices include discrimination for union activities, secondary boycotts, refusal to bargain.	National Labor Relations Board, Federal Mediation and Conciliation Service.

Table 1 continued

Law	Coverage	Major Provisions	Federal Agencies
Labor-Management Relations Act (cont'd)		National emergency dispute procedures.	
Landrum-Griffin Act (1959)	All private sector employers and labor organizations.	Specification and guarantee of individual rights of union members. Prohibits certain management and union conduct. Requires union financial disclosures.	U.S. Department of Labor.
Civil Service Reform Act, Title VII (1978)	All nonuniformed, nonmanagerial federal service employees and agencies.	Employees may choose bargaining representative for collective bargaining. Bargaining rights on noneconomic and nonstaffing issues. Requires arbitration of unresolved grievances.	Federal Labor Relations Authority

Source: Adapted from J. A. Fossum, *Labor Relations: Development, Structure, Process*, 4th ed. Homewood, IL: Irwin, copyright © 1989.

these jobholders to determine how best to achieve these goals. The owners of a pharmaceutical company may know little about organic chemistry, finance, or human resource management (HRM). They hire employees, in this case managers, with the expectation that these individuals will operate the business to the owners' benefit.

Useful insights on the employment relationship can come from considering how economists assume employees are oriented. Economic theories of employment assume that, in general, employees

Table 2

Civil Rights Laws and Regulations

Law or Order	Coverage	Major Provisions	Federal Agencies
Civil Rights Act of 1964, Title VII (as amended)	Private-sector employers with 15 or more employees, state and local governments, federal service workers; unions; employment agencies.	Discrimination in employment decisions prohibited on the basis of race, sex, religion, color, and national origin.	Equal Employment Opportunity Commission (EEOC).
Age Discrimination in Employment Act (as amended) (1967)	Persons over age 40 (except between 40 and 65 for bona fide executives).	Prohibits discrimination in employment decisions or mandatory retirement.	EEOC.
Executive Order 11246 (as amended) (1965)	Federal contractors and subcontractors.	Contractors underutilizing minorities and women must specify goals and timetables to affirmatively recruit, select, train, and promote individuals from underutilized groups.	Office of Federal Contract Compliance Programs (OFCCP).
Vocational Rehabilitation Act of 1973	Federal contractors and subcontractors.	Contractors must develop AA programs to employ handicapped persons.	OFCCP.
Veterans Readjustment Act of 1974	Federal contractors and subcontractors.	Contractors must develop AA programs to employ Vietnam era veterans. Job	OFCCP.

Table 2 continued

Law or Order	Coverage	Major Provisions	Federal Agencies
Veterans Readjustment Act of 1974		openings must be listed with state employment services which will give veterans priority on referrals.	
Equal Pay Act of 1963	Most employers.	Men and women must be paid equal pay for jobs requiring equal skill, effort, responsibility, and working conditions.	EEOC.

Source: Adapted from H.G. Heneman III, D.P. Schwab, J.A. Fossum, L.D. Dyer, *Personnel/Human Resource Management,* 4th ed. Homewood, IL: Irwin, copyright © 1989.

are risk averse while employers (and other capitalists) are risk neutral. For practitioners, this academic assumption can help them to understand the views employees express about how to structure the employment relationship. In unionized situations, employees can express preferences and may be able to bargain changes in the employment relationship that reduce risks for a majority of them. Employers also may recognize employees' preferences for risk aversion by developing employee relations policies which aim to reduce employees' exposures to risk.

Labor Relations

Labor relations has been defined in the federal statutes and their subsequent review and interpretation by the NLRB and the court system. In essence, labor relations regulations require that where employees desire representation by a union, collective bargaining ensues. Collective bargaining agreements require parties to meet at reasonable times and places to bargain over wages, hours, and terms and conditions of employment. This obligation extends beyond negotiations to include the administration of a contract. Thus, these issues require the joint attention of management and labor.

Table 3

Occupational Safety and Health Laws and Regulations

Law	Coverage	Major Provisions	Federal Agencies
Occupational Safety and Health Act (OSHA) (1970)	Private-sector employers except domestic service employers. Excludes employers covered by Federal Mine Safety Act.	Employers have a general duty to provide working conditions that will not harm their employees. So that employees may know specific standards of care they must use regulations and guidelines are published by the Department of Labor. Agents inspect workplaces with appropriate authorization and may issue citations calling for corrections and penalties. If an employer disputes a citation, a review commission determines its appropriateness. Enforcement authority may be given to states after they have passed laws consistent with OSHA.	Occupational Safety and Health Administration, National Institute for Occupational Safety and Health, Occupational Safety and Health Review Commission.
Federal Mine Safety Act (1969)	Employees in underground and surface mining operations.	Establishes procedures for identifying and eliminating exposure to toxic and other harmful materials and for inspecting mines.	Mine Safety and Health Administration, Federal Mine Safety and Health Review Commission.

Table 3 continued

Law	Coverage	Major Provisions	Federal Agencies
Federal Mine Safety Act (1969)		Mandates health and safety training. Provides benefits for pneumoconiosis (black lung disease).	

Source: Adapted from H.G. Heneman III, D.P. Schwab, J.A. Fossum, L.D. Dyer, *Personnel/Human Resource Management*, 4th ed. Homewood, IL: Irwin, copyright © 1989.

Issues involved in terms and conditions of employment include work rules, discipline procedures, opportunities to pursue grievances, entitlement to employment opportunities and jobs, and the like. Provisions regarding employment opportunities cover decisions about how and where the work will be produced, such as the establishment of new facilities and subcontracting.

Contracts are negotiated for a finite duration. Whenever a contract is renegotiated, the relationship between the represented employees and the employer is subject to change. In this volume, terms and conditions of employment are the primary focus. Each time a renegotiation takes place, the pattern of employee relations may change. From this standpoint, employee and labor relations involve a short-run perspective since the present state is bound by the length of the contract.

In the longer run, however, unions aim for continuing improvements in the employment relationship in future negotiations. Some employers also establish explicit employee relations statements and policies which constitute values that the organizations intend to live by. Organizations which establish these policies in the absence of collective bargaining (or the overt avoidance of it) have been termed "philosophy-laden" by one observer.[6]

Employee Relations

Employee relations involves the reciprocal expectations and behaviors between employers and employees. In practice, employee relations encompasses the operational processes implementing an employer's philosophical or policy approaches to employment. These processes may be influenced or modified by collective bargaining relationships and legal requirements. Among other things, employee relations would specify the manner in which the workplace is governed. Obviously, labor relations forms a segment of employee relations in unionized employment settings. A good deal of the implementation of employee relations focuses on handling exceptional cases of employee behavior—both the decisions and actions taken by managers and the behavior of the employee within his/her position responsibilities.

Alternative Approaches to Understanding the Employment Relationship

From a legal stance, employment in most jurisdictions is considered to be at will. An employer may hire or fire an employee for any reason as long as the action does not violate employment laws barring discrimination. However, despite explicit at-will employment statements in employee handbooks and other disclaimers, both employers and employees develop expectations of each other which are at variance with these specific disclaimers.

Labor Markets and Implicit Contracts

Employment and labor market studies suggest that employment opportunities are segmented into secondary and primary labor markets.[7] The secondary labor market consists of jobs of relatively short duration that offer few advancement opportunities and little experience of value for subsequent employment. The primary labor market, on the other hand, consists of job ladders with specific entry ports and modes of progression. Employment with a given employer is generally for an extended period. Primary labor market jobs generally require greater KSAs than secondary labor market jobs. Further, after employees complete a probationary employment period, an employer is likely to provide specific training (invest in specific human capital) as jobs become increasingly distinct from external labor market comparisons.

For employers, this investment in specific human capital would be lost if trained employees later quit. For employees, time and effort spent in acquiring specific human capital instead of KSAs more generally applicable in the external labor market (general human capital) follows from an expectation of continued employment in a particular organization. Economists have suggested that the employment relationship in a primary labor market employer can be characterized as involving an implicit contract.[8] In a secondary labor market situation, an employer is likely to hire and/or retain employees only in situations where the value of an employee's work product exceeds wage costs in the short run. Since secondary labor market employees neither need nor receive training, either because they possess the KSAs necessary or because the jobs require very few skills, an employer loses no investment in letting an employee go. In a primary labor market with job progression ladders, an employer may not see immediate payoffs from an employees' efforts while at other times, an employee's productivity may substantially exceed the pay provided. Over a career with a company, pay generally increases at a decreasing rate. The decreasing rate of increases for the average individual probably represents the decreasing probability of promotion as jobs require increasingly higher levels of KSAs and motivation. Some evidence also suggests that senior employees within jobs are not necessarily more productive than junior employees even though their pay is generally higher.[9]

For employers and employees, pay will likely exceed the value of productivity during early periods of time on the job (and within a career). Once an employee learns KSAs which form employer-specific human capital, productivity increases may substantially exceed pay increases during a significant portion of a career. Toward the end of a career, productivity may plateau or grow at a slower rate than pay increases. The implicit contract adopts a long-term perspective on the balance between productivity and pay, with the organization subsidizing an employee during early and late career stages in expectation of receiving productivity substantially in excess of pay during the middle of the employee's career.

Both employers and employees face risks in this relationship. If an employee leaves following acquisition of specific human capital characteristics, the employer loses the expected payback for its investment in training and development and the implicit contract is broken. For the employee, if an employer terminates senior employees when pay exceeds productivity levels, the preceding period of high productivity in relation to pay has earned no payoff for the employee. If employees do not trust an employer to carry out its late career obligations within the implicit contract, then commitment and productivity will be more difficult to engage during peak capability periods of employees. How an employer states and operationalizes the structure and management of careers establishes its commitment to the implicit contract. An employer's consistency in managing the relationship, including a willingness to terminate employees who violate their obligations under the implicit contract, should generate lower voluntary turnover rates.

Psychological Contracts

The implicit contract relates to another behavioral approach, the psychological contract.[10] The psychological contract embodies the sense of reciprocal commitment that an employee feels exists between him/her and the organization. What employees return to an organization may be a result of how they perceive the employment exchange. Employees may perceive the employment relationships as either coercive, calculative, or normative.[11] A coercive relationship is one in which employees perceive that noncompliance will result in punishments, but good performance earns few rewards. A calculative relationship is one in which the exchange is well known, with each party fulfilling its obligations on an essentially contractual basis. A normative relationship is one in which the parties practice employment based on their beliefs about their obligations to the other. With the cutbacks, layoffs, and restructurings employees experienced during the 1980s, a calculative relationship may be the best that employees can expect in many organizations. Demographic and social changes that occurred in the 1980s also will strongly influence employee relations in the 1990s. Other changes will result from continuing societal expectations that the workplace environment should include a balance in the power and obligations of both employers and employees.

Societal Issues and Employee Relations

The U.S. labor force has become increasingly diverse during the last several years. The first, and the most pervasive, change since World War II has been the increased participation of women in the labor force. This change reflects a number of factors, including equal employment opportunity requirements, the expanding number of occupations for women, the economic necessity of two-earner households, and the decreasing supply of labor available in the late 1980s and 1990s. A second shift occurred through the legal prohibition against racial barriers in employment. While affirmative action programs followed, relatively little evidence exists to indicate that higher-level opportunities have opened up, although at least one study suggests that unionized organizations have made substantially more progress than nonunion employers.[12] Legal and illegal immigration also has contributed to increasing diversity. Finally, the removal of mandatory retirement policies through the amendments to the Age Discrimination in Employment Act, together with more discretion included in early retirement programs, has contributed to more age diversity in work groups.

Diversity requires accommodation of different cultures and expectations. Some problems involve both employers and unions. People of different cultural backgrounds may differ in the extent to which they believe collective activity is appropriate in employment. Generally speaking, evidence suggests that women are more difficult to organize while racial minorities are more easily organized.[13] Women may not show interest in organizing when the union which seeks to represent them appears to be male dominated or when the majority of a proposed bargaining unit is male. Given the democratic nature of unions, and the requirement that candidates for office and contracts obtain a majority of voters to gain power or ratification, officers or contracts may not prove particularly beneficial to women when a majority of the unit are men. Evidence does exist, however, to indicate that relatively large, predominantly female units are interested in organization. The Yale clerical organizing campaign of 1983 is a recent example.[14]

Employment-at-Will

Under common law, U.S. employers have historically had the right to hire, promote, demote, transfer, reward, or terminate employees at will. The principal of employment-at-will is perhaps best summed up in an 1894 Tennessee court decision which stated: "All may dismiss their employee(s) at will, be they many or few, for good cause, for no cause, or even for cause morally wrong. . ."[15]

Employment-at-will has been increasingly narrowly construed through laws, regulations, and court decisions. Both the Railway Labor Act and the Wagner Act curtailed the right to fire or treat differently employees on the basis of involvement in union activities. Title VII of the 1964 Civil Rights Act forbids hiring, promotions, demotions, transfers, or terminations based on race, sex, religion, color, or national origin. The Age Discrimination in Employment Act forbids basing decisions on age for employees older than 40. Occupational Safety and Health laws, the Fair Labor Standards Act, and other protective legislation shields persons who report employers for unlawful activities.

Employment-at-will also has been eroded by several state courts. Major areas in which courts have limited the right to discharge include situations where the discharge occurs in retaliation for reporting illegal activity, where wording in employee manuals and other communications constitutes an implied contract, and where employers acted in bad faith, such as when employees have moved expecting to retain employment but are terminated shortly after starting at their new locations.[16]

State legislatures also have considered restricting the right of employers to discharge at will. In Montana, for example, recent legislation has been enacted which forbids discharges which punish employees for refusing to violate public policy or for reporting a violation of public policy, which violate the company's own written personnel policies, or which lack "good cause." A good cause dismissal requires evidence of legitimate reasons for the discharge, such as the employee failed to perform job duties satisfactorily or disrupted work operations. At the same time, the law limits liability for wrongful discharge to up to four years of lost wages and fringe benefits, and additional punitive damages where fraud or malice is proven. Interestingly, the legislation was supported by both employee groups, so as to restrict employers' powers, and by employers, so as to limit their liability. When the first case testing the constitutionality of the law was brought, the court upheld the statute and ruled in the employer's favor.[17]

Governance in the Workplace

In situations where collective bargaining exists, employees are entitled, through their representatives, to have a say in the governance of the work place. Rules and regulations and their implementation are governed by the negotiated collective bargaining agreement. In virtually all unionized settings, a grievance procedure exists and the final step requires that an impartial arbitrator settle unresolved grievances. Generally, unions have no say in a company's strategic decisions and are not represented on its board of directors except in special cases (for example, as a condition for agreeing to economic concessions offered in the Chrysler bailout).

Strategic decisions obviously have an ultimate effect on employment. However, the courts have not interpreted U.S. labor law to include business strategies within the scope of mandatory bargaining issues. In some western European countries, particularly Germany, laws require the establishment of works councils that include employee representatives. These bodies oversee strategic decision making and allow employee representatives a voice in the direction of an organization.

In many capitalist and democratic socialist economies, employees exercise an organized voice through political parties and/or administrative decision making. In Sweden, for example, the government establishes many wage rates, and employers and employees in individual establishments then work to improve productivity enough to pay for these wages. Virtually all employees are organized into unions and the dominant political party is closely associated with the trade union movement. However, in early 1990, the Swedish government, controlled by the Labor Party, asked unions to freeze wages and forego strikes. Another example is Australia, where most wages are set by arbitration councils. The government there also is closely associated with the labor movement and a majority of employees belong to unions. Recently, labor parties in both Australia and Sweden have suffered electoral losses or a reduction in popular support as their economies have encountered inflation and stagnation problems.

The preceding examples contrast considerably with the United States. The proportion of employees who belong to unions has been declining since the 1950s. Most of this drop is due to industrial and occupational changes;[18] however, it also reflects employer antipathy toward unions. Unions and employers are very involved in governance issues. Employers seek to maintain as much latitude in decision making as they can. From a union standpoint, national unions seek to exercise control over local unions and to structure negotiations in specific plants to fit an overall pattern. However, during the 1980s, if concessions proved necessary to preserve employment in individual plant situations, union members occasionally were able to convince national unions to allow them to negotiate their own economic arrangements.

Takeover activity during the 1980s has created an ironic situation. A Delaware Chancery Court decision held that takeovers of companies incorporated in Delaware could not go through without the approval of the company's board of directors unless the acquiring company held at least 85 percent of the outstanding shares.[19] Companies with employee stock ownership plans (ESOP) which allow employees the confidential right to decide whether or not to tender their shares could not be acquired against the wishes of employee shareholders if they held more than 15 percent ownership in the company. Several firms have taken advantage of this situation by creating ESOPs to reduce their vulnerabilities to takeovers. However, when these firms have been pressured by employees or their representatives for a seat on the board of directors, they have been reluctant to allow it.

The Role of Unions in Society

The political activities of national unions increased markedly in the 1980s. Activity is greatest among unions involved with public employers and those in which executive boards are democratically chosen.[20] Political action committees (PACs) have become important vehicles for providing financial support to election campaigns of individuals thought to favor PAC viewpoints. Evidence suggests that the receipt of PAC contributions by a candidate who subsequently becomes or remains an incumbent is directly related to roll-call voting records and indirectly related to the number of candidates elected.[21] PACs do not, however, give contributions to all who support their causes. Contributions to candidates appear to depend on the willingness of the organization to give, the compatibility of the candidate's ideology with that of the contributing PAC, the probability of the candidate winning (with more given when the race is close), and the magnitude of the candidate's vote margin in the last election (if an incumbent).[22] Contributions also appear related to the closeness of an incumbent's committee assignment to interests of labor, voting record, and electoral security.[23]

While unions (and corporations) are heavily involved in PAC activities, the attitudes of their members toward issues do not appear to be monolithic. In most cases, members' views seem less liberal than the positions espoused by their unions' PACs. Further, PACs appear to be more successful in influencing legislative outcomes peripheral to labor's interests, such as education, rather than outcomes directly affecting its environment, such as labor law reform.[24]

A recent Supreme Court decision may possibly limit the impact of union PACs in political campaigns.[25] This decision held that persons covered by a collective bargaining agreement can withhold the amount of union dues in excess of what is required for collective bargaining purposes. The argument noted that such funds might be used by a union to support political issues and/or candidates whose views differ from those of the dues payer.

Possible Scenarios for the Future

One analysis of the major changes that have occurred in employment in the late 1970s and 1980s, suggests four possible emerging scenarios.[26] The first possibility is a continuation of current trends, which would further reduce the unionized proportion of the labor force and concentrate unions in the public sector and in firms insulated from foreign competition. As a result, fewer innovations will take place in industrial relations and HRM since firms will face less competition from unions in employee relations.

A second scenario suggests that labor law reform will eliminate the delay tactics employers have used to circumvent union organization, thereby allowing employees a freer choice on whether or not to be represented. In Canada, where elections are held swiftly and where recognition may require only a card count, union representation is much higher. However, this change would not greatly affect most employers.

A third scenario suggests that employee relations innovations will spread to other organizations as it becomes apparent which practices contribute to organizational performance. Spillovers will occur across union boundaries as they have in the past.

Scenario four suggests that unions may develop new organizing strategies. These strategies might include vehicles such as associate membership which offers participants access to credit, group health insurance, and advocacy for their individual employment problems. Where sufficient numbers of people within a unit feel benefitted by this type of relationship, they may organize.

Parts of scenarios three and four seem most plausible. They are also consistent with organized labor's long-run involvement in advocating improvements in employment conditions. Despite the potential loss of collective bargaining advantage, unions would benefit from new laws and regulations recognizing the individual advocacy roles suggested by associate member status.

A fifth scenario also could occur. The Industrial Revolution heralded the pervasiveness of employment. Perhaps the post-industrial period that many say has begun will mark the demise of employment in its present form. Employment relationships have become much more flexible over the 1980s. Companies which have had longer-run career opportunities now prune employees and divisions with alacrity. Increasingly larger proportions of work forces are temporary employees. Organization and job design innovations such as self-managed work teams rely more on employee skills and eliminate managers. Employees are expected to tend to their own skills obsolescence problems. Products and services are changing rapidly. If technology changes rapidly without much attempt to adapt it to employees' needs, a return to Luddism may even emerge.[27]

This fifth scenario might suggest that employment will essentially be a relic by the middle of the 21st century. Individuals and groups may contract with organizations to provide services on an ad hoc basis. Managers will essentially negotiate and manage contracts. Employees will essentially act as "free agents." Given the increasing complexity of machinery and equipment, manufacturing will require decreasing amounts of labor. Thus, relatively few people will work outside of the home, except to manage or in cases where providing services requires substantial capital (such as transportation). To an extent, the future may come full cycle back to the days of the craft era, with masters and apprentices—albeit on an intellectual rather than a physical level.

◆

Notes

1. Heilbroner.
2. Dulles; Rayback.
3. Heilbroner.
4. Yoder.
5. Chamberlain and Cullen; Taft.
6. Foulkes.
7. Doeringer and Piore; Jacoby.
8. Rosen.
9. Medoff and Abraham.
10. Schein.
11. Etzioni.
12. Leonard.
13. Heneman and Sandver

14. Coulson.
15. *Payne v. Western & A.R.R. Co.*, 81 Tenn. 507 (1894).
16. Koys, Briggs, and Grenig.
17. *Meech v. Hillhaven West, Inc.*, 4 IER cases 737 (Mont., 1989). This case was brought by a disgruntled employee who argued that the Montana statute reduced the ability of an employee to gain satisfactory tort settlement from an employer.
18. Dickens and Leonard.

19. *Shamrock Holdings, Inc. v. Polaroid Corp.*, 559 A.2d 257 (Del. Ch., 1989).
20. Masters and Delaney (1985).
21. Saltzman.
22. Wilhite and Theilmann.
23. Grier and Munger.
24. Masters and Delaney (1987).
25. *Beck v. Communications Workers of America*, 487 U.S. ___, 128 LRRM 2792 (1988).
26. Kochan, Katz, and McKersie.
27. Glendenning; Grossman.

◆

References

Chamberlain, N.W., & D.E. Cullen. 1971. *The Labor Sector*, 2nd ed. New York: McGraw-Hill.

Coulson, C. 1985. "Labor Unrest in the Ivy League." *Arbitration Journal* 40(3): 53–62.

Dickens, W.T., and J.S. Leonard 1985. "Accounting for the Decline in Union Membership, 1950–1980." *Industrial and Labor Relations Review* 38: 323–334.

Doeringer, P.B., and M.J. Piore 1971. *Internal Labor Markets and Manpower Analysis*. Lexington, MA: D.C. Heath Co.

Dulles, F.R. 1966. *Labor in America: A History*. New York: Crowell.

Etzioni, A. 1961. *A Comparative Analysis of Complex Organizations*. New York: Free Press.

Glendenning, C. 1990. "Notes Toward a Neo-Luddite Manifesto." *Utne Reader* (March/April): 50–53.

Grossman, D. 1990. "Don't Just Say Yes to Technology." *Utne Reader* (March/April): 44–49.

Grier, K.B., and M.C. Munger 1986. "The Impact of Legislator Attributes on Interest-Group Campaign Contributions." *Journal of Labor Research* 7: 349–359.

Heilbroner, R.L. 1961. *The Worldly Philosophers*. New York: Simon and Schuster.

Heneman, H.G., III, and M.H. Sandver 1983. "Predicting the Outcome of Union Certification Elections: A Review of the Literature." *Industrial & Labor Relations Review* 36: 537–559.

Jacoby, S.M. 1985. *Employing Bureaucracy: Managers, Unions, and the Transformation of Work in American Industry, 1900–1945*. New York: Columbia University Press.

Kochan, T.A., H.C. Katz, and R.B. McKersie 1986. *The Transformation of American Industrial Relations*. New York: Free Press.

Koys, D.J., S. Briggs and J. Grenig 1987. "State Court Disparity on Employment-at-Will." *Personnel Psychology* 40: 565–577.

Leonard, J.S. 1985. "The Effect of Unions on the Employment of Blacks, Hispanics, and Women." *Industrial and Labor Relations Review* 39: 115–132.

Masters, M.F. and J.T. Delaney 1985. "Union Legislative Records during President Reagan's First Term." *Journal of Labor Research* 8: 1–18.

Masters, M.F. and J.T. Delaney 1987. "Union Political Activities: A Review of the Empirical Literature." *Industrial and Labor Relations Review* 40: 336–353.

Medoff, J.L., and K.G. Abraham 1981. "Are Those Paid More Really More Productive? The Case of Experience." *Journal of Human Resources* 16: 186–216.

Rayback, J.G. 1966. *A History of American Labor.* New York: Free Press.

Rosen, S. 1985. "Implicit Contracts: A Survey." *Journal of Economic Literature* 23: 1144–1175.

Saltzman, G.M. 1987. "Congressional Voting on Labor Issues: The Role of PACs." *Industrial and Labor Relations Review* 40: 163–179.

Schein, E. 1965. *Organizational Psychology.* Englewood Cliffs, NJ: Prentice-Hall.

Taft, P. 1964. *Organized Labor in American History.* New York: Harper & Row.

Wilhite, A., and J. Theilmann 1986. "Unions, Corporations, and Political Campaign Contributions: The 1982 House Elections." *Journal of Labor Research* 7: 175–186.

Yoder, D. 1948. *Personnel Management and Industrial Relations,* 3rd ed. New York: Prentice-Hall.

———— ◆ ————

4.2

The Role of Industrial Relations in Industrial Performance

Morris M. Kleiner

Understanding what people do at the workplace and how to improve their performance has the potential to affect long-term growth of private-sector businesses and the national economy. This aspect of human resource management is especially important in the United States, where labor costs account for approximately 75 percent of the national income. In a similar fashion, expenses related to human resources form the largest single cost in most organizations, and many employers consider their workers to be their most valuable asset.

Unfortunately for human resource (HR) practitioners, the link between human resource management (HRM) practices and bottom-line measures of organizational performance has received little attention. Most studies of HR practices examine only the performance of individual workers or work groups, not overall productivity. In addition, measures used to assess the success of HRM practices typically examine turnover rates or performance appraisals, not an organization's profitability.

In contrast, most line managers or corporate executives view the bottom line as a company's balance sheet or equity value. In fact, the goal of investor-owned corporations is to maximize shareholders' wealth.[1] While achieving this goal depends on a number of key constituent groups, such as suppliers, customers, managers, and shareholders, labor ranks as the most important factor in the production process. Other stakeholders within the organization, such as trade unions may argue that the real measure of the success of an organization is how it treats its employees.[2] Union leaders often argue that beyond making a profit or staying in business, the ultimate measure of performance is the ability of the employer to provide a good work environment. The criterion they would establish is the fairness of the organization, as well as the pay of the company and its ability to provide its workers with a "decent living."[3] Similar alternative measures of performance would include measures of equity or "economic welfare" or the morale of employees rather than measures of economic efficiency.

In investor-owned corporations, the goal as presented in most statements of policy or practice is to maximize the wealth of the shareholders. In fact, the basic assumption is that the goal of management is to maximize shareholder wealth.[4] In manufacturing, for example, team processes dominate. The output of one type of labor depends on the work of other types of labor. Each factor of production must be monitored because the cost of one factor's shirking is not borne by that factor alone, but is also shared by other members of the team.[5] The result is the formation of the firm and identification of a "residual claimant," or stakeholder; that is, the group that receives the surplus after the other factors have been paid. The management of human resources has a special place in the modern corporation. The manager must function to ensure the continued cooperation of labor and to maximize the wealth of shareholders. These two goals by managers are equally important, and to neglect either is to engage in poor management practice.[6]

This review examines the extent to which HRM contributes to firm wealth through enhanced productivity and profitability. It looks at the effects of specific types of HR practices, including the role of unions, union-related practices, voluntary turnover, information-sharing with employees, training, pensions, and hiring practices. Although this list is by no means exhaustive, it includes those HR practices that have received the most attention from researchers. The specific outcomes explored here include labor quality, as well as intermediate outputs, such as increased product quality and enhanced productivity; additional outputs, such as sales, revenues, and profits; and final outcomes like capital market assessments, market share, and an organization's stature and reputation.[7]

Linkages Between HRM and Organizational Performance

Table 1 lists several of the major HR policies that influence or have the potential to influence an organization's economic perform-

---

Table 1

Major Human Resource Policies with the Potential of Significantly Affecting Firm Performance

Compensation Policies (executive and nonexecutive)
Employer Information-Sharing
Employee Participation in Firm Decisions
Employee Training and Development
Fringe Benefits
Grievance Procedures
Internal Promotion
Job Design and Analysis
Performance Appraisal
Recruitment
Training
Turnover and Employment Security
Unionization
Union Policies (Strikes, Concession Bargaining, Work Rules)

Source: Adapted from M.M. Kleiner, et al., *Human Resources and the Performance of the Firm.* Madison, WI: IRRA, copyright © 1987; M.M. Kleiner, et al., *Labor Markets and Human Resource Management.* Glenview, IL: Scott Foresman, copyright © 1988; D. Lewin, "Human Resource Policy and Practice and Economic Performance of the Firm," mimeo, 1986.

---

ance. The practices and policies listed include those identified in the personnel literature as well as in academic research as having the greatest financial impact. They range from policies and practices found in unionized establishments, such as strikes, concession bargaining, and work rules, to ones found in both organized and unorganized settings, such as job design and analysis, and performance appraisal methods.

The following sections discuss specific research findings regarding the impact of these policies on an organization's productivity and profitability. However, before turning to this discussion, some mention of the limitations and problems affecting investigations in this area is necessary.

The amount of research conducted on the HR policies and practices listed in Table 1 varies considerably. For example, few studies have examined the link between an establishment's productivity or economic value and its internal promotion policies, employee training and development programs, performance appraisal methods, and job design and analysis. In other HR areas, such as employee participation in firm decisions or the impact of unionized work rules, research findings are scanty, unclear, or show only modest effects. In contrast, HR practices in the areas of compensation, recruitment, information sharing, training, turnover, employment security, and pensions have received more thorough investigation.

A major caveat in linking HR practices to organizational performance concerns questions of cause and effect. For example, a firm's performance in its product or financial market can have a major effect on the type of HR policy it employs. On the other hand, HR policies also can affect an establishment's economic performance. While some of the studies discussed here attempt to disentangle these cause-and-effect issues, most research in this area could benefit from more precise methodology, such as fixed effects research design or before-after studies.

Impact of Unionization on Industrial Performance

The effect of unionization is perhaps the most widely researched area of the link between HRM and organizational performance. Unionization of a work force generally increases employees' control over wage levels by giving monopoly power to the union as the single seller of labor to an establishment. Unionization also creates a "voice" mechanism for employees by establishing negotiated grievance procedures and the right to bargain collectively.[8]

Productivity Effects

The higher wages associated with unions raises a basic economic question; that is, how can a firm in a competitive product market pay more for labor and stay in business? One answer given by economists is that union firms are more productive than nonunion companies.[9] This higher productivity results from lower turnover, which in turn enhances employees' knowledge of the specific jobs they perform. Another possibility is that management in unionized businesses does a better job of monitoring this higher-priced labor, and invests more in these workers, who are less likely to quit.

Most managers, however, would argue that unionization produces a quite different effect on productivity growth. This side holds that even if productivity improves, the improvement never completely offsets union-generated wage increases. This imbalance raises unit costs and reduces productivity growth in the firm.[10] Finally, unions can cause reallocation of resources toward labor and away from research and development expenditures within the firm.[11]

Despite these arguments, statistical research regarding the impact of unions on productivity generally shows positive results on productivity levels and no impact on productivity growth. Most studies estimate productivity through measuring the output per hour or per employee, controlling for the capital-labor ratio and other variables related to labor quality. Other studies, however, use estimates of value-added per worker. Regardless of methodology, the research generally shows sizable productivity gains associated with the "voice" effects, as well as the shock effects to management, of unionization.[12]

Beyond these general findings, empirical studies suggest that the impact of unionism varies with the product market. Because of greater market constraints, unions have been shown to have greater productivity effects in the private sector than in the public sector. Other studies indicate that the effect of unionization also varies over time. Unfortunately, due to measurement problems, researchers have yet to determine the exact causes of unions' varying impacts on productivity.

Profitability Effects

If unions do in fact raise productivity, then why do organizations oppose unionization with such vigor? The apparent answer to this puzzle lies in the impact unions have on corporate profits. A number of studies support the argument that while unions may increase productivity, the wage increases associated with unionization exceed productivity gains.

Table 2 summarizes several studies analyzing the impact of unions and union practices on organizational performance. The first shows that a successful representation election tends to reduce shareholder value, at least relative to no election. The second study indicates that the expected wage settlements have no effect on shareholder equity, but any unanticipated wage settlements in favor of labor can cost shareholders one dollar for every dollar gained by union members. In a similar fashion, Table 2 also shows that nego-

Table 2

Impact of Union Activities on Organizational Performance (as reported in research studies)

Union Event	Productivity Effect	Profit/Share Price Effect	Time Period
Election (Ruback and Zimmerman)	N/A	Union loss reduces shareholder equity by 1.86%; union win reduces shareholder equity by 3.84%	1962–1980
"Unexpected" wage settlement (Abowd)	None	Each $1.00 gained by either side costs other side $1.00	1975–1982
Concession bargain (Becker)	N/A	Increases shareholder equity by 8%	1982–1983
Two-Tier Wage Agreement (Thomas and Kleiner)	N/A	Increases shareholder equity by .8% to 3.6%	1983–1986
Strikes (Neumann; Becker and Olson)	N/A	Reduces shareholder equity by 1.0% to 4.1%	1962–1982
Grievance Activity (Ichiowski; Katz, Kochan and Gobeille; Katz, Kochan, and Weber; Kleiner, Nickelsburg, and Pilarski)	1 standard deviation increase in filings reduces productivity by 1.5% to 6.7%	Increase from zero to average level of grievances reduces profits by 14.6% (Ichniowski)	1970–1988
	Higher productivity results from monitoring-related grievances	(Kleiner, Nickelsburg and Pilarski 1989a)	

tiations which end in strikes tend to reduce shareholder equity by one to four percent.

Studies of the impact of unionization on profitability have adopted different perspectives. For example, one pair of researchers examined price-cost margins and other measures of profitability at a number of establishments and found that unions reduce profit from 9 to 37 percent.[13] Another study, which used different profit measures and a private data set obtained from the

Harvard Business School, showed that unionized firms had not only lower profits but lower growth rates as well.[14]

Another test utilized data from the New York and American Stock Exchanges to evaluate the impact of new unionization on a company's stock price. This analysis found that an organizing drive reduced share price by 1.38 percent even when the union lost, while actually becoming organized cut share price by 3.84 percent.[15] These percentages translate into a total shareholder loss of $7,000 to $46,000 per unionized worker.

These research findings suggest that the average effect of new unionization is associated with a decline in shareholder wealth. Given the efficiency of capital markets in detecting the present value of future profits, this method of assessment may produce the most accurate estimates of the impact of unionization on shareholders. These negative effects also may explain more current studies showing that low-wage firms, which have the most to lose from an organizing drive, are most likely to engage in union avoidance techniques.[16] Further, they suggest that unions may serve to redistribute firm resources away from shareholders to unionized workers.

Union Policies Related to Industrial Performance

Once a company becomes organized, what are the policies that may enhance productivity or profitability? This section examines policies typically associated with union enterprises and evaluates the extent to which policy variations impact firm performance. In particular, the discussion focuses on the role of strikes, negotiations, concession bargaining, and grievance procedures.

Effects of Strikes

The impact of strikes on an organization and on society has generated a great deal of industrial relations research. Starting in the 1970s, a number of researchers began to link the effects of a strike to the economic value of an enterprise. Not surprisingly, most studies demonstrated that both shareholders and striking workers became major losers in this economic warfare.

One analysis, conducted over 1967 to 1975, found that strikes reduced cumulative average returns to shareholders by one percent.[17] More recent findings suggest that strikes have an even greater effect, decreasing shareholder wealth by 4.14 percent.[18] This percentage translates into an average profit reduction of $72 million to $87 million in strike-related costs borne by shareholders. In addition, each worker lost the equivalent of $21,000 for each strike event. Interestingly, this last study found that during the prestrike period, investors consistently underestimated the cost of strikes.

Consequences of Collective Bargaining

The outcome of collective bargaining can also have important consequences for shareholders and unions. Aspects of collective bargaining that have received investigation include unexpected negotiation outcomes, wage concessions, and two-tier wage and benefits programs.

Contract Negotiation Outcomes

A recent study, summarized in Table 2, examined the impact of alternative contract negotiations in considerable detail.[19] By developing an expected trend line for the negotiations, this investigation analyzed the effect that deviations from these expected outcomes had on shareholders and union members. The results proved to be highly symmetrical; that is, a one percent deviation in favor of shareholders resulted in a one percent reduction in the compensation package going to the union, and vice versa. Thus, events at the bargaining table can have important impacts on the economic welfare of both the firm and its workers.

Wage Concessions

Wage concessions are another aspect of collective bargaining that gained importance during the early 1980s. A number of analysts have attempted to determine the impact of the agreements on industrial performance. The key concern was whether financial markets viewed a concession agreement as meaning that a company was facing economic hardship, or that it had gained a benefit at the bargaining table.

One recent study of more than 166 collective bargaining agreements found that firms gained substantial economic benefits from signing a collective bargaining agreement that contained concessions.[20] In particular, the study showed that concession agreements raised average returns to shareholders by 8 percent. Moreover, this shareholder gain appeared to outweigh any negative signal that the concession agreement might have sent to financial markets.

Two-Tier Wage and Benefit Programs

Another type of concession bargaining involves two-tier wage and benefit programs, which pay new workers substantially less than continuing employees. Managers have debated the benefits of this compensation tool, since varying pay for workers who perform identical jobs may reduce work effort. A recent analysis found that the introduction of two-tier wage programs in collective bargaining agreements enhanced the economic value of the firm to shareholders.[21] However, the results of this study seem to be closely tied to the type of specification used in the analysis. Overall, the results suggest that although two-tier agreements add value to the firm, on average, the magnitude is about equal to the transactions value of such a trade. Consequently, it is not a way to significantly add value to the firm. This may have led to the decline in two-tier agreements during the later half of the 1980s as managers and investors came to realize and act upon this outcome.

Impact of Grievances

After contract negotiations, the most important part of a bargaining relationship involves the administration of the agreement. Most major companies utilize a grievance process containing three to five steps, with each successive step involving increasingly senior officials from labor and management. In most private-sector contracts, the final step involves arbitration of the grievance by an outside third party.

Grievance procedures result in a number of costs to a company. The first expense relates to time spent by supervisors and the employee in adjudicating the grievance. For example, a government report placed the average total cost to management of arbitrating a grievance at over $5,200.[22] Additional potential costs include lost productive time resulting from perceptions by workers that management is incompetent. Nonetheless, some analysts have argued that grievance procedures provide a voice mechanism that keeps workers productive and reduces turnover.[23]

Productivity Effects

All of the major investigations have shown that higher overall grievance activity is associated with lower productivity. However, only studies of the auto industry and paper mills have used appropriate controls for other firm characteristics.[24] In addition, most studies failed to rule out changes in the production process, the assembly line, or capital-labor ratios as possible causes of higher grievances. Finally, existing research overlooks situational factors that may lead unions to file grievances so as to appeal to their constituency. However, one study which controls for these factors finds that grievances due to managerial monitoring can enhance productivity.[25] Future studies on grievance activity should control further for the possible impact of union objectives and changes in production processes. Other issues meriting more study include questions regarding the optimal level of grievances for peak performance, and whether some production-related grievances reflect managerial monitoring and thus enhance plant performance.

Impact of HR Policies on Organizational Performance

HR managers in union and nonunion establishments must deal with numerous issues that can affect a company's economic performance. Recruitment methods, turnover rates, compensation practices, pension programs, employee training programs, and employee participation and information-sharing policies all have consequences on productivity and profitability.

Recruitment and Screening Practices

As most HR managers know, hiring procedures usually consist of two sets of activities: recruitment of applicants, followed by applicant screening and employee selection. Typical recruitment activities include soliciting referrals from current employees or other employers, posting "help-wanted" signs, placing ads in newspapers, and obtaining referrals from a variety of other sources. Screening activities often include reviews of written applications, interviews, physical examinations, cognitive or dexterity tests, and reference checks. Probationary periods also are commonly considered as part of the screening process.

Recent research on recruitment patterns provides some evidence on the effect of different types of HR hiring procedures on productivity and profitability.[26] One study of 3500 firms, summarized in Table 3, found that recruitment through referrals from current employees enhances both relative and absolute company productivity by around 2 percent.[27] In particular, the research showed that referrals from current employees and other employers produced new hires with better performance ratings, higher overall individual productivity, and lower turnover than other recruitment

Table 3

Impact of HR Policies and Practices on Industrial Performance (as reported in research studies)

HR Policy/ Practice	Productivity Effect	Profit/Share Price Effect	Time Period
Golden Parachute for executive (Larker)	N/A	Increases shareholder equity by 3%	1975–1982
Profit sharing for workers (Ehrenberg and Milkovich)	Unclear	Unclear	1970–1987
Pension plans (Allen and Clark)	No significant effect	Zero net effect on profits	1983
Turnover (Brown and Medoff)	Reducing turnover by 10% increases productivity by 1%	N/A	1972–1977
Information sharing (Kleiner and Bouillon)	No significant effect	Change from low to high information sharing reduces profits by 3%	1984
Training programs (Bartel)	Increase of .11% to .18%	N/A	1987
Recruitment (Holzer)	Using referrals from current employees increases productivity by 1.8% to 2.3%; Using external sources reduces productivity by 3% to 5%	N/A	1982

methods. In contrast, use of external sources, such as walk-in interviews or references from newspaper want ads, tends to reduce both absolute and relative productivity by 3 to 5 percent.

Relying on employee referrals for recruitment does pose some potential problems. This recruitment strategy tends to produce fewer applicants who are young, minorities, female, and less experienced. As a result, reliance on employee referrals may create efficiency-equity tradeoffs, enhancing an organization's economic performance while flouting public policy concerns such as equal opportunity laws.

Turnover Rates

While numerous authors in personnel psychology have addressed the impact of managerial styles and jobs on the likelihood of employee turnover, none of these studies have examined issues related to the economic effects of turnover. For example, does turnover help or harm the productivity and profitability of an organization? Can an employer use turnover to create optimal age and tenure profiles that enhance productivity?

The only study of these issues that used appropriate controls and a significant number of companies took place in the early 1970s.[28] The results show that manufacturing companies which reduced turnover by 10 percent achieved a 1 percent increase in productivity. However, this analysis did not examine the possibility that exceptionally low or high turnover levels could have the opposite effect on productivity.

A more recent review supports the possibility of a nonlinear relationship between turnover levels and organizational performance.[29] While the results are preliminary and sketchy, they suggest that the relationship looks much like an inverted U-shape. That is, very low turnover decreases profits since the retention of poor performers reduces productivity, while the increased recruitment and training costs caused by very high turnover levels also lowers profits.

Compensation Practices

The previous discussion raises the question of how an organization can achieve an optimal level of turnover. One method, discussed earlier, is through establishing grievance procedures.[30] A more obvious tool for changing turnover is wage compensation.

As mentioned in the introduction, employee compensation generally forms the single largest expense category for an organization and frequently accounts for more than half an organization's total expenses. Compensation also functions as the employee reward which an organization can control most easily and use to influence behavior related to organizational performance.

Given the large costs of compensation and its obvious ties to behavior, research in this area is surprisingly lacking. As one pair of reviewers pointed out, ". . . while a variety of theories exist about the effects of various compensation practices, surprisingly little evidence exists on the extent to which compensation policies vary across firms, and more importantly, on the effects of pursuing alternative compensation strategies."[31] With the exception of executive compensation, relatively few studies have investigated the link between compensation practices and an organization's economic performance.[32] The focus of industrial relations research is moving toward the examination of how compensation policies matter.[33] Moreover, as the following discussion demonstrates, the research that is available often suffers from methodological problems or produces mixed results.

Efficiency Wages

Proponents of efficiency wage policies, which pay above-market salaries, have suggested various economic benefits that might allow organizations to pay more for workers than the competition does. Such effects as reduced turnover, greater employee effort, higher productivity, and less need for supervision might result in no greater unit labor costs to organizations which pursue an efficiency wage policy.

In general, larger firms tend to be the primary users of efficiency wages. Some of the reasons given for this tendency include (1) larger firms use more advanced technologies and thus require a more highly skilled and disciplined work force; (2) employees' greater dislike of working in larger firms necessitates higher wages; (3) labor unions in larger firms have succeeded in reallocating some of the higher profits to employees; and (4) large firms pay higher wages to reduce employee "shirking" and supervision costs.[34]

Profit Sharing

Another type of nonexecutive compensation is profit sharing, or pay for productivity based on an organization's performance.

Studies on the role of merit pay generally have either lacked appropriate controls, utilized samples too small to produce clear outcomes, or demonstrated mixed effects on profits and/or share prices.[35]

As a result, hard evidence as to the overall impact of different types of profit sharing is scarce. However, considerable anecdotal information suggests that this method of compensation does in fact produce substantial productivity effects, and that profits increase when a large portion of compensation is tied directly to firm profits.

On the other hand, some analysts have suggested that most profit-sharing plans place too small an amount of compensation at risk to test the potential effects of this tool on firm productivity. In the United States, for example, most nonexecutive compensation plans tie less than 5 percent of an employee's salary to firm profitability.[36] In addition, the formulas used are generally too complex for employees to understand how their work effort directly affects their wages or the company's success.

Pensions

The effect of pensions on organizational effectiveness has generated a fair amount of discussion in the compensation field. Some evidence suggests that even firms in competitive markets can afford the additional expense of providing pensions because of the higher productivity resulting from pension plans.

An analysis conducted in the early 1980s showed that companies which provide pensions have age and tenure profiles that create a relatively more productive work force.[37] In particular, these employers had more employees at their peak years of productivity and with the tenure to know a lot about the organization. As a result of this human capital and higher productivity, organizations offering pension plans can just balance the cost of higher compensation. However, this study did not find any difference in the overall profitability of organizations that provide pensions relative to employers with no pension plans.

These findings on pensions suggest that this method of compensation, if used wisely, can generate a highly productive work force with no lower profits than other firms in the same industry. As a result, the percentage of private-sector companies providing pensions, which rose from 25 percent in 1950 to more than 50 percent in 1984,[38] seems likely to increase further.

Executive Compensation

In the area of executive compensation, one study of firms traded on the New York or American stock exchanges has shown that the use of "golden parachutes" to ensure executives' job security has a positive effect on shareholder equity.[39] While this effect may also reflect the higher takeover potential facing companies with such plans, the researchers nonetheless concluded that providing executives with stock options or job security (through golden parachutes) substantially improved the economic performance of the firms studied. However, only one study has attempted to link the method or level of compensation to executives' decisions.[40]

Employee Training Programs

The effect of employee training programs on organizational performance has received little investigation. The only rigorous study of this issue found that formal training programs in large publicly traded companies have a positive effect on labor productivity.[41] While the productivity levels of workers who received training remained less than those of experienced workers, the programs did significantly raise output per worker. Unfortunately, this analysis did not compare the costs of training programs relative to their productivity effects, a key issue.

Information-Sharing and Employee Participation Programs

Despite much speculation that information-sharing programs might lead to greater productivity and profitability,[42] the only empirical research in this area has produced mixed results. For example, a 1984 study of production employees in manufacturing companies found that information sharing was positively related to wage and benefit levels, unrelated to productivity, and had a modest negative relationship to profitability and cash flows.[43] However, additional research is needed to expand this analysis beyond manufacturing and to other kinds of employees.

Information sharing is often linked to employee participation programs and other forms of labor-management cooperation. While the personnel literature contains many claims that these programs enhance organizational performance,[44] no systematic study has investigated these claims. Since information sharing plays a key role in employee participation programs, the preliminary results suggesting no relationship between information-sharing programs and profitability may deter employers from establishing these forms of cooperation.

Future Research Requirements

Unlike most writings in the industrial psychology field,[39] this review has focused on economic measures of performance, such as productivity, profits, or shareholder equity, rather than individual-level measures. The reason for this focus is to provide the types of measures that upper-level management may use in assessing the effectiveness of HR programs. However, as the preceding discussion shows, the current state of knowledge provides no definitive conclusions regarding the effect of specific HR policies on organizational performance.

One problem with the studies conducted to date is that most analyses examine a cross-section of firms during one time period, rather than look at a particular organization over time. Through studying one group of workers over a long period, the effects of changes in specific HR policies become more apparent. In addition, the results allow detailed analysis of the human capital characteristics of the work force while controlling for variations in product type and demand. Organizations with the resources and research capabilities may want to conduct such longitudinal analyses on their own work force.[45]

In the absence of firm-specific studies, cross-sectional analyses of different plants or divisions within a single organization offer the next-best alternative. Relative to studies of different industries over different time periods, data on one organization, even if over different product lines, can provide important clues as to the effects of different compensation, grievance, performance appraisal, or employment and training programs. However, such studies should carefully control for differences in workers' skills, changes in capital-labor ratios, variations in product line and/or price, and alterations in the company's managerial culture or organizational design.

Another issue of particular importance concerns the timing of studies linking HR practices to organizational performance. To illustrate, from the early 1950s to 1970s, common wisdom held that unionization dramatically increased employees' wages and reduced profits with the first negotiated contract. However, a study using matched plant-level data over time has shown that during the 1980s, new unions were unable to raise wages much higher than wages and benefits in unorganized firms.[46] As a result, this "fact" in labor relations needs to be reevaluated.

In a similar fashion, the current impact of HR policies may differ considerably from the effects of such policies in the 1970s. Relative to the 1980s, employers in the 1970s had to deal with higher levels of inflation and unionization but lower levels of domestic and foreign competition. As a result, organizations paid less attention a decade ago to the effects of HR policies and allowed more leeway in implementing such policies.

Some researchers have begun to undertake these needed types of analyses. For example, a detailed study of HR practices and firm performance is currently underway at the Columbia Graduate School of Business. Using data from a number of organizations, the researchers are linking specific HR policies, such as staffing, selection, and job performance of different types of workers to various measures of productivity and profitability. Complementary studies, controlling for product line, and the mix of human capital characteristics among workers, are taking place at the plant level in order to capture the effect of changes in HR practices on smaller groups of employees. In combination, these studies should greatly enhance current knowledge regarding the impact of specific HR practices on the financial performance of American industry.

Conclusions

The linkage of HR policies to overall organizational performance relates to the most important factor in any organization, and in the national economy: labor. Although research in this area is still relatively new, a number of conclusions seem possible. Industrial relations and HR policies have important quantitative effects on the productivity and profitability of major organizations. As a result, variations in these policies and practices can have a major effect on an organization's success.

The union sector has attracted the greatest amount of research in this field. These studies suggest that while unionization may reduce an organization's overall profitability, the existence of a grievance process which acts as a check or balance on managerial authority can enhance both profitability and productivity. In addition, different practices with regard to unions may produce different effects.

HR practices found in union and nonunion establishments have received less attention. Still, research findings indicate that policies related to compensation, turnover, information sharing, recruitment, and pensions all have direct or indirect linkages to productivity and/or profitability.

Despite debate over how to measure an organization's success, share value tends to serve as the most accepted criterion for investor-owned corporations. Within this context, HR managers who hope to have a greater role in strategic management must be able to show how their function influences the organization's economic success. To progress from a reactive role as an "order filler" to the proactive role of developing firm strategic policies, greater knowledge of the linkage between HRM and organizational performance is essential. Achieving this knowledge will require the collaborative effort of both academics and practitioners in the HR field.

◆

Notes

1. Brealey and Myers, chapter 2.
2. Peters and Waterman suggest that "treating people—not machines or minds—as the natural resource may be the key to it all."
3. Freedman. 1987. Comments delivered to the session on Human Resources and Firm Performance, IRRA, Chicago.
4. Brealey and Myers.
5. Alchian and Demsetz.
6. See Kleiner, McLean, and Dreher, chapter 2, for a textbook treatment of the role HRM can play in maximizing shareholders' wealth and managing people.
7. Kleiner, Block, Roomkin, and Salsburg, pp. 319–343.
8. Freeman and Medoff.
9. Freeman and Medoff.
10. Allen.
11. Hirsch.
12. An excellent summary of these findings can be found in Allen, Tables 2 and 3.
13. Freeman and Medoff.
14. Clark.
15. Ruback and Zimmerman.
16. Freeman and Kleiner (1990).
17. Neumann.
18. Becker and Olson.
19. Abowd.
20. Becker.
21. Thomas and Kleiner.
22. Federal Mediation and Conciliation Service.
23. Freeman and Medoff.
24. Ichniowski; Katz, Kochan, and Gobeille; Katz, Kochan, and Weber.
25. Kleiner, Nickelsburg, and Pilarski (1989a and 1989b).
26. Holzer; Barron, Bishop, and Dunkelberg.
27. Holzer.
28. Brown and Medoff.
29. Osterman, pp. 275–318.
30. Spencer.
31. Ehrenberg and Milkovich.
32. For alternative views, see volume 3 of this series, *Compensation and Benefits*.
33. Ehrenberg and Milkovich.
34. Id.

35. Weitzman.
36. Allen and Clark.
37. Id.
38. Larker.
39. Larker.
40. Bartel.
41. Lawler.

42. Kleiner and Bouillon.
43. Gershenfeld.
44. Campbell and Campbell; Gordon and Johnson.
45. Kleiner, Nickelsburg, and Pilarski (1989a and 1989b).
46. Freeman and Kleiner (1989).

◆

References

Abowd, J. 1989. "The Effect of Wage Bargains on the Stock Market Value of the Firm." *American Economic Review* 79 (September): 774–809.

Alchian, A.A., and H. Demsetz. 1972. "Production, Information Costs, and Economic Efficiency." *American Economic Review* 62 (5) (December): 777–795.

Allen, S.G. 1988. "Human Resource Practices and Union-Nonunion Productivity Differences." Paper presented to the Academy of Management meetings, Anaheim, CA, August.

Allen, S.G., and R.L. Clark. 1987. "Pensions and Firm Performance." In *Human Resources and the Performance of the Firm*, eds. M. Kleiner, R.N. Block, M. Roomkin, and S.W. Salsburg. Madison, WI: Industrial Relations Research Association.

Barron, J.M., J. Bishop, and W.C. Dunkelberg. 1985. "Employer Search." *Review of Economics and Statistics* 67 (February): 45–52.

Bartel, A. 1989. "Formal Employee Training Programs and Their Impact on Labor Productivity: Evidence from a Human Resource Survey." NBER Working Paper 3026, July, p. 37.

Becker, B.E. 1987. "Concession Bargaining: The Impact on Shareholders' Equity." *Industrial and Labor Relations Review* 40 (January): 268–279.

Becker, B.E., and C.A. Olson. 1986. "The Impact of Strikes on Shareholder Equity." *Industrial and Labor Relations Review* 39 (April): 425–438.

Brealey, R., and S. Myers. 1984. *Principles of Corporate Finance*, 2nd ed. New York: McGraw-Hill.

Brown, C., and J. Medoff. 1978. "Trade Unions in the Production Process." *Journal of Political Economy* 86 (June): 355–378.

Campbell, J.P. and R.J. Campbell. 1988. *Productivity and Organizations*. San Francisco: Jossey-Bass, Inc.

Clark, K.B. 1984. "Unionization and Firm Performance: The Impact on Profits, Growth, and Productivity." *American Economic Review* (December): 893–919.

Ehrenberg, R.G. 1990. "Do Compensation Policies Matter?" *Industrial and Labor Relations Review* 43 (3) (February): 3-5–12-5.

Ehrenberg, R.G., and G.T. Milkovich. 1987. "Compensation and Firm Performance." In *Human Resources and the Performance of the Firm*, eds. M.M. Kleiner, R.N. Block, M. Roomkin, and S.W. Salsburg. Madison, WI: Industrial Relations Research Association, 87–122.

Federal Mediation and Conciliation Service. 1982. *Thirty-Fourth Annual Report, 1981*. Washington, D.C.: U.S. Government Printing Office.

Freeman, R.B., and M.M. Kleiner. 1989. "The Impact of New Unionization on Wages and Working Conditions: A Longitudinal Analysis." *Journal of Labor Economics* 7(3) (January): 5-8–5-25.

———. 1990. "Employer Behavior in the Face of Union Organizing Drives." *Industrial and Labor Relations Review* 43(4): (April) 351–365.

Freeman, R.B., and J. Medoff. 1984. *What Do Unions Do?* New York: Basic Books.

Gershenfeld, W.J. 1987. "Employee Participation in Firm Decisions." In *Human Resources and the Performance of the Firm*, eds. M.M. Kleiner, R.N. Block, M. Roomkin, and S.W. Salsburg. Madison, WI: Industrial Relations Research Association.

Gordon, M.E., and W.A. Johnson. 1982. "Seniority: A Review of Its Legal and Scientific Standing." *Personnel Psychology* 35: 255–280.

Hirsch, B.T. Forthcoming. "Firm Investment Behavior and Collective Bargaining Strategy." *Industrial Relations*.

Holzer, H.J. 1987. "Hiring Procedures in the Firm: Their Economic Determinants and Outcomes." In *Human Resources and the Performance of the Firm*, eds. M.M. Kleiner, R.N. Block, M. Roomkin, and S.W. Salsburg. Madison, WI: Industrial Relations Research Association, 243–274.

Ishniowski, C. 1986. "The Effects of Grievance Activity on Productivity." *Industrial and Labor Relations Review* 40 (October): 75–89.

Katz, H.C., T.A. Kochan, and K.R. Gobeille. 1983. "Industrial Relations Performance, Economic Performance, and QWL Programs: An Interplant Analysis." *Industrial and Labor Relations Review* 37 (October): 3–17.

Katz, H.C., T.A. Kochan, and M. Weber. 1985. "Assessing the Effects of Industrial Relations Systems and Efforts to Improve the Quality of Working Life on Organizational Effectiveness." *Academy of Management Journal* 28 (September): 509–526.

Kleiner, M.M., R.N. Block, M. Roomkin, and S.W. Salsburg, eds. 1987. "Industrial Relations and the Performance of the Firm: An Overview." In *Human Resources and the Performance of the Firm*. Madison, WI: Industrial Relations Research Association.

Kleiner, M.M. and M. Bouillon. 1988. "Providing Business Information to Production Workers: Correlates of Compensation and Profitability." *Industrial and Labor Relations Review* 41 (4) (July): 605–617.

Kleiner, M.M., R.A. McLean, and G.F. Dreher. 1988. *Labor Markets and Human Resource Management*. Glenview, IL: Scott Foresman/Little Brown College Division.

Kleiner, M.M., G. Nickelsburg, and A. Pilarski. 1989a. "Grievances and Plant Performance: Is Zero Optimal?" *Proceedings*. Madison, WI: Industrial Relations Research Association, 284–298.

———. 1989b. "Monitoring, Grievances, and Plant Performance." Unpublished manuscript, p. 34.

Larker, D. 1983. "The Association Between Performance Plan Adoption and Corporate Capital Investments." *Journal of Accounting and Economics* 5 (April): 3–30.

Lawler, E.E. 1967. "Secrecy about Management Compensation: Are There Hidden Costs:" *Organizational Behavior and Human Performance* 2: 182–189.

Neumann, G. 1980. "The Predictability of Strikes: Evidence from the Stock Market." *Industrial and Labor Relations Review* 33 (July): 525–535.

Osterman, P. 1987. "Turnover, Employment Security, and the Performance of the Firm." In *Human Resources and the Performance of the Firm*, eds. M.M. Kleiner, R.N. Block, M. Roomkin, and S.W. Salsburg. Madison, WI: Industrial Relations Research Association.

Peters, T.J., and R.H. Waterman. 1984. *In Search of Excellence: Lessons From America's Best-Run Companies*. New York: Warner Books.

Ruback, R., and M.B. Zimmerman. 1984. "Unionization and Profitability: Evidence from the Capital Market." *Journal of Political Economy* 92 (6) (December): 1134–1157.

Spencer, D. 1986. "Employee Voice and Employee Retention." *Academy of Management Journal* 29 (September): 488–502.

Thomas, S., and M. Kleiner. 1989. "Two-Tier Collective Bargaining Agreements and Shareholder Equity." Unpublished manuscript, University of Minnesota, p. 26.

Weitzman, M. 1984. *The Share Economy*. New York: Basic Books.

———— ♦ ————

4.3

Union-Management Cooperation

Michael Schuster

In recent years, American industrial relations have been transformed and one aspect of the transformation has been a significant increase in cooperation between companies and unions.[1] Increased union-management cooperation began in the 1970s and continued unabated throughout the 1980s. Although the traditional system of collective bargaining remains the most common mechanism for resolving important workplace issues, evidence suggests that increasingly diverse cooperative efforts are taking place. These efforts have occurred primarily at the plant or workplace, but some are also occurring throughout an entire company, industry, or region.

This chapter reviews the state of union-management cooperation by examining: (1) The historical evolution of cooperative efforts in the United States; (2) the stimulus for increased labor-management cooperation in the United States; (3) models of organizational change and cooperative behavior; (4) the forms that cooperation may take, including key issues and research findings in cooperation; and (5) the opportunities and difficulties in developing cooperative strategies.

Evolution of Union-Management Cooperation

The experience of the past decade continues a long-term evolution in industrial relations toward pragmatic, problem-solving approaches and away from ideological, class conflict oriented approaches to union-management relations. This seemingly new type of union-management behavior does have historical precedence in the United States. In the 1920s and 30s, cooperation frequently meant the arbitration of disputes in the hotel, electrical contracting, and garment industries. In the 1940s, some 9,000 wartime labor-management production committees handled disputes, while the 1950s saw the full development of automation committees to respond to technological change in such industries as coal, meat packing, longshore industries, and efforts to make grievance and arbitration procedures more effective. Cooperative efforts in general declined in the 1960s. However, one noteworthy exception is the steel industry, which following the 116-day strike in 1959, created a Human Relations Research Committee to study ongoing problems.[2]

Historical Forms of Cooperation

Union-management cooperation has previously fallen into eight categories.[3] At the national or regional level, cooperative efforts have taken the form of (1) presidential economic policy committees, (2) industry-level labor-management policy committees, (3) joint industry or companywide committees to develop responses to technological change, and (4) area- or communitywide labor-management committees.

The most frequent and far-reaching efforts at cooperation have occurred at the plant or workplace level. These efforts go beyond the traditional manufacturing environments of trade unionism and have influenced other sectors, such as health care and public employment. Four forms of workplace-level cooperation have become prevalent, each having a distinct structure, process, and scope of activity despite sharing similar goals. Forms of workplace cooperation include (1) safety committees; (2) in-plant labor-management committees and programs to improve union-management relations; (3) productivity committees, gainsharing, employee involvement, and quality circles, and (4) quality of work life and work redesign projects.

Several forms of cooperation may occur at the same location, simultaneously or as an outgrowth of initial efforts. For example, an employer and union may initiate a cooperative approach with a labor-management committee which later evolves into more in-depth employee involvement, job restructuring, and/or gainsharing. Such a committee frequently includes a safety subcommittee.

Each of these forms of cooperation poses potential benefits and difficulties that will be examined later in this chapter. But for any cooperative effort to succeed, certain factors favoring initiation of cooperation must be in place. The following section outlines these variables.

Present Stimuli for Union-Management Cooperation

Recent changes in the American industrial relations system have parallelled sweeping shifts in the economic environment. Since the early 1970s, foreign competition, the advantages of the non-union sector in terms of cost and modern equipment, and changing values, attitudes, and work behaviors among much of the labor force have increasingly shaken the foundations of the traditional system of collective bargaining. During the 1980s, harsh economic difficulties have accelerated the process of change and accommodation. Despite dramatic improvements in the economic fortunes of most manufacturing firms during 1987 and 1988, continued worldwide competition has fueled corporate cost cutting and further stimulated cooperative activities.

Whether, and to what degree, the increased levels of cooperation will continue is very much an open question. The impetus and publicity for many cooperative efforts came from the National Center for Productivity and Quality of Work Life (NCPQWL) during the 1970s and from the Bureau of Cooperative Labor-Management Programs in the 1980s. While, at present, economic conditions have stabilized, companies have had to increase their efficiency in order to enhance their competitiveness. One strategy for doing this is to expand the level of employee and union involvement in decision-making affecting the workplace. More importantly, the current situation provides an opportunity for a long-term reshaping of many bargaining relationships. The success of these cooperative efforts will likely determine whether such endeavors become part of the American industrial relations system or merely constitute a temporary interruption in traditional adversarial collective bargaining.

Factors Fueling Cooperation

Nearly all models of organizational change and union-management cooperation suggest an initial stimulus is necessary for cooperation or change to occur.[4] A series of factors have combined to make change in unionized settings more prevalent. These trends are outlined below.

Foreign and Domestic Competition

Overseas competition in the 1980s caused significant cost competition for unionized companies. Differences in the exchange rate value of the dollar relative to European and Japanese currencies further exacerbated this problem. In addition, domestic competition from nonunion companies primarily based in the South threatened union firms. Many of these nonunion facilities were subsidiaries of the same company, thus setting in motion high levels of internal competition.

Overcapacity

Many industries suffered from considerable overcapacity both within the United States and overseas. This problem placed considerable pressure on many union-represented facilities which tended to have dated capital and systems, as well as more mature workforces.

Technology and Systems

Many companies are seeking to install new systems of factory automation, robotics, and more modern production systems. These processes and systems require greater employee flexibility and their effectiveness improves when employers have the cooperation and involvement of employees. Firms that have sought to install work teams and manufacturing cells have found it necessary to achieve contractual changes that allow for more flexibility.

Drive for Quality

The focus of product competition in many industries has shifted to a greater emphasis on quality rather than simply pricing. Here again, employees and positive employee and union relations play a very critical role. For example, Ford Motor Company reflects this focus through its program of "Quality is Job One" and its emphasis on employee involvement and quality training programs, as well as vendor certification. In many instances, vendors have been encouraged to replicate their customers' cooperative programs.

Recognition of the Problem

For some time, widespread recognition that a problem existed in our industries proved difficult to obtain. That recognition now appears to exist throughout management and labor. Employees and unions are viewed as potential allies in management's efforts to create a competitive advantage.

Changes in Employee Needs, Values, and Concerns

The shifting composition of the work force has led to a new emphasis on employee initiatives. Employees want to get more involved in their jobs and express a desire to have more influence and control over their work. Many union leaders now see employee participation as a valuable goal and report that their members welcome the opportunity for expanded control over their jobs. One union leader has recently commented that workers have the right to share in the profits of their firms.[5]

Changes in Management and Union Philosophy

There is more willingness on the part of management to involve employees and unions in workplace decision-making. Many companies now staff facilities without the traditional first level of supervision, thus relying upon an expanded role for employees in daily operations.

Government Policy

Deregulation of such industries as trucking and the airlines has fundamentally shifted the rules of the game. Many companies and unions must work together in order to survive, as excess costs can no longer be passed on to the end user.

National vs. Workplace Trends

The increase in cooperative activity in the United States has, paradoxically, occurred at a time when relations between the labor movement and employers at the national level have been strained. Increased employer aggressiveness in political activity and at the workplace, as well as the apathy of the Reagan administration regarding labor management relations issues, have caused this rift.[6]

In addition, at some companies, such as Eastern Airlines, union-management relations hit a new low.

In the political arena, employer lobbying efforts have served to further contaminate the relationship between labor and management. During the 1970s, management's efforts resulted in the defeat of Common Situs Picketing and Labor Law Reform legislation, two bills actively sought by the labor movement. In the 1980s, the lack of a labor policy consensus encouraged employer opposition to minimum wage increases and plant-closing legislation, even though many companies had already voluntarily complied with many of the proposed provisions. This opposition further demonstrated to unions that cooperation on the factory floor does not guarantee partnership on issues beyond the workplace, leading some to question the benefit of cooperation and team concepts.[7]

In the workplace, management has launched increased, aggressive opposition to union organizing efforts in nonunion operations, as well as upped efforts to decertify existing unions. Even after waging a successful representation campaign, unions frequently face difficulty reaching a first contract.[8] Likewise, in collective bargaining, management demands for concession wage agreements and work rule changes have become widespread.[9] Although the economic environment has improved, management's aggressiveness at the bargaining table has declined only slightly.

Despite conflict at the national level, cooperation at the plant level has increased, propelled by the strong stimuli for change discussed earlier. The harsh competitive environment facing many firms, continuing overcapacity in some industries at home and worldwide, and the opportunity costs associated with off-shore production have prompted a reshaping of local collective bargaining relations, national activity notwithstanding. Moreover, management philosophy at the workplace level has shifted. Employers increasingly favor greater involvement by both employees and unions in workplace problem-solving and decision-making, and encourage a more team-oriented approach to achieving organizational effectiveness.

The Process of Cooperation and Change in Union Environments

Cooperation and change in union settings have received little theoretical or empirical examination. In fact, most authors have neglected to even provide a definition of cooperation. For the purposes of this discussion, cooperation is defined as: joint collaboration by a company and a union in problem-solving activities that aim to enhance organizational performance, improve quality, and reduce friction in union-management relations. Cooperation should serve to strengthen employee job security, increase employee earnings, and/or improve safety and the quality of work life. In practice, union-management cooperation most often takes the form of information-sharing policies, labor-management committees, employee involvement efforts, safety committees, gainsharing and profit-sharing programs, and expanded training activities.

Models of Cooperation and Change

Despite the relative lack of research, several theories regarding the development of union-management cooperation have emerged. One of the best models,[10] when combined with others,[11] suggests that cooperation evolves through a four-stage process of change in union settings. In stage one, a stimulus for cooperation emerges, leading to an initial decision for cooperation (stage two). The third stage sees the introduction of programs to operationalize cooperative efforts. Success at this stage will depend on factors related to the nature of the intervention introduced (for example, gainsharing success factors will likely be somewhat different from work restructuring). Finally, in stage four, the parties enter into an ongoing labor-management relationship. This model, shown in Figure 1, is elaborated in the following discussion.

A number of factors operate in favor of cooperation in union settings. For example, joint efforts between union and management may enhance support for, and the effectiveness of, quality of work life projects.[12] Cooperation would lessen employees' resistance to change, and offer the potential to achieve lasting change. In addition, the union could achieve noneconomic benefits for its members outside of collective bargaining, the overall union-management relationship would become less adversarial, and the threat of government-legislated involvement would lessen.

Nonetheless, cooperation is difficult to achieve for a number of reasons. The conflicting goals of labor (employment security, higher wages and benefits, job rights) and management (profit, productivity, organizational effectiveness and efficiency) and the adversarial nature of many relationships rank as longstanding obstacles. The relative novelty of cooperative efforts, and the lack of models of

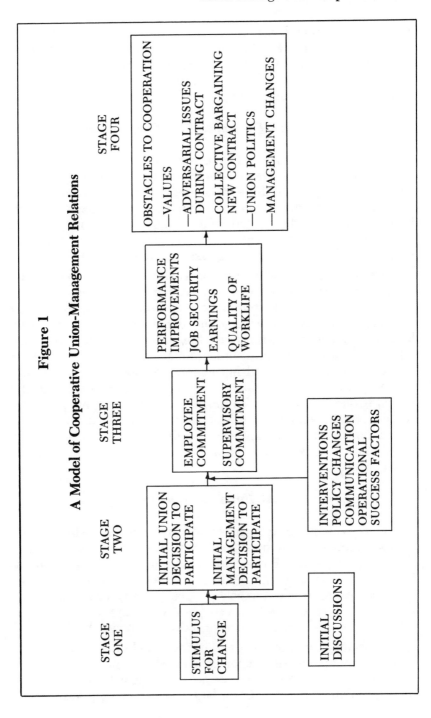

Figure 1

A Model of Cooperative Union-Management Relations

cooperation, research data on changes, and qualified consultants, also pose problems. Practical impediments include the potential loss of power for managers and union leaders, barriers in collective bargaining agreements to such programs as job redesign, and the time needed to plan and implement change.

Stage One: The Impetus for Cooperation

The conflicting goals between labor and management become less important when adverse stimuli affect both parties. As noted previously, the present drive for cooperation has arisen largely as a result of the difficult competitive environment facing many unionized companies in the United States. Many of these firms seek to utilize labor to create a greater competitive advantage, or at least to reduce or offset any disadvantage associated with labor.

The greater the internal or external pressure for change, the more likely the parties will consider a cooperative strategy.[13] One of the great sources of frustration to many observers over the last several years has been the magnitude of the difficulties facing many labor-management situations and the business as usual approach taken by many companies and unions. However, pressure for change in and of itself will not generate cooperation, since both parties probably will attempt to resolve issues first through the formal bargaining process. To the extent that traditional processes succeed, further efforts toward cooperation will probably not occur. When, however, standard processes prove ineffective in addressing the stimulus issues—as has often occurred in the 1980s—cooperation may occur.

Stage Two: An Initial Decision to Cooperate

Once both parties recognize that a problem exists which cannot be addressed through traditional bargaining they must formally decide to cooperate. First, both sides must view cooperation as instrumental to resolving the stimulus issues; then both sides must reach compromise as to the goals of a cooperative program. At any point, a decision to engage in a cooperative program can be undermined or thwarted by coalitions or individual power holders.

Unfortunately, the process is not as straightforward as it might seem. Many union-management players still do not view cooperative approaches as appropriate ways for dealing with labor-management problems. There exists a large degree of skepticism based upon ideological factors and an absence of trust that leads many on both sides to question the validity of cooperative approaches. Supervisory resistance to cooperation and employee involvement has been well-documented.[14]

Union Attitudes Toward Cooperation. Several studies of union and company attitudes toward cooperation have taken place in both the United States and Canada.[15] Union activists view collective bargaining as effective in addressing traditional workplace issues such as fringe benefits, earnings, job security, grievance procedures, safety, and hours. Thus, labor expressed less preference for collaboration with management on these matters. On the other hand, unions viewed collective bargaining as less effective in addressing issues such as interesting work, supervisors, control of work, productivity, better jobs, adequate resources, and work load. As a result, a distinct preference exists for pursuing joint programs with management outside collective bargaining to address these issues.

At the national level, union officials express divided opinions on the benefits of cooperation. One view, held by the auto workers and communications workers, considers joint union-management programs on the quality of work life as adding to a foundation of industrial democracy built through collective bargaining. Cooperative efforts are viewed as increasing worker dignity and providing an opportunity to influence decisions affecting one's job. Moreover, unions see cooperation as a method of "helping to shape management practices and policies while they are being formed rather than after the fact."[16]

The Machinists union has taken a different view. This view holds that management's belated desire to involve workers in efforts to increase organizational effectiveness stems from any of four factors: First, management has made errors, the responsibility for which it would like to share with the union. Second, when management wants to introduce new processes or technology, it seeks to involve the union to legitimize resulting unemployment. Third, management is looking for a speed-up, or fourth, it hopes to weaken the union by making its role unnecessary.[17]

Management Attitudes Toward Cooperation. Management attitudes toward cooperation have received less attention. One study asked executives of large companies whether they would favor returning to traditional bargaining once the economy became healthy or whether they would prefer giving unions and workers more say in company operations if employee compensation were tied to company performance. Overall, 50 percent of the executives would opt for greater union and employee involvement. Heavily unionized companies were more likely to favor employee participation than firms with less unionization. The number favoring participation increased from 42 percent to 58 percent as the degree of unionization in the company increased from 40 percent or fewer to more than 70 percent of employees. Differences also emerged among various industry groups. Utilities (87 percent) and electrical companies (73 percent) held the most favorable views toward cooperation, while the natural resources (27 percent) and retail industries (25 percent) were least likely to prefer cooperation.[18]

Stage Three: Program Success Factors

One analysis has dichotomized workplace management approaches as oriented toward either control or commitment.[19] A traditional control environment included elements like strict division of work, tight management hierarchy, treatment of labor as a variable cost, status symbols attached to organizational position, and the like. These characteristics produce adversarial employee relations, with unions acting to "protect the work force" from management excesses. The control model may prove inappropriate for achieving world-class competitive status, particularly in a high-wage country such as the United States.

The elements of a commitment approach are summarized as follows:

> [J]obs are designed to be broader than before, to combine planning and implementation, and to include efforts to upgrade operations, not just maintain them. Individual responsibilities are expected to change as conditions change, and teams, not individuals, often are the organizational units accountable for performance. With management hierarchies relatively flat and differences in status minimized, control and lateral coordination depend on shared goals, and expertise rather than formal position determines influence.[20]

Others have suggested that labor and employee relations strategy may be employed to create a unique competitive advantage.[21]

Research shows a relationship between organizational commitment and many positive organizational outcomes.[22] However, organizational commitment can prove difficult to achieve in union environments because of the conflicting institutional goals that separate unions and management. A considerable debate, dating back to the 1950s, has revolved around the issue of dual loyalty—allegiance to the company versus the union.[23] Recent research suggests that in good labor relations climates, employers will likely have dual loyalty and greater organizational commitment, while in poor labor relations climates, employee loyalty will normally run to the union.[24] In very poor situations, employees may experience disaffection toward both parties.

All of the cooperative interventions discussed in this chapter are designed to achieve heightened employee commitment to the organization. However, one precondition to success is the quality of the labor management relationship. In short, improving union-management relations is a precursor to substantial, long-term change in union environments.

Stage Four: Institutionalization of the Process

Institutionalizing cooperative union-management relationships is not an easy task. While the cooperative process is a fragile one, the following conditions may enhance the likelihood that cooperation will continue:

- Valued goals are achieved in the early stages.

- The probability that additional goals will be achieved in the future is high.

- Initial goals are not displaced by goals of a higher priority.

- The program stimulus or the reason for the cooperative effort remains strong.

- Benefits derived from the cooperation are equitably distributed.

- The union is perceived as instrumental in attaining program benefits.

- The cooperative effort does not infringe on traditional collective bargaining issues.

- The program does not threaten management prerogatives.

- The program does not overlap the grievance procedure.

- Union leaders are not viewed as being co-opted.

- The cooperative effort is protected from use of bargaining tactics and maneuvers.

- Union leaders continue to pursue member goals on traditional economic issues.[25]

Forms of Union-Management Cooperation

Cooperative efforts may take a diversity of forms. Some types of cooperation occur primarily at a national level; others are more oriented toward the plant or facility level. Each form of cooperation tends to encompass a different focus and thus, each usually has a different structure and impacts on a different set of variables. In recent years, the most far-reaching cooperative labor-management efforts have occurred at the facility level; therefore these initiatives receive greater attention in the following discussion.

National- and Industry-Level Cooperation

Cooperation between employers and unions at the national level has taken three forms. These efforts have included presidential labor-management committees, industry labor-management policy committees, and joint responses to technological change.

Presidential Labor-Management Committees

The United States experienced national labor-management conferences at the beginning and end of both World Wars.[26] In addition, periodic tripartite bodies were established with charters to address specific issues. In 1961, recurring recessions, inflation and industrial disputes (for example, the steel strike of 1959-60) prompted President Kennedy to found an Advisory Committee on Labor-Management Policy. Unlike the previous one-time conferences, the advisory committee was intended as a continuing vehicle for addressing diverse issues, including unemployment, manpower policies, collective bargaining, and tax policy. The advisory committee made recommendations on manpower programs and supported an administration-inspired tax cut.

Following Kennedy's death, President Johnson initially allowed the committee to falter. But as Vietnam spending programs heated up the economy, Johnson revived the advisory body to address wage-price and other economic policy issues. This group recommended a tax increase, which the Johnson administration subsequently endorsed.

Because the Kennedy-Johnson committee had an uneven record of accomplishment, the Nixon administration created a series of tripartite committees, including the National Commission on Productivity; the Construction Industry Stabilization Committee, which reviewed wage and contract settlements; and the National Commission for Industrial Peace, which aimed to improve the process of bargaining and to find ways to protect the public interest. The Nixon administration also instituted a wage-price freeze in August 1971, followed by a period of controls. A tripartite Pay Board, comprising five members each from the labor, business, and public sectors, took on the task of making pay policy and reviewing wage increases. After labor members resigned from the Pay Board, its duties fell to a new Cost of Living Council which contained a ten-member (five labor, five business) Labor-Management Advisory Committee. These business and labor representatives also served on the commissions on Productivity and Industrial Peace, making the commissions somewhat interlocking and giving members authority over a broader spectrum of issues.

The Ford administration's Presidential Labor-Management Committee took a broader approach, but maintained the representatives appointed during the Nixon period. Designed to battle inflation, the committee made recommendations for tax cuts and energy policy. It also worked to encourage bargaining reforms in several industries and to resolve jurisdictional disputes in the construction industry. When President Ford vetoed the common situs picketing legislation, Secretary of Labor John Dunlop resigned and the Committee severed its ties with the administration and operated independently.

In the Carter administration, the Labor-Management Committee operated independently, but did review the administration's economic policies. The group recommended policies on energy and illegal aliens, and worked to resolve labor problems in the maritime industry and on the construction of nuclear power plants. In 1978, Douglas Fraser, president of the Autoworkers Union, resigned to protest business actions which had led to the defeat of labor law reform and other anti-union actions. The Reagan administration—and Bush administration to date—did not create a national forum for cooperative issues.

Although these committees did not produce a series of important and successful accomplishments, they have generated high-level discussion, as well as recommendations on tax policy, manpower, energy, and collective bargaining. While the committees have impacted various sectors (e.g., retail food, construction, and maritime) of the economy, they were notably unsuccessful in producing agreement on wage-price policies.

Industry Labor-Management Policy Committees

Labor-management committees at the industry level offer several advantages to the parties that can only come from a level of analysis and detachment from day to day negotiations. They permit broad discussion of underlying industry problems, focused study and analysis of problems, the opportunity to experiment with new programs, and the potential to impact the overall climate facing labor and management. Because these committees are often detached from day-to-day politics and the stresses of normal collective bargaining, they can offer the basis for broad change throughout a particular sector of the economy.

In recent years, the construction, retail food, and health care industries have operated labor-management committees. The retail food committee addressed issues such as technological changes, work rules, transportation and distribution, productivity, and the structure of bargaining. When successful, industry committees can minimize the cost disadvantages that a single firm would incur if it made changes that were not followed throughout its industry.[27] Still, for these committees to succeed, they must gain the cooperation and participation of a broad spectrum of company and union officials.

Joint Responses to Technological Change

Historically, as industries mechanize through automated machinery or robotics, employee displacements occur and a substantial number of jobs often are lost. This has also been the case as many firms have undergone widespread rationalizations resulting in severe displacement of employees. To ease the effect of loss of employment, several industries have formed joint committees to smooth the displacement of employees. These committees have addressed issues of retraining, health and welfare, and income security. Industries utilizing automation funds and committees include coal mining, meat packing, and long shore.[28] More recently, the auto industry and state governments have established these bodies.[29]

Area Labor-Management Committees

During the 1970s, a unique format for cooperation developed: the areawide labor-management committee. Although several communities—Toledo, Ohio and Louisville, Kentucky—have had such committees since the 1940s, the concept did not catch on until the success of the Jamestown and Buffalo, New York committees in the 1970s. In both cities, the committees are widely credited for improving the labor relations climate in the local community.

The increasing use of area labor-management committees (AL-MCs) represents an important new institutional arrangement in industrial relations. Such committees have been characterized as a grass-roots approach to resolving difficult labor relations problems at the local level. Communities have created AL-MCs in response to excessive strike activity, plant closings (threatened and actual), and an area reputation as a bad labor town. These factors are believed to reduce a community's economic viability by affecting its ability to recruit new industry and to expand existing facilities.

Committee Functions

The AL-MC members typically include a community's key union leaders, top operating management, and in some cases, elected officials. A professional staff directs the primary work of a committee and its day-to-day operations. AL-MC activities generally encompass the following functions:

- Sponsoring social and educational events to increase communication and understanding between labor and management and to demonstrate the mutual benefits of cooperation

- Serving as informal neutrals in difficult collective bargaining negotiations

- Acting as an integral part of the area's economic development program

- Stimulating and facilitating the creation of in-plant labor-management committees.[30]

This last function ranks as the most important activity of an area committee.

Political Sponsorship

These local efforts received federal recognition through the passage of the Labor-Management Cooperation Act of 1978.[31] The Act is designed to encourage plant-, area-, and industrywide cooperation through the following union-management efforts:

(1) to improve communication between representatives of labor and management;

(2) to provide workers and employers with opportunities to study and explore new and innovative joint approaches to achieving organizational effectiveness;

(3) to assist workers and employers in solving problems of mutual concern not susceptible to resolution within the collective bargaining process;

(4) to study and explore ways of eliminating potential problems which reduce the competitiveness and inhibit the economic development of the plant, area or industry;

(5) to enhance the involvement of workers in making decisions that affect their working lives;

(6) to expand and improve working relationships between workers and managers; and

(7) to encourage free collective bargaining by establishing continuing mechanisms for communication between employers and their employees through Federal assistance to the formation and operation of labor-management committees.

The Federal Mediation and Conciliation Service (FMCS) was empowered to provide financial and technical assistance to companies and unions to facilitate this process. The FMCS allocated limited amounts of funds, most of which went to support area labor-management committees. However, budget restrictions kept actual funding for the program well below authorized levels. As a result, the federal government has served a primarily informational role in efforts to stimulate cooperation between companies and unions. This situation has, to some extent, limited the potential success and diffusion of cooperative strategies given the shortage of qualified resources to assist parties in developing cooperative strategies.

Several states (such as Pennsylvania, Ohio, and Illinois) and local communities (such as Erie County, NY) presently have legislation to provide funds for cooperative efforts, particularly through area labor-management councils. This funding is used to provide technical assistance, education, training, and other funding for cooperative efforts. Despite scarce resources, more than 100 area labor-management committees have emerged across the country, including several in large metropolitan areas like Buffalo, Philadelphia, and St. Louis.[32]

Facility-Level Cooperation and Change

Efforts at cooperation and change at the facility level have taken four basic, but overlapping forms: safety and health committees; programs to improve union-management relations; productivity gainsharing, profit sharing, and employee involvement; and quality of work-life programs. As previously noted, these distinctions can seem arbitrary, since efforts discussed in this section frequently overlap.

Union-Management Safety Committees[33]

One of the most common areas of union-management cooperation deals with safety and health issues. Safety and health committees have a rich history in the United States, since both parties can readily gain from safety improvements brought about by cooperation. Further stimulus for health and safety committees has come through the Occupational Safety and Health Act. This act has given employee representatives more power in forcing employers to address safety concerns.

Maintaining continuing interest has been a long-standing problem affecting safety committees. Factors enhancing the effectiveness of safety committees include management commitment to safety improvements, a willingness to work with union representatives, employee interest in safety as an issue, external pressure from federal regulators, and mechanisms to shield the safety committee from the traditional adversarial process.[34]

Programs to Improve Union-Management Relations

The 1970s saw the evolution of two strategies to improve union-management relationships and to bring about organizational change. One program, Labor-Management Relationships by Objectives (RBO), was developed and administered by the Federal Mediation and Conciliation Service (FMCS). The second strategy, labor-management committees, arose largely through private efforts.

RBO Programs. The RBO program marked the first attempt to adapt organizational development techniques and approaches (for example, laboratory training) to labor-management relations. It focused on producing attitudinal change and problem-solving approaches as conceptualized in the Walton & McKersie Model.[35] The goal was to move labor-management relations from antagonism to constructive problem-solving through clarifying and diagnosing intragroup images and through building intergroup teams. RBO interventions utilized off-site, intensive, three-day sessions, involving ten to fifteen participants from each party and three to five mediators.

After working to improve perceptions and attitudes, mediators helped develop joint goals for improving the parties' relationship. Improvements typically targeted five areas: communications, grievance handling, supervisory and steward training needs, company attitudes and practices, and the union. A recent evaluation has shown that the RBO programs have produced new roles and attitudes, better plant morale, fewer political grievances filed, improved productivity, and smoother contract negotiations.[36] Union and company representatives attributed much of the program's success to the mediators' skill and expertise.

Labor-Management Committees. Labor-management committees represent a redirection of earlier efforts. Historically, labor-management committees have tended to focus on single issues or purposes. For example, at one time, joint productivity committees were used extensively; other labor-management committees have been used to maintain communication.

The labor-management committees of the 1970s and 1980s have aimed to improve attitudes and to increase trust. Once these goals have been achieved, the committees serve to facilitate organizational change. Committee members usually include key operating managers and local union leaders, who meet periodically to discuss noncontractual issues, that is, issues expressly excluded from the collective agreement. The general objectives of plant labor-management committees include the following activities:

- Providing for regular broad ranging contact and communications between the parties during contract term

- Focusing contact and communication on positive problem-solving and achievement-oriented activity

- Building informal relationships, trust, and understanding

■ Recognizing the union as a communication link with employee/members[37]

Other than avoiding contractual issues, mature labor-management committees face no limit or restriction in the nature of issues discussed. Representative items might include introductions of new processes or equipment, quality or productivity improvements, job redesign, alcoholism and substance abuse programs, skill training, and the like.

Other Efforts

Other facility-level forms of cooperation include gainsharing, profit-sharing, and employee involvement plans. Due to the scope of information available, these cooperative efforts will receive separate discussion in the following sections.

Gainsharing, Profit Sharing, and Employee Involvement

Relative to other forms of cooperation, profit sharing, gainsharing, and employee involvement have generated more plentiful and better-quality research. This section takes advantage of those data to provide a more in-depth review of these programs.

Evolution of Gainsharing and Profit-Sharing Plans

Productivity-sharing plans (more recently called gainsharing) and profit-sharing are organizational systems which utilize regular cash bonuses to share the benefits of improved productivity, cost factors, quality, and/or overall business performance. In many cases, gainsharing plans also incorporate mechanisms for employee involvement.[38] Although many organizations have only recently begun to consider gainsharing and profit sharing as an element in their HR strategy, the concepts are not new. Profit-sharing plans date back as early as the first part of the 19th century. The first use of gainsharing, the Scanlon Plan, has been on the American industrial scene since the late 1930s.

Since then, two additional forms of productivity sharing have emerged: Rucker plans in the 1940s and Improshare plans in the 1970s. The plans differ greatly in philosophy, structure, and the type of organizations in which they are installed. In recent years, local adaptations of these plans, such as the Scanlon multi-cost plan and hosts of others, have been developed.

The first productivity-sharing plans arose largely as attempts to save companies from financial collapse. However, by the 1950s many gainsharing plans reflected a different management philosophy and a different approach by unions—namely, mutual cooperation and greater utilization of human resources.

Profit-Sharing Plans. Profit sharing could be considered one form of gainsharing. However, profit-sharing plans tend to operate in two distinct fashions: deferred and cash distribution. Deferred distribution plans do not pay current bonuses to employees. Instead, these plans defer the profit-sharing monies owed to employees in order to fund a pension plan or provide additional funding for a supplemental retirement vehicle. Cash distribution plans pay bonuses in the period in which they are earned. As a result, this type of profit-sharing plan shares some of the same motivational potential as gainsharing plans. Finally, some profit-sharing plans adopt a mixed form, distributing a portion of monies earned to employees in the current period, while deferring the remainder.

Gainsharing Plans. Gainsharing plans differ from piecework incentives and profit sharing in several important ways. Unlike individual incentives, gainsharing plans measure group, not individual, performance. Thus, they encourage teamwork, employee flexibility, and cooperation, as well as enhance standards of quality and workmanship. Gainsharing plans also do not entail the substantial start-up and ongoing administrative costs involved in individual incentive plans. Relative to piecework incentives, gainsharing plans produce far less workplace conflict for three reasons.[39] First, gainsharing bonuses affect a smaller amount of employee compensation than piecework plans. Second, gainsharing uses broad measures of organizational performance rather than individual standards, and third, management often participates in the plans.

Gainsharing, though conceptually similar, also offers the following advantages over profit sharing: First, it uses measures of organizational performance that are more readily understood by the work force. Second, gainsharing plans measure and reward performance more often, thus providing greater motivational leverage. Third, gainsharing does not require disclosure of unduly sensitive information. Finally, gainsharing plans within large companies are better suited for application in facility and business units, particularly if those units are cost, rather than profit, centers.

Scanlon Plans. The first gainsharing plan, the Scanlon Plan, was developed by Joseph Scanlon of the United Steel Workers

Union. Because of its union heritage, the Scanlon Plan enjoys a wide acceptance by labor organizations. The philosophy behind the plan focuses on three concepts: (1) an organization should function as a single unit; (2) workers are capable and willing to contribute ideas and suggestions; and (3) improvements should be shared. The goal is for workers to identify with an organization and thus raise employee commitment. The Scanlon Plan includes a two-tiered employee committee structure (departmental and plantwide), an employee suggestion system, and a plantwide productivity bonus. The bonus formula, which includes all employees (production, clerical, professional, and managerial), is calculated monthly, based upon the ratio of labor costs to the sales value of production.[40]

Improshare Plans. Improshare Plans operate on an entirely different philosophy. These plans tie economic rewards to performance without any attempt at meaningful employee participation. Because Improshare Plans typically do not attempt employee involvement, they tend to resemble traditional incentive systems organized around plant or large-group performance. The bonus formula is based upon the relationship between industrial engineering standard hours earned and total actual hours worked.[41]

Rucker Plans. Rucker Plans appear to fall between the humanistic Scanlon Plans and the economically rewarded and driven worker under Improshare systems. Rucker Plans have most of the same participatory elements of Scanlon Plans, but in smaller doses or degrees. Rucker Plans have a single plantwide committee, an employee suggestion system, and a bonus formula based upon the relationship between labor costs and added value.[42]

Interest in gainsharing waned during the 1960s, but declining productivity growth rates, eroding positions in world markets, and the resulting need to improve productivity and the quality of work life led to a marked increase in gainsharing plans during the 1970s and 1980s. In recent years, employers have used gainsharing as a vehicle to tie compensation to organizational performance. Although originally used only in manufacturing and union environments, gainsharing has made inroads in the service and not-for-profit sectors, including government agencies and health care organizations.

Uses of Gainsharing

One review of gainsharing plans has noted that the growth of gainsharing plans does not arise from one single source or theme.[43]

Instead, multiple factors, including the growing business orientation of the personnel profession, have contributed to the growth of these plans.

In some companies, particularly in Scanlon Plan firms or firms adopting a Scanlon-like approach, gainsharing is a *philosophy of management*. These companies use gainsharing to increase employee identification, commitment, and loyalty through significant and meaningful employee participation in decision-making and financial outcomes.

Other companies use gainsharing merely as a management tool to increase hourly productivity. In these cases, gainsharing is most likely to constitute a short-term strategy, applicable for a one- to three-year period. Still other firms have utilized gainsharing as a vehicle for organizational *change* and development. These firms have found that financial rewards can induce changes in long-standing attitudes and behavior, thus revitalizing older and more mature facilities.

Gainsharing also can provide an excellent way to relate employee compensation to organizational performance, i.e., to create variable pay. In firms using gainsharing in this fashion, annual pay increases are more modest, but employees receive sizable bonuses in good business years and small or no bonuses in years when the business climate is unfavorable. This approach is receiving increased attention and support from economists. Proponents argue that such gainsharing plans make labor costs more sensitive to economic cycles, thus reducing inflation, and reducing unemployment during recessionary periods by lowering the cost savings from layoffs. [44]

Yet another application occurred during the recent rounds of concession bargaining. A number of companies and unions agreed to institute gainsharing plans to offset concessionary reductions of wages and benefits. Higher productivity, cost reductions, and improved quality were used to generate bonuses to compensate employees for reduced wages.

Finally, a significant number of firms utilize gainsharing as a replacement for, or an alternative to, an individual incentive system. These firms have found that the existing individual systems were costly and produced many dysfunctional results. However, these firms still believed they needed some form of economic incentive to manage their employees. Gainsharing became the alternative in hopes that the group bonus would be easier to administer and would encourage more positive employee work behavior.

Impact of Gainsharing and Profit Sharing

Despite a 50-year history, few research studies have investigated the impact of gainsharing and profit-sharing plans on organizational effectiveness and employee work attitudes and behavior. In the case of gainsharing, the vast amount of research has focused on organizations with Scanlon Plans. Because the consultants who install Scanlon Plans employ very rigid selection criteria (for example, evidence of management commitment and votes by employees), research on Scanlon Plan companies has questionable applicability to more traditional firms.

As much of the previous commentary suggests, the uniqueness of the Scanlon Plan lies in a highly developed philosophy of management. The failure of a Scanlon Plan frequently results from management's unwillingness to recognize the plan as something more than a committee structure and bonus-sharing plan. Firms with successful Scanlon Plans share a common philosophy and set of values. Managers in these plans focus on the value of the individual. Scanlon Plans recognize the value and contribution of each member of the organization, encourage decentralized decision-making, and seek to get each employee to identify with the company's goals and objectives. Scanlon committees are authorized to spend limited amounts of money to implement each project they work on.

Attitudinal Effects. This strategy seems to pay off. Research on gainsharing has shown generally favorable outcomes. One study found that employees believed that the Scanlon Plan encouraged people to work harder, improved the company's financial situation, helped employees to do their job better, increased employee knowledge of the company, and boosted trust and confidence in the company.[45] Interestingly, managers in this study expressed greater confidence in the plan's benefit to the company's financial situation than did supervisors and hourly employees.

Other research shows that the amount of employee participation is higher in firms that use a Scanlon Plan than in those that do not.[46] Managers in more traditional environments may find that other forms of gainsharing with less emphasis on employee involvement are philosophically better suited to their situations. These plans are more compatible in their work place environment. Retention of the Scanlon Plan also seems to be related to managers' confidence in the capabilities of their employees and their general attitudes toward participation.[47] Managers in firms that had *dropped* the Scanlon Plan perceived rank-and-file employees as demonstrating less dependability, initiative, long-range perspective, and willingness to change, as well as possessing less judgment, responsibility, pride in performance, and alertness.

Organizational Effectiveness. Four recent studies have examined the impact of gainsharing plans on organizational effectiveness. The General Accounting Office (GAO) surveyed 36 firms with gainsharing plans, obtaining "hard" data from about two-thirds of the firms. The GAO reported that gainsharing improved performance by between 16.4 percent (sales more than one hundred million dollars) to 17.3 percent (sales less than one hundred million dollars).[48] A second survey by the New York Stock Exchange found that 15 percent of respondents with 500 or more employees had a gainsharing plan, and 70 percent of these firms reported that gainsharing resulted in improved performance.[49] However, the limited data employed in these two studies have caused some analysts to question how seriously these results should be taken.[50]

More recently, another survey by the American Productivity Center of 212 firms asked the impact of four types of gainsharing plans: Scanlon, Improshare, profit sharing, and custom-designed. The survey reports the results of those firms indicating "positive" or "very positive" results. Several findings are noteworthy:

- Gainsharing plans produced greater productivity improvements than profit sharing.
- Scanlon Plans had a slightly bigger impact than other forms of gainsharing.
- Scanlon Plans affected costs and quality more favorably than profit-sharing or Improshare Plans.
- Improshare Plans had the greatest impact on employee pay.[51]

These results would appear consistent with what is known about these gainsharing plans. Profit-sharing plans pay out infrequently (annually) and involve elements over which employees have little or no control. Therefore, they presumably would have less impact on productivity. Since Scanlon Plans encourage the use of employee involvement teams, they should have a more favorable impact on quality and costs than Improshare, which is primarily a "time-savings" system. Because Improshare more closely resembles traditional incentive systems, with a 30 percent leverage goal, it should have a larger impact on employee pay than the other plans, which normally encourage conventional wage administration.

One major evaluation of gainsharing involved 28 firms that used some form of financial sharing.[52] The sample included nine Scanlon, seven Rucker, eight Improshare, and two locally developed plans, along with one profit-sharing plan. The study examined formal performance measures before and after the introduction of the gainsharing plans. Of the firms evaluated, about 50 percent achieved significant performance improvements over the expected level of improvement without a gainsharing plan. A leveling effect occurred, with firms experiencing an immediate level change followed by a modest upward trend in productivity. Other favorable effects included more stable employment when compared with the firm's overall industry, enhanced quality, and improved labor relations and attendance.

The study also observed that in all types of gainsharing, some plans succeeded, while others failed. This finding suggests that the type of plan is not the key determinative factor in successful plans. Instead, the "fit" of the plan to the location, management style and commitment, and the quality of the plan's implementation and its sustaining activities are more likely to determine plan success.[53]

A final observation must be noted. Despite rigorous evaluation procedures, it is nearly impossible to isolate the contribution of gainsharing (or any other labor-management intervention) from other organizational variables contributing to performance outcomes. Indeed, factors such as capital investment, changes in management and union leadership, and the general state of the economy can have more of an impact on organizational performance than some gainsharing plans.[54]

A limited amount of research on profit sharing also shows favorable results. One study found that profit sharers outperformed nonsharers in 8 of 9 industries in a sample of 175 companies for the period 1948 through 1966.[55] A similar study examined the performance of 202 companies in 6 industries between 1958 and 1977.[56] In two-thirds of the cases investigated, firms with profit sharing outperformed non-profit-sharing firms. The results were consistent across three of the six industries in the sample.

Employee Involvement

Employee involvement has long been part of several of the interventions discussed above, such as Scanlon Plans, safety committees, and labor-management committees. In recent years, however, employee involvement has taken on a separate distinction of its own. One analyst, in a review of employee participation, referred to this process as a "structured, systematic approach to the involvement of employees in group decisions affecting work and the work environment with goals that include reducing product cost, improving product quality, facilitating communication, raising morale, and reducing conflict."[57] Along with the traditional structures already discussed, interventions such as quality circles, employee involvement teams, problem-solving teams, task forces, and participation teams would fall within this definition.

Major issues associated with employee involvement programs include the level of participation, performance outcomes, and the impact on employees and unions. Each of these issues is briefly discussed below.

Employee involvement has become very visible. Major collective bargaining agreements in the auto, communications, and steel industries provide for team and group approaches to decision-making. Studies have shown that as many as 35 percent of all firms in the United States now utilize forms of employee involvement, and as much as 25 percent of the American work force is covered by involvement programs.[58]

As with other labor-management interventions, establishing cause-and-effect relationships between employee involvement and performance proves difficult. One review has suggested that only 20 percent of the studies on participation related employee involvement to improved performance.[59] Some of the more detailed analyses appear to suggest that while participation, by itself, makes only a small contribution to the success of an organization, when combined with other management and HR approaches, it can contribute significantly to organizational performance.[60]

Strong evidence indicates that union involvement and support are critical to the success of an employee involvement effort. One study has found that since employee involvement leads to commitment, which in turn enhances employees' identification with a firm, unions which support such programs and share responsibility and ownership with management also strengthen union identification.[61] However, when the union is not involved, employees' preferences for involvement in decisions affecting them will likely prompt them to participate but their identification with the union will decline.

Quality of Work Life

Quality of Work Life (QWL) projects are more varied and, therefore, more difficult to define. QWL interventions have focused on such matters as: the physical environment, like cafeteria and lighting improvements; human systems, including the way people are treated; organizational policies, such as parking and salaried status; supervisory style changes; and revisions in work rules or schedules. Other QWL interventions have targeted organizational systems, including the structure of jobs (for example, job design), the organization and flow of work and/or decisions (for example, autonomous work groups), and individual reward policies that reinforce these systems such as pay for knowledge.

In a sense, all of the cooperative efforts discussed in this chapter are types of QWL projects. Some observers might even argue that separating employee involvement from QWL projects is an arbitrary distinction. Indeed, as a recent study of pay-for-knowledge systems has shown, many of these interventions are used concurrently as part of a total systems approach.[62] Regardless of the debate over terminology, this section examines two of the more significant and substantial changes taking place: work restructuring and pay-for-knowledge systems.

Work Restructuring. The origin of work restructuring dates back to the sociotechnical systems thinking of European writers during the 1950s and 1960s. In recent years, the combination of the need for enhanced quality and productivity, job flexibility, and changes in technology and systems have necessitated a redesign of work. In addition, manufacturing strategies such as "Just In Time," which often involve the use of manufacturing cells (work teams with product-dedicated machinery and people), have caused companies and unions to re-examine the structure and design of jobs.

Different approaches to job redesign fall into four categories: (1) job rotation—the movement of employees on a regular basis to similar tasks; (2) job enlargement—the addition of tasks of the same variety to a job; (3) job enrichment—the addition of more significant tasks to an employee's duties, such as inspection or planning; and (4) autonomous work teams: the organization of work around group-oriented tasks, with the responsibility and accountability for task completion falling to team members, normally with little or no supervision.[63]

In many cases, autonomous work teams are now called self-managed teams. This approach reflects a new desire on the part of management and labor to further push decision-making to the shop floor and to reduce the costs associated with layers of organizational control. Autonomous work teams represent the most sophisticated form of employee involvement. Organizations with high commitment work designs often employ these principles.

Pay-for-Knowledge Systems. Pay for knowledge represents a departure from traditional pay systems. Instead of tying pay levels to specific jobs, pay-for-knowledge systems compensate employees for the "number, kind, and depth of skills that they develop."[64] Two basic approaches to pay for knowledge are multi-skill plans and increased-knowledge plans. Multi-skill plans, which are particularly appropriate for factory settings, link pay levels to the number of specific skills an employee learns. In contrast, increased-knowledge plans attach pay levels to increased knowledge and skill within a job category. Knowledge-based plans are considered more appropriate for skilled jobs such as skilled trades. Many pay systems combine elements of both approaches.

Pay-for-knowledge plans purportedly offer a number of benefits. Advantages include greater employee flexibility, reduced need for staff and supervision, and less restrictive work rules, all of which may improve productivity.[65] Reduced staffing is possible because the broader array of skills possessed by the work force enables an organization to cover inefficiencies, such as absenteeism and turnover, and to adapt more readily to overtime needs. Because pay-for-knowledge companies often operate with high commitment work teams, the pay structure frequently includes managerial functions, thus reducing the need for supervisors and other staff employees. Pay-for-knowledge systems have fewer and broader job classifications, which can enhance production efficiencies by facilitating employee movement. Finally, the greater flexibility and breadth of work rules permits new approaches to work design and further rewards for teamwork and cooperation such as gainsharing.

The Success and Failure of American Cooperation

The odds seem to weigh heavily against long-term institutionalization of cooperative projects. One study of QWL projects with at least five years' experience found that 75 percent of the projects were no longer functioning and that none in unionized settings were in operation.[66] A second study of the life-cycle of 10 plants revealed similar findings.[67]

In most instances, when cooperation fails, neither the company nor the union has a real commitment to change. In other cases, the parties meet often, but lack either the internal expertise to get the process moving or the wisdom to seek outside assistance. The absence of models upon which to base cooperative activity no doubt hampers such efforts.[68]

Gainsharing plans often end when changes initiated by management lead to the perception that the bonus formula has been manipulated. One study found that only three out of ten gainsharing efforts survived after six years.[69] However, the surviving plans continued to operate successfully after eight, twelve, and twenty-seven years.

Obstacles to Cooperation

Problems associated with implementing and sustaining cooperative programs can occur at three stages in the process.[70] The first stage involves getting the cooperative process started. A second set of problems can arise during efforts to reconcile the cooperative process and traditional process of collective bargaining. Finally, long-term commitment to the effort can run afoul due to a variety of internally created difficulties.

Difficulties in Establishing a Cooperative Framework

Several national collective bargaining agreements (for example, the steel and auto industries) have mandated cooperation at the plant level. However, these efforts, not surprisingly, have not always succeeded, as plant-level cooperation is difficult to impose by actors external to the immediate bargaining relationships. More cooperation has occurred in the auto industry where the national leadership (company and union) have made concerted efforts to convince plant-level participants of the need for change.

To obtain an initial commitment to cooperate, both parties must agree on the goals of the cooperative program.[71] However, a more fundamental problem stems from the parties' failure to agree on what the problems actually are. As noted earlier, many participants have refused to acknowledge the existence of any problem.

A final, but very common problem, is lack of skill in devising and implementing cooperative strategies. Although parties can utilize external consultants, many consultants are not qualified to work in unionized settings. Unionized and nonunion settings have inherent differences which must be recognized when devising change strategies. Neutrals and consultants must possess a wide array of behavioral science training and a thorough background in the mechanics and implications of the collective bargaining agreement to assist parties in the change process. Such consultants appear to be in short supply.

Reconciling the Cooperative and Adversary Processes

The theoretical and conventional wisdom has held that the cooperative process should be kept separate from the negotiations process and the grievance procedure.[72] This principle is frequently raised as a means of reducing resistance to initial participation in a cooperative venture. As a practical matter, however, companies and unions find this separation difficult to achieve and maintain. Since the processes are often intertwined, separating cooperative efforts can only work when the parties are addressing relatively minor problems. However, once the cooperative process begins to address meaningful questions, it inevitably overlaps the negotiations and grievance procedures. An often-used strategy to resolve this difficulty gives the grievance process sole jurisdiction over active grievances, but allows the cooperative process to address the underlying issues causing the grievance.

Meaningful change frequently requires modification of, or additions to, the collective bargaining agreement. This situation occurs when participants in the cooperative process decide to memorialize their accomplishments in the "web of rules" contained in the collective bargaining agreement. In some instances, this process requires executing a memorandum of understanding and appending it to an existing agreement. In other cases, however, the parties delay change until the next round of negotiations and incorporate it into a new agreement.

A third issue concerns whether the cooperative process should be suspended during negotiations. In these situations, parties sometimes fear that aggressive tactics at the bargaining table in the pursuit of distributive goals will upset the tentative trust and good faith established in the cooperative process. No clear evidence has emerged regarding abandoning or maintaining cooperation during negotiations. However, when the cooperative process is effective, it clearly reduces the conflict inherent in the traditional collective bargaining process.

Obtaining Continuing Commitment

One of the most serious obstacles to cooperation has been the failure to adequately prepare both sides for major changes. Agreements reached by the plant management and union leadership may later earn acceptance from their respective constituencies. However, unless these agreements address long-standing attitudinal and managerial issues, no trust will develop.

The difficulties stemming from this problem should not be underestimated. Many managers and union members are very skeptical of the benefits to be derived from cooperation. In short, these persons prefer to continue behaving as they have historically—in an authoritarian (in the case of managers and supervisors) or an adversarial (in the case of union stewards and members) manner. For cooperative strategies to work, a sufficient number of these actors must see the instrumentality of the effort *prior* to its implementation.

Political pressures within the union can pose difficulties for even the most secure union leadership. Although opponents often only represent a vocal minority, they can constrict the maneuverability of the leadership. Union leaders have found ways to reduce the likelihood of this problem occurring:

- Leaders should assure from the outset that the rank and file has realistic understandings of what the cooperative process means. This education effort can defuse discussion that the leadership has been co-opted or has sold out to management.

- Vocal skeptics may have their fears allayed if they participate in the process. This strategy may be accomplished by seating skeptics on committees or allowing them to serve as visiting attendees at meetings.

- Union members should be kept informed of progress through the posting of committee minutes and other communications from the union and the company.

- Most important of all, management representatives should recognize the credibility problem facing union leaders and avoid creating situations which might compromise them.

- Finally, union leaders can opt to play an oversight, rather than direct, role in the program's operation.

Another obstacle to long-term commitment and institutionalization of cooperative efforts arises from turnover of key union and management participants. Finally, where productivity-sharing plans are used, the perceived fairness of the bonus formula can affect worker commitment to the participatory structure. The evidence continues to mount that unfair administration of the bonus formula or actual manipulation of the format or ratios causes an abrupt loss of worker support.

Conclusions

Cooperation between companies and unions has a long history in the United States. Cooperation has occurred at national, industry, community, and facility levels on a wide range of issues. In recent years, the greatest amount of cooperation has occurred at a facility level and has taken the form of safety committees, programs to increase trust, improve labor-management relations, and/or enhance productivity; and efforts to improve the quality of the work environment through physical, human, and systems improvement. Recent surveys and discussion in the media strongly suggest that cooperative activities are currently widespread.

The theme of cooperation at the facility level has centered on employee involvement. These efforts at achieving greater employee involvement and commitment aim to encourage those behaviors that will increase the efficiency, productivity, and financial performance of an organization. The available data suggest that such programs produce positive results.

Given the traditionally adversarial nature of union-management relations, the recent popularity of cooperation stems largely from the sweeping economic changes that have impacted bargaining relationships over the last 10 to 20 years. Cooperation has offered a pragmatic approach to problems affecting the economic viability of companies, the job and income security of their employees, and the institutional future of their unions.

In spite of strong stimuli for change in labor-management relations, cooperative behavior still runs contrary to the inherent values and ideology of the American industrial relations system. As a result, companies and unions embarking on strategies for change find the path to success difficult to achieve and sustain. The limited data available suggest that a majority of the cooperative activities engaged in by labor and management do not continue beyond the first five years.

As the decade of the 1980s comes to a close, cooperative activity nonetheless appears to be well-entrenched in our system. While recent years have seen some internal union opposition to cooperation and employee involvement, this resistance does not appear to be widespread. Management likewise appears unlikely to dispense with its strategy of involving employees and enhancing cooperation with their representatives.

At present, the future economic success of the unionized base of our industry remains challenged by foreign and internal competition, deregulation, new technology and manufacturing systems. These pressures and other unforeseen factors which may accelerate the pace of social and economic change make it likely that efforts at cooperation will continue.

◆

Notes

1. Kochan, Katz, and McKersie.
2. Healy.
3. Schuster (1984b).
4. Kochan and Dyer.
5. Majerus.
6. Kochan, Katz, and McKersie, pp. 184, 188.
7. Parker and Slaughter.
8. Cooke.
9. See, e.g., Cappelli.
10. Kochan and Dyer.
11. For other models, see Goodman (1973); Lawler and Drexler; and Nadler, Hanlon, and Lawler.
12. Lawler and Drexler.
13. Kochan and Dyer.
14. Klein.
15. Dyer, Lipsky, and Kochan; Ponak and Fraser.
16. Watts.
17. Poulin.
18. *Business Week.*
19. Walton.
20. Ibid., p. 59.
21. See, e.g., Mills and Lovell, pp. 429–454.
22. Mowday, Porter, and Steers; Steers.
23. Stagner.
24. Fukami and Larson.
25. Kochan and Dyer.
26. Maye.
27. Kochan, pp. 420–422.
28. Healy.
29. Kochan.
30. Leone et al.
31. 29 U.S.C. 175(a).
32. Telephone conversation with Vern Talbott, executive director, Na-

tional Association of Area Labor-Management Committees, May 12, 1989.

33. Readers interested in a comprehensive review of union-management safety committees should consult Kochan, Dyer, and Lipsky.

34. Kochan, pp. 425–427.

35. Walton and McKersie.

36. Hoyer.

37. Ahern.

38. Bullock and Lawler.

39. Schuster (1986).

40. Schuster (1983a).

41. Schuster (1984b), p. 80; Fein.

42. Schuster (1984b), pp. 80–81.

43. Schuster (1987).

44. Mitchell.

45. Goodman, Wakely, and Ruh.

46. White.

47. Ruh, Wallace, and Frost.

48. United States General Accounting Office.

49. New York Stock Exchange.

50. Ehrenberg and Milkovich, p. 111.

51. O'Dell, p. 38.

52. Schuster (1984b).

53. Bullock and Lawler.

54. Schuster (1984b), chapter 3.

55. Howard and Deitz.

56. Howard.

57. Gershenfeld, p. 124.

58. Ibid, pp. 130–131.

59. Locke and Schweiger.

60. Kochan, McKersie, and Katz, pp. 261–276.

61. Verma and McKersie.

62. United States Department of Labor.

63. Cummings and Molloy.

64. Lawler and Ledford, p. 6.

65. Locke and Schweiger.

66. Goodman (1980), pp. 487–494.

67. Schuster (1983b); Schuster (1984a).

68. Lawler and Drexler, pp. 23–28.

69. Schuster (1983b); Schuster (1984a).

70. Schuster (1984a).

71. Kochan and Dyer.

72. Ibid.

◆

References

Ahern, R.W. 1979. *Positive Labor Relations: Plant Labor Management Committees and the Collective Bargaining Process*. Report prepared for the Buffalo-Erie Labor-Management Council, November.

Bullock, R.J., and E.E. Lawler. 1984. "Gainsharing: A Few Questions, and Fewer Answers." *Human Resource Management* 23 (1): 23–40.

Business Week. 1982. "Concessionary Bargaining: Will the New Cooperation Last?" June 14: 66–69.

Cappelli, P. 1985. "Plant Level Concession Bargaining." *Industrial and Labor Relations Review* 39: 90–104.

Cooke, W.N. 1985. *Union Organizing and Public Policy*. Kalamazoo, MI: The Upjohn Institute.

Cummings, T.C., and E.S. Molloy. 1977. *Improving Productivity and the Quality of Work Life*. New York: Praeger.

Dyer, L., D.B. Lipsky, and T.A. Kochan. 1977. "Union Attitudes Toward Management Cooperation." *Industrial Relations* 16(2): 163–172.

Ehrenberg, R.G., and G.T. Milkovich. 1987. "Compensation and Firm Performance." In *Human Resources and the Performance of the Firm*, eds. M.M. Kleiner, R.N. Block, M. Roomkin, and S.W. Salsburg. Madison, WI: Industrial Relations Research Association, 87–122.

Fein, M. 1980. *Improshare: An Alternative to Traditional Managing*. Norcross, GA: Institute of Industrial Engineers.

Fukami, C.V., and E. Larson. 1982. "The Relationship between Union Commitment and Organizational Commitment: Dual Loyalty Reexamined." Paper presented at the annual meeting of the Academy of Management, August.

Gershenfeld, W.J. 1987. "Employee Participation in Firm Decisions." In *Human Resources and the Performance of the Firm*, eds. M.M. Kleiner, R.N. Block, M. Roomkin, and S.W. Salsburg. Madison, WI: Industrial Relations Research Association.

Goodman, P.S. 1973. "The Scanlon Plan: A Need for Conceptual and Empirical Models." Paper presented to the American Psychological Association, September.

―――. 1980. "Quality of Work Life Project in the 1980s." In *Proceedings of the 1980 Spring Meeting of the Industrial Relations Research Association*. Madison: WI: Industrial Relations Research Association.

Goodman, P.S., J.H. Wakely, and R.H. Ruh. 1972. "What Employees Think of the Scanlon Plan." *Personnel* 49(2): 282–289.

Healy, J. 1965. *Creative Collective Bargaining*. Englewood Cliffs, NJ: Prentice Hall.

Howard, B.B. 1979. *A Study of the Financial Significance of Profit Sharing, 1958–1977*. Chicago: Profit Sharing Council of America.

―――, and P.O. Deitz. 1969. *A Study of the Financial Significance of Profit Sharing*. Chicago: Profit Sharing Council of America.

Hoyer, D.T. 1982. *Relations by Objectives: An Experimental Program of Management-Union Conflict Resolution*. Unpublished doctoral dissertation, University of Michigan.

Klein, J.A. 1984. "Why Supervisors Resist Employee Involvement." *Harvard Business Review* 62(September/October): 87–95.

Kochan, T.A. 1980. *Collective Bargaining and Industrial Relations*. Homewood, IL: Irwin.

Kochan, T.A., and L. Dyer. 1976. "A Model of Organizational Change in the Context of Union-Management Relations." *Journal of Applied Behavioral Science* 12(2): 59–78.

Kochan, T.A., L. Dyer, and D.B. Lipsky. 1977. *The Effectiveness of Union-Management Safety and Health Committees*. Kalamazoo, MI: The Upjohn Institute.

Kochan, T.A., H.C. Katz, and R.B. McKersie. 1986. *The Transformation of American Industrial Relations*. New York: Basic Books.

Kochan, T.A., R.B. McKersie, and H.C. Katz. 1985. "U.S. Industrial Relations in Transition: A Summary Report." *Proceeding of the 37th Annual Meeting, Industrial Relations Research Association.* Madison, WI: Industrial Relations Research Association.

Lawler, E.E., III, and J.A. Drexler. 1978. "Dynamics of Establishing Cooperative Quality of Worklife Projects." *Monthly Labor Review* 101(3): 23–28.

Lawler, E.E., III, and G.E. Ledford, Jr. 1984. *Skill-Based Pay.* Working paper no. 8, University of Southern California, Center for Effective Organizations.

Leone, R.D., et al. 1981. *The Origins of Areawide Labor-Management Committees.* Report submitted to the Labor-Management Services Administration, United States Department of Labor.

Locke, E.A., and D.M. Schweiger, 1979. "Participation in Decision Making: One More Look." In *Research in Organization Behavior,* vol. 1, ed. B.M. Staw. Greenwich, CT: JAI Press.

Majerus, R.E. 1984. "Workers Have a Right to a Share of Profits." *Harvard Business Review* 62 (September/October): 42–50.

Maye, W.T. 1980. "Presidential Labor-Management Committees: Productive Failures." *Industrial and Labor Relations Review* 34(1): 51–66.

Mills, D.Q., and M.R. Lovell, Jr. 1985. "Competitiveness: The Labor Dimension." In *U.S. Competitiveness in the World Economy,* eds. B.R. Scott and G.C. Lodge. Boston: Harvard Business School Press.

Mitchell, D.J.B. 1982. "Gainsharing: An Anti-Inflation Reform." *Challenge* 25 (July/August): 18–25.

Mowday, R.T., L.W. Porter, and R.M. Steers. 1982. *Employee-Organization Linkages.* New York: Academic Press.

Nadler, D.A., M. Hanlon, and E.E. Lawler III. 1980. "Factors Influencing the Success of Labor-Management Quality of Work Life Projects." *Journal of Occupational Behavior* 1(1): 53–57.

New York Stock Exchange, Office of Economic Research. 1982. *People and Productivity: A Challenge to Corporate America.* New York: New York Stock Exchange.

O'Dell, D. 1987. *People, Performance, and Pay.* Houston, TX: American Productivity Center.

Parker, M., and J. Slaughter. 1988. *Choosing Sides: Unions and the Team Concept.* Boston: South End Press.

Ponak, A.M., and C.R.P. Fraser. 1979. "Union Activists' Support for Joint Programs." *Industrial Relations* 18(2): 197–209.

Poulin, G.J. 1982. "Three Survival Issues." Remarks to the International Association of Machinists and Aerospace Workers Western States Conference, July 15.

Ruh, R.A., R.L. Wallace, and C.F. Frost. 1973. "Management Attitudes and the Scanlon Plan." *Industrial Relations* 12: 282–292.

Schuster, M. 1983a. "Forty Years of Scanlon Plan Research: A Review of the Descriptive and Empirical Literature." *International Yearbook of Organizational Democracy* 1: 53–71.

———. 1983b. "The Impact of Union-Management Cooperation on Productivity and Employment." *Industrial and Labor Relations Review* 36(3): 415–430.

———. 1984a. "Cooperation and Change in Union Settings: Problems and Opportunities." *Human Resource Management* 23(2): 145–160.

———. 1984b. *Union-Management Cooperation: Structure, Process, and Impact.* Kalamazoo, MI: The Upjohn Institute.

———. 1986. "Gainsharing: The State of the Art." *Compensation and Benefits Management* 2(4): 285–290.

———. 1987. "Gainsharing: Do It Right the First Time." *Sloan Management Review* 29(2): 17–26.

Stagner, R. 1954. "Dual Allegiance as a Problem in Modern Society." *Personnel Psychology* 1: 41–47.

Steers, R.M. 1977. "Antecedents and Outcomes of Organizational Commitment." *Administrative Science Quarterly* 22(1): 45–56.

United States General Accounting Office. 1981. *Productivity Sharing Programs: Can They Contribute to Productivity Improvement?* Washington, DC: GAO.

United States Department of Labor. 1988. *Exploratory Investigations of Pay-for-Knowledge Systems.* Washington, DC: Superintendent of Documents.

Verma, A., and R.B. McKersie. 1987. "Employee Involvement: The Implications of Non-Involvement by Unions." *Industrial and Labor Relations Review* 40(July): 556–568.

Walton, R.E. 1985. "From Control to Commitment in the Work Place." *Harvard Business Review* 63(March/April): 57–74.

Walton, R.E., and R.B. McKersie. 1965. *A Behavioral Theory of Labor Negotiations.* New York: McGraw-Hill.

Watts, G.E. 1982. "Quality of Work Life." Remarks to the National Labor Management Conference, Washington, DC, September 9–10.

White, J.K. 1979. "The Scanlon Plan: Causes and Correlates of Success." *Academy of Management Journal* 22(2): 292–312.

———— ◆ ————

4.4

Due Process

Elizabeth C. Wesman
Dana Edward Eischen

As the member of management most likely to deal with the company's union, employment laws, and employee complaint procedures, an HR manager bears the responsibility for knowing the due process rights of employees and assuring that those rights are not violated. HR managers who do this job well may improve employee morale and avoid costly lawsuits; if they do the job poorly, organizational as well as financial costs may result.

This chapter addresses the many situations in which employees' rights to due process may arise. It first considers grievance procedures in both union and nonunion work environments. The next section examines employees' statutory entitlements to due process as found in various employment laws and related court cases. The discussion then moves to specific issues concerning an employee's right to privacy, right of access to his or her personnel files, and rights in the event of discipline or discharge.

Legal Basis of Due Process

Due process is a fundamental tenet of the North American legal environment, rooted in early English Common Law. Sometimes difficult to define, due process at its most basic level is exemplified in a 17th century case involving a physician and the Royal College of Physicians. The College levied fines against Dr. Thomas Bonham for practicing "physic" before being admitted to practice by the college. Since the college sat as *both* accusers *and* judges in the circumstance, Chief Justice Coke in the Court of Common Pleas found a violation of Dr. Bonham's right to due process, particularly since one half of the fines levied accrued directly to the college itself.[1]

Legislation in the United States, specifically the Fourteenth Amendment to the U.S. Constitution, and numerous court cases[2] have specified the rights which constitute due process.[3] Due process in legal proceedings provides individuals with the right to:

- Prior notice of prohibited conduct

- Timely procedures adhered to at each step of the procedure

- Notice of the charges or issues prior to a hearing

- Impartial judges or hearing officers (persons with interests in a proceeding may not act as judges in that proceeding)

- Opportunity to confront and cross-examine adverse witnesses and evidence, as well as to present proof in one's own defense

- Representation by counsel

- Notice of rulemaking proceedings (opportunity for hearing and comment by interested parties)

- Notice of decision (may include right to written decision)

- Protection from retaliation for utilizing a complaint procedure in a legitimate manner[4]

Due Process in Labor-Management Relations

Contrary to some popular notions, most employees have no constitutional right to due process in their work environments. Constitutional due process protects individual rights with respect to state, municipal, or federal government processes and does not normally apply in non-governmental situations, such as a private employment relationship.

Accordingly, employee rights to due process stem either from a collective bargaining agreement, from legislative protections, or, on occasion, from procedures provided unilaterally by an employer.[5] These nonconstitutional sources can still provide employees with considerable due process rights. For example, a carefully crafted grievance procedure in a collective bargaining agreement may provide for very elaborate employee protections in discipline proceedings. These protections, however, are matters of contractual, rather than Constitutional due process.

Collective Bargaining Agreement Procedures vs. Unilateral Appeals Mechanisms

Nearly all collective bargaining agreements in the United States contain a provision establishing a grievance procedure which culminates in arbitration of unresolved disputes.[6] Such a provision serves to compensate a union for relinquishing its chief economic weapon by agreeing to a no-strike provision. In a nonunion environment, mechanisms by which employees may air and resolve their work-related disputes can serve as a "safety valve," decreasing the potential for serious employee-employer conflict.

Collectively Bargained Procedures

Most collectively bargained grievance procedures define what constitutes a grievance. Typical language is the following definition:

> The term "grievance" shall mean any dispute between the Company and the Union, or between the Company and any employee concerning the interpretation, application, claim of breach or violation of the Agreement.[7]

The procedure to be followed by an employee and the responding company representatives following filing of a grievance is also clearly specified in most agreements. The process usually contains several steps, with rules outlining the levels of union and company management involved at each step, timelines for responses and appeals, and other requirements. Figure 1 gives an example of such contractual requirements.

As Figure 1 shows, most collectively bargained grievance procedures culminate in binding arbitration. Both employers and unions prefer arbitration to the use of strikes or litigation for dispute resolution, which no doubt explains its widespread usage in labor-management relationships.[8]

A code of professional responsibility governs arbitrators who belong to the National Academy of Arbitrators, the American

---

Figure 1

Procedures for Filing a Grievance

Step 1. The aggrieved employee and/or his Shop Steward shall first take up the complaint or grievance orally with his foreman. If the complaint or grievance is not settled, it shall, within three (3) working days thereafter, but put in writing setting forth the nature of the grievance and the provision(s) of the Agreement alleged to have been violated; and presented to the foreman who shall, within three (3) working days after receipt of the written grievance, give his written answer.

Step 2. If the grievance is not settled in Step 1, it shall be presented to the Plant Manager within five (5) working days after receipt of the foreman's written answer. The Plant Manager shall discuss the grievance with the Union Shop Chairman and shall give his written answer to the grievance within five (5) working days after the close of the discussion.

Step 3. If the grievance is not settled in Step 1, it shall be returned to the Plant Manager within five (5) working days. The grievance shall be taken up within the next fifteen (15) calendar days between the Union's Grievance Committee and their representative, and the Plant Manager or his representative. The Company's written answer shall be given within five (5) working days after the meeting is held. . . .

Step 4. If the grievance is not settled in Step 3, it may be appealed to arbitration in accordance with the procedure and conditions set forth under "Arbitration" in this article. Either party may submit the grievance to arbitration by written demand given to the other party within fifteen (15) working days after the Company's representatives have given written answer in Step 3. This time period may be extended by mutual consent.

From agreement between Printing Specialties and Paper Products Union Local No. 754 and Arnold Corporation (1983–86).

Arbitration Association (AAA), the Federal Mediation and Conciliation Service (FMCS), and the National Mediation Board.[9] This code and other provisions in a collectively bargained grievance and arbitration procedure can provide employees with considerable rights to due process. In a nonunion environment, due process issues are more unsettled.

Management-Established Grievance Procedures

Management may attempt to establish a credible grievance procedure in a nonunion environment, but it will often encounter difficulties not associated with collectively bargained grievance mechanisms. From the start, employee skepticism poses problems, simply because the procedure exists at the forebearance of management. Under such systems, at least in theory, management can withdraw from, modify, or ignore the procedure at will.[10] Nevertheless, many nonunion companies have created mechanisms by which employees may have their complaints heard.

Advantages of establishing employee complaint mechanisms include the following:

- Improved worker satisfaction and productivity

- Lower turnover (provision of an outlet other than "walking" for serious employee complaints)

- Cost savings by avoiding possible litigation

- Feedback on how well lower and middle management implement company policies and procedures[11]

Nonunion complaint procedures include "open door" policies, peer or peer/management review committees, nonunion grievance procedures culminating in arbitration, and ombudsmen.

"Open Door" Policies

These policies offer access to management, up to and including the top of the organization, in an effort to redress a complaint. While most policies require an employee to proceed step-by-step up the managerial ladder, some open-door programs allow skipping of steps, particularly when the immediate supervisor is the subject of the employee's complaint. In most open-door processes, the top executive's decision is final—no further appeal is available.[12]

Peer or Peer/Management Review Committees

These committees, sometimes simply called grievance committees, review employees' complaints and make recommendations or rulings concerning redress, if appropriate. In a peer review committee, panelists are normally either workers elected by employees to serve for a specific term or volunteers selected on an *ad hoc* basis by the grieving employee.[13] Almost without exception, the committee's disposition of the grievance is final.

A committee typically has a narrow scope; it rarely has the power to change company policies, work rules, or pay policies.[14] Another significant problem associated with peer review committees concerns ensuring effective representation. With no union backing, a grieving employee often feels intimidated by the prospect of going alone before a committee, even if it does include other workers.[15]

Despite some limitations, peer or peer/management review committees have been successfully adopted by many nonunion organizations, including General Electric, Borg-Warner, and Allied Bendix.[16] However, the credibility of review committees and employees' willingness to use them largely depends upon the extent to which management involves workers at the formative stages. Peer or peer-management review systems established by executive fiat, rather than through worker-management cooperation, are unlikely to succeed.[17]

Nonunion Grievance Procedures Culminating in Arbitration

In their most common form, nonunion grievance procedures resemble those found in collective bargaining agreements. The process consists of several steps, with time limits for appeals and responses by management at each level, and ends in binding arbitration.[18] (See Appendix A for an example.) In nonunion arbitration, as in union/management arbitration, an arbitrator may be selected directly or through referral agencies such as the AAA or FMCS. Resolution of other cases may go before a panel of arbitrators consisting of two members selected, respectively, by the employee and the employer and a third impartial member selected by the other two.[19]

Nonunion arbitration does have some drawbacks. Without a collective bargaining agreement, arbitrators lack a contractual basis for their decisions. Moreover, arbitrators have considerable leeway in crafting remedies. Unless arbitral jurisdiction and authority are carefully defined, an arbitrator may infringe upon functions which would be considered exclusive rights of management under a collective bargaining agreement.[20]

Ombudsmen

The term ombudsmen, or "ombuds" originally referred to a neutral government official responsible for investigating complaints lodged by citizens against government agencies or officials. The ombuds were totally independent of the officials or agencies they were investigating.[21] Ombudsmen employed by companies to investigate workplace disputes, by virtue of their affiliation with management, lack complete independence. Nevertheless, most corporate ombudsmen provide confidential dispute resolution assistance to employees apart from the traditional management structure.[22]

Ideally, an ombudsman offers employees an informal source of counseling, serves as an advocate for employees' grievances, mediates workplace disputes, and improves top-down and bottom-up communication. As a rule, an ombudsman reports directly to upper management, outside the normal personnel department channels. This direct access to the "ear" of upper management considerably enhances an ombudsman's credibility with employees.[23] An equally important feature is the complete confidentiality with which an ombudsman treats employee concerns and complaints. Ombudsmen can be effective only if employees have great confidence in their integrity. Because ombudsmen owe their employment to management, they must scrupulously maintain the privacy of matters brought to their offices. Only in illegal or life-threatening situations, should an ombudsman consider breaching this confidentiality.[24]

Besides serving employees, an ombudsman may improve management's HR function. By acting as a "lightning rod" for employee complaints, an ombudsman may pinpoint emerging problems before they become seriously disruptive.[25]

Summary

Nonunion programs of grievance resolution which encourage airing and potential settlement of workplace disputes at an early stage can improve unorganized employees' access to due process. Since any issue may be raised as a grievance, nonunion employees may have greater opportunity for redress than do unionized employees. However, management may have greater flexibility with respect to settling employee grievances than it in fact exercises. Without a collective bargaining agreement, employers face no contractual obligation to relinquish any of their rights. As a result, unless management and employees sign an arbitration agreement or a similar contract guaranteeing management's commitment to redress employee grievances, any of the programs described above can be withdrawn by management at will.[26]

Statutory Entitlement to Due Process

Employee entitlement to due process is enunciated or implied in many of the employment-related federal laws. Employees may also have rights to due process under state and municipal laws. Since the latter are so many and so varied, however, this section deals only with federal statutes, including the National Labor Relations Act, employment discrimination laws, the Occupational Safety and Health Act, and the Equal Pay Act. It also covers the related topics of employee insulation against retaliatory discharge and workers' right to fair representation. The discussion will focus largely on public-sector employees since the common law of fair procedure, or due process, rarely has been applied to private employment situations. Moreover, application usually has been limited to professional organizations or associations in which membership is a requisite to earning a living or akin to licensing; for example, state bar associations or medical associations.[27]

National Labor Relations Act

In 1937, the Supreme Court of the United States considered the constitutionality of the Wagner Act,[28] the first of three acts which would eventually form the National Labor Relations Act (NLRA).[29] Among other concerns, the Court addressed the adequacy of due process for employees under the statute. In upholding its constitutionality, the Court also found that the Wagner Act did not violate the Fifth Amendment to the Constitution.[30]

The Taft-Hartley Act, passed in 1947, extended unfair labor practice coverage to unions, including provisions prohibiting discrimination against employees who do not engage in union activity.[31] The third act, the Landrum-Griffin or Labor Management Reporting and Disclosure Act (LMRDA), deals most directly with employee rights to due process within their union or representative labor organizations.[32] The LMRDA contains a "bill of rights" for union members, including the right to secret ballots, protection from arbitrary or excessive dues assessments, and freedom of speech.[33]

Many of the employee rights guaranteed under the NLRA cannot be waived by unions during collective bargaining. While unions can cede some rights, such as the right to strike or to use other economic weapons like work slowdowns, those rights enumerated in sections 7 and 8 of the NLRA, such as the right to join a union and the right to be free from company domination of the representative union may not be waived.[34] A rule of thumb is that rights which guarantee employees access to the protections and remedies contained in the NLRA may not be waived, while rights which are primarily economic in their effect may be waived. In most collective bargaining agreements, the right to strike is waived explicitly or by inference when the agreement contains an arbitration clause.[35]

Employment Discrimination Laws

In theory, prohibition of discrimination in employment appears to guarantee protected classes of employees due (or fair) process in their work environments. As a rule, however, federal laws dealing with employment discrimination establish procedures to be followed by complainants, not any due process entitlement.

Under both Title VII of the Civil Rights Act of 1964 (Title VII)[36] and the Age Discrimination in Employment Act (ADEA),[37] for example, aggrieved persons must adhere to federal time limits when filing their charges. In addition, under Title VII, employees must file complaints with their state antidiscrimination agency before seeking redress from the Equal Employment Opportunity Commission (EEOC). Complainants under the ADEA may file with the appropriate state agency before or after submitting their complaint to the Secretary of Labor, but must file with the EEOC prior to commencing suit against their employer.[38]

The Rehabilitation Act of 1973 requires employers to make reasonable accommodation for handicapped employees as they are defined in the act.[39] Such accommodation does not mean that an employer must incur undue expense, tolerate sub-standard productivity, or risk the welfare of other employees in order to employ a handicapped worker. Rather, the purpose of the act is to assure handicapped applicants and employees a fair opportunity to compete for jobs and receive fair treatment once employed.[40] Similar standards under Title VII apply to situations involving employees whose religious beliefs may require flexible scheduling on the part of their employer.[41]

Occupational Safety and Health Act

Employees' rights to due process under the Occupational Safety and Health Act (OSHA),[42] have been enunciated through the act itself and in subsequent court cases. In addition, many states have "right-to-know" laws governing hazardous substances in the workplace. Typical provisions include requirements that employers notify workers prior to use of toxic substances in the workplace, train employees in the safe handling of toxic substances, maintain detailed records of workplace accidents and worker injuries, and disseminate literature to workers at risk.[43] OSHA also protects employees from retaliatory discharge or discipline for exercising their rights under the act.[44] Employees' rights to insulation against retaliatory discharge receive more lengthy discussion in later sections of this chapter.

Other Employment Laws

Protections afforded employees and procedural requirements for complainants under the Equal Pay Act (EPA) amendment to the Fair Labor Standards Act (FLSA)[45] resemble those under Title VII, although somewhat more complex. An employee with an EPA complaint may either file with the EEOC or proceed directly to a federal or state court for relief. If the EEOC elects to pursue the charge, however, the employee relinquishes his/her right to take the case to court. As with Title VII and OSHA, an employee exercising rights under the EPA or FLSA is protected from retaliatory discharge.

Under the Veterans Reemployment Act of 1976,[46] veterans receive protection from arbitrary discharge for one year after release from service. Besides restricting an employer's freedom to discharge a veteran except for just cause, this act also entitles veterans to return to the job they held prior to service for one year after leaving the military.

Most federal civil service employees enjoy similar protection against arbitrary discharge under the Civil Service Reform Act of 1978.[47] In addition, the Equal Employment Opportunity Act of 1972 extends Title VII protection to a majority of federal, state and municipal employees.[48] Federal employees must file their discrimination complaints with the Civil Service Commission rather than with the EEOC.

Insulation Against Retaliatory Discharge

While many statutes ostensibly protect employees against arbitrary or unfair treatment, to be effective these statutes must also afford some protection to those employees seeking redress under their provisions. In recent years, federal and state bodies have enacted legislation to insulate employees against retaliatory discharge when they refuse to violate public policy or when they act to enhance public policy (as in so-called "whistleblowing").[49]

Statutory or common law protection against retaliatory discharge generally has greater relevance for nonunion employees than for employees covered by a collective bargaining agreement. In the latter case, employees have an established, contractual grievance system for enforcing the traditional "just cause" discipline clause in their agreement. At-will employees, on the other hand, enjoy no such protection and, therefore, may be discouraged from taking actions which would imperil their already tentative rights to employment.[50]

Courts generally have recognized an employee's right to sue an employer for compensatory and punitive damages when discharged for refusing to engage in such illegal acts as perjury.[51] In other situations, however, establishing a claim of retaliatory discharge can be difficult. Employees may have a problem making a case when the retaliatory action falls short of discharge. For example, if an employer simply passes over the employee for promotion or allocates unattractive work assignments, the worker may be hard pressed to succeed in a retaliatory action suit.[52]

The distinction between retaliatory discharge and arbitrary discharge is an important one. Except in those jurisdictions with specific employment-at-will legislation, nonunion employees enjoy no protection from arbitrary discharge, unless they can show an employer's apparently arbitrary discharge was in reality a retaliatory discharge.[53]

A particularly thorny problem involves employees who take it upon themselves to report employer conduct which violates federal, state, or municipal laws. The dilemma arises because such employees have no legal duty to act, and their behavior unquestionably constitutes disloyalty to the employer. On the other hand, allowing an employer to punish workers for voluntarily furthering public policy condones the employer's illegal actions.[54]

Courts are not uniform in their sympathy for whistleblowers. In some jurisdictions, whistleblowers have been denied protections against retaliatory discharge for exercising their rights under wage and hour, safety, or other employment laws.[55] In general, whistleblowers have had greater success gaining protection when the issue involved theft or violation of antitrust or consumer credit laws, than when employers flaunted health and safety or financial practice regulations.[56] Even in jurisdictions which protect such whistleblowing, once the employer complies with the law in question and has so informed the complaining employee, the worker loses further protection. He or she may be subsequently discharged for refusal to resume regular work duties once compliance with the law is established.[57]

Several issues surrounding whistleblowing remain unresolved, to wit:

(1) Is blowing the whistle to the media protected?

(2) Is the employee obligated to report to management before going to government or to the public at large?

(3) Must the employee limit his whistleblowing effort to the least disruptive means of enforcing public policy?

(4) Is the employee protected if he blows the whistle on conduct that reasonably appears to be, but is not, illegal?

(5) Must the employee's purpose be legitimate when he blows the whistle, or can he act out of self-serving motives and still be protected?[58]

Right to Fair Representation

Unions are bound by a common-law tradition to represent fairly all members of the bargaining unit in both contract negotiations and grievance handling. This court-developed doctrine, the "duty of fair representation," predates Title VII by 20 years. In 1944, the Supreme Court held that exclusivity—the right of a union to be sole bargaining agent for a group of employees—imposed upon the union a commensurate responsibility to represent all of those employees "without hostile discrimination, fairly, impartially, and in good faith."[59]

An employee who feels the union has breached this duty may file an unfair labor practice complaint with the appropriate regulatory agency (for example, the National Labor Relations Board or the Public Employment Relations Board). As an alternative, an employee may sue the employer for breach of the collective bargaining agreement, and in the course of reviewing the case, the federal court may determine if the union breached its duty of fair representation in handling the grievance.[60] Access to the courts for resolving a grievance is allowed on the theory that a union's breach of fair representation renders the grievance and arbitration machinery useless. Remedies for breach of fair representation may include an award of back pay, some or all of which may be charged to the union.[61]

In considering an employee's right to fair representation, an important distinction concerns the difference between unfair representation and incompetent or careless representation.[62] While negligence may occasionally be a pretext for unfair representation, incompetence is often no more than it appears. Union members may protest such failures by unseating the offending union officer in the next election, but ordinarily cannot prevail in a fair representation suit for mere incompetence.

In general, the duty of fair representation encompasses the following obligations:

- A union must process equal grievances in the same manner, including settlement short of arbitration.

- A union cannot refuse to process an employee's grievance because of personal dislikes, prejudice (racial or other), or political reasons.

- A union will not "swap" grievances—drop one meritorious grievance in the hope or on promise of winning another.

Employees' Rights to Privacy

Privacy, as it applies in a workplace setting, is a difficult concept to define, let alone to administer. It encompasses more than the traditional Fourth Amendment guarantees against unlawful search and seizure.[64] Employees' concerns include employer acquisition and dissemination of information about workers and job applicants, "personal" behavior on and off the job, surveillance on and off the job, testing of body fluids and neural responses, and access to information about other employees.[65] Employers, for their part, are concerned about the job safety risks inherent in employee substance abuse, prompt detection and discharge of dishonest employees, liability for exposure of employees to cigarette smoke and life-threatening diseases, rising costs of medical benefits, maintenance of good public relations/public image, and control over the quality of their product.[66] The particular issues dealt with in this section are polygraph testing, drug and genetic testing, smoking in the workplace, employees with AIDS, and employees' off-duty conduct.

Polygraph Testing

The essential premise behind the polygraph machine is that measurements of a subject's pulse rate, breathing patterns, blood pressure, and perspiration, yield valid conclusions about the subject's truthfulness.[67] However, the accuracy of polygraph results, whether used in crime detection or in an employment situation, is hotly disputed.

Since 1923, polygraph test evidence has been inadmissible in most state and federal courts,[68] although some states leave the question of admissibility to the judge's discretion.[69] Critics of polygraphs suggest that, at best, a polygraph can only measure accurately the change in a subject's arousal level when asked different questions. They also point out the frequency with which polygraphs report truthful subjects to be lying.[70]

The questionable validity of polygraph tests and the personal indignity suffered by employees subjected to these tests has prompted 21 states to pass legislation which prohibits or restricts the use of polygraphs in an employment setting.[71] Many states also prohibit the use of other "truth tests" such as psychological stress evaluators—written tests which purport to accomplish the same end as polygraph tests.[72]

At the federal level, on June 27, 1988, then-President Reagan signed into law the Employee Polygraph Protection Act of 1988. That act, effective December 27, 1988, prohibits private employers from using polygraph tests to screen job applicants. It also forbids employers from disciplining or otherwise retaliating against a current or prospective employee who refuses to take a polygraph test. Under the new law, an employer investigating a theft or other costly workplace incident may request that an employee submit to a polygraph exam, but may not take action against that employee based solely upon the results of such an exam. An exception is made in the statute for private security firms and drug companies. Federal, state, and local employers also are exempt from coverage by the polygraph law with respect to their employees. Furthermore, public employers are permitted, under the law, to test private parties who serve as consultants or advisors to them.[73]

Some researchers have suggested that when used conscientiously, the polygraph can be a useful tool in investigating and preventing corporate theft. They maintain that an employee's right to privacy must be balanced against an employer's right to make a legitimate investigation into workplace crime.[74] Of particular concern to employees, however, is the nature of the questions asked in the course of polygraph or psychological stress tests. For example, examiners frequently ask immaterial questions regarding a subject's personal life-style or sexual habits. Such incursions into a subject's privacy may, in certain circumstances, constitute a cause of action against the employer for defamation of character or infliction of psychological trauma.[75]

Since management often interprets an employee's refusal to take a polygraph test as admission of guilt, polygraphs involve an unavoidable element of coercion, even if an employee or applicant "voluntarily" submits to a test. In a labor relations setting, most arbitrators will not sustain a discharge based solely upon an accused employee's refusal to take a polygraph, unless there was a prior agreement by the employee to submit to one if requested to do so.[76] When such an agreement constitutes part of an employment application, however, the "voluntary" nature of the agreement becomes suspect, since few applicants will jeopardize their chances of employment by refusing to sign the agreement.

Drug and Alcohol Testing

A reason employers frequently give to justify drug or alcohol testing of employees is the legally imposed obligation to maintain a safe and healthy work environment. Under such federal laws as the Occupational Safety and Health Act (OSHA)[77] and numerous state and municipal laws, employers must protect their employees from fellow workers whose impaired judgment may pose a safety or health risk.[78]

Substance abuse may considerably reduce not only safety, but also efficiency and profitability of the workplace. Substance abusers account for more accidents, greater absenteeism, and lower product quality than their non-abusing co-workers.[79] In addition, employee theft is frequently associated with substance abuse, since an addicted employee must often find ways to "supplement" his/her wages.[80] An employer is clearly justified in trying to minimize the ramifications of substance abuse in the workplace. A controversial way to do that is through routine testing of employment applicants and random testing of current employees for drug and alcohol abuse.

Counterbalancing the concerns of employers on this issue are the rights of employees to privacy and due process. State and federal employers must weigh the use of drug and alcohol testing, whether via blood, urine or breath analysis, against employees' Fourth Amendment rights to privacy. Accordingly, the government's need to detect substance abuse by its employees must be strong enough to outweigh the employees' rights to privacy.[81] The courts have found that such a need exists when employees operate buses or trains, for example, but no consensus has emerged on the issue of testing clerical or custodial employees.[82]

Opponents of both mandatory and "voluntary" employee drug testing rely upon three principal arguments: (1) drug testing cannot detect on-the-job impairment; (2) test procedures and results frequently are seriously inaccurate (particularly in yielding false-positive results); and (3) acquisition of bodily fluids for drug testing violates employees' statutory rights to privacy.[83] Advocates point to the epidemic abuse of drugs and alcohol at all levels of society, the responsibility of employers to provide a hazard-free environment for their employees, and the employer's legitimate concern with rising medical and insurance expenses.[84]

Under labor law, drug or alcohol abuse testing is normally subject to collective bargaining. In a formal advice memorandum, the general counsel to the National Labor Relations Board found drug and alcohol testing to be mandatory subjects of bargaining under section 8(a)(5) of the National Labor Relations Act.[85] He stated that employers and unions must bargain over the contents of the test, the purpose of the test, and how test results, or refusal to submit to a test, will affect employment.[86] Therefore, absent restrictive language in a collective bargaining agreement, an employer who wishes to institute a drug testing program must bargain in good faith with the union before commencing testing.[87]

A further management issue with respect to drug testing, even absent specific statutory restrictions, concerns federal and state handicap or disability discrimination laws. Alcoholism and drug addiction constitute handicaps under federal and most state legislation.[88] In theory, this employment discrimination legislation may limit an employer's latitude in testing current employees or job applicants for alcohol or drug abuse.[89] The Rehabilitation Act of 1973, for example, specifies that employers may not require medical exams prior to an offer of employment. However, the act does allow employers to condition a job offer by requiring an employee to pass a medical exam verifying his/her ability to perform the job with reasonable accommodation.[90]

Dismissal of employees for proven intoxication or drug abuse on the job will usually be sustained in arbitration, provided that the employer had a standing rule against substance abuse at the time of the incident, had clearly communicated the rule to all employees, and consistently applied the rule. Discharge for use of drugs or intoxication off company premises and not on company time will generally not be sustained unless the employer can show that the employee's behavior adversely affected the employer's ability to conduct business (for example, by damaging the company's reputation in the community).[91]

An employer who has legitimate reason to believe a worker is under the influence of alcohol or drugs clearly has the right to require that employee to submit to a test. Some authors have suggested that observed performance impairment should be the only basis for drug testing.[92] The catastrophic implications of drug-impaired performance in certain jobs such as transportation, air traffic control, or the health professions, however, continue to generate pressure for random testing for drug and alcohol abuse.

In 1986, then-President Reagan issued Executive Order 12564 to address the "serious adverse effects [of drug use] upon a significant proportion of the national work force."[93] In that document, the President ordered each executive agency to develop a plan for achieving a drug-free workplace and to "establish a program to test for the use of illegal drugs by employees in sensitive positions."[94] Agencies responding to the executive order included the Federal Aviation Administration and the Federal Railroad Administration, which issued regulations prohibiting the use of alcohol and drugs in the workplace; authorizing drug tests for preemployment screening, accident investigations, and just cause; and establishing policies regarding troubled employees.[95] In addition to regulations concerning drug testing, federal agencies also have established elaborate and rigorous procedures for assuring the integrity of their testing programs.[96]

Much of the controversy surrounding drug and alcohol testing involves random testing of incumbent employees. In six out of the seven states with drug testing laws, random testing is allowed only for workers in hazardous or safety-related jobs. In the city of San Francisco, public and private employers cannot require blood and urinalysis tests unless they can show evidence of on-the-job worker impairment.[97]

Random urinalysis tests are particularly objectionable to most employees. In order to maintain the "chain of custody" of a urine sample—that is, to preclude possibility of tampering or substitution, a "monitor" must be present while an employee produces the sample. As one author put it, ". . . [that is] treatment generally reserved for inmates of correctional institutions."[98] (An example of a "Urine Custody Control Form" from the Department of Transportation appears in Appendix B.) Moreover, even if a "clean" sample is obtained, the lack of established standards for testing laboratories and laboratory procedures leads to an error rate estimated to be as high as 40 percent.[99]

An effective drug testing program must, from the outset, be clearly communicated to the employees concerned. The following recommendations for a substance abuse testing program are based upon two fundamental principles. First, employers should only test employees (1) who hold positions where impairment could endanger themselves, fellow employees, the consumer public, and (2) who appear to be behaving in an impaired manner. Second, an employer must always recognize the need to balance interests of employee privacy with the necessity to provide a safe work environment. Specific ways to put these principles into practice include the following procedures:

- An employer must have a legitimate state or interest in testing employees.

- An employer must have a reasonable suspicion of a widespread problem or a problem with a specific group of employees.

- The scope of a program must be limited to detecting only those problems which will adversely affect job performance.

- Tested employees must receive equal treatment.

- An employee's consent must be obtained prior to testing.

- Specimen collection must be under controlled but private conditions.

- The integrity of the sample must be scrupulously maintained from the time of collection until lab analysis.

- The testing laboratory must be a reputable one which performs additional tests to confirm positive results.

- An employer must maintain complete confidentiality regarding test results, releasing information on a strict need-to-know basis.[100]

Employment Testing

Employment testing is covered at length in Volume 3 of this series. The issue of primary importance to employee due process rights concerns the "fairness" of employment tests. Definitions of fairness appear in federal legislation (Title VII of the Civil Rights Act of 1964) and in the Uniform Guidelines for Employment Selection,[101] as well as in numerous court cases.[102] As generally defined, fair employment tests must be job related and must not intentionally discriminate against protected classes of employees. For example, a selection device designed to eliminate female, black, or Jewish applicants from candidacy would be illegal.

Even seemingly neutral selection devices—not obviously intended to discriminate unfairly—may have adverse impact upon protected groups. Unintentional or indirect discrimination occurs when applicants belonging to a protected class score disproportionately poorly on an apparently neutral employment test.[103] When an employment test results in adverse impact, an employer must be ready to prove that the test is reliable (gives consistent results across time), valid (actually predicts subsequent job performance), and that no other test with less adverse impact is equally reliable and valid.[104]

Finally, even fair employment tests may be erroneously interpreted. Accordingly, an employee's right to due process may be abridged by a supervisor whose interpretation of a test is biased, arbitrary, or simply uninformed.[105] In most companies, an HR department bears the responsibility for monitoring use and interpretation of employment tests.

Military and Criminal Records

A particularly problematic conflict between employees' rights to privacy and an employer's legitimate need for "sensitive" information involves an employee's military or criminal record. Numerous cases have held employers culpable for illegal acts of employees with prior criminal records, even if the company had no prior knowledge of the employees' record. Employers have consistently been found to have breached their duty to customers or clients when employees with prior criminal convictions commit similar crimes while in the employer's hire.[106] Such law suits maintain that the employer failed to check adequately the applicant's background before employing him or her.

Employers therefore have a compelling interest in discerning convicted criminal applicants among job candidates. At the same time, however, employers are finding it increasingly difficult to obtain even the most basic information concerning criminal and military records of prospective employees. This difficulty occurs not only because of privacy legislation but also because of former employers' fears of defamation suits (discussed later in this chapter).[107]

Many states forbid inquiry into a prospective applicant's criminal record unless it bears directly upon the job in question. A particular concern in restrictive legislation is the applicant's arrest record. Since arrests do not always lead to convictions, and protected groups are disproportionately represented in annual arrest statistics, acquisition of that information may lead to indirect discrimination.[108] Under these statutes an employer has no obligation to obtain the criminal history of a prospective employee if the job in question does not involve carrying a weapon (such as a law enforcement officer), or financial or personal security responsibility (such as a bank teller or armored car driver). On the other hand, jobs which affect public safety obligate an employer to take special care in reviewing an applicant's background. Such jobs would arguably include day-care teachers, people working with disturbed or delinquent children, and bus and train operators.[109] Recent cases also have indicated that in limited circumstances, employers may rely on the release or pardon of a convicted criminal as an indication of society's recognition of the fitness of that individual to return to the work force.[110]

Some employers have ready access to information on prospective employees' arrest and conviction records. The Federal Bureau of Investigation's (FBI) Identification Division maintains an extensive data base on more than 20 million people. These data are released to banks and power plant operators, for example, since they are viewed as particularly vulnerable to employees with "criminal histories." Until recently, records of arrests which did not lead to conviction were not released after a year had passed. However, the FBI recently has considered lifting the one-year statute of limitations on release of arrest records, irrespective of whether the arrest led to a conviction. Critics fear that change in FBI policy will lead to abuse of the information and indirect discrimination for the reason already noted.[111]

An employer's desire for information concerning an applicant's military career may only reflect an attempt to gather data on job-related military experience. However, an employer often is seeking additional information concerning the nature of an applicant's discharge from military service: Was it an honorable or dishonorable discharge? If dishonorable, what were the circumstances? By making such inquiries prior to a hiring decision, an employer hopes to avoid taking on a problem employee—one who may have a history of drug or alcohol abuse, psychological difficulties, or insubordination. As explained in Vol. 2 of this series, this area of preemployment inquiry may easily run afoul of employment discrimination laws, since dishonorable discharges occur disproportionately among nonwhite military personnel.[112]

Genetic and AIDS Testing

Since both genetic testing and AIDS testing allegedly stem from employers' concerns with the future health of the employees tested, they are covered together in this section. Apart from the obvious difference in media attention given these two topics, the rationale of basing employment decisions on an applicant's health prognosis is essentially the same in both cases.

Genetic Testing

Genetic monitoring and genetic screening are two types of genetic tests. Genetic monitoring involves periodic checking of employees for changes in their genetic material brought about by their working environment. Genetic screening, on the other hand, involves testing applicants or incumbent employees before placing them in positions which may, because of an individual's genetic make-up, place his or her health at risk.[113]

Genetic testing has developed sufficiently to allow reliable predictions of an employee's predisposition to heart disease and cancer.[114] It may also predict predisposition to racially related diseases such as sickle cell anemia. Employers favoring genetic testing assert that the results are used only to prevent placing hypersensitive employees in hazardous work environments. However, critics suggest that genetic testing may offer a way to reject applicants on the basis of projected health problems, even though the problems may never actually develop during an employee's entire working life. Further, since many of the genetic diseases are race- or ethnicity-specific, genetic testing poses one more threat to equal employment opportunity.[115]

The controversy surrounding genetic testing can be expected to intensify as techniques become more accurate and knowledge about toxic hazards in the workplace increases. Employers will be caught between fears of liability for placing genetically hypersensitive employees in high-risk work environments and fears of EEO suits for using screening devices which disproportionately affect certain racial and ethnic minorities. To date, OSHA has remained silent on the subject of genetic testing for fear that employers will use it to exclude protected class employees from their work force. Nor has the agency addressed the difficult question, frequently raised by opponents of genetic screening, of employees' rights to waive employer liability once genetic tests have shown them hypersensitive to their current work environment.[116]

AIDS in the Workplace

Disputes over Acquired Immunodeficiency Syndrome (AIDS) in the workplace generally center upon one or more of the following issues: 1) hiring employees who test seropositive for AIDS or ARC (AIDS-Related Complex); 2) concerns of fellow employees about exposure to a worker with AIDS; 3) client/customer contact with employees who have AIDS; 4) employee reluctance to work with AIDS-infected clients or customers; 5) testing of applicants and incumbent employees for the HTLV-III virus (indicative of a likelihood of developing AIDS); and 6) the employer's duty to a worker with AIDS.[117]

Since the U.S. Supreme Court's decision in *School Board of Nassau County v. Arline*,[118] AIDS may arguably be considered a handicap covered under the Rehabilitation Act of 1973 (although the *Arline* case involved tuberculosis rather than AIDS). While the Rehabilitation Act applies only to federal employers, 21 states to date have also declared AIDS to be a handicap. In addition, some cities, such as San Francisco, Los Angeles, Cincinnati, and Philadelphia, have passed laws prohibiting discrimination against employees on the basis of having AIDS or even being perceived as having AIDS. Yet, unlike most other "handicaps," AIDS is communicable and, at present, almost certainly fatal once contracted. [119]

According to the U.S. Surgeon General, AIDS is transmitted only through sexual intercourse, blood exchange (such as blood transfusions or needle-sharing by drug abusers), or from AIDS-infected mothers to infants either through the umbilical cord or during childbirth. [120] Nonetheless, many workers fear even casual contact with AIDS-infected employees or clients. Accordingly, employers often must reconcile their obligation to obey federal, state, and municipal antidiscrimination laws, their duty to current concerned non-infected employees, and their responsibilities—ethical, humane, and legal—to applicants and incumbent employees with AIDS.

While discomfited employees may refuse to work with AIDS-infected co-workers or clients, they likely will have little success seeking redress if they are disciplined for their action. For example, in order to claim protection under OSHA for such refusal to work, an employee must show that working with an AIDS-infected client or co-worker presents a recognized (documented) hazard under the act. Given the current state of knowledge, only in unusual circumstances—perhaps an actor filming a "love scene"—could an employee prevail under OSHA or any of the state and municipal handicap legislation. [121]

Employers would be well advised to treat AIDS victims as they would any other employees with a degenerative disease. Provided that an AIDS-infected employee can perform his or her job satisfactorily and does not present an imminent threat to the health of fellow employees, he or she should be retained. As their health deteriorates, employees with AIDS should receive reasonable accommodation, as would other handicapped employees, in their work load, scheduling, and sick leave. Companies who combine a rational AIDS policy with a general education effort are meeting increasing success. [122]

Determining which employees are AIDS carriers presents employers with a further dilemma. At present, the preferable alternative is voluntary disclosure by the affected employee. AIDS testing is less than totally reliable, and a positive result—even if later proven a false-positive result—may cause untold trauma for an employee and his/her family. Further, revelation of the names of employees who test positive for the HTLV-III virus, may well expose an employer to a costly discrimination and/or defamation suit.[123]

AIDS testing and genetic testing, as health and safety issues, are generally considered mandatory subjects of bargaining.[124] Even in a collective bargaining situation, however, a union has no established right to the identity of specific AIDS victims or of employees whose genetic testing shows them to be at risk. At least to date, the privacy right of tested employees has outweighed the desire of a union to oversee perceived health risks to its membership.[125] As a rule, applicants are not protected by the collective bargaining agreement. However, an applicant aggrieved by such preemployment testing may seek redress through applicable local, state, or federal legislation.

Smoking Policies

The hazards smoking poses for smokers includes increased risk of cancer, heart diseases, lung disease, and problem pregnancies. Similar risks to passive smokers (people who inhale smoke from others' cigarettes) are lower, but not insignificant. Passive smoke also affects a larger number of people, since nonsmokers outnumber smokers in the work force by approximately two to one.[126]

Employers incur direct and indirect costs associated with employees' increased risk of illness from smoking. Chronic and acute illnesses related to smoking are responsible for approximately $22 billion per year in health care costs. Further, missed workdays due to the increased illness rate result in lost productivity of approximately $43 billion per year.[127] Thus, employers have many good business reasons to curtail or eliminate on-the-job smoking.

Smoking in the workplace remains a hotly contested issue, despite essentially uncontroverted evidence of the harm to cigarette smokers themselves and to passive smokers. Smokers allege that depriving them of the right to smoke infringes upon their civil liberties, and nonsmokers argue that permitting smoke to pollute the work area infringes upon *their* civil liberties.[128]

In some industries, such as mining and petroleum, smoking on the job is prohibited by federal law (OSHA). Some states and municipalities also have passed laws prohibiting or restricting smoking in the workplace. In addition, an increasing number of private companies have implemented no-smoking or restricted-smoking policies and a few companies have instituted a policy of not hiring smokers.[129] In lawsuits filed against their employers to compel a smoke-free work environment, nonsmokers have prevailed in some cases and lost in others.[130]

While the debate between smokers and nonsmokers remains heated and emotional, some general trends have emerged with respect to employers' rights to restrict smoking. In most reported cases, employers have been upheld in efforts to restrict or prohibit smoking in the workplace.[131] Employers generally do not have the right, however, to penalize or discharge employees for smoking off the job if the employees' off-the-job smoking does not impair their ability to function effectively at work.[132] A more positive approach is to encourage current smokers to quit. Many employers have instituted quit-smoking programs, bonuses for employees who quit on their own, and/or general health habits counseling. These employers often have reduced their insurance costs (fire and medical) and report employees overwhelmingly in favor of these efforts.[133]

Social Relationships and Lifestyle Preference

Most employees feel their employer has no right to regulate their private living accommodations or sexual preference. However, recent court cases indicate that even those very personal matters may be grounds for discipline or discharge.[134] In a widely publicized case, an employee sued the J.C. Penney Co. for wrongfully discharging him after he refused to cease dating a female coworker. The woman in question was not under the direct or indirect supervision of the discharged man. According to the Oregon Supreme Court this discharge was not "actionable outrageous conduct" and therefore was allowed to stand.[135]

In the public sector, two federal circuit courts of appeals have found that police officers' private lives may lawfully come under considerable scrutiny by their departments. The courts have upheld the firing of police officers for cohabiting outside of marriage, for committing adultery, and for having sexual relations with a minor three years before joining the police force [in the latter case, the minor had attained majority while still involved with the officer and prior to the time of his induction].[136] However, the Ninth Circuit Court of Appeals found questions regarding the off-duty sexual conduct of a police officer applicant to be constitutionally impermissible and thus invalid grounds for denying her admission to the police academy.[137] The cases which held off-duty sexual conduct and life-style preference to be just cause for dismissal rested on the premise that private-sector standards of privacy do not apply because of the heightened visibility of law enforcement officers and the threat their off-duty behavior may pose to the department as a whole.[138]

Similar reasoning has appeared in cases involving discharge of employees for homosexual lifestyles. In 1984, the District of Columbia Circuit Court upheld the discharge of a U.S. Navy sailor who admitted homosexuality, because his conduct was deemed a threat to maintaining discipline, morale, and national security.[139] However, in a more recent case, the Ninth Circuit Court of Appeals found that a United States Army regulation disqualifying homosexuals from Army service violated the "equal protection" portion of the Fifth Amendment. The Court held that the Army had failed to show a "legitimate compelling governmental interest" in banning homosexuals from its ranks.[140]

Employer rules prohibiting nepotism, contact with a competitor's employees, fraternization among employees, or dealing with more private issues such as life-style preference or sexual activity all must be premised upon the employer's ability to conduct business. The greater public responsibility of law enforcement agencies or government organizations may justify a more stringent code of conduct and less tolerance of divergent life-styles. However, such incursion into employee privacy by most private-sector companies would appear difficult to justify.[141]

Most employers have understandable concerns about maintaining a good public image and a competitive position. Accordingly, employers often have rules concerning various employee behaviors such as wearing of company uniforms off company premises, public or quasi-public statements concerning company strategy or technological breakthroughs, and employee grooming standards governing hair length, beards, and obesity. All such rules must be nondiscriminatory in content and application. In a collective bargaining relationship, these rules must also stand the test of reasonableness. In general, reasonable rules must be demonstrably related to health and safety or to a company's ability to conduct business in an efficient and profitable manner, and the rules must not intrude upon employee privacy any more than necessary to effect these ends.[142] Many non-union employers espouse a similar standard of intrusion as well.[143]

Employee Searches

In an effort to curb theft and improve security, some employers have instituted employee searches. These procedures may consist of random searches, department-wide searches, or routine searches as an employee exits the work premises. The issue of employee searches involves employees' reasonable expectations of privacy of person or possessions (such as lockers or tool boxes) and an employer's right to prevent and detect theft.[144]

In the public sector, an employee may invoke Fourth Amendment protections against unreasonable searches. The test of reasonableness in the public employment sector includes an evaluation of the employee's subjective expectation of privacy under the circumstances and of whether the search was conducted in a reasonable manner and in response to probable cause. However, if a private employer with no strong government nexus conducts the search, an employee will not have recourse to claims of a constitutional violation.[145]

Nonetheless, even private employers must take care that searches do not violate other rights of employees, including the right to be free from false imprisonment. Detention of employees during a search or physical contact with an employee without the person's consent, for example, may expose an employer to serious legal consequences, including charges of battery. Further, an employee must freely consent to the search, a condition difficult to prove if the search occurs in the coercive and intimidating environment of suspicion.[146]

In a collective bargaining relationship, arbitrators generally uphold an employer's right to search employees' lockers, purses, lunch boxes, or briefcases where a reasonable suspicion exists. However, the search must not be conducted in a discriminatory, capricious, or arbitrary manner. Unions also may grieve unilaterally promulgated search policies even prior to their enforcement.[147]

Union and nonunion employers should take several steps in establishing a search policy:

- An employer should keep the concepts of due process in mind when initiating a search policy.
- The search policy should stem from a legitimate employer interest.

- The policy should be drafted with legal counsel and cover all types of searches—lockers, purses, lunch boxes, and so on.

- Incumbent employees should have adequate notice of impending implementation of the policy, and new employees should be apprised of the policy once hired.

- Employers should post the policy in a prominent place, and include it in the employee handbook with an explanation of the rationale for the policy.

- Security personnel should be fully trained in legal and ethical search procedures, including emphasis on minimizing physical contact.[148]

Employee Surveillance

An issue related to employee searches is surveillance of employees. Surveillance can take place through electronic and more traditional methods, such as the use of "spotters"—employees or outside agents hired to observe other employees surreptitiously. During the past decade, employers have acquired the ability to monitor employees' behavior through video cameras and electronic surveillance of computer and telecommunications, often without the employee's knowledge or consent.[149]

This increased interest in employee monitoring reflects mounting concerns about theft, product security, and plant productivity. Acquisition of data is easier than ever before, transfer of data is facilitated by computer programs, and plant security is compromised more easily than ever before. By the same token, monitoring, either at the worksite or from a remote location, can occur in ways not previously contemplated—even employees using office computers in their homes may be under electronic surveillance.[150]

The ease with which monitoring can be accomplished does not mean that it is always a good policy. The negative effects on employees often outweigh the anticipated positive effects of increased employer control. Monitoring may have a deleterious effect on morale and productivity; it may encourage workers to devise ways to "beat the system," or to substitute quantity of output for quality of product.[151] In addition, federal and state laws prohibit or regulate the interception of written and telephone communication by outside parties. Such a violation can occur in the workplace when an employer intercepts the telephone communication of an employee who had a reasonable expectation of privacy in his/her communication.[152] If employees are engaged in an organizing campaign, surveillance by the employer may violate the NLRA, because it arguably interferes with employees' right to organize.

In just cause arbitration under a collective bargaining agreement, surveillance evidence may be admitted in support of the employer's case against the accused employee, even if such evidence were not admissible in a court of law. Nor does a grievant necessarily have the "due process" right to confront the spotters whose testimony (usually offered by deposition) implicates the employee. An arbitrator may determine that the necessity of maintaining the secrecy and integrity of the surveillance process outweighs the grievant's traditional right to confront his/her accuser.[153]

As a rule, employers should restrict surveillance to situations in which the organization has a legitimate and reasonable concern regarding employee theft or product security. In most reported cases, when an employer has bona fide concerns and carries out surveillance in a reasonable manner, employee challenges have failed.[154] In general, an employer should observe the following standards in instituting and maintaining a system of employee surveillance:

- A clear need for surveillance should exist, either because of legal requirements (OSHA, for example) or an employer's past experience.

- Only information pertinent to the job should be collected.

- Employees should receive advance notice of monitoring and of the mechanisms for appeal.

- Mechanical surveillance procedures should undergo thorough pre-testing before installation.

- Workers should have access to information about themselves and the right to correct or appeal information which they feel is erroneous.

- An employer should be prepared to provide monetary redress to employees whose rights are violated or who are adversely affected by erroneous surveillance information.

- A statute of limitations should apply to all information collected—it should be removed from an employee's record after a specific period of time, or immediately, if the monitoring system is proven defective.[155]

Employees' Rights and Access to Personnel Records

Another dilemma with respect to due process and employee privacy concerns employers' needs versus employee rights in the acquisition, maintenance, and disclosure of employees' records. Employers can easily accumulate sensitive information on incumbent employees or job applicants since employees often feel obligated to reveal such information in order to obtain or retain their jobs.[156] In addition, an employer often adds information to employees' files—data on performance, discipline, promotability, and salary prospects—during the employment period. Without access to their own files, employees cannot assess whether they received due process in employment decisions. On the other hand, an employer may feel understandably reluctant to reveal performance ratings, promotability estimates, or comparative salary information. Some answers to these problems are found in applicable legislation.

Federal and State Privacy Laws

All privacy legislation has its roots in the Bill of Rights and the Fourteenth Amendment to the Constitution. The most significant federal privacy legislation is the Privacy Act of 1974.[157] Under this law, federal-sector employees have the right to know the type of information collected on them, to review the information in their files, to correct or have removed erroneous information, and to restrict distribution of the information.[158]

While the Privacy Act applies only to federal employees, its guidelines regarding employee privacy and access to personnel files have been adopted by some state legislatures and private employers. Private employers, as users of credit bureau reports, may face additional restrictions under one federal privacy law—the Federal Fair Credit Reporting Act.[159] Under this law, employers must notify employees or applicants whenever credit information is sought. Employees or applicants in turn have the right to obtain from the investigating agency the results of the credit investigation.[160]

Except in the area of labor relations, federal law has little direct impact upon employer acquisition of and employee access to records in the private sector. In *Detroit Edison Co. v. NLRB*,[161] the U.S. Supreme Court held that an employer is not obligated to release information from employees' personnel files to a union without the employees' consent. The union's interest in the information did not take precedence over the employees' privacy rights. In later cases, however, two federal circuit courts of appeals have held that an employer's reluctance to reveal employee information must stem from a credible concern for confidentiality and not from an attempt to avoid disclosure prior to an arbitration.[162]

Several states' constitutions recognize individual privacy rights, and a dozen states have laws according private-sector employees the rights to view their own personnel files, to know what information an employer adds to their files, and to restrict an employer's release of that information.[163] The most stringent of these state laws, Connecticut's, prohibits release of any information "other than the employee's dates of employment, title, and salary" without the employee's authorization.[164] Many states also permit employees to copy records from their files and to correct any erroneous entries. Most states, however, limit employees' access to such information as letters of recommendation, results of security investigations, collective records which may relate to other employees, or supervisors' estimates of promotability or salary potential.[165]

Employees' Access to Files in the Private Sector

The Privacy Act of 1974 established the Privacy Protection Study Commission to assess whether some or all of the act's provisions should be applied to the private sector. The commission recommended that private-sector employers should comply with the act, but only on a voluntary basis. Specific recommendations concerning employees' personnel files made by the commission include the following:

- Employers should collect only job-related information.

- Employees should have access to their personnel files.

- Employees and applicants should be told how an employer intends to use the information collected.

- Employees should have the right to correct inaccurate information.

- Employers should strictly limit release or disclosure of employee information to third parties without an employee's consent.

- Employers should restrict internal use of employee records.[166]

According to a 1984 Prentice-Hall/ASPA survey, private employers are increasingly allowing employees access to their own personnel records. Procedures for viewing files vary, as does the right to copy, amend, or delete certain documents. In general, however, employees have access to preemployment records, performance appraisals, salary records (but not salary recommendations), and disciplinary records. Medical records are not generally kept in personnel files, and investigatory reports, if kept in the files, are not normally accessible to employees.[167] The survey data indicated at least two positive results of increased employee access to their files. First, employees had fewer suspicions concerning employer use of personnel information and better morale. Second, employers improved their methods of information gathering and storage, including updating and verification of the information gathered.[168]

Third-Party Access to Employee Files

Employers have an additional responsibility to safeguard personnel records from unauthorized intrusion. In assigning access privileges to persons other than the employee him/herself, the HR department should determine each individual's "need to know" and vary access accordingly. For example, some persons may possess rights only to view the information, others may have rights to record or copy the information, and a few individuals may be permitted to remove, add to, or change the information.[169]

Employers should pay close attention to the maintenance and security of employee medical records. Federal court cases and certain employment-related federal and state legislation have specifically recognized an employee's right to privacy concerning medical records. The protection accorded medical records includes an employee's past or present enrollment in a drug abuse or alcohol abuse program.[170] Yet, the need for detailed data on employees' medical and accident histories has increased due to the interest of prospective employers, the demands of unions looking for bargaining chips, and the legal requirements of OSHA and other state and municipal employment safety regulatory agencies.[171] An employer's best recourse might be to maintain medical and insurance files separate from other personnel files, restricting access to managers who clearly require the information for decision making and to government agencies or employee organizations with a legal right to know.[172]

Defamation Suits and Disclosure of Employee Information

During and subsequent to a worker's tenure, an employer may be asked to release some or all of its accumulated information on that worker to prospective employers or others, such as credit agencies, banks, or worker compensation agencies. Most of these requests are legitimate in nature, made in the normal course of doing business or investigating a worker's compensation claim. Nevertheless, defamation suits brought by employees against present or former employers have made managers increasingly reluctant to release any records beyond minimal information.[173]

Defamation can occur when an employer publicly discloses information which injures an employee's reputation. In order to prevail in a defamation suit, an employee must prove the following conditions:

- The employer publicly disclosed facts pertaining to the employee.

- The facts disclosed were private facts.

- The disclosure would have been highly offensive and objectionable to any person of reasonable sensibilities.

- The disclosure did not serve any legitimate public interest.[174]

In addition, because an employer's communications about employees are usually regarded as privileged, an employee generally must prove malice in order to recover damages from the employer. In order to retain the privileged status of its communication, however, an employer must prove that the communication at issue was made in good faith and was limited to the legitimate scope and to the appropriate parties.[175]

Fear of defamation suits has prompted many employers to limit the personnel information they will release to the "bare bones": name, job held, and dates of employment with the company. Yet even this spartan approach may not provide sufficient protection against suit. Failure to reveal certain information about an employee may subject a prior employer to a suit by the present employer.[176]

The problem becomes even more complex when the situation involves the public welfare and constitutional rights—such as when a teacher, fired for pupil abuse, is rehired by another school district.

A further issue concerns the problem of "compelled self-publication." Compelled self-publication occurs, for example, when an employee is forced to reveal defamatory information about him- or herself. An example would be an employee falsely accused of theft and fired who must reveal that false accusation to a prospective employer. If the prospective employer consequently declines to hire the individual, the employee may have a legitimate cause to initiate a defamation suit against the former employer, even though the actual defamatory information was "self-published."[177]

To avoid such problems, the following recommendations may help users and providers of reference information. Users of reference information should:

- Request only specific job-related information

- Avoid requesting or using subjective information and

- Obtain written consent from applicants before making reference checks

Providers of reference information should:

- Document all information released (date, specific information, and to whom released)

- Release only specific, objective information

- Obtain written consent from employees before releasing information

- Confirm the identity of the reference requestor (do not give reference information over the telephone)

- Avoid "blacklisting" employees

- Refuse to answer if asked whether they would rehire the employee (either a "yes" or a "no" answer may create a problem)[178]

Discipline and Discharge

Most collective bargaining agreements acknowledge an employer's right to discipline or terminate employees for misconduct or negligence under the standard of "just cause" or "proper cause." As developed in thousands of arbitration decisions over the last 60 years, the concept of just cause requires an employer not only to produce persuasive evidence of the employee's culpability or negligence, but also to provide the employee a fair hearing and to impose a penalty appropriate for the proven offense.[179]

This "common law" definition of just cause has become so well established that it is universally accepted by labor relations practitioners, even though collective bargaining agreements rarely define the term "just cause." A more detailed examination of just cause arbitration is beyond the scope of this section, but practitioners will find the following "questions" provide a useful checklist of the criteria followed by most arbitrators in deciding just cause discipline and discharge cases. Unless the contract states otherwise, each question below must be answered "Yes" if the employer's disciplinary action is to be upheld in just cause arbitration:

- Did the company give to the employee forewarning or foreknowledge of the possible or probable disciplinary consequences of the employee's conduct?

- Was the company's rule or managerial order reasonably related to (a) the orderly, efficient, and safe operation of the company's business and (b) the performance that the company might properly expect of the employee?

- Did the company, before administering discipline to an employee, make an effort to discover whether the employee did in fact violate or disobey a rule or order of management?

- Was the company's investigation conducted fairly and objectively?

- At the investigation did the "judge" obtain substantial evidence or proof that the employee was guilty as charged?

- Has the company applied its rules, orders, and penalties evenhandedly and without discrimination to all employees?

- Was the degree of discipline administered by the company in a particular case reasonably related to (a) the seriousness of the employee's proven offense and (b) the record of the employee in his service with the company?[180]

Fair Dismissal and Employment-at-Will

Until very recently, in the absence of a collective bargaining agreement or applicable antidiscrimination legislation, employers were as free to terminate employees as the employees were to quit.[181] This doctrine of employment-at-will, with the relationship severable by either party for good, bad, or no reason, governed employer-employee relations in most of the English-speaking world for several hundred years.[182] Commencing in the 1980s, however, a number of state courts in the United States began recognizing suits, finding violations, and awarding remedies in "wrongful discharge" actions brought by employees challenging the "fairness" of their termination.[183] Informed observers agree that employment-at-will soon may be viewed as just another relic of Victorian times.[184]

At this time, nearly all reported wrongful discharge cases in which employees have prevailed involve termination from employment rather than lesser disciplinary actions. State courts which permit wrongful discharge suits vary in their analytical approach, but three distinct bases for recovery have been recognized to date. The first basis is an implied contract of employment, in which the employer's words and actions constitute an implied promise not to discharge except for "just cause."[185] Second, public policy may restrict an employer's right to terminate employees who refuse to engage in illegal conduct or who "blow the whistle" on illegal, unsafe, or unhealthy employer conduct.[186] Third, the courts may find a "tort of bad faith dealing" if, by analogy from insurance industry cases, the employment relationship contained an implied "covenant of good faith and fair dealing" which would prohibit arbitrary, unreasonable, or capricious termination.[187]

Some state legislatures and Congress are considering enactment of "fair dismissal" laws defining standards, rights, and duties for employers and employees and also providing for administrative and regulatory review, rather than case-by-case lawsuits. At the present time, however, state courts remain the primary forum for discharged employees who are not covered by collective bargaining agreements.[188] Whether fair dismissal and wrongful discharge issues continue to be litigated case by case in the judicial arena or under administrative law and regulations, the "common law" of "just cause" standards used in collective bargaining cases will likely influence decisions.

Conclusion

In order to perform effectively, today's HR manager must fully recognize the complex and constantly evolving issues influenced by considerations of "due process." While most employees have no constitutional right to due process in the workplace, many employees are entitled to due process under collective bargaining agreements, employer-established grievance mechanisms, and/or employment-related federal and state legislation.

At bottom line, adherence to the concepts implied by due process contributes to an HR system that will meet not only the requirements of employment law, but also employees' desire for rational and nondiscriminatory procedures. Moreover, as the issues of AIDS in the workplace, drug testing, and privacy generate increasing concern among employees in general and for HR managers in particular, the importance of according potential and incumbent employees due process will increase as well.

◆

Notes

1. 8 Co.Rep. 1066, 77 Eng.Rep. 638 (1610). Cited in Linde and Bunn, at 810–11.
2. For a complete analysis of due process rights under the U.S. Constitution, see Linde and Bunn.
3. For a recent case on this issue, see *Cleveland Bd. of Educ. v. Loudermill*, 470 U.S. 532 (1985); see also Gulas.
4. See, for example, Administrative Procedure Act, 60 Stat. 237 (1946) as amended. See also Rowe, pp. 139–140.
5. Bedikian, p. 4.
6. Basic Patterns, p. 33.
7. From agreement between Philips Medical Systems, Inc. and Local 1270, Communications Workers of America (1982–85).
8. Fossum, p. 399.
9. *Code of Professional Responsibility for Arbitrators of Labor-Manage-* *ment Disputes.* See also Elkouri and Elkouri, p. 67.
10. Herman, Kuhn, and Seeber, p. 401. For a thorough discussion of resolution of grievances in a nonunion environment, see Ewing.
11. Diaz, Minton, and Saunders, p. 14.
12. Fossum, p. 467.
13. Caras, p. 54.
14. Caras, p. 57.
15. Diaz, Minton, and Saunders, p. 14.
16. Caras, p. 57.
17. Caras, p. 58.
18. Herman et al., p. 401.
19. Florey, p. 14.
20. Florey, p. 16.
21. Robbins and Deane, p. 15.
22. Rowe, p. 127.
23. Rowe, p. 127; Robbins and Deane, p. 18.
24. Rowe, p. 129; Robbins and Deane, p. 20.
25. Robbins and Deane, p. 23.

26. Edwards, p. 673, 676.
27. Holloway and Leech, p. 113, 335.
28. 49 Stat. 449 (1935).
29. *NLRB v. Jones & Laughlin Corp.*, 301 U.S. 1, 1 LRRM 703 (1937).
30. For a thorough discussion of this issue see Taylor and Whitney, p. 170.
31. Public Law 101, 80th Congress, Chapter 120, 1st sess.
32. 73 Stat. 519.
33. See *Finnegan v. Leu*, 456 U.S. 431 (1982), with respect to union officer's rights to due process in removal from office.
34. Phillips, p. 809.
35. Phillips, pp. 794–818. See also *Metropolitan Edison v. NLRB*, 460 U.S. 693, 112 LRRM 3265 (1983).
36. 42 U.S.C. §2000e et seq.
37. 29 U.S.C. §623 (a)(1).
38. Friedman and Strickler, pp. 627–630. *Oscar Meyer & Co. v. Evans*, 441 U.S. 750 (1979).
39. 29 U.S.C. §793(a).
40. Ledvinka, pp. 79–81.
41. See, for example, *Trans World Airlines v. Hardison*, 432 U.S. 63, 14 FEP Cases 1697 (1977).
42. 29 U.S.C. §660(c).
43. Holloway and Leech, p. 283.
44. See *Whirlpool Corp. v. Marshall*, 445 U.S. 1 (1980).
45. 29 U.S.C. §215 (a)(3).
46. 38 U.S.C. §2021(a).
47. 5 U.S.C. §2301 et seq.
48. 42 U.S.C. §2000e-2(a)(1) (1976 & Supp. V 1981).
49. An extensive listing of such legislation may be found in Holloway and Leech, pp. 423 ff.
50. Holloway and Leech, pp. 249, 259.
51. See *Petermann v. Teamsters*, 174 Cal. App. 2d 184, 344P.2d 25 (1959); *Pierce v. Ortho Pharmaceutical Corp.*, 84 N.J. 58, 417 A.2d 505 (1980).
52. Holloway and Leech, pp. 260–261.
53. Id.
54. Id., at p. 290.
55. For a thorough discussion of this issue and numerous case citations, see Holloway and Leech, pp. 290ff.
56. Id., at 291.
57. *Pierce v. Ortho Pharmaceuticals Corp.*, *supra* note 51.
58. Holloway and Leech, p. 292.
59. *Steele v. Louisville & Nashville R.R.*, 323 U.S. 192 (1944); *Wallace Corp. v. NLRB*, 323 U.S. 192 (1944).
60. *Vaca v. Sipes*, 386 U.S. 171, 64 LRRM 2369 (1967); *Amalgamated Ass'n of Street Employees v. Lockridge*, 403 U.S. 274, 77 LRRM 2501 (1971).
61. Taylor and Whitney, p. 429. See also *Bowen v. U.S. Postal Serv.*, 459 U.S. 212, 112 LRRM 2281 (1983).
62. Holzhauer, pp. 255ff.
63. Summers; see also McKelvey.
64. See Linde and Bunn, pp. 787–797, for discussion of case law supporting Fourth Amendment protections.
65. Duffy, Pepe, and Gross, p. 31.
66. *Business Week*.
67. Flanagan, p. 357.
68. *Frye v. United States*, 293 F. 1013 (D.C. Cir. 1923); see also *United States v. Alexander*, 526 F. 2d 161 (8th Cir. 1975).
69. Flanagan, pp. 360–362.
70. Weimer, pp. 52–54.
71. Weimer, p. 58.
72. Duffy, Pepe, and Gross, p. 41.
73. Bureau of National Affairs, Inc. (1988).
74. Flanagan, *passim*; and Weimer, pp. 77–79.
75. Weimer, pp. 51 and 61.
76. Weimer, p. 59; Elkouri and Elkouri, pp. 315–316.
77. 29 U.S.C. §§651–678 (1986).
78. Duffy, Pepe, and Gross, p. 45.
79. Cecere and Rosen, p. 860.
80. Duffy, Pepe, and Gross, p. 43.
81. Cecere and Rosen, pp. 860–861.

82. Cecere and Rosen, p. 862.

83. Bills, p. 620. Frequently reported false positives include poppy seed consumption yielding a positive reading for heroine and some herbal teas yielding a positive reading for cocaine.

84. Bills, p. 620.

85. A formal advice memorandum is not binding Board policy, but a statement by the General Counsel of how his office will pursue this category of unfair labor practice charges.

86. Advice Memorandum, at 8, *cited in* Vaughan, Axelrod, and Gorman III, p. 29.

87. See *Steelworkers v. Marshall*, 647 F.2d 1189 (D.C. Cir. 1980) *cert. denied*, 453 U.S. 913 (1981).

88. See, for example, Pub. L. No. 93-112, 87 Stat. 355 (codified as amended at 29 U.S.C. §§701–796 (1982)).

89. Cecere and Rosen, pp. 866 ff.

90. Cecere and Rosen, p. 869.

91. Duffy, Pepe, and Gross, pp. 44–45.

92. Duffy, Pepe, and Gross, p. 51.

93. 51 *Federal Register*, no. 180, 32889.

94. *Id.*, at 32890.

95. See, 14 CFR Parts 61, 63, 65, 121, and 135; 49 CFR Part 219.

96. See, for example, 49 CFR Part 40, "Procedures for Transportation Workplace Drug Testing Programs."

97. *Business Week*, p. 65; Duffy, Pepe, and Gross, p. 36.

98. Bills, p. 624.

99. *Business Week*, p. 65.

100. Adapted from Cecere and Rosen, pp. 875ff and 870, and Rothstein (1987A), pp. 734 ff.

101. *Uniform Guidelines on Employee Selection Procedures*, 29 Code of Federal Regulations, Part 1607.

102. See *Griggs v. Duke Power Co.*, 401 U.S. 424, 3 FEP Cases 175 (1971) for seminal decision on this issue.

103. Ledvinka, pp. 39–41.

104. Milkovich and Boudreau, Chapter 11.

105. Elkouri and Elkouri, pp. 619–620.

106. Silver, pp. 72–73. See also *DiCosala v. Boy Scouts of Am.*, 450 A.2d 508 (N.J. 1982) and *Pruitt v. Pavelin*, 685 P.2d 1347 (1984).

107. Reibstein.

108. Green and Reibstein, p. 76; Holloway and Leech, p. 276.

109. Silver, p. 74; see also *Burch v. A & G Associates*, 333 N.W. 2d 140 (1983).

110. See, for example, *Hunter v. Port Authority*, 277 Pa. Super. 4, 419 A.2d 631 (1980).

111. *Business Week*, p. 64.

112. See *Gregory v. Litton Indus.*, 316 F. Supp. 401 (C.D. Cal. 1970), *aff'd*, 472 F.2d 631 (9th Cir. 1972).

113. Williams, pp. 182–183.

114. *Business Week*, p. 65.

115. *Business Week*, p. 65.

116. Williams, pp. 181–182, 189, 204–205.

117. Stein, p. 22; and Lorber and Kirk, p. 28.

118. 480 U.S. 273, 43 FEP Cases 81 (1987).

119. Lorber and Kirk, pp. 26–28.

120. U.S. Department of Health & Human Services.

121. Lorber and Kirk, pp. 31 ff.

122. Koepp.

123. Bureau of National Affairs, Inc. (1986).

124. Fossum, p. 174.

125. Williams, pp. 186–187; Bureau of National Affairs, Inc. (1986), p. 1103.

126. Rothstein, 1987b, pp. 941–943; Hutchins, p. 42.

127. Rothstein, 1987b, pp. 945–946.

128. Hutchins, p. 42.

129. Rothstein, 1987b, pp. 946ff., p. 951; Bureau of National Affairs, Inc. (1987), pp. 1–7; Hutchins, pp. 42–43.

130. See *Shimp v. New Jersey Bell Tel. Co.*, 145 N.J. Super. 516, 368 A.2d

408 (N.J. Super. Ct. Ch. Div. 1976), and *Federal Employees for Non-Smokers' Rights*, 446 F. Supp. 181. Rothstein, 1987b, pp. 946 ff.

131. Rothstein, 1987b, p. 955.

132. Id.

133. Rothstein, 1987b, p. 964; Hutchins, p. 43; Bureau of National Affairs, Inc. (1987).

134. McClenahen, p. 52.

135. *Patton v. J.C. Penney Co.*, 301 Or. 117, 719 P.2d 854 (1986).

136. See *Shawgo v. Spradlin*, 701 F.2d 470 (5th Cir. 1983, *cert. denied*, 464 U.S. 965 (1983); *Andrade v. City of Phoenix*, 692 F.2d 557 (9th Cir. 1982); and *Fleisher v. City of Signal Hill*, 829 F.2d 1491 (9th Cir. 1987).

137. *Thorne v. City of El Segundo*, 726 F.2d 459, 33 FEP Cases 441 (9th Cir. 1983), *cert. denied*, 469 U.S. 979, 36 FEP Cases 234 (1984).

138. Korando, p. 318.

139. *Dronenburg v. Zech*, 741 F.2d 1388 (D.C. Cir. 1984). For thorough coverage of this topic, see Dressler.

140. *Watkins v. U.S. Army*, 837 F.2d 1428 (9th Cir. 1988).

141. Korando, p. 318; Elkouri and Elkouri, p. 763.

142. Elkouri and Elkouri, pp. 764–771.

143. McClenahen, pp. 50 ff.

144. Nobile, p. 89.

145. Duffy, Pepe, and Gross, p. 49–50; Nobile, p. 91; see also, for historical reference, *Burdeau v. McDowell*, 256 U.S. 465 (1921).

146. Nobile, p. 92; see also, *General Motors Corp. v. Piskor*, 340 A.2d 767 (MD 1975), *aff'd*, 381 A.2d 16 (Ct. of App. of MD 1977); Barnes and Palmer, p. 833.

147. Nobile, p. 96; Elkouri and Elkouri, p. 790.

148. Adapted from Nobile, p. 96.

149. *Business Week*, p. 65.

150. Marx and Sherizen, pp. 32–35.

151. *Id.*, p. 35.

152. For example, see Omnibus Crime Control and Safe Streets Act of 1968, Pub. L. 90-351, 82 Stat, 197, cod. as am. [18 U.S.C. §§2510–2520 (1982 & Supp. III, 1985)]; Holloway and Leech, p. 276.

153. Elkouri and Elkouri, pp. 330–331; 788.

154. *Id.*, pp. 330–331; Barnes and Palmer, p. 832.

155. Adapted from Barnes and Palmer, p. 832, and Marx and Sherizen, p. 37.

156. S. Cook, p. 62.

157. 5 U.S.C. §552a (1982 & Supp. III 1985).

158. Ledvinka, p. 255.

159. 15 U.S.C. §§1681–1681t (1982 & Supp. III 1985)

160. Barnes and Palmer, pp. 839 ff.

161. 440 U.S. 301 (1979).

162. See *NLRB v. Pfizer, Inc.*, 763 F.2d 887 (7th Cir. 1985), and *Salt River Valley Water Users' Ass'n v. NLRB*, 769 F.2d 639 (9th Cir. 1985), analyzed in detail in Finner, pp. 579–580.

163. Ledvinka, p. 255.

164. Conn. Gen. Stat. Ann. §31–128f, discussed at length in Finner, p. 573.

165. Barnes & Palmer, pp. 840–841; Finner, pp. 573–575.

166. Ledvinka, p. 257.

167. Prentice-Hall/ASPA survey, pp. 922–925.

168. Prentice-Hall/ASPA survey, p. 921.

169. Milkovich and Boudreau, p. 304.

170. See *E.I. du Pont de Nemours & Co. v. Finklea*, 442 F. Supp. 821 (S.D. W. Va. 1977) and *United States v. Westinghouse*, 638 F.2d 570 (3d Cir. 1980); Holloway and Leech, p. 224; the Drug Abuse Protection and Treatment Act of 1972 (21 U.S.C. §§801, 801(a) (1973)); Barnes and Palmer, p. 841; and Cal. Lab. Code. §1025 (West 1971).

171. Duffy, Pepe, and Gross, pp. 42, 49.

172. Goddard, p. 20; S. Cook, p. 65.

173. Finner, p. 569; Prentice and Winslett, p. 208.

174. Adapted from Restatement (Second) of Torts §652D (1976), cited in Barnes and Palmer, p. 842.
175. Finner, pp. 569, 571.
176. *Business Week*, p. 64; Finner, p. 578; Goddard, p. 19.
177. Prentice and Winslett, p. 207; see also *Lewis v. Equitable Assurance Soc'y of the U.S.*, 389 N.W.2d 876 (Minn. 1986).
178. Ledvinka, pp. 257–258.
179. Elkouri and Elkouri, pp. 651–655.
180. 46 LA 359 (1966), at 363–364. See also Elkouri and Elkouri, pp. 651–655; Holloway and Leech, pp. 112–133; and Redeker, pp. 22, 45–47.
181. Bradshaw and Deacon, p. 74.
182. Jacoby, *passim*.
183. See, for example, *Weiner v. McGraw-Hill, Inc.*, 57 N.Y.2d 458, 443 N.E.2d 441 (1982); *Shah v. American Synthetic Rubber Corp.*, 655 S.W. 2d 489 (Ky. 1983); and *Pine River State Bank v. Mettille*, 333 N.W.2d 622 (Minn. 1983).
184. McOmber, p. 343.
185. See *Weiner, supra*.
186. Holloway and Leech, pp. 290–296.
187. Holloway and Leech, pp. 66–68.
188. St. Antoine, p. 43.

Editor's Note: In addition to the references shown below there are other significant sources of information and ideas on due process.

Books

Lewicki, R.J., and J.A. Litterer. 1985. *Negotiation*. Homewood, IL: Richard D. Irwin.

Twomey, D.P. 1986. *A Concise Guide to Employment Law: EEO & OSHA*. Cincinnati: Southwestern Publishing Co.

Articles

Abbasi, S.M., K.W. Hollman, and J.H. Murrey, Jr. 1987. "Employment at Will: An Eroding Concept in Employment Relationships." *Labor Law Journal* (January): 21–32.

Cook, R.W. 1987. "Reaffirming the Employer's Right to Fire at Will: Patton v. J.C. Penney Co." *Willamette Law Review* 23(1) (Winter): 179–192.

Finney, M.I. 1988. "A Game of Skill or Chance?" *Personnel Administrator* (March): 38–43.

Gilkey, R. 1987. "Alternative Dispute Resolution: Hazardous or Helpful?" *Emory Law Journal* 36: 575–578.

Green, R.M., and R.J. Reibstein. 1987. "It's 10 p.m. Do You Have to Know Where Your Employees Are?" *Personnel Administrator* (April): 70–76.

Klug, M. 1987. "The Alternative Dispute Resolution Promotion Act of 1986: A Critical Analysis." *St. Louis University Law Journal* 31: 981–1000.

Mauer, G.W., and J. Flores. 1986. "From Adversary to Advocate." *Personnel Administrator* (June): 53–58.

Mazadoorian, H.N. 1987. "On Implementing ADR: One Company's Experience Putting Theory Into Practice." *The Compleat Lawyer* (Spring): 45–47.

Millhauser, M. 1987. "The Unspoken Resistance to Alternative Dispute Resolution." *Negotiation Journal* 3 (January): 29–35.

Mur, R. 1984. "Using Alternative Methods to Resolve Corporate Disputes." *The Arbitration Journal* 39 (4) (December):

Reibstein, L. 1987. "Firms Face Lawsuits for Hiring People Who Then Commit Crimes." *The Wall Street Journal* (April 30): 31.

Wasson, R.P., Jr. 1987. "AIDS Discrimination Under Federal, State and Local Law After *Arline*." *Florida State University Law Review* 15: 221–278.

Yoder, D., and P.D. Staudohar. 1984. "Testing and EEO: Getting Down to Cases." *Personnel Administrator* (February): 67–76.

Pamphlets

Acquired Immune Deficiency Syndrome: 100 Questions and Answers. 1987. New York State Department of Health, May.

Code of Professional Responsibility for Arbitrators of Labor-Management Disputes. 1974, amended 1985. American Arbitration Association, National Academy of Arbitrators, and Federal Mediation and Conciliation Service.

◆

References

Barnes, T.J., and G.M. Palmer. 1986. Private Matters in Private Employment." *Detroit College of Law Review* 3: 825–845.

Bedikian, M.A. 1986. "Safeguarding the Interests of At-Will Employees: A Model Case for Arbitration." *Detroit College of Law Review* 1 (Spring).

Bills, R.D. 1987. "Mandatory Employee Drug Testing: The War on Drugs Invades the Workplace." *Western State University Law Review* 14: 617–629.

Bradshaw, D.A., and L.V.W. Deacon. 1985. "Wrongful Discharge: The Tip of the Iceberg?" *Personnel Administrator* (November): 74–76.

Bureau of National Affairs, Inc. 1986. *Employee Relations Weekly* 4 (September 4): 1103–4.

———. 1987. "ASPA-BNA Survey No. 51 Smoking in the Workplace: 1987 Update." *Bulletin to Management* 38 (45) (November 26).

———. 1988. *Daily Labor Report* 124 (June 28): A-10, A-11.

———. 1989. *Basic Patterns in Union Contracts*, 12th ed. Washington, DC: BNA Books.

Business Week. 1988. "Privacy." March 28: 61–68.

Caras, H.S. 1987. "Peer Review Grievance Procedure Bolsters Employee Support." *Personnel Journal* (June): 54–58.

Cecere, M.S., and P.B. Rosen. 1987. "Legal Implication of Substance Abuse Testing in the Workplace." *Notre Dame Law Review* 62 (5): 859–878.

Cook, S.H. 1987. "Privacy Rights: Whose Life Is It Anyway?" *Personnel Administrator* 32 (April): 58–65.

Diaz, E.M., J.W. Minton, and D.M. Saunders. 1987. "A Fair Nonunion Grievance Procedure." *Personnel* 64 (April): 13–18.

Dressler, J.B. 1988. "*Bowers v. Hardwick*: No Constitutional Protection for Private Consensual Homosexual Intimacy." *North Carolina Central Law Journal* 17 (1): 100–118.

Duffy, J., S.P. Pepe, and B. Gross. 1987. "Big Brother in the Workplace: Privacy Rights Versus Employer Needs." *Industrial Relations Law Journal* 9 (1): 30–56.

Edwards, H.T. 1986. "Alternative Dispute Resolution: Panacea or Anathema?" *Harvard Law Review* 99: 668–684.

Elkouri, F., and E.A. Elkouri. 1985. *How Arbitration Works*, 4th ed. Washington, DC: BNA Books.

Ewing, D.W. 1989. *Justive on the Job: Resolving Grievances in the Nonunion Workplace*. Boston: Harvard Business School Press.

Finner, W. 1986. "Privacy of Employment Records in the Private Sector." *1986 Annual Survey of American Law*: 569–586.

Flanagan, S.M. 1987. "Employer-Employee Relations—The Employee Polygraph Protection Act: Polygraph Testing in Private Employment Is Not the Answer." *Southern Illinois University Law Journal* 11: 355–380.

Florey, P. 1985. "A Growing Fringe Benefit: Arbitration of Nonunion Employee Grievances." *Personnel Administrator* (July): 14–18.

Fossum, J.A. 1985. *Labor Relations: Development, Structure Process* 3d ed. Plano, TX: Business Publications, Inc.

Friedman, J.M., and G.M. Strickler. 1987. *The Law of Employment Discrimination: Cases and Materials*, 2d ed. Mineola, NY: The Foundation Press.

Goddard, R.W. 1987. "Shedding Light on Employee Privacy." *Management World* 16 (January): 18–20.

Gulas, A.M. 1987. "Due Process—Constitutional Guarantee, Not Legislative Grace." *Duquesne Law Review* 25 (345).

Herman, E.E., A. Kuhn, and R.L. Seeber. 1987. *Collective Bargaining and Labor Relations*, 2d ed. Englewood Cliffs, NJ: Prentice-Hall, Inc.

Holloway, W.J., and M.J. Leech. 1985. *Employment Termination: Rights and Remedies*. Washington, DC: BNA Books.

Holzhauer, J.D. 1987. "The Contractual Duty of Competent Representation." *Chicago Kent Law Review* 63 (2): 255–278.

Hutchins, D. 1986. "The Drive to Kick Smoking at Work." *Fortune* (Sept. 15).

Jacoby, S.M. 1982. "The Duration of Indefinite Employment Contracts in the United States and England: An Historical Analysis." *Comparative Labor Law*, 3: 85–128.

Koepp, S. 1986. "Living With AIDS on the Job." *Time* (August 25): 48.

Korando, K.J. 1985. "Professions and Occupations: Dismissal for Sexual Activities—Should Police Officers Be Held to a Higher Standard of Conduct than Other Employees?" *Oklahoma Law Review* 38 (2) (Summer): 301–322.

Ledvinka, J. 1982. *Federal Regulation of Personnel and Human Resource Management*. Boston: Kent Publishing Company.

Linde, H.A., and G. Bunn. 1976. *Legislative and Administrative Processes*. Mineola, NY: The Foundation Press, Inc.

Lorber, L.Z., and R.J. Kirk. 1987. *Fear Itself: A Legal and Personnel Analysis of Drug Testing, AIDS, Secondary Smoke, VDT's*. Alexandria, VA: The ASPA Foundation.

Marx, G.T., and S. Sherizen. 1987. "Corporations That Spy on Their Employees." *Business and Society Review* 60 (Winter): 32–37.

McClenahen, J.S. 1985. "The Privacy Invasion: In a Job Setting, How Personal Is Too Personal?" *Industry Week* (November 11).

McKelvey, J.T., ed. 1985. *The Changing Law of Fair Representation*. Ithaca, NY: ILR Press.

McOmber, R.A. 1986. "Emerging Issues in Employment Law: The Debate Shifts to the States." *Cooley Law Review* 4: 329–345.

Milkovich, G.T., and J. Boudreau. 1988. *Personnel/Human Resource Management: A Diagnostic Approach* 5th ed. Plano, TX: Business Publications, Inc.

Nobile, R.J. 1985. "Employee Searches in the Workplace: Developing a Realistic Policy." *Personnel Administrator* (May): 89–98.

Phillips, P. 1986. "The Contractual Waiver of Individual Rights Under the National Labor Relations Act." *New York Law School Law Review* 31: 793–850.

Prentice, R.A. and B.J. Winslett. 1987. "Employee References: Will a 'No Comment' Policy Protect Employers Against Liability for Defamation?" *American Business Law Journal* 25: 207–239.

Prentice-Hall/American Society for Personnel Administration. 1984. "P-H/ASPA Survey: Employee Access to Records." Englewood Cliffs, NJ: Prentice-Hall, Inc.

Redeker, J.R. 1983. *Discipline: Policies and Procedures*. Washington, DC: BNA Books.

Robbins, L.P. and W.B. Deane. 1986. "The Corporate Ombuds: A New Approach to Conflict Management." *Negotiation Journal* 2(2): 15–27.

Rothstein, M.A. 1987a. "Drug Testing in the Workplace: The Challenge to Employment Relations and Employment Law." *Chicago Kent Law Review* 63: 683–743.

———. 1987b. "Refusing to Employ Smokers: Good Public Health or Bad Public Policy?" *Notre Dame Law Review* 62(5): 940–968.

Rowe, M.P. 1987. "The Corporate Ombudsman: An Overview and Analysis." *Negotiation Journal* 3(2): 127–140.

St. Antoine, T.J. 1982. "Protection Against Unjust Discipline: An Idea Whose Time Has Long Since Come." In *Arbitration Issues for the 1980s:* Proceedings of the Thirty-Fourth Annual Meeting, National Academy of Arbitrators, eds. J.L. Stern and B.D. Dennis. Washington, DC: BNA Books.

Silver, M. 1987. "Negligent Hiring Claims Take Off." *ABA Journal* (May 1): pp. 72–78.

Stein, R.E. 1987. "Strategies for Dealing with AIDS Disputes in the Workplace." *The Arbitration Journal* 42(3) (September): 21–29.

Summers, C.W. 1977. "The Individual Employee's Rights under the Collective Agreement: What Constitutes Fair Representation?" In *The Duty of Fair Representation*, ed. J.T. McKelvey. Ithaca, NY: ILR Press.

Taylor, B.J., and F. Whitney. 1987. *Labor Relations Law*, 5th ed. Englewood Cliffs, NJ: Prentice-Hall.

U.S. Department of Health and Human Services. 1988. "Understanding AIDS." HHS Publication No. (CDC) HHS-88-8404.

Vaughan, D., J. Axelrod, and E.J. Gorman III. 1988. "Positive/Negative: Examining Drug Testing Cases in the District of Columbia." *The Washington Lawyer* 2(4) (March/April).

Weimer, D. 1987. "Common Law Remedies of Employees Injured by Employer Use of Polygraph Testing." *University of Richmond Law Review* 22: 51–81.

Williams, J.F. 1987. "A Regulatory Model for Genetic Testing in Employment." *Oklahoma Law Review* 40(2) (Summer): 181–208.

Appendix A

Nonunion Grievance Procedure of a Western Bank

A new Internal Review Procedure, designed to handle work-related concerns of staff members, will soon be implemented. It will be provided for the use of the general staff.

The new two-step procedure should resolve most work-related problems within two weeks.

The new procedure is a supplement to the usual means of resolving staff concerns. Staff members are encouraged to review their problems first with the branch/department and region/division channels.

If this isn't sufficient, a staff member may informally express concern to a Labor Relations representative by calling (phone number) or by using Expressline (toll free number).

If the staff member feels a formal review is necessary, the Internal Review Procedure is set in motion.

A Review Request form, which will soon be available at all work locations and from the Labor Relations Section, is filled out and mailed to Labor Relations, 11th floor, HOB.

Labor Relations will acknowledge receipt of the Review Request immediately in a letter to the staff member, the branch/department and the region/division.

Within seven working days, a Labor Relations representative will visit the work location to gather facts and consult with the staff member, meet with the supervisor and recommend a solution if that is appropriate. It is hoped most concerns will be resolved at this stage.

If a resolution is not achieved during this "discovery visit," the Labor Relations representative will consult with the region/division office and attempt to solve the problem at that level.

The next step in the process is a review meeting. If no solution to the problem is found within ten working days of the "discovery visit," the Labor Relations representative will prepare a report which includes a statement of the problem, the remedies sought by the staff member and the respective viewpoints of both the staff member and the supervisor.

This report will be submitted to each member of a three-person committee. The committee will consist of a peer of the person requesting the review, an administrative officer from a region/division other than from where the Review Request originated and the manager of the Labor Relations Section, who acts as chairperson for the committee.

The peer will be selected from among all staff members of the same pay grade and the same region/division as the person who requested the review. The person requesting the review will have the right to refuse the first person selected.

Within 15 days of the "discovery visit," the committee will hold a review meeting attended by the staff members, the line supervisor/manager and the Labor relations representative who made the visit. The committee will issue a final written decision within five working days of the hearing.

Each step of this internal process will be fully documented, but no record of the Review or any associated documents will be part of the staff member's personnel file.

Staff members who utilize and participate in this procedure shall suffer no reprisals for doing so and need not be concerned about adverse consequences because a Review Request was filed, regardless of the outcome.

It should take no more than a month to go through the entire process, from the time the formal review is requested to the time the decision is mailed out.

We think the new procedure is an objective way to resolve any problems encountered by staff members regarding fair treatment at the Bank.

The Internal Review Procedure is scheduled to go into operation later this month. More information will be made available by Informative Letter. (Western bank)

DIAGRAM OF PROCEDURE:

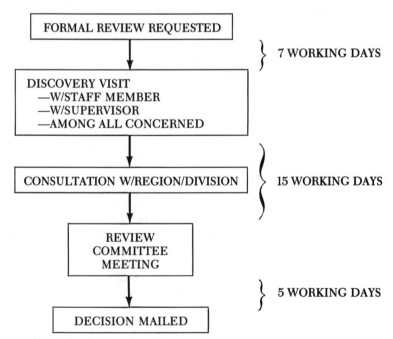

Source: Reprinted from "Personnel Management," BNA *Policy and Practice Series*, Washington, DC: The Bureau of National Affairs, Inc., pp. 263: 803–263: 804.

Appendix B

DOT Urine Custody Control Form

URINE CUSTODY AND CONTROL FORM

STEP 1—TO BE COMPLETED BY EMPLOYEE/APPLICANT

Employee I.D. # _____ [PRE-PRINTED SPECIMEN I.D. #]   Employer Name: _____
    Social Security No.
    or Employee No.

STEP 2—TO BE COMPLETED BY EMPLOYER REPRESENTATIVE/OR COLLECTOR   Reason for Test (Check One)

☐ Pre-employment   ☐ Post Accident   ☐ Random   ☐ Periodic Medical

☐ Other (Specify) _____

STEP 3—COLLECTOR MUST NOTE THAT TEMPERATURE OF SPECIMEN HAS BEEN READ. RECORD IF NOT WITHIN

THE RANGE OF 32.5–37.7C/ 90.5–99.8F: _____   ☐ WITHIN RANGE

STEP 4—TO BE INITIATED BY THE PERSON COLLECTING SPECIMEN AND COMPLETED AS NECESSARY THEREAFTER:

Purpose of Change	Released By Signature/Print Name	Received By Signature/Print Name	Date
Provide Specimen for Testing	DONOR		

STEP 5—(SEE BELOW—TO BE COMPLETED BY EMPLOYEE)

STEP 6—BEFORE COMPLETING THIS STEP HAVE EMPLOYEE COMPLETE STEP 5 BELOW. To be completed by person collecting specimen:

Collector's Name _____   Date of Collection _____
    Print (First, M.I., Last)

Collection Site _____   ( ) _____
    Facility Name and Location   Telephone

Remarks concerning collection: _____

    I certify that the specimen identified on this form is the specimen presented to me by the employee providing the certification below, that I have certified that it bears the same identification number as that set forth above, and that it has been collected, labeled and sealed as required by the instructions provided.

_____
Signature of collector

STEP 7—TO BE COMPLETED BY THE LABORATORY: Accession No. _____

    I certify that the specimen identified by this accession number is the same specimen that bears the identification number set forth above, that the specimen has been examined upon receipt, handled and analyzed in accordance with applicable Federal requirements, and that the results attached are for that specimen.

Printed Name	Signature	Date

Copy No. 1: Original

URINE CUSTODY AND CONTROL FORM

STEP 1—TO BE COMPLETED BY EMPLOYEE/APPLICANT

Employee I.D. # _____   [PRE-PRINTED SPECIMEN I.D. #]   Employer Name: _____
       Social Security No.
       or Employee No.

STEP 2—TO BE COMPLETED BY EMPLOYER REPRESENTATIVE/OR COLLECTOR   Reason for Test (Check One)

☐ Pre-employment   ☐ Post Accident   ☐ Random   ☐ Periodic Medical
☐ Other (Specify) _____

STEP 3—COLLECTOR MUST NOTE THAT TEMPERATURE OF SPECIMEN HAS BEEN READ. RECORD IF NOT WITHIN
THE RANGE OF 32.5–37.7C/ 90.5–99.8F: _____   ☐ WITHIN RANGE

STEP 4—TO BE INITIATED BY THE PERSON COLLECTING SPECIMEN AND COMPLETED AS NECESSARY
THEREAFTER:

Purpose of Change	Released By Signature/Print Name	Received By Signature/Print Name	Date
Provide Specimen for Testing	DONOR		

STEP 5—(SEE BELOW—TO BE COMPLETED BY EMPLOYEE)

STEP 6—BEFORE COMPLETING THIS STEP HAVE EMPLOYEE COMPLETE STEP 5 BELOW. To be completed by
person collecting specimen:

Collector's Name _____   Date of Collection _____
       Print (First, M.I., Last)

Collection Site _____   ( ) _____
       Facility Name and Location   Telephone

Remarks concerning collection: _____

I certify that the specimen identified on this form is the specimen presented to me by the employee providing the
certification below, that I have certified that it bears the same identification number as that set forth above, and that it has been
collected, labeled and sealed as required by the instructions provided.

_____
Signature of collector

STEP 7—TO BE COMPLETED BY THE LABORATORY: Accession No. _____

I certify that the specimen identified by this accession number is the same specimen that bears the identification number set
forth above, that the specimen has been examined upon receipt, handled and analyzed in accordance with applicable Federal
requirements, and that the results attached are for that specimen.

Printed Name	Signature	Date

STEP 5—TO BE COMPLETED BY EMPLOYEE OR APPLICANT PROVIDING SPECIMEN:

Name _____   Duty Location _____
       Last/First/M.I.

Job Title: _____   Date of Birth _____

If you wish to have prescription or over-the-counter medications that you may have taken or been administered within the past
30 days considered as your test results are reviewed, you may list them here or provide that information separately to your
employers' Medical Review Officer:

_____

_____

I certify that the urine specimen identified on this form is my own; that it is fresh and has not been adulterated in any
manner; and that the identification information provided on this form and on the collection bottle is correct. I consent to the
submission of this specimen to the certified laboratory designated by my employer, to the analysis of the specimen for controlled
substances as provided by Federal requirements, and to the release of test results from that analysis to the Medical Review Officer
designated by my employer.

_____   _____
       Signature   Date

Copy No. 2: Medical Review Officer

URINE CUSTODY AND CONTROL FORM

STEP 1—TO BE COMPLETED BY EMPLOYEE/APPLICANT

Employee I.D. # _____ [PRE-PRINTED SPECIMEN I.D. #] Employer Name: _____
　　　　　　Social Security No.
　　　　　　or Employee No.

STEP 2—TO BE COMPLETED BY EMPLOYER REPRESENTATIVE/OR COLLECTOR Reason for Test (Check One)

　　☐ Pre-employment　　☐ Post Accident　　☐ Random　　☐ Periodic Medical
　　☐ Other (Specify) _____

STEP 3—COLLECTOR MUST NOTE THAT TEMPERATURE OF SPECIMEN HAS BEEN READ. RECORD IF NOT WITHIN
　　THE RANGE OF 32.5–37.7C/ 90.5–99.8F: _____　☐ WITHIN RANGE

STEP 4—TO BE INITIATED BY THE PERSON COLLECTING SPECIMEN AND COMPLETED AS NECESSARY
　　THEREAFTER:

Purpose of Change	Released By Signature/Print Name	Received By Signature/Print Name	Date
Provide Specimen for Testing	DONOR		

STEP 5—(SEE BELOW—TO BE COMPLETED BY EMPLOYEE)

STEP 6—BEFORE COMPLETING THIS STEP HAVE EMPLOYEE COMPLETE STEP 5 BELOW. To be completed by
　　person collecting specimen:

Collector's Name _____　　Date of Collection _____
　　　　　Print (First, M.I., Last)

Collection Site _____　　( ) _____
　　　　　Facility Name and Location　　　　　　　　Telephone

Remarks concerning collection: _____

　　I certify that the specimen identified on this form is the specimen presented to me by the employee providing the
certification below, that I have certified that it bears the same identification number as that set forth above, and that it has been
collected, labeled and sealed as required by the instructions provided.

_____
Signature of collector

STEP 7—TO BE COMPLETED BY THE LABORATORY: Accession No. _____

　　I certify that the specimen identified by this accession number is the same specimen that bears the identification number set
forth above, that the specimen has been examined upon receipt, handled and analyzed in accordance with applicable Federal
requirements, and that the results attached are for that specimen.

Printed Name	Signature	Date

STEP 5—TO BE COMPLETED BY EMPLOYEE OR APPLICANT PROVIDING SPECIMEN:

Name _____　　Duty Location _____
　　　　Last/First/M.I.

Job Title: _____　　Date of Birth _____

If you wish to have prescription or over-the-counter medications that you may have taken or been administered within the past
30 days considered as your test results are reviewed, you may list them here or provide that information separately to your
employers' Medical Review Officer:

_____

_____

　　I certify that the urine specimen identified on this form is my own; that it is fresh and has not been adulterated in any
manner; and that the identification information provided on this form and on the collection bottle is correct. I consent to the
submission of this specimen to the certified laboratory designated by my employer, to the analysis of the specimen for controlled
substances as provided by Federal requirements, and to the release of test results from that analysis to the Medical Review Officer
designated by my employer.

_____
　　Signature　　　　　　　Date

URINE CUSTODY AND CONTROL FORM

STEP 1—TO BE COMPLETED BY EMPLOYEE/APPLICANT

Employee I.D. # _____ [PRE-PRINTED SPECIMEN I.D. #] Employer Name: _____
        Social Security No.
        or Employee No.

STEP 2—TO BE COMPLETED BY EMPLOYER REPRESENTATIVE/OR COLLECTOR Reason for Test (Check One)

☐ Pre-employment ☐ Post Accident ☐ Random ☐ Periodic Medical
☐ Other (Specify) _____.

STEP 3—COLLECTOR MUST NOTE THAT TEMPERATURE OF SPECIMEN HAS BEEN READ. RECORD IF NOT WITHIN THE RANGE OF 32.5–37.7C/ 90.5–99.8F: _____ ☐ WITHIN RANGE

STEP 4—TO BE INITIATED BY THE PERSON COLLECTING SPECIMEN AND COMPLETED AS NECESSARY THEREAFTER:

Purpose of Change	Released By Signature/Print Name	Received By Signature/Print Name	Date
Provide Specimen for Testing	DONOR		

STEP 5—(SEE BELOW—TO BE COMPLETED BY EMPLOYEE)

STEP 6—BEFORE COMPLETING THIS STEP HAVE EMPLOYEE COMPLETE STEP 5 BELOW. To be completed by person collecting specimen:

Collector's Name _____   Date of Collection _____
        Print (First, M.I., Last)

Collection Site _____   ( ) _____
        Facility Name and Location   Telephone

Remarks concerning collection: _____

   I certify that the specimen identified on this form is the specimen presented to me by the employee providing the certification below, that I have certified that it bears the same identification number as that set forth above, and that it has been collected, labeled and sealed as required by the instructions provided.

_____
Signature of collector

STEP 7—TO BE COMPLETED BY THE LABORATORY: Accession No. _____

   I certify that the specimen identified by this accession number is the same specimen that bears the identification number set forth above, that the specimen has been examined upon receipt, handled and analyzed in accordance with applicable Federal requirements, and that the results attached are for that specimen.

Printed Name	Signature	Date

STEP 5—TO BE COMPLETED BY EMPLOYEE OR APPLICANT PROVIDING SPECIMEN:

Name _____   Duty Location _____
        Last/First/M.I.

   I certify that the urine specimen identified on this form is my own; that it is fresh and has not been adulterated in any manner; and that the identification information provided on this form and on the collection bottle is correct. I consent to the submission of this specimen to the certified laboratory designated by my employer, to the analysis of the specimen for controlled substances as provided by Federal requirements, and to the release of test results from that analysis to the Medical Review Officer designated by my employer.

_____   _____
        Signature   Date

Copy No. 4: Collector

URINE CUSTODY AND CONTROL FORM

STEP 1—TO BE COMPLETED BY EMPLOYEE/APPLICANT

Employee I.D. # _____ [PRE-PRINTED SPECIMEN I.D. #]   Employer Name: _____
Social Security No.
or Employee No.

STEP 2—TO BE COMPLETED BY EMPLOYER REPRESENTATIVE/OR COLLECTOR   Reason for Test (Check One)

☐ Pre-employment   ☐ Post Accident   ☐ Random   ☐ Periodic Medical

☐ Other (Specify) _____.

STEP 3—COLLECTOR MUST NOTE THAT TEMPERATURE OF SPECIMEN HAS BEEN READ. RECORD IF NOT WITHIN THE RANGE OF 32.5–37.7C/ 90.5–99.8F: _____   ☐ WITHIN RANGE

STEP 4—TO BE INITIATED BY THE PERSON COLLECTING SPECIMEN AND COMPLETED AS NECESSARY THEREAFTER:

Purpose of Change	Released By Signature/Print Name	Received By Signature/Print Name	Date
Provide Specimen for Testing	DONOR		

STEP 5—(SEE BELOW—TO BE COMPLETED BY EMPLOYEE)

STEP 6—BEFORE COMPLETING THIS STEP HAVE EMPLOYEE COMPLETE STEP 5 BELOW. To be completed by person collecting specimen:

Collector's Name _____   Date of Collection _____
Print (First, M.I., Last)

Collection Site _____   ( ) _____
Facility Name and Location   Telephone

Remarks concerning collection: _____

I certify that the specimen identified on this form is the specimen presented to me by the employee providing the certification below, that I have certified that it bears the same identification number as that set forth above, and that it has been collected, labeled and sealed as required by the instructions provided.

_____
Signature of collector

STEP 7—TO BE COMPLETED BY THE LABORATORY: Accession No. _____

I certify that the specimen identified by this accession number is the same specimen that bears the identification number set forth above, that the specimen has been examined upon receipt, handled and analyzed in accordance with applicable Federal requirements, and that the results attached are for that specimen.

Printed Name	Signature	Date

STEP 5—TO BE COMPLETED BY EMPLOYEE OR APPLICANT PROVIDING SPECIMEN:

Name _____   Duty Location _____
Last/First/M.I.

Job Title: _____   Date of Birth _____

I certify that the urine specimen identified on this form is my own; that it is fresh and has not been adulterated in any manner; and that the identification information provided on this form and on the collection bottle is correct. I consent to the submission of this specimen to the certified laboratory designated by my employer, to the analysis of the specimen for controlled substances as provided by Federal requirements, and to the release of test results from that analysis to the Medical Review Officer designated by my employer.

_____   _____
Signature   Date

Copy No. 5: Employer

[FR Doc. 88-26611 Filed 11-15-88; 3:48 pm]
BILLING CODE 4910-62-C

4.5

Union Organizing and Representation

John J. Lawler

This chapter focuses on the processes related to union growth and decline. These processes are vital, since the viability of unions as organizations depends on their ability to attract and hold members. In the United States, trade unions have always represented a relatively small proportion of the labor force, at least when compared to labor movements in most other industrialized democracies. At their peak, U.S. unions had organized only about one-third of the work force, although their power and influence was clearly greater than this number suggests. Yet American unions have experienced a major slump for at least 20 years. In addition to eroding political and bargaining power, the unionization rate is currently about 17 percent. In contrast, unionization rates in western European countries are often two to three times greater, even though most of these labor movements were well-established long before unions caught on in the United States. And union membership in Canada, currently around 40 percent of the labor force, has grown continuously over the same period in which U.S. unions have lost strength.[1]

The decline in union membership has been attributed to a number of factors, including economic, political, and social conditions beyond the control of either unions or employers. But despite unfavorable conditions, the legal practice of granting a union the exclusive right to represent all employees within a defined bargaining unit remains a central feature of the American industrial relations system. Unions and employers have always made active attempts to affect organizing outcomes at the bargaining-unit level. However, the current period of union decline has generated widespread employer opposition of a level not witnessed in this country for well over half a century. Union organizing techniques have also been undergoing profound change, particularly since the early 1980s.

To many observers, the use of such strategies and the intensity of these efforts by unions and employers have become even more important than external forces in determining whether or not a union will secure and maintain representation rights among a group of employees. These institutional mechanisms relating to union recognition are the principal concern of this chapter. Issues examined include the strategies pursued by employers and unions before, during, and after organizing efforts; the impact of such strategies on the likelihood of union recognition; and the procedures and legal restrictions related to organizing and counter-organizing activity.

Union Growth and Decline

To understand contemporary management and union action in the organizing arena, it is necessary to have a general understanding of recent patterns of union growth and decline, as well as an appreciation for the forces which shape membership trends.

Union Membership

Several sources provide union membership data. Historical data are available on a continuous basis back to the late 19th century.[2] The Bureau of Labor Statistics (BLS) published a biannual directory of American unions, based on surveys of national and international unions, which broke down membership data by industry, occupation, region, and several other categories. While the BLS' publication was suspended by the Reagan administration, the Bureau of National Affairs (BNA) now issues a similar document.

One drawback with using data collected from union surveys is that unions may either under- or overstate true membership figures. A more reliable, though somewhat limited, source of information on membership is the Current Population Survey (CPS). The CPS ascertains the union membership and contract coverage of respondents at least once a year and publishes results of its survey in the January issue of *Employment and Earnings*.[3] In addition, the CPS data may be used to generate fairly detailed breakdowns of union membership.

A standard measure of the aggregate level of union membership, termed union density, is the proportion of unionized workers in the nonagricultural labor force. Despite some significant downturns—most notably during the 1920s—union density in the United States trended upward throughout the first half of this century (see Figure 1). Forces associated with the Depression, along with passage of the Wagner Act and formation of the CIO, prompted the take-off of the labor movement in the mid-1930s and its ascent from weakness to a position of strength and influence.

In contrast, the latter part of the 20th century has seen an initially gradual, but more recently precipitous, decline in union density. At first, union membership continued to increase in absolute numbers, but at a rate less than the growth of the labor force. During the early 1980s, the absolute, as well as relative, number of workers organized declined substantially. By the late 1980s, union membership was estimated at about 17 million, down from a high of around 23.5 million members in 1979.[4] However, the rapid losses experienced in the early part of the decade had abated by 1985 and

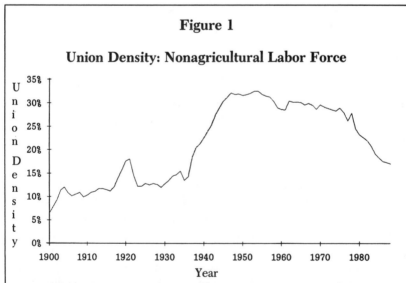

Figure 1

Union Density: Nonagricultural Labor Force

Source: Reprinted with permission from L. Troy and N. Sheflin, *U.S. Union Sourcebook: Membership, Finances, Structure, Directory.* West Orange, NJ: Industrial Relations and Data Information Services, copyright © 1985, Appendix A.

unions have begun to gain members, although growth continues to be small. Despite this increase in absolute membership, relative union membership continues to drop.

Union density has declined in virtually all major sectors of the economy. Figure 2 depicts union density by industry for 1953, 1975, and 1985. Rates of unionization in major union strongholds (manufacturing, mining, construction, and transportation) has dropped to between one-half and one-quarter of what they were in the early 1950s. Even the government sector, the only major source of union expansion over the past quarter century, has actually experienced a reduced level of unionization.

Sources of Union Decline

The precipitous decline in union membership over the past decade, like most social phenomena, is linked to a complex of factors

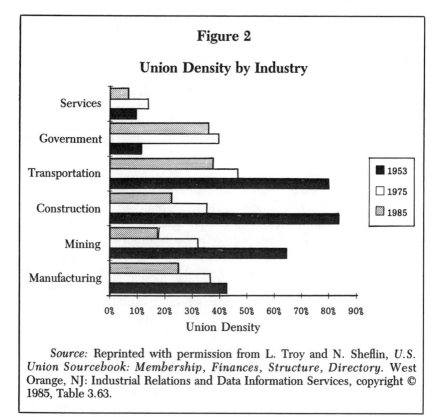

Figure 2

Union Density by Industry

Source: Reprinted with permission from L. Troy and N. Sheflin, *U.S. Union Sourcebook: Membership, Finances, Structure, Directory.* West Orange, NJ: Industrial Relations and Data Information Services, copyright © 1985, Table 3.63.

rather than a single cause. As this chapter is concerned with the organizing process, the principal focus will be to analyze the nature and impact of management and union strategies and tactics in connection with unionization and deunionization efforts. Yet other factors also are at work, many of which are beyond the control of either employers or unions.[5]

Union Organizing Efforts

Following World War II, many observers of the labor movement recognized that unions faced certain limits in their ability to expand.[6] As these limits appeared to be fast approaching, analysts argued that unions needed to restructure goals and strategies in order to extend union protection to unorganized workers. However, unions' interest in organizing new workers began to wane in the 1950s, as labor organizations placed greater emphasis on servicing existing members rather than recruiting new ones. The merger of the AFL and CIO in 1955 all but eliminated the interunion rivalries which had driven much of the organizing effort since the mid-1930s. Despite conflicting evidence as to whether or not actual organizing resources dwindled,[7] the commitment to and enthusiasm for organizing on the part of high-level union officials declined substantially. In addition, external conditions continued to worsen, reducing unions' bargaining power and political clout and undermining labor's institutional strength. This trend ultimately led to the significant decline in union density that has occurred over the past two decades.

The succession of Lane Kirkland to the presidency of the AFL-CIO, following the retirement of George Meany in 1979, ushered in a new era of pragmatism and innovative strategic thinking within the labor movement. Kirkland has placed a number of highly professional and competent individuals in key AFL-CIO staff positions. His efforts at renewal led to a series of strategic initiatives, culminating in a "white paper" issued by the AFL-CIO in 1985.[8] This report defined key strategic concerns for labor unions and had considerable input from nationally renowned authorities in industrial relations, a rather unusual step for the federation. Among other things, the report called upon unions to rejuvenate and expand their organizing programs.[9]

The new policies and concern with strategic thinking ushered in by the report seem to have had a positive impact on union organizing effectiveness. However, the extent and staying power of these changes are not yet clear. Some unions clearly display an increased concern with strategic planning,[10] and a resulting willingness to utilize innovative organizing methods.[11] Yet the report has not been well-received within all quarters of the labor movement. Unions affiliated with the AFL-CIO are independent organizations and several leaders of national unions felt the report contradicted traditional union values and practices. Critics have argued that the report's advocacy of union mergers and interunion cooperative programs, often coordinated by the AFL-CIO, would promote greater centralization within the labor movement and reduce national union autonomy. Implementation of the report's proposals has also met resistance from grassroots union officials, who feel politically threatened and resent what they see as the elitist manner in which the report was generated.[12] Thus, the long-term prospects for strategic change within the labor movement and a corresponding increase in the effectiveness of organizing efforts remain unclear.

Employer Opposition

While American management has never shown much enthusiasm for unionism and collective bargaining, the post-war era saw something of an accommodation between labor and management. After an initial period of uncertainty and conflict, many firms built strong and relatively amicable relationships with the unions that represented their employees. Overtly aggressive union-avoidance practices, while always present, were not commonplace.

This post-war trend has clearly been reversed. Contemporary organizations, confronting uncertain and complex environments, often rely on structures that promote flexibility and encourage discretionary action by employees. These new organizational forms and the related expectation of employee commitment are not so readily compatible with the strictures imposed under conventional collective bargaining, thus leading to greater employer animosity. At a more fundamental level, ideological opposition to unionism by management seems to have increased.

Evidence of employers' new hostility toward unions appears in two Conference Board surveys of corporate executives in several hundred of the nation's largest firms.[13] Among other issues, the surveys queried respondents as to whether their firms attached greater priority to forestalling unionization or achieving the best bargaining results in contract negotiations. The first survey, conducted in 1978, found that only about one-third of the unionized firms reported "keeping the company as nonunion as possible" (versus "achieving the most favorable bargain possible") to be the principal labor relations objective. Yet only five years later, 45 to 50 percent of these firms had shifted to the union avoidance position.

This new hostility to unionism has spawned a variety of management techniques designed either to preclude the organization of nonunion facilities or to oust already established unions. In fact, management aggressiveness in this area is argued to be a leading cause of union decline.

Occupational Structure

The growth of white-collar and professional employment relative to the blue-collar sector has resulted in a greater proportion of workers whose values and needs do not always match traditional union goals. Greater use of temporary workers and flexible employment arrangements may also reduce the appeal of unionism to employees who lack a long-term interest in a given company.

Labor Force Demographics

The increasing proportion of women in the labor force has created problems for unions. Labor organizations are not used to dealing with issues of concern to women workers, although this situation seems to be changing as certain unions now aggressively seek to organize women. The large number of young workers in the labor force has also reduced the appeal of unions, though this trend may change as the baby-boom generation ages. The substantial increase in the numbers of Hispanic and Asian workers, more difficult to organize for reasons of language and culture, is also an important demographic constraint.

Product Market Conditions

Increased competition from foreign producers has clearly ranked among the most serious pressures facing the unionized sector. Unions have generally had greater success in more concentrated industries, but these industries have been among the most severely impacted by foreign competition. Domestic nonunion competitors have emerged, further challenging unionized companies. The growth sectors of the economy tend to be highly competitive and more resistant to unionization.

Labor Market Conditions

The availability of a world labor market means that employers seeking to reduce labor costs or to avoid unionization may locate production facilities abroad. The shift of the population to the Sunbelt has encouraged firms to locate domestically in areas traditionally hostile to union organization. Outsourcing by union firms to foreign producers and domestic nonunion companies has much the same effect in reducing union employment.

Political and Legal Environments

The National Labor Relations Board (NLRB), taxed by a growing workload and more aggressive employer action, is less able to enforce the National Labor Relations Act in a timely and effective manner.[14] Efforts to amend the act in the late 1970s to provide greater protection for unions failed. Appointees of the Reagan administration to the NLRB have generated a series of rulings highly unfavorable to union interests, prompting AFL-CIO President Lane Kirkland to speculate that unions might be better off if the act were repealed.[15] The public sector is one area, of course, in which political and legal support for unionism has substantially increased since the 1950s, a factor clearly responsible for the general success unions have had organizing government employees.[16]

Government Regulation of the Organizing Process

American labor relations law is complex in that different statutes apply to different types of workers. Its centerpiece is the National Labor Relations Act (NLRA). A federal law enacted in 1935, the NLRA has been amended several times since. The original Wagner Act established basic rights for employees, a mechanism for recognizing unions, and prohibitions against conduct by employers which might thwart the objectives of the law. The Taft-Hartley Act, passed in 1947, greatly expanded the provisions of the NLRA and, most agree, added balance to the law by restricting the actions of unions.

The NLRA applies only to the private sector and not all private-sector employees fall under its umbrella. Several states have enacted their own private-sector laws to cover some of the employees excluded from the NLRA. Employees of railroads and airlines fall under the federal Railway Labor Act of 1926. Civilian employees of the U.S. government are covered under the relatively weak provisions of Title VII of the Civil Service Reform Act, passed in 1978 and administered by the Federal Labor Relations Authority. States are free to grant or withhold bargaining rights to their employees and those of other governmental units within the state. A number of states have enacted public-sector laws, typically patterned after the NLRA, usually administered by a public employee relations board or similar agency.

Despite the multitude of laws and jurisdictions, this discussion will focus on the NLRA. Its provisions have the greatest relevance to private-sector HR managers and serve as the model for most other pieces of legislation. The NLRA governs several important aspects of labor-management relations, including the determination of union representation rights within a company, collective bargaining, and industrial conflict. Since this chapter focuses on union growth and decline, only aspects of the law primarily related to unionization and deunionization will be treated here.

Basic Employee Rights

The heart of the NLRA is section 7, which establishes a set of rights for employees covered under the Act, including the right to:

- Organize themselves

- Form, join, or assist labor organizations

- Bargain collectively through representatives of their own choosing; and

- Engage in concerted activity (including strikes) for the purpose of collective bargaining

The Taft-Hartley Act also extended to employees the right to refrain from engaging in protected activities. However, this right is limited to some extent by provisions allowing for union-security clauses which mandate some level of union membership for all bargaining unit employees[17] (except in states that have passed so-called right to work laws).[18]

A key consideration in the drafting of the law and in its implementation is an effort to balance employees' rights against concerns for economic efficiency and the free flow of commerce. Indeed, a stated intent of the law is to limit interference with interstate commerce by encouraging peaceful settlement of labor-management disputes through collective bargaining. Thus, while employees' right to free choice in selecting a bargaining agent is central to questions of union recognition, this right may be to some extent subordinated to other considerations. For example, the designation of relatively small and homogeneous bargaining units within a company enhances the likelihood that all employees will be represented in the manner they most prefer. Yet small units generate inefficiencies in bargaining and promote instability. Hence, the Board generally prefers to establish larger, more inclusive units when called upon to resolve unit composition questions.

Union Recognition

Under the provisions of the NLRA, unions are recognized at the bargaining unit level. A bargaining unit consists of a group of workers deemed, either by the parties or by the relevant labor relations authority, to have a sufficient "community of interests" to justify negotiating a contract establishing rules applicable to all within the unit. A union is designated as the exclusive bargaining representative for all employees within the bargaining unit if the union can demonstrate that the majority of employees within the unit want it to be their representative. A union thus can represent even those who oppose collective bargaining or who choose not to join the organization (even in right-to-work states). It is also possible for an incumbent union to lose its representation rights in an established bargaining unit.

A union can gain recognition as an exclusive bargaining agent in one of three ways: voluntary recognition by the employer, victory in a NLRB representation election, or issuance of a bargaining order by the NLRB as a remedy for certain types of unfair labor practices.

Voluntary Recognition

An employer may recognize a union directly if the union can establish its majority status in an appropriate bargaining unit. Demonstrating majority status generally involves collecting cards signed by a majority of unit employees authorizing the union to represent them. While the NLRA does not obligate employers to recognize a union which claims majority status, an employer which undertakes certain steps to verify the authenticity of the signatures on the cards may be bound to grant recognition if a union majority is confirmed. Once an employer extends voluntary recognition to a union, management cannot withdraw recognition without reasonable cause to believe the union no longer represents a majority in the unit.

Representation Elections

The most common method of union recognition occurs through victory in secret-ballot certification election conducted by the NLRB. A union or group of workers may request an election by filing a petition with the NLRB and demonstrating a sufficient showing of interest among unit employees. In general, at least 30 percent of the unit employees must have signed authorization cards or cards requesting an election. An employer may also request an election if a union has demanded recognition. A union is certified as bargaining representative only if a majority of those voting in the election cast ballots in favor of the union.

In cases where more than one union may claim to represent a majority in the unit, multi-option elections must be held. A run-off election takes place if a clear majority fails to emerge in the initial election. Similar rules apply if an outside union seeks to replace an incumbent union. In addition, disgruntled unit employees may seek to return to nonunion status by means of a decertification election. Alternatively, an employer may request a decertification election if it has reasonable cause to doubt a union's continuing majority status.

A serious problem confronting American unions is their declining capacity to win certification elections. Unions typically won 60 percent or more of the certification elections held during most of the period following passage of the Wagner Act. That figure has now dropped to a union victory rate of 46 to 48 percent. The number of elections in which unions have participated has also declined sharply since the late 1970s (see Figure 3). The impact of this trend appears in the decreased number of new members organized through election activity (see Figure 4).

As shown in Figure 3, the number of decertification elections has remained relatively constant over the past decade, with unions winning about 25 percent of such elections. However, the number

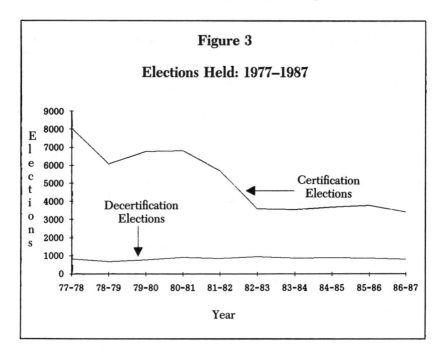

Figure 3

Elections Held: 1977–1987

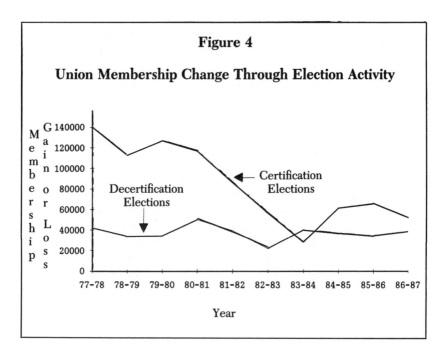

Figure 4

Union Membership Change Through Election Activity

of workers added through certification now only slightly exceeds the number lost through decertification (see Figure 4). Thus, unions now are barely able to compensate for membership loss through decertification, once an insignificant problem, much less to offset other sources of union decline, such as plant closings and layoffs.

Board-Ordered Recognition

Under certain conditions, the NLRB can order an employer to bargain with a union, even though the union fails to win an election. The so-called *Gissel* doctrine establishes union recognition as a remedy when an employer's unfair labor practices have undermined a previously existing union majority and made a free election impossible.[19] Consequently, a union which actually loses an election may earn certification if it once had a card-based majority but the employer engaged in severe and persistent unfair labor practices which caused employees to vote against the union.

Procedures in Representation Elections

The procedures governing NLRB representation elections are elaborate and various options are available to the parties involved (see Figure 5).[20] However, certain choices may preclude a party from pursuing particular courses of action at subsequent points in time. Therefore, the advice of legal counsel familiar with NLRB rules is clearly desirable. In addition to specifying the steps to follow in resolving a question of union recognition, the board regulates the conduct of those involved in representation elections; these rules will be discussed in the next section.

Types of Representation Elections

Once an election petition is submitted to the appropriate NLRB regional office,[21] a staff member from that office will seek to arrange an election. The level of NLRB involvement in representation elections will vary, depending on whether a consent election, a stipulated election, or a directed election occurs.

Consent Elections. In general, the NLRB prefers that the parties agree to a consent election, which is possible when the issue of union recognition is the only major outstanding dispute. That is, the parties agree as to the composition of the bargaining unit, absence of election or certification bars, and related matters. With-

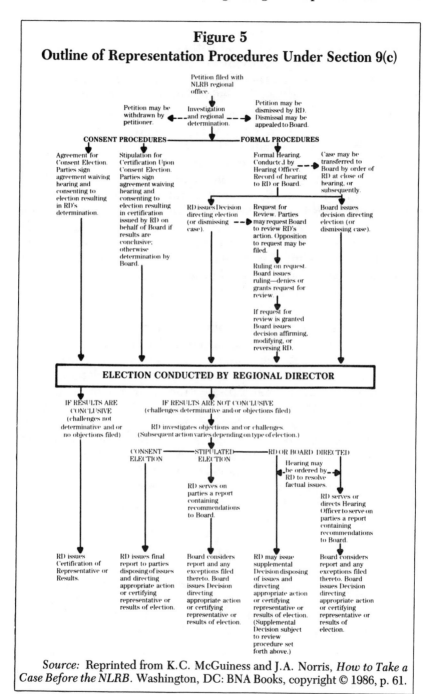

Figure 5
Outline of Representation Procedures Under Section 9(c)

Source: Reprinted from K.C. McGuiness and J.A. Norris, *How to Take a Case Before the NLRB*. Washington, DC: BNA Books, copyright © 1986, p. 61.

out the need for pre-election hearings, consent elections accelerate the process and are usually held within a month or so of petition filing. Parties agreeing to consent elections also waive their right to a post-election hearing on campaign irregularities or challenges and must accept the findings of the regional director on these questions.

Stipulated Elections. In an era of aggressive opposition to unions, employers are no longer very willing to enter into consent election agreements. An alternative, which still avoids lengthy and costly hearings, has the rather cumbersome name: stipulation for certification upon consent election. While the parties must agree to major pre-election questions, such as the composition of the bargaining unit, questions that arise out of the election or pre-election campaign are ultimately settled by the NLRB itself rather than its regional directors. Given that the board has become increasingly sympathetic to business interests in recent years (while regional offices are seen as more inclined to favor unions), stipulated elections have supplanted consent elections as the most common type of election.

Directed Elections. In a significant number of cases, profound disagreements over basic issues must be resolved before an election may take place. In fact, questions may center on whether an election should even take place. Such cases require more elaborate procedures, including formal pre-election hearings at which the regional director or, in some instances the NLRB, settles issues and determines how matters will proceed. Resolving pre-election questions under formal procedures may take several months, and many unionists argue that employers abuse NLRB procedures to delay elections. In general, the likelihood of union victory in certification elections declines with the length of any election delay.[22] Elections resulting from formal, as opposed to consent, procedures are termed directed elections.

Pre-Election Procedures

Several types of pre-election questions may require formal procedures to resolve. Issues regarding the NLRB's jurisdiction and disputes over bargaining-unit composition rank among the most common questions raised in directed elections.

NLRB Jurisdiction. The most basic issue relates to the jurisdiction of the NLRB for the employees or firm in question. Along with all public agencies, private-sector firms which are not significantly involved in interstate commerce do not fall under the NLRA's coverage. The NLRB has various business volume tests to determine whether a firm in a covered industry participates sufficiently in interstate commerce for purposes of the act.[23] In addition, an employer may claim that although the firm falls within the jurisdiction of the NLRB, the employees proposed for inclusion in the bargaining unit are in part or total excluded from the law. The NLRB may thus have to decide which, if any, of the workers are supervisors, independent contractors, and other employees excluded from inclusion in a bargaining unit under the act.[24] If all or virtually all bargaining unit employees fall into the excluded category, the election request will be dismissed. Finally, an election bar exists if a representation election has been held within the preceding 12 months. A valid contract, within certain limits, creates a contract bar to a decertification election or challenge by an outside union.

Bargaining-Unit Composition. The most common and involved type of dispute concerns the composition of the proposed bargaining unit. Questions of unit composition are typically raised for strategic reasons, since the configuration of the bargaining unit will likely affect the outcome of an election. For example, a union with strong local support may recognize that it will have a hard time winning an election which includes employees in all plants of a multiplant firm and thus will propose that each plant should be treated as a separate bargaining unit. Conversely, management may press for a companywide unit, recognizing this requirement will likely result in a defeat for the union.

The NLRA includes broad guidelines and some specific restrictions regarding unit determination questions, but most of the standards have been developed by the NLRB applying the community of interests criterion. Factors used in making unit determinations include the following considerations:

- Similarities in skills, interests, duties, and working conditions of the employees in question

- The nature of the employer's organization (functional integration of subunits, organizational and supervisory structure, interchange of personnel, the physical proximity of different employee groups)

- Employee desires

- The extent of union organization among employees[25]

Election Procedures

Representation elections generally take place on an employer's premises and are conducted by NLRB staff members. Elections normally follow a period of active campaigning on the part of both the union(s) seeking recognition and the employer. To facilitate union campaigning, an employer must supply the participating union(s) with a list of the names and addresses of all bargaining unit employees, known as Excelsior lists,[26] once an election has been set.

Under the provisions of the original Wagner Act, the NLRB initially barred virtually all employer campaigning, although the courts often found such restrictions unconstitutional. However, the so-called "free speech amendment" of the Taft-Hartley Act specified that campaign statements by either side which do not contain threats or bribes do not constitute unfair labor practices.[27] Still, the NLRB, under its "laboratory conditions doctrine," holds both parties to certain standards of conduct. Actions which violate these standards may result in the nullification of the election results and the ordering of a new election, even though the conduct in question does not constitute an unfair labor practice. This matter will receive more detailed discussion in later sections.

Post-Election Procedures

The outcome of an election is not final until certified by the regional director or the NLRB. Disputes which arise during balloting and/or the course of the election campaign may delay certification for several more months, especially in directed election cases. Three principal types of disputes are resolved through post-election procedures.

Voter Eligibility Challenges. First, union or management representatives may challenge the eligibility of certain voters. Some questions of unit composition may remain unresolved at the time of an election, even in consent cases. Even when consensus exists regarding what types of employees are in the unit, questions may arise as to whether a given employee meets the criteria. Other issues might involve the participation of employees on leave. Of course, strategic considerations motivate voter eligibility challenges. Since a significant proportion of representation elections are closely contested, a shift of a few votes either way could alter the outcome. Challenged ballots are kept apart and the NLRB makes a determination as to their validity in post-election proceedings should they have the potential for affecting the outcome of the election.

Unfair Labor Practice Charges. Objections to election conduct may come in the form of unfair labor practice charges. An unfair labor practice is a violation of specific provisions of the NLRA,[28] such as the firing of a union supporter, and is resolved through formal system of adjudication. If the regional office finds merit to the charges, it issues a complaint and orders the offending party to stop engaging in the illegal activity. An appropriate remedy may be specified as well. For example, if an unfair labor practice impacted the outcome of the election, then the regional office may order a new election; in extreme cases, a bargaining order may be issued without a new election. After an initial complaint is issued, unfair labor practice cases are handled by the office of the NLRB's General Counsel rather than by the regional director.[29] Multiple levels of appeal exist within the NLRB and through the courts.[30]

Election Interference Charges. Election interference cases involve allegations that one party violated administrative procedures established by the NLRB to regulate the election process. Unlike unfair labor practice charges, election interference cases are resolved through the internal administrative procedures of the NLRB and are not subject to review directly by the courts. Resolution of election interference allegations and voter challenges depends on the type of election. In the case of a consent election, the regional director's findings and certification are final and binding. In stipulated or directed elections, the director's findings and certification are subject to review by the Board.

In election interference cases, the regional director may initiate an investigation if the charging party files sufficient evidence. A hearing may take place at the discretion of the regional director, but this is not usually the case. Instead, written objections typically serve as the basis for the regional director's finding and recommendations.

A finding of election interference can only be remedied through setting aside election results (if the interference materially affected the election outcome) and ordering a new election. Imposition of stronger measures requires a finding that an unfair labor practice also occurred. Thus, a party may file both election interference and unfair labor practice charges in connection with the same actions, although such cases are often consolidated into a single unfair labor practice case. Election interference cases normally are more rapidly resolved than unfair labor practice cases; the latter may require several years to adjudicate, the former usually a few months or less.

Employer and Union Misconduct

The statutory provisions of the NLRA are, for the most part, very general. Unfair labor practices, broadly defined in the act, are clarified through board interpretations of the law in specific cases. Requirements designed to preserve employee free choice and prohibitions against election interference developed through NLRB case law and are not specifically stated in the NLRA. Thus, understanding the NLRA requires some familiarity with the complex and frequently shifting doctrines of the NLRB.

The NLRB is an independent administrative agency and not part of the Labor Department. Its chair and four additional members are appointed by the president, subject to Senate confirmation, for five-year terms. As with other autonomous administrative agencies, members can only be removed for neglect of duty or malfeasance. Unlike many agencies, the board does not normally rely on formal rule-making procedures to promulgate the regulations through which the law is implemented. Instead, doctrines governing conduct in most aspects of labor-management relations within the purview of the NLRB develop through the resolution of specific cases. The NLRB has quasi-legislative rule-making authority but it has exercised this authority only once in its history.[31]

The body of NLRB case law is voluminous and its interpretation requires expert assistance, particularly since NLRB "doctrines" have a tendency to flip-flop in some areas. Indeed, many observers argue that NLRB is among the most politicized of all federal administrative agencies. At least one study of board decisions in unfair labor practice cases found that little mattered in predicting how Board members would vote other than their political party and the political party of the president who appointed them.[32]

Conduct related to unionization and deunionization efforts is governed both by the NLRA's provisions on unfair labor practices and the NLRB's administrative policies relating to election interference. Activities prohibited as unfair labor practices are generally treated as more serious offenses which, if unabated, would thwart the purposes of the law. Individual as well as collective rights are safeguarded by the unfair labor practice provisions of the law. For example, an employee discharged for supporting a union organizing effort would qualify for reinstatement with back pay regardless of whether the discharge affected election results. Election interference restrictions relate only to the integrity of the election process and cannot be used to compensate injured parties for losses. Examples of conduct proscribed as unfair labor practices or election interference are considered below.[33]

Unfair Labor Practices

The unfair labor practices defined in sections 8(a) (related to employer conduct), 8(b) (related to union conduct), and 8(e) (related to joint union-employer conduct) of the NLRA concern a wide range of issues. Along with the regulation of unionization and deunionization activity, the NLRA's unfair labor provisions address the bargaining process and industrial conflict. However, a large proportion of unfair labor practice charges, most of which are brought against employers, involve issues linked to unionization or deunionization efforts. The NLRB does not initiate investigations of unfair labor practices; an aggrieved party must first file a charge with the agency. While the NLRB can specify remedies for unfair labor practices, it cannot award punitive damages.[34]

Discriminatory Employment Actions. Unfair labor practices relating to unionization or deunionization activities can occur even in the absence of a formal election campaign. Nonunion employers who screen out applicants based on prior union membership, a practice sometimes used to reduce the likelihood of unionization, violate the NLRA's antidiscrimination provisions.[35] Discharging employees for union activity or engaging in other personnel practices which discriminate against employees because of union activity also violates these provisions. In a similar fashion, employers cannot provide favorable treatment to employees who oppose unionization. In discrimination cases, the remedy will generally involve compensating the adversely affected employees for lost wages, as well as offering to rehire or reassign such employees in a nondiscriminatory fashion. However, an employer may defend itself against these charges if it can establish that discharge or other action was for justifiable cause and consistent with past practice.

Campaign Misconduct by Employers. Other charges may relate to conduct during a certification or decertification election campaign.[36] Employers may not issue statements which contain explicit or veiled threats of retaliation should the union win. The interpretation of this provision can be difficult. An employer which threatens to fire everyone and move its plant abroad just because employees vote in a union clearly violates the law. However, if an employer predicts that the plant will close because it will no longer be competitive, then determining whether the law has been broken must rest on other factors. Other prohibited employer actions include bribing employees to work against a union or vote in opposition to bargaining, surveillance of employees with respect to protected activities, and interrogation of employees to obtain information on union activities. Employers may restrict union activity in the workplace (e.g., solicitation, distribution of literature, wearing of union insignia) and prohibit nonemployee union representatives access to the campany property, but these rules must be properly drawn and enforced.[37] Employers may not establish a "company union" or assist a union during a campaign.[37] In a similar fashion, employers cannot provide substantive assistance to employee groups which seek union decertification nor may the employer promote and orchestrate a decertification campaign.

Campaign Misconduct by Unions. Unions also face restrictions, although they generally have fewer limits than employers. Threats, bribes, and other forms of interference with employees' free choice are prohibited.[38] Employers also receive protection under the NLRA. Unions cannot strike or boycott a third-party employer in order to force it to pressure the company that is involved in a certification or decertification action.[39] An employer with a certified union may not be struck to force it to recognize another union[40] and picketing related to certification is also restricted.[41] Finally, an employer which is engaged in a dispute with a union over recognition may file unfair labor practice charges against the union and another organization if they enter into an agreement to boycott the employer.[42]

Election Interference

As noted earlier, objections to election conduct are filed immediately following a certification or decertification election. Unlike unfair labor practice charges, election objections can only relate to conduct during the formal election campaign (which begins as of the date an election petition is filed with the NLRB). If a review shows that actions inconsistent with the "laboratory conditions" standard occurred and could have affected the outcome of the election, then the results may be set aside and a new election ordered. Election interference issues are often resolved without formal hearings and appeal rights are quite limited. Various unfair labor practices can constitute election interference, if they impact on the election outcome (e.g., threats, bribes, discriminatory treatment of union activists) and serve as the basis for election objections. Yet other actions which are not unfair labor practices can also nullify election results.

A very significant and controversial class of election objections is *"misrepresentation of fact."* The NLRA specifies that statements made by employers and union representatives cannot be construed as unfair labor practices unless they contain threats or inducements, a standard which even applies to outright lies.[43] However, the board has changed its position on how it will treat misrepresentations several times in recent years,[44] creating considerable confusion and resentment. Under its original *Hollywood Ceramics* doctrine, the NLRB established a series of tests to determine when misrepresentations would constitute election interference (e.g., Was the misrepresentation substantial and material to the election issues? Did the opposing party have time to respond?). However, the board reversed its position on misrepresentation in 1977, holding that misleading campaign statements would no longer be the basis for setting aside election outcomes.[45] The Board again returned to the *Hollywood Ceramics* standard in 1978, then reversed itself again in 1982 in the *Midland National Life Insurance* case.[46] *Midland* established the current standard, that is, misrepresentations will not be the basis for election reversals.

Implications for HR Managers

Even HR managers not directly involved in labor relations work must be aware of the general standards under the NLRA which govern the treatment of employees and unions. Although a company may take a union avoidance stance and operate on a union-free basis, disregard for the law could have serious implications. At the extreme, an employer which shows callous disregard for the provisions of the law may find itself confronting a bargaining order under the provisions of the *Gissel* doctrine despite the failure of a union to win an election. While Reagan appointees to the NLRB have generally favored management, experience suggests that Board positions can shift abruptly with the change of a single member. Thus, what may seem acceptable conduct today could later be determined to violate NLRB standards.

Several specific implications for action by HR managers follow from an understanding of the law. Among the most important guidelines are the following five recommendations:

1) Train supervisors in appropriate conduct. Supervisors who are unaware of the provisions of the law could make statements or take action against employees supporting unions which constitute unfair labor practices or election interference.

2) Document and justify actions taken against union supporters and avoid discriminatory treatment. Any employee may be subject to disciplinary action or discharge under company rules or union contract provisions. However, it is an unfair labor practice to discriminate against individuals based on their support or opposition to unionization. In an organizing situation, management must take care to establish a case against an employee and the disciplinary action must be consistent with policies and past practices.

3) Avoid unilateral changes in personnel policies during organizing campaigns. Employers sometimes raise wages or make other adjustments during campaigns in order to appease employees. However, depending upon the circumstances, these actions may be viewed as an unfair labor practice or election interference during a campaign.

4) Avoid assisting rival unions in campaigns or providing direct support to employee committees opposed to unionization. Both actions are unfair labor practices.

5) Be careful in accepting the recommendations of labor relations consultants. Committing unfair labor practices can be costly, despite the absence of punitive damages. Employees discharged in violation of the NLRA can collect lost wages plus interest. Even if an employer does not have to pay monetary damages as the result of an adverse NLRB ruling, the public relations consequences can be substantial and undermine management credibility with employees. Not all management consultants specializing in the area of union avoidance take care to avoid suggesting illegal or unethical options to their clients. In such instances, the employer, not the consultant, will generally be held responsible for illicit conduct and bear the costs of remedying such action.

Management and Union Strategy

As mentioned earlier, the strategies of employers and unions with respect to unionization and deunionization are generally viewed as some of the most significant contributors to the recent drop in union membership. Therefore, an understanding of how both sides formulate and implement unionization and deunionization strategies can prove beneficial. This understanding is all the more important for HR managers, as they deal most directly with the effects of union and management strategies. This section provides an overview of strategic action as it relates to unionization and deunionization processes. How these strategies and tactics operate in practice, along with their effects on unionization and deunionization outcomes, will be taken up in the following sections.

Unionization and Deunionization Strategies

Unionization outcomes (that is, whether a union wins a representation election) and deunionization results (that is, whether an incumbent union loses a decertification effort) depend, for the most part, on the preferences of bargaining unit employees.[47] Employee support for bargaining depends largely on many of the contextual influences discussed earlier, such as work force demographics, labor and product market conditions, political and legal pressures, and the like. If market conditions, for example, do not favor the exercise of union power or if the NLRB is seen as unable or unwilling to protect employees from employer retaliation, then bargaining unit employees as a group are less apt to support unionization.

Unions and management utilize specific strategies to influence unionization or deunionization outcomes in ways consistent with their respective institutional objectives. Union and management strategies may involve activities directed toward one another, toward bargaining unit employees, or toward the individuals and entities which constitute the context within which the organizing effort takes place.[48] In addition, a union or an employer may be in the position to determine certain outcomes unilaterally.

The strategy concept has become popular in both the general management and HRM fields. The term "strategy" most often refers to fairly high-level organizational decisions which define the organization and its future directions.[49] The concept is used here in a more limited sense, since it refers to specific efforts to organize or remove an established union. Strategic choice concepts, however, are quite useful in comprehending what transpires during unionization and deunionization efforts. Thus, the broader strategic management framework can be adapted to the analysis of unionization and deunionization processes.

Strategy Formulation

Strategies are influenced by the external environment, the internal characteristics of union and management organizations (such as distribution of political power, planning systems, and so on), and existing levels of employee support for bargaining. Yet these factors are not the only determinants of union and employer strategy. In recent years, authors have stressed the importance of the dominant values and preferences of key decision makers in strategy formulation. That is, unionization and deunionization strategies are, to a considerable extent, discretionary and represent the strategic choices of management and union leaders.[50]

Strategic action may be either *adaptive* or *proactive*. An adaptive strategy involves working within existing contextual constraints, while a proactive strategy consists of efforts to alter the context so as to make conditions more favorable to one's preferred outcome. Thus, causation runs in both directions between contextual influences and strategy. While strategies may be formulated in an analytical and deliberate fashion, they may also emerge as the natural extension of past action.[51] Moreover, strategic decision making may fall subject to information processing distortions, emotionalism, and nonrationality. As a result, the strategy pursued by a party in connection with a unionization or deunionization effort could prove inappropriate and counterproductive.

Both union and employer strategies may be influenced by external advisers. Labor relations consultants represent the most important type of external advisers on the management side; consultants for unions, while more prevalent than in the past, are still relatively rare and usually provide highly specialized services.[52] While many labor relations consultants are attorneys, other types of professionals are also involved, usually individuals with training in psychology, organizational behavior, or industrial relations.

Labor relations consultants typically specialize in providing management with various union avoidance programs. Their degree of involvement with management may vary from simply holding open seminars for company representatives to designing and orchestrating a specific union avoidance effort. Consultants can be quite expensive. Practitioners estimate that a fully developed campaign designed by a consultant to counter a union organizing drive might cost $500 or more per employee.[53]

Needless to say, the role of consultants has stirred considerable controversy. Unionists and union advocates argue that "union busters" are a primary cause of union decline.[54] Despite calls for greater regulation of consultants and stronger sanctions for those engaged in illicit activities,[55] little headway has been made in that direction. In any event, the jury is still out as to whether consultants have all that much of an impact on unionization or deunionization outcomes. This last point is explored further in following sections.

Implementing Strategy

Unionization and deunionization strategies, whether planned or emergent, are the overall and relatively self-contained courses of action by which employers or unions seek to affect outcomes. Strategies are translated into action through elementary tactics; these tactical methods used to execute strategies fall into four principal categories.

Influence Tactics

Influence tactics involve efforts to persuade others to change their attitudes or behaviors without altering actual conditions. For example, both unions and employers commonly use various communications techniques in an attempt to influence bargaining unit employees either to support or oppose union representation. Mass rallies, "captive audience" speeches, letters, posters, and small group meetings all are forms of influence tactics. Influence tactics may also be directed at groups outside the bargaining unit. For example, unions recently have begun to rely on a technique known as the corporate campaign. These campaigns typically feature a public relations effort designed to generate adverse publicity for an employer engaged in a union avoidance effort.

Contextual Control Tactics

Influence tactics involve attempts to alter perceptions regardless of any change in the actual conditions which give rise to those perceptions. But employers and unions may be able to alter such conditions via *contextual control tactics.* Changing compensation policies, improving working conditions, and adopting management techniques to reduce employee discontent are all examples of common contextual control tactics used by employers. Other contextual control tactics involve organizational design considerations, since certain types of organizational structures (such as centralized and rule-laden systems) may promote unionization. As discussed below, the selection and training of first-line supervisors in implementing union avoidance programs also can play a critical role. Both employers and unions use NLRB procedures to affect the composition of the bargaining unit and the constraints imposed on the other side during certification and decertification elections.

Besides changing existing contexts, another tactic is to select favorable new contexts. Employers frequently make plant site decisions which reflect union avoidance considerations, such as locating in areas with low levels of union activity. Unions also are increasingly likely to screen potential organizing sites thoroughly before committing resources to a campaign.

Monitoring Tactics

An important strategic objective in almost all unionization or deunionization efforts is the acquisition of reliable information via *monitoring tactics.* Unions and employers monitor each other's actions, the actions of employees in the election unit, and relevant external influences. Both sides make widespread use of surveys and polls. Union organizers will contact employees, usually away from the work location, to develop an understanding of the social dynamics of the firm and employee sentiments. Employers are frequently advised by consultants to train first-line supervisors in proper and effective means of discerning union activities at the shop floor level.

Direct Action Tactics

Finally, a union, but more often an employer, may be able to determine the outcome of a unionization or deunionization effort unilaterally via direct action tactics. An employer may close a unionized facility, outsource materials produced by union workers, automate their functions, or file for reorganization under federal bankruptcy laws (allowing, under some circumstances, the voiding of a labor contract). The voluntary recognition of a union by an employer or an employer's withdrawal of recognition also constitute examples of direct action tactics. The most common direct action tactic by unions is withdrawal from an organizing campaign when continued effort appears futile.

Unionization and Deunionization Strategies in Practice

The unionization and deunionization strategies wielded by employers and unions have changed substantially in recent years and researchers have shown a keen interest in the nature and impact of these strategic choices. Unfortunately, research does not always generate unambiguous answers to questions of greatest concern to HR professionals. This section covers the essential components of typical unionization and deunionization strategies, while research relating to the impact of organizing and counterorganizing activity is covered in the following section.

Strategy in Nonunionized Settings

While union-management competition may be intense during representation election campaigns, actions taken long before any active organizing drive begins may have profound effects on the likelihood of a given workplace ever being unionized. Significant developments have taken place over the past dozen or so years with respect to both management and union strategies in nonunion settings prior to the onset of an organizing drive.

Positive Labor Relations

Management strategies in union-free settings are largely preemptive in character. Nonunion firms frequently implement sophisticated HRM programs to maintain union-free status; many companies with some level of unionization have adopted similar programs in their nonunion facilities in order to preclude the expansion of union influence. The nature of such positive labor relations programs has generated a great deal of writing, largely by management consultants specializing in the union avoidance field.[56] Unfortunately, consultant publications tend to be "cookbooks" which, for the most part, treat issues in a superficial manner. As one observer has pointed out, author-consultants sometimes make claims which have lacked substantiation by independent studies.[57]

One of the leading academic studies of positive labor relations strategies in nonunion corporations, while qualitative in character, illustrates well how the various types of tactics identified earlier are used in union avoidance efforts.[58] A cornerstone of successful preventive labor relations strategies is the use of influence tactics, especially those intended to convert rather than intimidate employees. These companies articulate corporate philosophies which express a commitment to operating on a nonunion basis and place great weight on employee welfare as a corporate objective. Orientation programs and the use of quality circles serve as culture building devices, promoting employee sentiments which do not support unionization.

Contextual control tactics also play an important role in firms with successful union avoidance strategies. Personnel management systems are well designed and address employee needs. Firms tend to offer attractive compensation packages, have structured internal labor markets which provide for career advancement, and numerous channels of communication between lower-level employees and upper management. In addition, nonunion companies often choose contexts which are hostile to unionism. Plant site selection and choices regarding production technology and product market focus may reflect union avoidance considerations.

Companies with little or no unionization have long favored positive labor relations strategies. But the current decline of American unions also stems from increased union avoidance efforts in firms that already have significant levels of unionization.[59] While these companies sometimes pursue very aggressive deunionization campaigns within established bargaining units, the preferred route these days is to establish new, and enhance existing, nonunion facilities. At the same time, these firms have effectively disinvested in their unionized plants.[60] A good example of this process is found in the construction industry, where unions have experienced the most significant losses. While large numbers of nonunion contractors have entered the market in recent years, many established union firms now operate on a "double-breasted" basis, that is, to have nonunion subsidiaries.

Union Approaches

On the union side, organizing efforts have traditionally arisen in one of two ways: (1) a group of disenchanted employees approaches a union and requests assistance or (2) a union targets a particular unit for strategic reasons.[61] In both cases, the union organizer must make some initial assessment as to the likelihood of winning the election and, given victory in the election, of achieving an acceptable contract at reasonable cost. Thus, unions rely heavily on monitoring and information-gathering tactics in the early stages of an organizing effort. For example, a union representative may try to get a job in the targeted firm to see if conditions are ripe for initiating an organizing drive. In either case, the organizer may visit employees at home or other places away from the unit in order to discern their feelings regarding unionization. Once a decision has been made to pursue unionization, the organizer will seek to build an employee committee (contextual control), which serves to effect both monitoring and influence objectives. Secrecy is a key element in this early stage, as the union is seeking to identify or build a solid majority of support within the unit.

The 1985 AFL-CIO report addresses the issue of strategy in unorganized settings. It urges unions to screen targets thoroughly, show greater selectivity about the units targeted for organizing, and provide increased training for organizers. But the most controversial proposal is the report's recommendations that unions establish a special category of membership (associate membership) for employees in nonunion settings. Most unions have traditionally limited membership to employees in established bargaining units or in units with active campaigns. The associate membership program would provide workers in nonunion settings with certain membership benefits, such as group insurance, access to AFL-CIO sponsored product discounts, and low-interest, no-fee credit cards. The intention is to develop workers' attachment to a union before initiating any organizing effort. However, many union officials are uncomfortable with this concept and the program has been implemented in only a handful of unions.

Election Campaigns

The increased intensity of union avoidance activity by management is most evident in the degree of opposition that unions regularly encounter during representation election campaigns.

Employer Campaign Activities

Positive labor relations programs are long-term efforts designed to create a climate unreceptive to unionism. In contrast, actions undertaken in response to an active organizing drive quite frequently represent stop-gap measures which can only serve temporarily to deflect a unionization effort. Experience suggests that when an employer prevails in an election but fails to remediate the grievances which spurred the organizing drive, unionization efforts are likely to recur. While unions win less than 50 percent of first-time certification elections, the probability of victory increases quite substantially in follow-up elections.

Organizing campaigns historically were often marred by violence on both sides. The protection afforded workers under the NLRA served to reduce, though not completely eliminate, the likelihood of violent clashes. The general shift toward noncoercive management techniques and sophisticated behavioral strategies also influenced employers' methods during organizing campaigns. Yet while employers and consultants may rely primarily on noncoercive campaign techniques, management often keeps more aggressive options ready. And some techniques, while not coercive, are clearly manipulative. Employer strategies vary, depending upon circumstances specific to the particular bargaining unit. However the substantial number of guidebooks detailing union avoidance methods,[62] coupled with the extensive use of consultants by employers, has generated some degree of conformity in employer response across campaigns.

Employer election campaigns rely heavily on influence tactics, which include small group and individual meetings, "captive audience" speeches,[63] and the distribution of written materials. Common campaign themes include the high costs of unionization (dues, strikes, fines and sanctions against members), the inability of the union to guarantee that it will succeed in negotiations, and portrayals of union representatives as outsiders concerned more with collecting dues than serving members' interests. Employers may stress union corruption or attribute plant closings in unionized companies to irresponsible union action. In more positive campaigns, employers may point to relatively high wages, desirable working conditions, and the willingness of management to listen to employee complaints ("open-door" policies).

In addition to influence tactics, employers may use certain contextual control tactics. However, the types of contextual control tactics typically applied at this stage usually differ from those used in preventive labor relations programs. One reason is that preventive contextual control tactics usually target improved working conditions and may take too long to implement during an election campaign. Moreover, the NLRA bars employers from making unilateral changes in wages, hours, and working conditions while a question of representation exists.

Typical contextual control tactics used by employers at this stage aim to hinder the union's effort to achieve recognition. NLRB procedures are often employed to delay elections as long as possible, since the likelihood of union victory declines the longer an election is postponed. The number of consent elections also has declined, as employers have aggressively sought to obtain favorable unit determinations and/or to reverse union election victories through NLRB administrative procedures. Other contextual control tactics include establishing and enforcing strict rules limiting organizing activity during working time and prohibiting access of outside organizers to company property. While not in general illegal, these measures can violate provisions of the NLRA under certain circumstances. Of course, employers may and apparently often do engage in such patently illegal activities as discharging or in other ways discriminating against union activists.

Monitoring tactics are very important in management campaigns and first-line supervisors are often trained in information gathering. However, overly zealous supervisors may engage in actions that constitute NLRA violations, such as interrogation and surveillance. Employee attitude surveys are another common monitoring technique.

Emerging Union Campaign Strategies

Traditional union organizing strategies, at least subsequent to passage of the NLRA, typically revolve around activities within the bargaining unit.[64] Once sufficient support is obtained to request recognition, the organizer continues to work with the plant committee to build and consolidate support for an election. Influence tactics, such as mass rallies, home visits, parties, and written communications, are the mainstay of most within-unit campaigns. Contextual control tactics include using NLRB procedures (unit determination, unfair labor practice and election interference charges), making sure union supporters vote in the election, and enforcing internal discipline within the organizing committee. Structuring the committee to reflect important constituencies is also important. Monitoring of employer activities plays a key role, since unions have a special interest in discerning the presence of a labor relations consultant on the management side. Consultants often maintain a low profile and knowing whether, and which, consultant is involved can assist the union in anticipating management's next move.

Unions have increasingly begun to augment the traditional intraunit strategy with non-workplace strategies.[65] Such strategies rely largely on externally directed influence and contextual control tactics designed to pressure recalcitrant employers into recognizing the union without an election or into agreeing to remain neutral during the election campaign. The popularity of these strategies reflects unionists' view that the NLRB is inadequate and unwilling to protect union interests.

One venerable tactic, the consumer boycott, has seen increased use over the past couple of decades. A newer approach, which was highlighted in the AFL-CIO report and served as the basis for the ultimately successful effort to organize J.P. Stevens, is the corporate campaign.[66] This multi-faceted tactic relies on a mixture of public relations and direct pressure techniques. Unions may appeal to stockholders, perhaps by purchasing stock in order to raise the issue of the company's actions at annual stockholder meetings. Extensive research on the company's business activities may reveal illegal or unethical practices that a union can use to generate adverse publicity. A union also may act against a firm's business partners to induce them to pressure the company into moderating its antiunion stance.

The AFL-CIO also has advocated programs of interunion cooperation, and several unions have undertaken such programs. For example, construction craft unions pursued a joint organizing effort in Houston for several years (with mixed results), and several unions involved in organizing white-collar and office workers have initiated a joint effort to unionize workers in the insurance industry. Perhaps the most successful of the current joint organizing efforts is a program under the general direction of the Industrial Union Department of the AFL-CIO, which concentrates on organizing in southeastern states.[67]

Deunionization Strategies

In the past, most challenges to an incumbent union came either from another union ("raiding") or from disgruntled employees who wished to return to nonunion status. Decertifications were rare and a no-raiding agreement limited challenges among AFL-CIO affiliates. Now, however, employers are increasingly likely to move against a certified union. Direct action tactics include familiar steps, such as plant closings and relocations. These actions constitute unfair labor practices if undertaken solely to undermine a union, but strategic business considerations often may serve as a justification. While employers in principle may not promote decertification efforts, considerable evidence suggests that employers often do so, especially in new bargaining units where an initial contract has not yet been negotiated.[68] A common scenario seems to be for an employer to forestall negotiating a contract for the 12-month period in which the election bar is in effect. Employees, discouraged by the lack of movement and the costs of union membership, may then petition for decertification (perhaps with employer backing).

Unions have developed a variety of techniques to counter employer deunionization efforts, particularly those associated with aggressive employer bargaining or refusal to bargain.[69] Corporate campaigns, while used in connection with initial organizing drives, are probably even more common in response to deunionization attempts. Some unions have experimented with preemptive measures designed to preserve and enhance rank-and-file loyalty. Known as internal organizing programs, these measures are analogous to employer positive labor relations programs and utilize similar influence tactics. Given that strikes can be self-defeating in the face of determined employer opposition, some unions have also begun experimenting with in-plant strategies. While related to corporate campaigns, in-plant strategies involve, for the most part, activities carried on within the unit, in contrast to the external focus of the corporate campaign.

Research Findings

Numerous empirical studies have examined union growth and decline. Much of this research, which has been reviewed in several places,[70] has focused on fairly broad contextual determinants of unionization rates or attitudinal correlates of employee support for bargaining. More recent research in this area, which will be reviewed here, has dealt directly with the impact of employer and union strategies on unionization and deunionization efforts and on employee sentiments.[71]

Employer Preemptive Measures

How effective are positive labor relations strategies for employers in preempting unions organizing efforts? Unfortunately, quantitative studies on this topic are quite limited. In addition, research to date examines only the effects of employer initiatives and neglects the impact of union activities prior to the onset of formal campaigns on unionization and deunionization outcomes.

One analysis used Conference Board survey data to examine both the determinants and the impact of innovative personnel practices frequently found in preventive labor relations programs.[72] The findings suggest that an employer's sentiments toward union avoidance predicted whether these techniques would be implemented in nonunion facilities. In addition, the study found that the number of innovative methods employed significantly reduced the probability that a nonunion facility would be unionized.

A related study, which also utilized the Conference Board data, assessed the impact of specific HRM policies on the likelihood that a union would win an election and on the proportion of nonunion facilities successfully organized.[73] A variety of HRM techniques were found to have significant independent effects on both outcomes, generally in the expected direction of reducing union success. The presence of participative management systems and employee communications programs proved particularly successful in reducing union support.

Campaign Effects

The impact of tactics associated with various election campaign strategies has generated quite extensive research. Unfortunately, some studies report conflicting results, so a clear picture of what actions lead to which outcomes does not always emerge. Of the various analyses published in this area, the present discussion will consider two principal categories: (1) individual-level studies relating to the impact of campaign tactics on employee support for bargaining, and (2) bargaining unit and aggregate-level studies relating to the effects of tactics on union organizing success.

Micro-Level Research

A number of studies have identified factors related to employee support for bargaining. While early work generally involved simple correlation analysis, more recent studies evaluate causal models rooted in expectancy theory or a related framework.[74] In general, these studies tend to show that worker support for collective bargaining will increase with job dissatisfaction,[75] the perceived instrumentality of unions for improving employment conditions, limited alternative employment and influence opportunities, and the degree of social supportiveness for bargaining. However none of these motivational studies examined how campaign activities influenced employees' perceptions.

The first major quantitative analysis of effects of campaign activities was a behavioral study published in 1976.[76] The researchers started from the premise that NLRB campaign interference rules reflect implicit assumptions that workers engage in both rational information processing and rational decision making. The study tested the validity of these assumptions by examining the impact of several legal influence tactics (e.g., the use of letters and posters, mass meetings, and individual discussions) on workers' belief systems and on their voting behavior. In addition, certain illegal employer activities (e.g., threats, discharges) are also studied. Using a panel study design, the researchers interviewed several hundred workers in about 30 elections at the beginning of formal certification election campaigns and again just after the election. Employees were asked questions regarding how they voted (or intended to vote), job and union attitudes, the campaign tactics to which they had been exposed, and their general level of familiarity with themes developed by both sides in the campaign.

The study found that campaign tactics had little impact upon the way people ultimately voted in elections. About 80 percent of those surveyed voted in the elections as they had said they would before the campaigns began. Those who did change largely did so for reasons unrelated to campaign activities. Even those who had been uncommitted in the first wave of interviews were only marginally swayed by these efforts. In some instances, the commission of unfair labor practices by employers during the campaign actually appeared to increase the chances of union victory.

Given these results, the researchers proposed a revised model of information processing and choice in organizing campaigns that is based on behavioral decision theory concepts. While they did find campaign familiarity to be related to exposure to campaign tactics, they attributed this finding to individuals intentionally choosing to attend to campaign messages supportive of their pre-existing intentions. Furthermore, employees may distort messages received so as to maintain their belief structures.

Unfortunately, this study has generated only limited follow-up research. One reviewer reanalyzed the data after arguing that the original analysis was methodologically flawed.[77] This reanalysis demonstrated that employer tactics had some impact on voting behavior, though employees' voting intentions remained fairly stable. However, this analysis did not examine the impact of union tactics. Another study which partially replicated the original research found that, despite an active and vigorous campaign, a remarkable 70 percent of the respondents in a panel study voted as they had intended when interviewed at the onset of the campaign five years earlier.[78] Moreover, influence efforts, measured in terms of oral and written communication, were found to have impact on changes in voting intentions.

Macro-Level Studies

Several studies have explored the effects of campaign activities on election outcomes and on union growth and decline. Unfortunately, these studies have certain limitations. Most are tactical rather than strategic in focus, examining only a limited set of campaign tactics rather than the broad array of actions typically utilized by both sides. Moreover, virtually all the studies focus exclusively on employer conduct during campaigns, so little is known about the direct impact of union conduct or about the interplay of union and employer actions. The macro-level studies are important, however, since they capture a variety of effects that individual-level studies cannot.

Studies at the bargaining unit level are probably most relevant to HR managers, as they relate immediate organizational and contextual influences, along with unit-level campaign activities, to organizing outcomes. One series of studies suggests that the likelihood of union victory in NLRB representation elections decreases a) the longer the delay between the filing of a petition for an election and the holding of the election, b) when the election is not a consent

election, and c) when the employer engaged in discriminatory practices in violation of section 8(a)(3) of the NLRA.[79] Another analysis
considered several different employer tactics, including influence
efforts, contextual control, and monitoring.[80] It found that most
employer tactics had some negative impact on the likelihood of
union victory and, collectively, such tactics had a pronounced effect.
Studies of aggregate election activity demonstrate, for the most
part, similar effects.[81] Two researchers have found that the overall
propensity of management to oppose unionization substantially
reduces the probability of union victory.[82] However, this effect was
more pronounced in the case of white-collar than blue-collar
workers.

Several investigators have examined the effects of union strategy on union growth and decline. One study demonstrated that, at
least at an aggregate level, organizing success increases the greater a
national union's real expenditures on organizing (relative to unorganized employees within its natural jurisdiction).[83] In another
study of union campaign activity, the personal and psychological
characteristics of organizers appeared to impact the probability of
union victory in certification elections.[84] In particular, organizers
who possess a high sense of self esteem, who have a desire for
control, and who are not highly manipulative are more effective than
organizers with the opposite characteristics.

The most immediate question raised by these studies is the
apparent conflict between the micro- and macro-level analyses.
With one exception, micro-level work suggests campaign activities
do not matter much since employees tend to be committed to a
position before the onset of the campaign. One explanation could be
that the macro-studies tap effects that go beyond shifts in employee
attitudes. Campaign strategies are designed to affect not only
employees' views but also the mobilization and deployment of a
party's (and its opponent's) support. For example, one side often
raises unit determination questions with the hope of restructuring a
unit to maximize its support. Intimidation and coercion tactics may
dissuade an opponent's supporters from casting their ballots. Neither of these cases changes employees' attitudes, but both clearly
impact on who will actually vote.

As for the impact of labor relations consultants, the limited
research available produces a somewhat ambiguous picture. Two
separate studies found that, under certain circumstances, management's use of consultants during an election reduces the probability

of union victory.[85] Yet these studies also discerned evidence of a "backfire effect." That is, overly aggressive employer opposition could generate a reaction on the part of employees which increases the chances of the union winning. Indeed, consultants usually maintain a low profile in campaigns, as unions often can exploit the presence of a "union buster" as a campaign issue.

Deunionization Efforts

Only a few empirical studies have examined the effects of deunionization efforts. Research on the negotiation of initial contracts suggests that employers who engage in aggressive union opposition campaigns are most successful in precluding unions from obtaining a first contract.[86] Thus, employer tactics during and immediately following an election campaign may nullify the impact of a union's victory, as union certification absent a contract is relatively meaningless. However, a study that relied on both case analyses and survey data found that, contrary to popular belief, employer actions during decertification election campaigns do not seem to increase the chances of the union losing the election.[87] Ironically, when management tactics had any effect, they seemed to promote the probability of union victory through some type of backfire effect. However, the authors did find that union tactics reduced the chances of union decertification.

Conclusion

This chapter has examined the processes of union growth and decline in the United States from several different perspectives. Several implications for HR managers would seem to follow from this analysis.

First, American unions are in a state of unprecedented decline. The drop in union membership was especially pronounced in the early 1980s, but has abated in recent years. While weakened, unions now seem to be at least holding their own. Nonetheless, many of the economic, social, political, and technological factors that contributed to this decline will likely continue to present the labor movement with a hostile environment in the foreseeable future.

Employers have become more overtly antagonistic toward unions over the past 20 years. They are now much more likely to pursue aggressive strategies intended to preclude organization in nonunion settings and to weaken or eliminate unions in organized facilities. This trend is linked in many ways to increased management concern with strategic decision making, both in general and within the HRM function. It also reflects the emergence of the HRM field and the corresponding decline in the labor relations and traditional personnel areas. In most instances, union-avoidance strategies involve HRM activities and HR managers.

Union-avoidance strategies raise serious questions for HR managers. An employer clearly has a right to oppose union organization and this right is an integral part of American labor law. Yet many union-avoidance tactics are illegal or at least unethical. Engaging in such activities can only serve to undermine the professional standing of the HRM field. Furthermore, HR managers involved in very hostile union-avoidance activity run the risk of compromising themselves in the eyes of employees. It seems unlikely that individuals engaged in such conduct will be viewed as credible advocates by the workers they also serve. Unfortunately, pressure from upper management on HR managers to engage in union avoidance activities is only likely to increase.

Statutory and regulatory provisions relating to the conduct of unions and employers during organizing efforts are complex, shifting, and often contradictory. For private-sector firms under the jurisdiction of the NLRB, management now enjoys considerable freedom and a favorable Board. This situation is not the case, however, in other jurisdictions.

Research to date suggests that what unions and employers do in connection with unionization and deunionization efforts can have some impact on outcomes. However, studies have produced contradictory findings and results are highly qualified. It appears that, under some circumstances, intense employer opposition to unionization may generate a kind of backfire effect in which employees actually become more supportive of bargaining. Unions are developing new strategies and tactics to counter employer union-avoidance efforts, but the efficacy of most of these techniques (for example, corporate campaigns and in-plant strategies) is still largely untested.

◆

Notes

1. Huxley, Kettler, and Struthers, pp. 3–38.
2. Various membership series are presented in Troy and Sheflin.
3. Unfortunately, the CPS does not inquire as to the specific union to which a member or covered individual belongs.
4. Current figures based on Current Population Survey data reported in *Employment and Earnings*. Membership data for 1979 from Troy and Sheflin, Appendix A.
5. For additional discussion of factors related to union decline, see Kochan, Katz, and McKersie; Troy.
6. See, for example, Bell; Barkin.
7. Voos (1984).
8. AFL-CIO.
9. The report is wide-ranging and also touches on issues other than organizing such as union structure and administration, collective bargaining and representation practices, and the enhancement of rank-and-file involvement in union affairs.
10. Dunlop, pp. 3–52.
11. Stratton and Brown.
12. See, for example, Apcar.
13. Freedman (1978, 1985).
14. Weiler.
15. *New York Times* (1985).
16. In addition, admendments to the NLRA passed in 1974 extended coverage of the act to private-sector health care organizations, which has facilitated the unionization of workers in this industry.
17. NLRA §8(a)(3).
18. Right-to-work laws are covered under NLRA §14(b).
19. *NLRB v. Gissel Packing Co.*, 395 U.S. 575, 71 LRRM 2481 (1969).
20. For a fairly detailed discussion of election procedures, see McGuiness, pp. 51–230.

21. The NLRB has 33 regional offices. Both unfair labor practices and representation cases are initially handled at the regional level, with the regional director making initial determinations in both instances. Depending on the type of case, there are various avenues of appeal beyond the regional director, with the five-member board in Washington ultimately resolving contested cases within the NLRB. Unfair labor practice cases may be appealed to the federal courts.
22. See Prosten, pp. 240–249.
23. See Schlossberg and Scott, pp. 27–29.
24. For example, drivers who lease cabs on a daily basis from cab companies and who are not paid a wage by the company are, on the face of things, independent contractors and thus excluded from the law. However, a union attempting to organize such a group of drivers may be able to establish, contrary to management's contention, that certain personnel practices do, in fact, make these individuals "employees" in the sense of the law.
25. For a thorough treatment of unit determination questions, see Abodeely, Hammer, and Sandler, pp. 11–86.
26. McGuiness, p. 180–181.
27. NLRA §8.
28. Unfair labor practices are covered under NLRA §§8(a) and 8(b).
29. In order to avoid conflicts of interest in the adjudication of unfair labor practice cases, the General Counsel's office functions relatively independently of the NLRB.
30. NLRB unfair labor practice procedures are described at length in McGuiness, pp. 283–453.

31. This exercise of rule-making authority took place quite recently when the NLRB sought to deal with questions regarding appropriate bargaining units within the health care industry. See Delaney and Sockell for further discussion.

32. Cooke and Gautschi III.

33. For a more complete treatment of these issues, see Schlossberg and Scott, pp. 68–113 and 281–314; Williams.

34. Parties which fail to comply with NLRB remedies may be enjoined to do so by a federal court; failure to comply then may be sanctioned as contempt of court.

35. NLRA §8(a)(3).

36. NLRA §8(a)(1).

37. NLRA §8(a)(2).

38. NLRA §8(b)(1)(A).

39. NLRA §8(b)(4)(B).

40. NLRA §8(b)(4)(C).

41. NLRA §8(b)(7).

42. So-called "hot cargo" agreements are covered under NLRA §8(e).

43. NLRA §8(c).

44. Williams, pp. 25–63.

45. *Shopping Kart Food Mkts*, 228 NLRB 1311, 94 LRRM 1705 (1977). This reversal of the NLRB's previous position was prompted in part by the landmark study of Getman, Goldberg, and Herman.

46. *Midland Nat'l Life Ins.*, 263 NLRB No. 24, 110 LRRM 1489 (1982).

47. The conceptual framework presented here is developed more fully in Lawler (1990), chapter 2.

48. For example, a union may seek to influence public opinion through a public relations effort or by means of a consumer boycott so as to place pressure on management and to encourage employees in their resolve to unionize.

49. For a discussion of strategic management in general, see Mintzberg, pp. 7–92. For more on HR and industrial relations, strategies,

see Dyer and Holder; Kochan, Katz, and McKersie, pp. 2–20.

50. This theme is developed with respect to management strategy formulation in Kochan, Katz, and McKersie, pp. 3–20.

51. See Mintzberg, pp. 25–42.

52. See Lawler (1990), chapter 5.

53. Bureau of National Affairs, Inc. (1985).

54. Bernstein; McDonald and Wilson.

55. See Bethel.

56. See, for example, Hughes; Kilgour; Meyers.

57. See discussion in Gordon and Nurick.

58. Foulkes.

59. Kochan, Katz, and McKersie, pp. 47–80.

60. See, for example, Verma.

61. For example, the unit may be seen as vulnerable and the union may want to increase its membership. More likely, the unit bears some relationship to other units which are already represented by the union, and organization of the unit would increase its overall bargaining power.

62. See, for example, Kilgour; DeMaria.

63. So termed because these meetings are held on the employer's premises during work time and employee attendance is mandatory. Captive audience speeches are, in general, legal, although certain restrictions apply (for example, these speeches cannot be held within 24 hours prior to the election).

64. For a thorough treatment of union campaign activities at the bargaining unit level, see Gagala.

65. For a discussion of the nature of non-workplace strategies and their effectiveness, see Craft and Extejt.

66. For an in-depth discussion of various types of corporate campaigns,

as well as several illustrative case studies, see Perry.
67. See Bureau of National Affairs, Inc. (1988).
68. Cooke (1985).
69. For more detail, see Lawler (1990), chapter 8.
70. See, for example, Fiorito and Greer; Block and Premack, pp. 31–70.
71. For a more detailed review of this literature, see Lawler (1990), chapter 9.
72. Kochan, McKersie, and Chalykoff.
73. Fiorito, Lowman, and Nelson.
74. See, for example, Kochan; Walker and Lawler (1979); Youngblood, DeNisi, Molleston, and Mobley; Zalesny.
75. Workers vary in terms of which job satisfaction facets are most salient in generating support for bargaining. For example, Kochan finds

that blue-collar workers are more likely to support unionization as a result of dissatisfaction with wages and other extrinsic rewards. Conversely, white-collar workers, particularly professionals, are more responsive to intrinsic sources of dissatisfaction, especially lack of autonomy and influence.
76. Getman, Goldberg, and Herman.
77. Dickens.
78. Walker and Lawler (1986).
79. Cooke (1983, 1985b).
80. Lawler and West.
81. See, for example, Hunt and White; Seeber and Cooke.
82. Maranto and Fiorito.
83. Voos (1983).
84. Reed.
85. Lawler (1984); Lawler and West.
86. Cooke (1985a).
87. Anderson, Busman, and O'Reilly III.

♦

References

Abodeely, J., R. Hammer, and A. Sandler. 1981. *The NLRB and the Appropriate Bargaining Unit*. Philadelphia: Industrial Research Unit, Wharton Business School, University of Pennsylvania.

AFL-CIO. 1985. *The Changing Situation of Workers and Their Unions*. Washington, DC: AFL-CIO.

Anderson, J.C., G. Busman, and C. O'Reilly III. 1982. "The Decertification Process: Evidence from California." *Industrial Relations* 21 (Spring): 178–193.

Apcar, L. 1985. "AFL-CIO's Novel Program to Expand Union Membership Meets Resistance." *Wall Street Journal* (October 30): 7.

Barkin, S. 1961. *The Decline of the Labor Movement and What Can Be Done about It*. Santa Barbara, CA: Center for the Study of Democratic Institutions.

Bell, D. 1953. "The Next American Labor Movement." *Fortune* 47: 120–126.

Bernstein, J. 1980. "Union Busting: From Benign Neglect to Malignant Growth." *University of California (Davis) Law Review* 14: 3–77.

Bethel, T. 1984. "Profiteering from Unfair Labor Practices: A Proposal to Regulate Management Representatives." *Northwestern Law Review* 79 (3): 506–565.

Block, R. and S.L. Premack. 1983. "The Unionization Process: A Review of the Literature." In *Advances in Industrial and Labor Relations*, vol. 1, eds. D.B. Lipsky and J.M. Douglas. Greenwich, CN: JAI Press.

Bureau of National Affairs, Inc. 1985. *Labor Relations Consultants: Issues, Trends, and Controversies.* Washington, DC; Bureau of National Affairs, Inc.

————. 1988. "AFL-CIO's IUD Points to Success of Southern Organizing Drives." *Daily Labor Report* (November 11): A4.

Cooke, W. 1983. "Determinants of the Outcomes of Union Certification Elections." *Industrial and Labor Relations Review* 36 (April) 402–414.

————. 1985a. "Failure to Negotiate First Contracts." *Industrial and Labor Relations Review* 38 (January): 163–178.

————. 1985b. "The Rising Cost of Discrimination Against Union Activists." *Industrial Relations* 24 (Fall): 421–442.

Cooke, W., and F.H. Gautschi III. 1982. "Political Bias in NLRB Unfair Labor Practice Decisions." *Industrial and Labor Relations Review* 35 (July): 539–549.

Craft, J.A. and M. Extejt. 1983. "New Strategies in Union Organizing." *Journal of Labor Research* 4 (Winter): 1–32.

Delaney, J.T. and D. Sockell. 1988. "Hospital Union Determination and the Preservation of Employee Free Choice." *Labor Law Journal* 39 (May): 259–272.

DeMaria, A.T. 1980. *How Management Wins Union Organizing Campaigns.* New York: Executive Enterprises.

Department of Labor. 1989. *Employment and Earnings* 36 (January): 226.

Dickens, W. 1983. "The Effect of Company Campaigns on Certification Elections: 'Law and Reality' Once Again." *Industrial and Labor Relations Review* 36 (July): 560–575.

Dunlop, J.T. 1990. *The Management of Labor Unions.* Lexington, MA: Lexington Books.

Dyer, L., and G. Holder. 1988. "Toward a Strategic Perspective of Human Resource Management." In *Human Resource Management: Evolving Roles and Responsibilities.* Washington, DC: BNA Books.

Fiorito, J. and C. Greer. 1982. "Determinants of U.S. Unionism: Past Research and Future Needs." *Industrial Relations* 21 (Winter): 1–32.

Fiorito, J., C. Lowman, and F. Nelson. 1987. "The Impact of Human Resource Policies on Union Organizing." *Industrial Relations* 26 (Spring): 113–126.

Foulkes, F. 1980. *Personnel Policies in Large Nonunion Companies.* Englewood Cliffs, NJ: Prentice-Hall.

Freedman, A. 1978. *Managing Labor Relations.* New York: The Conference Board.

————. 1985. *The New Look at Wage Policy and Employment Relations.* New York: The Conference Board.

Gagala, K. 1983. *Union Organizing and Staying Organized.* Reston, VA: Reston Publishing.

Getman, J., S.B. Goldberg, and J.B. Herman. 1976. *Union Representation Elections: Law and Reality*. New York: Russell Sage Foundation.

Gordon, M. and A.J. Nurick. 1981. "Psychological Approaches to the Study of Unions and Union-Management Relations." *Psychological Bulletin* 90 (2): 293–306.

Hughes, C. 1976. *Making Unions Unnecessary*. New York: Executive Enterprises Publications Co.

Hunt, J.C. and R.A. White. 1982. "The Effects of Management Practices on Union Election Returns." *Journal of Labor Research* 21 (January): 1–32.

Huxley, C., D. Kettler, and J. Struthers. 1986. "Is Canada's Experience 'Especially Instructive'?" In *Unions in Transition: Entering the Second Century*, ed. S.M. Lipset. San Francisco: Institute for Contemporary Studies.

Kilgour, J. 1981. *Preventive Labor Relations*. New York: AMACOM.

Kochan, T. 1979. "How American Workers View Labor Unions.: *Monthly Labor Review* 102 (April): 23–31.

Kochan, T., H.C. Katz, and R.B. McKersie. 1986. *The Transformation of American Industrial Relations*. New York: Basic Books.

Kochan, T., R. McKersie, and J. Chalykoff. 1986. "The Effects of Corporate Strategy and Workplace Innovations on Union Representation." *Industrial and Labor Relations Review* 39 (July): 487–501.

Lawler, J.J. 1984. "The Influence of Management Consultants on the Outcome of Union Certification Elections." *Industrial and Labor Relations Review* 38 (October): 38–51.

———. 1990. *Unionization and Deunionization: Strategy, Tactics, Outcomes*. Columbia, SC: University of South Carolina Press.

Lawler, J.J. and R. West. 1984. "The Impact of Union-Avoidance Strategy in Representation Elections." *Industrial Relations* 24 (Fall): 406–420.

Maranto, C. and J. Fiorito. 1987. "The Effect of Union Characteristics on the Outcome of NLRB Certification Elections." *Industrial and Labor Relations Review* 40 (January): 225–240.

McDonald, C., and D. Wilson. 1979. "Peddling the 'Union Free' Guarantee." *American Federationist* 86 (April): 12–19.

McGuiness, K.C., and J.A. Norris. 1986. *How to Take a Case Before the National Labor Relations Board*, Fifth ed. Washington, DC: BNA Books.

Meyers, M.S. 1976. *Managing Without Unions*. Reading, MA: Addison-Wesley.

Mintzberg, H. 1989. *Mintzberg on Management*. New York: Free Press.

———. 1985. *New York Times* (February 19): 2.

Perry, C. 1987. *Union Corporate Campaigns*. Philadelphia: Industrial Research Unit, Wharton Business School, University of Pennsylvania.

Prosten, R. 1979. "The Longest Season: Union Organizing in the Last Decade, a.k.a. How Come One Team Has to Play With Its Shoelaces Tied Together?" In *Proceedings of the Thirty-First Annual Meeting of the Industrial Relations Research Association,* ed. B. Dennis. Madison, WI: Industrial Relations Research Association.

Reed, T. 1989. "Do Organizers Matter? Individual Characteristics and Representation Election Outcomes." *Industrial and Labor Relations Review* 41 (October): 89–104.

Schlossberg, S. and J. Scott. 1983. *Organizing and the Law.* Washington, DC: BNA Books.

Seeber, R. and W. Cooke. 1983. "The Decline in Union Success in NLRB Representation Elections." *Industrial Relations* 22 (Winter): 34–44.

Stratton, K. and R.B. Brown. 1988. "Strategic Planning in U.S. Labor Unions." Paper presented at the Forty-First Annual Meeting of the Industrial Relations Research Association, New York.

Troy, L. 1986. "The Rise and Fall of American Trade Unions: The Labor Movement from FDR to RR." In *Unions in Transition: Entering the Second Century,* ed. S.M. Lipset. San Francisco: Institute for Contemporary Studies.

Troy, L. and N. Sheflin. 1985. *U.S. Union Sourcebook: Membership, Finances, Structure, Directory.* West Orange, NJ: Industrial Relations and Information Services.

Verma, A. 1985. "Relative Flow of Capital to Union and Nonunion Plants within a Firm." *Industrial Relations* 24 (Fall): 395–405.

Voos, P.B. 1983. "Union Organizing: Costs and Benefits." *Industrial and Labor Relations Review* 36: 576–591.

_____. 1984. "Trends in Union Organizing Expenditures, 1953–1977." *Industrial and Labor Relations Review* 38 (October): 52–63.

Walker, J.M. and J.J. Lawler. 1979. "Dual Unions and Political Processes in Organizations." *Industrial Relations* 18 (Winter): 32–43.

_____. 1986. "Union Campaign Activities and Voter Preferences." *Journal of Labor Research* 7 (Winter): 19–40.

Weiler, P. 1983. "Promises to Keep: Securing Workers' Rights to Self-Organization under the NLRA." *Harvard Law Review* 96 (June): 418–476.

Williams, R. 1981. *NLRB Regulation of Election Conduct.* Philadelphia: Industrial Research Unit, Wharton Business School, University of Pennsylvania.

Youngblood, S., A.S. DeNisi, J.L. Molleston, and W.H. Mobley. 1984. "The Impact of Work Environment, Instrumentality Beliefs, Perceived Labor Union Image, and Subjective Norms on Union Voting Intentions." *Academy of Management Review* 27 (September): 576–590.

Zalesny, M. 1985. "Comparison of Economic and Noneconomic Factors in Predicting Faculty Vote Preference in a Union Representation Election." *Journal of Applied Psychology* 70 (2): 243–256.

4.6

Collective Bargaining

Peter Cappelli

Observers of United States industrial relations since World War II have often referred to collective bargaining as a "mature" system since it represents an evolving relationship that eventually became capable of addressing virtually all employee relations issues and containing conflict on those issues within the bargaining relationship. Perhaps the most striking development in the 1980s has been the breakdown of this system. Many important issues now arise outside of the collective bargaining relationship; the bargaining system no longer contains conflicts; and the rules governing appropriate behavior in collective bargaining seem to be in flux. Management has gained the initiative because of shifts in basic priorities for dealing with organized labor, fundamental changes in the economic environment, and new strategies for combatting unions. This chapter outlines resulting changes in the terms and conditions of employment and in the relations between unions and management. These new management strategies and labor's reaction to them take labor relations beyond the usual boundaries of collective bargaining and into uncharted terrain.

Changes in the Environment for Bargaining

Several shifts in the external environment have contributed to the erosion of collective bargaining relationships over the past decade. Management's tolerance of organized labor declined as public support for unions fell off and as new strategies for enhancing employees' job satisfaction emerged. Changes in the economic environment, brought on by increased competitive pressures at home and abroad, further fueled the eroding support for bargaining.

Changes in Management's Attitude Toward Labor[1]

Although American management as a group never quite accepted unions in principle, from the end of the New Deal through the 1970s a great many employers accepted unions in practice. Employers saw unionization as inevitable and collective bargaining as something that the public and the government accepted as part of the rules of fair play governing industry. Indeed, unions played an integral role in stabilizing wages under New Deal economic policies. As a result, the costs of trying to eliminate unions did not seem worth the benefits. Instead, firms trying to secure favorable terms and conditions through collective bargaining focused on establishing stable and predictable relations with unions. As pointed out in an early classic on collective bargaining, labor relations could not be stable and peaceful unless the unions were also stable and secure.[2] Strategies designed to get rid of or destabilize unions seemed senseless since such efforts might only lead to new and more radical labor organizations with even more troublesome demands.

Impact of Boulwarism

The change in management's priorities from stable labor relations to union avoidance began so slowly that the trend becomes apparent only with the benefit of hindsight. Perhaps the first, and in some ways the most important, step came with the rise of Boulwarism. This employer strategy in collective bargaining initially emerged at General Electric when management reacted to unions' attempt to dominate negotiations by presenting a single offer to all of its unions and refusing to bargain from it.[3] The success of a major American corporation like General Electric in pursuing such a policy certainly notified the business community that management could take the lead and change labor relations. Boulwarism thus marked a shift in management's negotiating strategy from a reactive to a proactive stance.

Shifts in Public Support for Labor

About the same time that Boulwarism developed, the gradual erosion of public support for organized labor began. After the McClelland hearings in the late 1950s brought graphic accounts of union corruption into the living rooms of America, annual public opinion polls began to show a steady decline in public support for labor, from an approval rating of about 60 percent to current ratings of about 30 percent. Since management attitudes and policies are very sensitive to public opinion,[4] this decline in public support for labor facilitated management's switch from accommodative strategies to ones that more aggressively opposed unions. Not surprisingly, the rapid rise of management unfair labor practices since the 1950s closely parallels this shift in public perceptions of organized labor.[5]

Public support for labor eroded even faster in the 1970s as unions took much of the blame for the rise of cost-push inflation. With this erosion, the range of management behavior that appeared acceptable expanded. By the 1980s, unions found themselves portrayed as the cause, rather than the victims, of structural economic changes. For example, organized labor bore the blame for failure of the steel and auto industries, where lower-wage foreign competition was presented as the problem. In addition, President Reagan's 1981 decision to fire the striking air traffic controllers and the apparent public support for this action sent the same signal to the management community that Boulwarism had, namely, that new and more aggressive tactics for dealing with unions were now acceptable.

Rise of the Behavioral Model of Employee Management

The final development influencing management's approach toward unions involved the rise of psychological models of employee management, or what some people refer to as "behavioral" or nonunion models of management. The quality of worklife movement in the early 1970s contributed to the popularity of this model by linking widespread job dissatisfaction to problems in the organization of work and in social relations at work, particularly among blue-collar positions.

The proposed behavioral solutions for this employee dissatisfaction indirectly provided a kind of manifesto for union-free management. Because much of the job dissatisfaction occurred in unionized industries, the industrial relations practices and material gains associated with collective bargaining appeared to make little contribution to employee satisfaction. Instead, remedies for job dissatisfaction, according to the behavioral argument, should attempt to reorganize jobs, increase the variety of tasks and the amount of autonomy workers have, make decisionmaking more participative, and so on.[6]

The behavioral model not only offered an alternative to unions and collective bargaining; it also encouraged anti-union attitudes. Unions were seen by many as obstacles to changes that could increase job satisfaction, such as creating broader and more flexible task assignments that might cut across existing job and craft union boundaries. Unions did in fact resist many of these changes because they violated the traditional system of contractual workrules which defined jobs narrowly and protected against management abuses of flexibility (e.g., working employees too hard). In addition, the collective bargaining system drew sharp lines between management and workers, which complicated the participatory decision making required under the behavioral model.

These arguments favoring the behavioral model gave rise to a nonunion manifesto for enlightened HRM, part of what became known as "The New Industrial Relations."[7] First, theories regarding what workers want from their jobs shifted from the material concerns of the union model toward psychological needs which could be met through more informed management practices. The resulting system of industrial relations could save money, since it would replace material rewards with less costly psychological rewards and increase productivity as a result of making workers more satisfied. Second, the traditional industrial relations system that emphasized material rewards not only had no role in the new model but in fact made it more difficult to satisfy employees' behavioral needs. These arguments made it easy for even enlightened management to say, as they did, "We believe that a union-free environment is in the best interests of our workers."[8]

Changes in the Economic Environment

The economic pressures posed by growing low-cost competition further induced management to seek new relations with unions. To see the development of this change, it is again helpful to contrast the current economic environment with the period prior to 1980.

Foreign Competition

After World War II, the United States dominated the world economy, and foreign competitors played almost no role in its domestic markets. Within the United States, union coverage in most manufacturing industries was virtually complete. Since most competitors received the same union contract, almost no low-wage domestic competition took place. In product markets, competitors simply passed labor costs on to consumers. Markets regulated by the government, such as transportation and communications, were automatically granted price increases to cover wage settlements. In manufacturing, especially in the heavily unionized, industrial core of the economy (steel, autos, rubber), oligopolies dominated the product markets and jointly increased prices to cover higher labor costs.[9] As a result, management had less reason to resist unions and union demands because no firm faced a disadvantage because of organized labor.

The rise of foreign competition in U.S. domestic markets significantly altered the economic environment for collective bargaining. Since foreign competitors did not participate in the U.S. system of administered pricing, they easily gained ever-increasing shares of the market by underpricing U.S. firms. Soon U.S. business had to match the price cuts of their foreign competitors. In the auto industry, for example, Japanese firms cut prices during downturns while U.S. automakers tended to maintain prices and reduce production. But by 1978, the U.S. producers were forced to follow the Japanese lead and cut prices, introducing manufacturer rebates for the first time in recent memory.

Because foreign businesses are not covered by U.S. union contracts, their presence means that wages are no longer common across competitors. As domestic firms fight to lower prices to the level of foreign competition, their union contracts clearly create a competitive disadvantage. As a result, U.S. producers have looked to unions for relief. This pressure to cut union labor costs varied directly with the intensity of the foreign competition.

Nonunion Domestic Competition

The rise of low-cost competition did not result solely from foreign competition. New domestic competitors which began and managed to stay unorganized have produced low-cost market competition which in turn has created competition to union wage rates. Even in industries virtually free from foreign competition, such as meat packing, a substantial nonunion presence has developed. These firms have managed to stay nonunion by starting up in the South and other areas with weak union support, then opposing organizing even in areas of union strength in part through aggressive anti-union policies. Similar developments have occurred more recently in the longshoring industry, where nonunion operations are putting great pressure on unionized docks to cut costs.

Rising union wage differentials in the mid 1970s also facilitated the introduction of nonunion systems[10] These differentials meant firms could pay high wages relative to community rates and still have labor expenses well below union wages and costs. Thus, the financial advantages of being union free became even greater. The cost-cutting pressures on unionized firms imposed by the growth of foreign competition and the rise of nonunion domestic competition explained about half of the incidence of concession bargaining through 1982.[11]

Deregulation

The deregulation of many product markets, especially those in transportation, created at least two challenges to existing union relationships. First, deregulation made it very much easier for new nonunion competitors to enter any individual market. For example, new, nonunion over-the-road trucking companies have effectively taken the market for full-load freight operations, although the expensive terminal facilities required by partial load freight has kept many of the new, nonunion operations out of this end of the business.[12] Similar competition has also arisen among airlines, especially in local, commuter markets. In telecommunications, the deregulation of selected product markets, such as equipment sales, created an explosion of new, nonunion entrants. Even heavily unionized operating companies are competing in these product markets by developing nonunion subsidiaries.[13] Major carriers in the railroad industry also have spun off "short-line" operations, typically new, short-haul routes, which operate without unions.

The second major impact of deregulation on union relations came about as a result of greater price, and therefore cost, competition. Since regulations had essentially prevented competitors from cutting prices, management had less incentive to resist union demands. Businesses could pass high labor costs on to consumers and could not turn any savings on labor into a competitive price advantage in the product market. But under deregulation, even the major airlines, which are almost entirely organized, found that low costs translated into low fares and a competitive advantage. As a result, all carriers now need to match the lowest costs of their competitors by matching their labor contracts.

Recession

The severity of the 1980 recession intensified all of these other economic pressures on union contracts. As many firms struggled to stave off bankruptcy, labor costs ranked among the few expenses that businesses could alter in the short run. Concessions therefore offered a much-needed means to improve cash-flow. On the union side, mass layoffs convinced many union members that the focus of bargaining efforts should shift to help reduce the risk of job loss. Layoffs no longer affected only the most junior members. Laid-off workers accounted for as much as half the membership of some unions, such as the United Auto Workers and the United Steel Workers; in cases where plants closed, entire locals found themselves out of business. Moreover, income security provisions, such as supplemental unemployment insurance, proved inadequate for the severity of the layoffs. In short, job security provisions no longer protected even a majority of union members from layoffs.

Collective Bargaining

Changes in the economic environment and the resulting competitive pressure to cut costs made management pursue more aggressive demands in collective bargaining. At the same time, membership losses prompted unions to reduce their demands and consider concessions as a means of reducing layoffs.[14] These developments helped produce a profound shift in power toward management that gave rise to new management tactics and new bargaining structures. In many cases, these changes altered the basic nature of the relationship between unions and management.

The Shift in Power: New Management Tactics

While economic pressures lessened the influence of organized labor, management's more powerful bargaining position has continued to reduce settlement levels, even where the economic environment has returned to more normal conditions. This change in power has resulted largely from new management tactics which developed due to changing management attitudes toward unions. New management strategies for handling unions appear in responses to industrial action, communication programs, and efforts to develop nonunion operations.

Responses to Industrial Action

Throughout the 1970s, many firms routinely shut down most or all of their operations during strikes. Beginning in the late 1970s, however, management began to adopt new strategies for operating during strikes.[15] The air transport industry clearly illustrates this change. While virtually no airline tried to operate during a strike by any of its employees for decades prior to 1978,[16] it is difficult to think of any case since then where management has not tried to operate during a strike.

The most obvious component of this new posture is the dramatic increase in the hiring of replacements for strikers. While this option had always existed, management almost never used it in previous decades, largely because of concern about a backlash in public opinion. The rise of this tactic in the early 1980s no doubt related to the large numbers and desperate situations of unemployed workers, but it has continued even as labor markets have tightened. A BNA survey reports that by 1987, only 22 percent of employers surveyed said that they would not hire strikebreakers in the event of a strike.[17]

In addition to replacing strikers, management has also resurrected the use of lockouts, most notably in a 1986 dispute between USX Corporation and the Steelworkers. Lockouts typically occur where contracts have expired but unions have not struck, generally because of a lack of bargaining power, and instead continue working under the conditions of the previous contract. Employees can return to work under management's terms, and if employees do come back, the union often is broken.

These more aggressive tactics by management have also played a deterrent role by making strikes dangerous tactics for unions to use. The Bureau of Labor Statistics reports that strikes declined in the 1980s to their lowest level since the BLS began keeping records in 1947. New record lows have been reported virtually every year, including 1987, when only 46 strikes or lockouts involving more than 1,000 workers and lasting more than one day were recorded. This statistic translates into 0.02 percent of work days lost due to industrial conflict.[18]

Communication Programs

Another new strategy in collective bargaining involved management's attempts to deny the union its traditional role as the spokesman and sole representative of worker interests in negotiations. In many ways, this development reflects the rise of the behavioral model. The tactic often begins with sophisticated attitude surveys of employees to identify their true interests on a range of issues and the strength of their feelings on those issues. Such information provides a great advantage in bargaining because it prevents the union from using management uncertainty about employees' preferences to gain an edge in bargaining. For example, unions may claim that their members are willing to strike over an issue, but through surveys, management can determine whether this possibility truly exists.

Management's efforts have gone beyond mere gathering of information toward shaping attitudes by communicating directly with workers on negotiating issues. Many companies now routinely address employees about the firm's economic situation in an effort to make them understand its problems. Burlington Northern Railroad, for example, hired a finance professor to teach its employees about the problems of raising capital in the railroad industry. These programs sometimes include elaborate multimedia presentations, although simple addresses by the CEO or another corporate official are equally common. These presentations have generally occurred during poor economic conditions and are designed to make workers recognize the need to cut labor costs. Whether management will abandon such presentations if conditions improve and how workers will view such abandonments remains to be seen.

Management has also launched communication programs that take place during contract negotiations. These programs rank as perhaps the most important management communication efforts and present the greatest threat to unions. Traditionally, unions not only presented demands to management on behalf of their members but communicated management's positions and actions back to the members and interpreted what those communications meant. For example, union negotiators might convey a management ultimatum with the caveat that the threat was a bluff. Now, however, management communicates its bargaining positions directly to the workers.

Management has used such programs not only to undercut the union's interpretation but in some cases, to attack union negotiators (e.g., "they are not representing your interests on this issue."). Indeed, some employers have gone so far in their communications as to suggest that workers should press their unions for a vote on certain contract issues. While other communication efforts help shift bargaining power to management, this last tactic is particularly dangerous because it may divide the union, undermine the leadership, and ultimately destabilize the bargaining unit. Management avoided such tactics when labor relations goals included stabilizing unions, but this current change illustrates the extent to which management has abandoned that earlier goal. Now, destabilizing a union is often a management goal in itself.

Development of Nonunion Capacity

Between 1978 and 1983, a Conference Board survey found that 20 percent of unionized firms had adopted union avoidance, rather than collective bargaining gains as their top industrial relations priority.[19] The most important mechanism for avoiding unions involves shifting capital and jobs away from areas of union control. While this strategy clearly affects unions (by reducing membership, for example), it also has a powerful effect on collective bargaining.

By the mid-1970s, management began to shift jobs and production away from union operations, even within their traditional lines of business, and to do so routinely.[20] The firms in the Conference Board survey that placed greater priority on union avoidance are building plants at twice the rate of companies whose priority is collective bargaining. These new facilities begin nonunion, and firms work hard to keep them that way. For example, by adopting policies associated with the behavioral model, companies can significantly reduce union organizing success.[21] In fact, the Conference Board survey found that union avoidance firms were about six times less likely to have their new plants organized than firms which ranked bargaining as the top priority.[22]

The ability to develop nonunion capacity has important effects on collective bargaining. In the tire industry, for example, management's efforts to open new plants in the South and to keep them nonunion paid off in collective bargaining during the 1976 industrywide strike. Management won at the bargaining table, largely because they had been able to keep nonunion operations in production during the strike. General Motors' southern strategy during this period went a step further by developing production capacity in nonunion plants and implementing the behavioral model in those plants. The productivity-enhancing innovations developed in those plants then were applied to the company's unionized facilities.[23]

Recent rulings by the National Labor Relations Board and the courts have substantially increased management's ability to transfer existing work from the bargaining unit,[24] and, in the process, to threaten employment and unions at existing facilities. Even profitable employers have pursued these tactics, in some cases manipulating financial and ownership provisions to close plants temporarily in order to influence union decisions. This greater ability of management to transfer resources and jobs appears to affect even nonunion facilities by creating a significant chilling effect on the interest of employees in unionizing.[25]

A final development involves the use of "double-breasted" operations, where unionized firms open nonunion subsidiaries in the same business. These operations have now spread from the construction industry to transportation; they are ubiquitous in trucking and common among airlines, most notably Continental. Unions charge that the nonunion, "short-line" railroads, spun-off by major carriers, constitute a type of double-breasted operation, at least when the carriers retain financial interests in the short-lines. The legality of some of these operations remains questionable, given the possibility that the corporate structure was designed simply to develop a nonunion work force.

Management's ability to shift work away from the unions certainly contributed to the increase in concession bargaining. At the plant-level, for example, management used the threat of plant closings to force local unions to compete against each other in an effort to lower costs and to stay open.[26] Similar decisions, such as whether to outsource operations, drop particular product lines, and the like, were presented to unions as hinging on whether management received labor cost concessions. These strategies proved particularly powerful where management combined the threat of layoffs if concessions were denied with a promise of at least some job security if concessions were granted. American Airlines, for example, threatened to abandon much of its route system if its unions refused to accept two-tier wage plans and other changes but promised to add routes and guarantee employment if they accepted. In the process, American secured perhaps the most sweeping changes in modern airline collective bargaining.[27]

Bargaining Structure

The structure used for negotiations also has played an important role in the continuing decline of union power. Bargaining structure refers to the array of bargaining units covered by a given agreement and the relationship between agreements (for example, pattern bargaining). American unions generally have tried to reduce wage competition by covering as many competitors as possible under common contracts. Thus, plants doing similar work within the same firm would operate under common, "master contracts," while competing firms would be covered by separate but basically identical agreements negotiated through so-called pattern bargaining.

When successful, this arrangement meant that no employer faced a competitive disadvantage by paying the union rate. In addition, centralized bargaining appeared to offer an advantage to employers who wanted to avoid being picked off, one by one, in strikes while their competitors stayed open and took their business. Many industries (such as railroads, trucking, steel, coal) responded by forming associations that bargained collectively for all of the employers. In other industries, such as airlines, strike insurance plans took the place of these associations and provided collective, financial support for employers whose workers were on strike.

One of the clearest, most striking developments in collective bargaining since 1980 has been the near-complete collapse of this system of centralized bargaining. The extraordinary and varying demands of employers for concessions—and the threats of associated job losses—drove the unions to make so many special deals that contracts across competitors lost much of their uniformity. These pressures generally pitted local unions, which favored concessions to prevent job losses (and, in many cases, complete firm or plant shutdowns), against their international unions, which often opposed such concessions for fear that they would spread to other locals. The success of the internationals depended largely on their constitutional control over locals; decentralized unions, like the airline pilots, had considerably less success than more centralized unions, such as the machinists.

The Conference Board survey discussed earlier indicates that the number of companies rating industry settlement patterns as the most important influence on their negotiations dropped by 50 percent between 1978 and 1983.[28] Industry settlement patterns topped the list of negotiating influences on the 1978 survey but had slipped to fourth place by 1983, behind company-specific factors (productivity and labor cost trends, profits, and local labor market trends, respectively). When setting wage objectives, firms responding to the 1983 survey ranked industry settlements dead last (out of 11 items) in importance. Given these survey findings, it comes as no surprise that bargaining patterns between industries that were common in the 1960s and early 1970s are now almost nonexistent.

The decline of employer associations has accelerated the decentralization of bargaining. Weaker employers saw the union concession trend and rightly thought they could get a better deal by negotiating outside of the associations. All of the major employer associations have lost a significant share of their members. For example, the association of over-the-road trucking companies has lost about half its members since deregulation, and in 1987, several firms left the Basic Coal Operators group. Even several of the major railroads have indicated that they will try, for the first time in more than a generation, to secure agreements outside of national bargaining. As noted above, decentralized bargaining within firms and plant-level concessions have led to the decline of master agreements across plants in the same firm.

In terms of immediate impact, decentralized bargaining structures have made it more difficult for unions to raise wages and settlements. The wide variance in settlements at present and the number of struggling firms that have received substantial concessions has prompted competing companies to demand similar deals in order to remain competitive in labor costs. As a result, wages throughout an industry get pulled down to the lowest common denominator. For example, one study has shown that unions are not able to raise wages in newly organized facilities above those prevailing in nonunion facilities.[29] This exact pattern created the wave of concessions in the airline industry as profitable carriers sought and secured many of the concessions that their struggling competitors had received.[30] The United Food and Commercial Workers Union addressed this problem in 1982 by negotiating wage concessions across even profitable firms as a way to regain some standardization of contracts in the meat packing industry. Until contract costs are at least reasonably common across competitors, higher settlements will place firms at a competitive disadvantage and will be strongly resisted.

An important long-run consequence of the decentralization of bargaining concerns its effects on unions as organizations. As bargaining becomes driven less by patterns in industries and in the economy as a whole and more dependent on the circumstances of individual employers, unions will find their own fortunes more closely tied to their employers'. In turn, unions may become less interested in the issues affecting unions elsewhere, develop more parochial concerns, and begin to look more like enterprise unions.

Outcomes in Collective Bargaining

Changes in the economic environment and in negotiating power have had profound effects on the settlements secured in collective bargaining. These effects include a significant erosion of the material gains which unions had secured in the period since WWII, as well as a considerable expansion of management's control over the way work is performed.

Wages

The decline in union wage increases certainly ranks as the most noticeable of these effects on material gains. What is considered normal for union wages has undergone significant change.[31] Within the union sector, manufacturing is no longer the settlement leader; total compensation in the manufacturing industry rose only 2.4 percent in 1987 versus 3.9 percent for all union contracts. But the most telling comparison is with the nonunion sector. Union wage increases actually amounted to less in percentage terms than wage increases in the nonunion sector for the last *seven* years. In 1987, for example, unions achieved wage increases of only 2.6 percent versus 3.6 percent in the nonunion sector. This development clearly erodes whatever union wage premiums remain.[32]

The decline in union wage gains continued even after the 1981 recession faded and the economy moved into a prolonged expansion. For example, the Bureau of Labor Statistics reports that union wage increases during the mid-1980s dropped to the lowest levels on record. As recently as 1986, a majority of major new agreements had either wage cuts or no increases in the first year of the contract. This trend further suggests that developments in collective bargaining level, and not simply economic conditions, are the cause of declining union wage increases.

Reductions in wage increases reflect a general effort by management to reduce the fixed costs associated with labor through the use of alternative pay arrangements (see Table 1). The 1981 abandonment of the annual improvement factor, which had effectively

---

Table 1

Alternative Pay Arrangements

	Union View	*Management View*
Concessions	May be advantageous when coupled with job security guarantees. Most likely to be agreed to when senior employees would be laid-off in their absence.	Sought when competitive pay is lower and/or profit levels are unsatisfactory. May be associated in longer run with lower employee quality.
Gainsharing	Advantageous where product demand, production technology, and employee population is relatively stable.	Increased pay occurs only as a result of increased employee productivity. May have to pay bonuses during periods of high productivity but low product demand.
Profit Sharing	Advantageous where product market environment is relatively stable and growing. Less closely related to individual worker productivity than gainsharing.	Increases proportion of variable compensation. Results in decreased pay during periods of poorer organizational performance.
Lump sum bonuses	Relatively large amount of cash paid immediately. Wage-tied fringes do not increase.	Maintains wage base at present level.
Two-tier pay plans	Creates representation problems since workers in same jobs receive different rates of pay.	Lowers compensation costs if expansion or turnover is anticipated.

---

guaranteed a minimum percentage wage increase in the auto industry every year (and through pattern bargaining, in other industries as well), marked a symbolic step in this trend. The elimination of cost-of-living adjustments (COLAs) also demonstrates the trend toward reducing basic wage costs. The Bureau of Labor Statistics reports that COLA provisions have been dropping from contracts steadily for the past ten years; in 1987, only 38 percent of agreements had COLAs, compared to 61 percent in 1977. Firms find COLAs particularly burdensome because they add uncertainty to labor costs. However, the continued elimination of COLAs, even though inflation has hit its lowest point in a generation, may indicate not only how much management objected to COLAs but also how much bargaining power has shifted to management.

As a substitute for wage and COLA increases, many firms are using lump-sum payments, which have the advantage of not raising the base of fixed costs of labor. The Bureau of Labor Statistics reported that 27 percent of major agreements had lump-sum provisions in 1987, and the trend toward using these in lieu of wage increases is growing. The Bureau of National Affairs found that 38 percent of firms surveyed in 1987 planned to use lump-sum payments, versus only 13 percent in 1986.[33] Still, lump-sum payments only account for a fraction of total pay (less than 1 percent), and serious questions, such as whether these payments must be included in the base for calculating overtime pay, may retard their use.[34]

Two-Tier Wage Plans[35]

Two-tier wage plans are another concession that reduces basic wage costs. These plans depress the level of pay or slow the rate of increase for workers hired after some arbitrary cutoff date. Workers hired after that date are governed by a new pay schedule which establishes lower rates of pay for equivalent levels of seniority. The practice of paying new hires less than workers with greater seniority has been around for generations in the form of seniority-based pay schedules. Instead, the defining characteristic of two-tier plans is that workers hired after the cutoff date receive less pay than employees who have identical positions and seniority but were hired earlier. In other words, two-tier wage plans treat cohorts differently.

Impetus for Two-Tier Plans. Two-tier pay plans first came to the public's attention in the 1980s as part of the general trend in union concessions. No doubt many of the same factors that led to union concessions provided the impetus for two-tier pay plans. For example, an analysis of contracts conducted by the Bureau of National Affairs found that settlement levels were significantly lower in contracts with two-tier plans than in contracts without them.[36] Unions accepted these plans more easily than other concessions because they cost current workers nothing, and current workers are the ones who ratify contract concessions. However, many observers find these plans objectionable since they appear to discriminate against new hires and violate traditional union concerns for equal treatment across the work force. Indeed, some analysts wonder whether two-tier plans conflict with a union's duty of fair representation because they divide workers into classes based on arbitrary hiring dates and then treat the classes differently. Permanent two-tier agreements, which never merge new-hire rates with the previous schedule, may be much more vulnerable to this charge than plans which merge schedules.[37] However, the long-standing acceptance of disparate treatment based on seniority may protect most two-tier plans.

Perhaps the most important boost for two-tier agreements came in 1984, when an arbitrator awarded a two-tier plan for the 600,000 postal workers. Since then, the proportion of two-tier plans among new, nonconstruction contracts has grown, from 5 percent in 1983 to 11 percent in 1985, before leveling off at 10 percent in 1986 and then dropping off to 9 percent in 1987.[38] A 1986 survey found two-tier plans in 28 percent of responding firms,[39] while a 1987 survey reported two-tier plans in 43 percent of firms surveyed.[40]

Effectiveness. Two-tier plans gradually reduce average labor costs as the ranks of workers in the lower-paid tier grow. As a result, these plans are much more useful to firms in industries characterized by rapid turnover. In fact, data suggests that two-tier pay plans are concentrated in service industries where turnover is high. For example, the industry with the largest number of two-tier agreements in 1987 was the retail food industry, where employee turnover is very great.[41] Within firms, two-tier agreements predominate for production workers, but rarely cover skilled trades and maintenance workers.[42] Two-tier plans for skilled workers offer employers little advantage because the strong external labor market makes such workers difficult to replace, especially at lower rates of pay. Thus, two-tier plans are useful only to firms which can attract new hires at wages well below those currently paid, that is, firms which currently pay wage rates well above market levels.

An important distinction concerns the difference between permanent plans, where "B" tier workers will always be on a lower wage schedule, and merging or temporary plans, where "B" tier workers eventually get on the "A" tier's wage schedule. The vast majority of two-tier pay plans are merging plans; a 1987 survey found that only 14 percent of two-tier plans have permanent B tiers,[43] while other data suggests that most temporary plans merge in approximately five years and that B-tier workers earn about 25 percent less than A-tier employees at the entry level.[44]

A recent study suggests that management in the airline industry pushed very hard for two-tier wage plans with the idea that they could cut costs without damaging the morale of current workers.[45] But anecdotal evidence indicates that these plans are divisive; in particular, B-tier workers are unhappy about being in a separate, lower-paid tier and generate pressure to eliminate it. Whether they are in general less happy with work-related issues than A-tier workers is another matter, however. One survey of workers in a long-standing, permanent two-tier plan concluded that B-tier workers had lower pay satisfaction and union commitment than A-tier workers.[46] However, a survey of workers covered by a merging plan found that B-tier workers were in fact more satisfied with their work and pay and more committed to their employer.[47] A possible explanation for these conflicting results is that the B-tier workers had different referents. Workers covered by the merging plan were new to their jobs, and therefore had different (lower) expectations than A-tier employees covered by the same plan and B-tier workers covered by a long-standing permanent plan. Permanent plans might generate morale problems, but temporary ones may merge workers onto the A tier before such problems develop.

In recent years, some companies have raised wages in B tiers. American Airlines, for example, moved from a permanent to a merging two-tier system and raised the entry rates in the process. In most cases, however, these revisions appear due to increased market wages rather than to conflict or morale problems in the B tier. Indeed, as union wage premiums continue to erode, the rationale for two-tier plans also erodes. If the use of two-tier plans does decline, this erosion of union wages, rather than morale problems, may well be the reason.

Benefits

The benefits associated with traditional compensation packages account for as much as 40 percent of total wage costs and obviously account for a large part of fixed labor costs. Not surprisingly, these benefits continue to be a target of management cost reduction efforts, especially insurance costs where liabilities are uncertain. Figure 1 outlines the planned changes in insurance benefits found among a recent survey of employers.

Of firms surveyed, 39 percent already require employee deductibles and copayments. The trend is to expand these require-

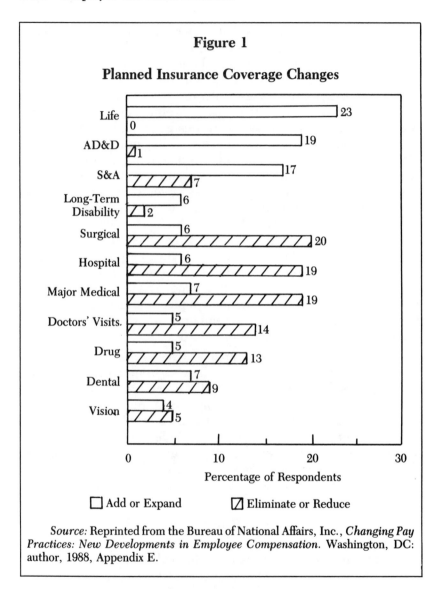

Figure 1

Planned Insurance Coverage Changes

Percentage of Respondents

☐ Add or Expand   ▨ Eliminate or Reduce

Source: Reprinted from the Bureau of National Affairs, Inc., *Changing Pay Practices: New Developments in Employee Compensation.* Washington, DC: author, 1988, Appendix E.

ments, as well as screening, second-opinion, and other review policies for health insurance programs. The survey also indicated significant management interest in reducing paid time off, although parental leave and child care assistance programs appear to be on the rise.

Making Labor Costs Flexible

In addition to holding down absolute labor costs, management is also interested in linking labor costs to the economic condition of the firm. For example, miners in the copper industry and workers at Kaiser Aluminum both have their pay vary directly with the prices of those commodities, reflecting employers' revenues and ability to pay. More common, however, are efforts to share the gains from increased productivity or reductions in labor costs. A 1988 study reported that 37 percent of firms surveyed have profit sharing, while 14 percent have other forms of gainsharing.[48] Managers rated such plans among the most effective pay innovations[49] and as the most popular among employees. Many of these plans have their roots in Scanlon-type plans and date back to the 1930s. They may be more common among unionized firms.

The 1986 telecommunications contracts offered a variety of these performance-based pay plans as a substitute for basic rate increases. The contracts illustrate how these plans can hold down basic wages. Agreements offering very generous lump-sum and gainsharing plans became very cheap once the contracts expired because the increase in basic rates was held to a minimum.

Plans that tie pay to firm performance not only impart flexibility but also try to enhance employee productivity and commitment by linking a worker's financial incentives to those of the firm. As a result, such plans reinforce efforts at participation and often are introduced together.[50]

Other compensation programs vary pay with individual performance as well. Most U.S. compensation systems attach pay rates to jobs, rather than to individuals, something trade unions have encouraged in order to prevent pay from fostering competition between workers. However, the use of skill-based pay or pay-for-knowledge plans is on the rise. These compensation programs offer wage premiums to encourage workers to learn new skills and to take on new tasks at work. A U.S. Department of Labor survey indicated that in 1986, 8 percent of firms had such plans.[51] These plans reinforce changes in the organization of work (see below) and appear to be well-received by employees. The main problems associated with them relate to coordination with skill and tasks demands; the pay plans have to be flexible enough to meet changes in skill needs and in work organization without simply adding additional premiums forever. For example, suppose an acquired skill is eliminated by automation. Do the payments continue?

Unlike skill-based plans, which do not place workers in direct competition with each other, merit-based pay, which differentiates pay increases according to the performance of individual workers, does create such competition. Merit pay plans are a serious concern to unions given their traditional interest in reducing such competition. A 1988 survey found that just under half of all firms have such plans, although they appear to be almost exclusively in the nonunion sector.[52] Management negotiators are increasingly pushing for merit pay in the belief that it will improve individual worker performance. Given the problems associated with running merit-based pay systems (for example, high administrative costs) and the conflicts they generate (for example, equity issues) even in nonunion settings,[53] such enthusiasm may be unwarranted.

Revisions in Workrules[54]

During the recession of the early 1980s, management's concession demands targeted wage and benefit cuts because the resulting cost savings proved useful for meeting immediate, cash flow crises. However, compensation can be cut only so far, and those cuts can have an immediate, negative effect on morale. Lowered morale in turn can reduce productivity through a variety of channels, such as higher absenteeism, increased turnover, and so on. In addition, pressures soon mount to restore wage and benefit cuts when periods of crisis pass.

Because of these concerns, management's efforts to reduce labor costs began to shift to the issue of workrules in the mid-1980s as recession-based crises gave way to recovery and longer-run concerns of competitiveness and growth. Employees typically find workrule changes a more acceptable means of reducing labor costs than either wage changes or benefits cuts,[55] since these changes do not affect their standard of living. In addition, workrule changes are less visible and therefore have less symbolic importance for unions. For management, workrule changes, especially those associated with a systematic redesign of jobs, tend to become permanent as it is more difficult to revert to the older system. Workrule changes have also become a crucial source of comparative cost advantage since they cannot easily be identified and copied by competitors, in part because of the idiosyncracies of organizations and jobs. In contrast, wage concessions are well publicized and have spread quickly across competitors.

Changes in Job Descriptions

One of the most common workrule changes is to broaden the tasks that certain workers can be assigned as well as the circumstances under which they can be assigned. Broader job descriptions explicitly attempt to reduce the number of workers needed for a particular operation by eliminating idle time when a particular set of tasks might not need to be done. These efforts work best for tasks that are done in the same area but at different times, such as maintenance work.[56] However, reductions may prove especially difficult if the change affects jobs represented by different unions since elimination of a job classification may eliminate an entire union. Still, changes are in the works even where jobs span different unions. For example, Hollywood's motion picture unions have recently agreed to broaden some jobs so that workers will perform tasks that span union jurisdictions. Although such changes may increase worker satisfaction, management's motive appears to be the opportunity to eliminate jobs.

Other workrule changes push tasks down the job ladder to less-skilled, lower-paid workers. The air transport, for example, has shifted the task of walking planes from the gate to the runway from mechanics to lower-paid members of the ground crew. Plumbers and pipefitters unions have agreed with the Mechanical Contractors Association to add a semi-skilled grade below journeyman to take over many of the simpler tasks.

A related effort attempts to transfer some managerial authority to workers and, in the process, eliminate many of the traditional first-line supervisory positions. Such programs may come as part of more comprehensive changes, such as quality of worklife plans (QWL) or autonomous workgroups, and vary in the amount of authority they give to the workers. Some employers, like TRW's Lawrence, Kansas plant and Digital Equipment's Enfield, Connecticut facility, even allow workers to make personnel decisions about hiring, training, and production standards for the group. One argument for these arrangements is that they shorten communications lines, especially on questions of scheduling and coordinating tasks, and make for quicker, more effective decisions.[57] Further, participation may increase satisfaction and, in turn, improve performance. One study conducted in 1983 found higher product quality at GM units with better QWL performance,[58] while more recent research suggests that participation may also improve workers' views of their unions.[59] Again, however, management appears interested in these programs as much for their ability to eliminate supervisors as for any direct benefits from participation.

New Placement Policies

Other policy changes give management greater control over the movement of employees in an organization, from hiring to transfers and dismissals. Rules governing selection have changed in part because of the increased demands that new job designs place on workers. Companies like Rohm and Haas now use elaborate testing and screening systems to select workers for their team-based plants. Other common revisions reduce the role of seniority, especially seniority-based reassignments or "bumping" that typically follows layoffs. Management has argued that transfers and promotions based solely on seniority, especially where jobs are specialized, often mean that unqualified people end up with the jobs; bumping is even worse because it shifts workers out of current jobs, disrupting workgroups and often requiring vast amounts of retraining. For example, Xerox recently secured limits on the extent of bumping in return for a no-layoff clause.

Employers have introduced a variety of contractual changes to help better address fluctuations in production levels. Virtually all of the major airlines rapidly followed American's lead and have increased their ability to hire part-time workers (at lower rates of pay and benefits) to staff the erratic flight schedules at less busy airports. The agreement between GM and the UAW for the new Saturn project creates a second category of employees without the job security enjoyed by the primary group; employment fluctuations for the second group help provide job protection for the other. The Newspaper Writers Guild and the Associated Press recently agreed to let employees share jobs as a way of dealing with job losses. Further, many contracts now reduce or eliminate premium pay for shift work since such payments pose a financial impediment to these changes. The United Transport Union, for example, recently agreed to eliminate many of these premium payments in the railroad industry.

Revised Production Policies

Finally, management has sought and secured changes in production standards. These standards not only cover output requirements, such as quality standards and work pace, but also may include such matters as manning levels and crew sizes for certain jobs (such as in the service sector). In some cases, these new standards may not make the job any harder for workers. For example, for jobs having a broad scope, new production standards may simply cover more issues. In other cases, the standards impose a kind of "speed up" that may make jobs harder for workers. An increasingly popular provision attempts to reduce absenteeism and employee misconduct. A 1988 survey by the Bureau of National Affairs found that 39 percent of responding firms had contractual provisions to reduce absenteeism, and 12 percent were planning to introduce them.[60] Such programs generally provide incentives (often a pay premium) for good attendance and discipline (sometimes discharge) for excessive absenses.

Potential Pitfalls

Securing workrule changes entails a different bargaining process from securing wage cuts since it precisely raises employment issues. Experience indicates that employees have no interest in changing workrules unless they receive some assurance that the changes will not result in layoffs. Any promise of job security requires a supportive business strategy—typically, a plan for business expansion, such as taking back functions previously subcontracted. In the U.S. airline industry, for example, only those carriers which could offer prospects for growth and employment security, contingent on new workrules secured extensive workrule changes through negotiations. In contrast, carriers that lacked such prospects could not change workrules as readily, even if severe employment losses were threatened.[61]

In addition to job security, acceptance of the union and its role within a firm is certainly necessary to secure any workrule changes. For example, General Motors could not get the UAW to consider work redesign efforts in the 1970s when the company was pursuing its strategy of opening nonunion plants in the South. The complete redesign of traditional workrules at GM's new Saturn plant represents a reversal of this situation. The UAW played an active role in the job redesign process at Saturn largely because GM agreed, before the plant was ever built, to have the UAW represent Saturn's employees.

Even with union support, introducing and administering a new system of workrules is a complex and idiosyncratic process. Transition to a new system occurs more smoothly when an organization has an existing model of alternative workrule arrangements where many problems unique to the firm have already been worked out.[62] GM's current cooperative enterprise with Toyota in California (NUMMI) is designed in part to create a new internal model—based on Japanese practices—for manufacturing. As is often the case, many of the innovative work designs that GM is currently installing in union plants first came about as experiments in nonunion facilities during the 1970s.[63] TRW and Best Foods also recently transferred work systems established at nonunion facilities to their unionized plants.

The success of workrule changes depends on whether they can be fit together into an effective system. Some workrule changes are more difficult to introduce than others. For example, horizontal and vertical restructuring requires systematic changes in other workrules to support the new work arrangements.[64] The greater flexibility of broader jobs, for example, is lost if supervisors still have to stand over employees and tell them what to do. These broader jobs also may require different kinds of workers—specifically, individuals with a wider range of skills and the capacity to learn new ones—and new methods of selection. The management at Borg-Warner calculates that their broadened production jobs require 10 times as much training as positions under the old system. Performance standards also must change to focus less on individuals and more on group or organizational performance as the tasks associated with particular jobs become harder to define and less routine. These changes, in turn, force revisions in compensation systems. For example, when the content of the job is changing almost daily and workers in the same classification may be performing quite different tasks, how can the usual wage/effort bargain be maintained?

Workrule changes introduce powerful dynamics to the employment setting which may have unintended consequences. For example, expanding the horizontal job structure may create jobs that are idiosyncratic and very difficult to replace, thus increasing the power of workers in those jobs. Changes such as the ones outlined above increase management's discretion and may lead to charges that decisions are made subjectively. Recent strikes at GM's Wentzville, Missouri and Lake Orion, Michigan plants apparently were associated with resentment and charges of favoritism in management's handling of job assignments and pay for knowledge increases. However, discretion appears to benefit whichever side has power at the moment. In the 1950s, for example, when unions were much more powerful, management worked hard to get work practices into contracts in order to eliminate discretion and the resulting shopfloor bargaining. If work groups regain power on the shopfloor, this discretion may come back to haunt management.

Of all these changes in collective bargaining outcomes, management appears to have been most concerned about reducing base wage and fixed labor costs, especially in the worst of the recession. Figure 2 from a 1985 Conference Board survey illustrates management bargaining priorities with regard to non-wage issues and how they have changed since the late 1970s.

The Union Response

The previous section outlined the shift in bargaining power toward management and the consequent changes in contracts that better serve management's interests. Although management clearly has the initiative, unions have often responded in innovative ways, some of which help address union problems and expand their influence.

Some union initiatives have taken place in the context of collective bargaining, even in the context of concession bargaining. In fact, when firms truly need labor cost cuts to survive, unions may have considerable power because management needs their help and should be willing to give something to get it.[65] Employers cannot give things that raise current labor costs—doing so would defeat the purpose of concessions—but virtually everything else is fair game.

Alternative Compensation Policies

The most obvious swap that workers can make in concession bargaining is to trade current labor cost cuts for future wages. Workers at LTV Steel, for example, have made concessions in the form of loans that are to be paid back when business picks up; Eastern Airline's variable earnings plans, which operated for most of the 1970s, swapped wage cuts for a share of future corporate earnings.

Figure 2

Shift in Management's Nonwage Objectives between 1978 and 1983

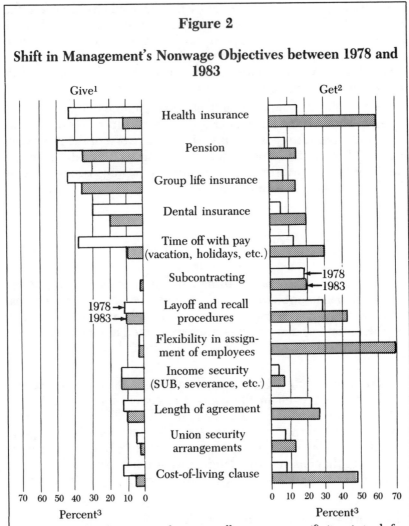

[1]Proportion of companies that were willing to use a specific item in trade for another item.

[2]Proportion of companies that wanted to tighten existing provision or get a more favorable one.

[3]100% = all companies with the same bargaining unit for both years, with an objective in the subject area in 1978 and in 1983. (e.g., Health benefits, 130 companies; subcontracting, 86 companies.)

Source: Reprinted with permission from A. Freedman, *The New Look in Wage Policy and Employee Relations.* New York: Conference Board, 1985, p. 15.

A related exchange trades labor cost concessions for stock ownership, a practice especially common in the airline and trucking industries. Employee stock ownership plans (ESOPs) are often the vehicle for these exchanges, in part because they create favorable tax advantages for the employers. Stock ownership also is thought to create a sense of involvement among employees, but research suggests that the plans do not necessarily have this effect.[66] Other studies have found that many stock ownership plans actually give employees nothing of value, partly because many companies offering these swaps are almost bankrupt.[67] Due to union involvement with these plans, labor has developed much greater expertise in financial matters.[68] Whether a result of this expertise or improvements in corporate performance, the popularity of stock deals appears to have declined since the 1980 recession.

The real motive behind union support for many of these ESOP deals may have aimed at ensuring jobs by increasing investment. For example, the Teamsters and the Steelworkers have swapped concessions for indirect improvements in job security that came through increased corporate investment in unionized operations.[69] More direct deals for job security have occurred in the airline and auto industries. United's pilots gave workrule concessions in 1981 in return for job security for the life of the contract. The UAW's auto contracts since 1984 also have included job security provisions: The 1984 agreement required management to provide lifetime salary protection for laid-off workers; the 1986 agreement placed restrictions on plant closings and layoffs; and the 1988 agreement basically guaranteed current job levels.

Union Voice on Management Strategies

The more interesting union efforts, however, have targeted some of the management strategies that are causing so many problems for unions. These efforts try to link collective bargaining issues with management tactics that take place outside of bargaining. In the area of union organizing, for example, unions at B.F. Goodrich, Dana Corporation, and other companies secured neutrality agreements that basically require management to remain neutral in any forthcoming union elections. The UAW accepted a more moderate contract in return for GM's agreement to build the Saturn car line in the United States and to allow the UAW to represent those workers. Airline unions got most major carriers to agree to prohibit double-breasted operations that threaten existing unionized operations.

Unions, first at Chrysler and then at several airlines and other companies, also have secured worker representation on the board of directors in exchange for concessions. These positions offered unions access to the highest level of decision making, as well as information, possibly even input, about those decisions. However, the effectiveness of these experiments remains uncertain, perhaps because board-level activity is rarely made public.[70]

Since most of these innovations took place at firms faced with relatively severe economic difficulties, unions had some leverage. However, the expansion of union influence into these areas of traditional management control appears to have been a temporary phenomenon. As the economy improved and firms regained their financial strength, these kinds of union innovations declined. One reason for this decline is the legal division between mandatory and permissive bargaining topics which basically prohibits bargaining on these traditional management issues unless both sides agree.[71] Management objects in principle to these inroads and only agreed to negotiate over them when economics problems were intense. Unions likewise may have found relatively little tangible benefits from some of these innovations, such as board membership and ESOPs.

Corporate Campaigns

A second type of union innovation that operates outside of the traditional collective bargaining arena is the corporate campaign. These campaigns seek to bring pressure on management when unions have had little success through traditional channels of union representation elections or collective bargaining. The compaigns try to influence management directly through public relations, customer boycotts, and stockholder-related challenges, as well as indirectly through pressure from affiliated business, such as corporate holding companies and financial institutions. Many corporate campaigns are designed to secure union recognition or first contracts, although some campaigns concern the terms and conditions of employment as traditionally handled through collective bargaining. Although elements of corporate campaigns have been used for years, the ACTWU's 1977 campaign against J.P. Stevens is widely recognized as the first, full-fledged corporate campaign. This tactic became increasingly popular in the mid-1980s, no doubt due in part to unions' lack of success through traditional channels.

One study examining several of the most important corporate campaigns concluded that this strategy works best at firms concerned with their public and customer image.[72] For example, campaigns proved successful at the nursing home chain of Beverly Enterprises and Campbell Soup but met failure at Louisiana-Pacific and Phelps-Dodge, in part because these firms do not sell to the general public. Unlike other union initiatives, corporate campaigns have not declined as economic conditions have improved. Unlike other innovations, which are secured through collective bargaining, management cooperation is clearly not a prerequisite to a corporate campaign. Indeed, lack of cooperation appears to be the necessary condition.

Conclusions

At no time since the 1930s has management possessed such control over labor relations. Changes in attitudes toward unions and in the economic environment have combined with new, more aggressive tactics to shift bargaining power sharply toward management, reshaping the system of labor relations. In some cases, the resulting changes are simply rollbacks of some union gains. In other instances, the changes amount to a wholesale revision of not only the terms and conditions of employment but also the process of rule setting and the union's role in this process. Moreover, these changes can take place simultaneously—bargaining can take place as usual while management is working hard to get rid of the union by moving jobs away from it.[73] In such cases, unions often wake up too late and find themselves representing only a small, declining section of a firm's business, such as the partial-load component of now double-breasted, over-the-road trucking firms.

Management generally has succeeded in reshaping labor relations along the lines it wanted. However, introducing wholesale changes can prove dangerous, even to management. While traditional collective bargaining arrangements certainly had problems, such as low productivity, these rules and procedures at least provided a means to address employee concerns and most employee relations issues in a predictable forum where conflict was contained. In addition, the task of introducing new terms and conditions of employment that can fit together in a system that is reinforcing and not self-defeating can pose enormous difficulties. For example, evidence suggests that at least some of management's favorite contract concessions failed to produce improved financial performance.[74] Perhaps most importantly, the process of introducing concessions and other changes has led, in many cases, to bitterness and a decay in employee morale.[75]

From a long-term view, contract concessions simply reflect the ebb and flow of any bargaining process. Other developments, however, threaten to alter the underlying premises of the collective bargaining relationship. Management in some firms has become so preoccupied with destabilizing unions that it does not appear to care what happens when the unions are gone. To illustrate, many plant managers informally report that since the threat of union organizing has disappeared, their corporate superiors are pushing to withdraw the often elaborate and expensive behavioral system of personnel practices in their nonunion facilities.

Indeed, many firms seem to believe that simply getting rid of their unions will make all of the employee relations effective and competitive. This view certainly is shortsighted. Sharp reductions in the terms and conditions of employment and losses of participation and control can cause workers to take out their frustrations and bitterness in costly ways, even in the absence of unions and strikes. Conflict simply emerges in a different form, such as in behaviors associated with lack of commitment and dissatisfaction like absenteeism, turnover, and low productivity. Corporate campaigns and the explosion of litigation by unions after collective bargaining breaks down, and by employees over violations of even "implicit" employment agreements also illustrate forms of conflict. Such bitterness and frustration seems likely to increase if employers remove the behavioral personnel plans which substitute for unions in many plants.

From the perspective of workers, the decline of contract outcomes and collective bargaining as a process causes nothing but problems. Even employees in nonunion facilities can suffer because of the spillover effect noted above. Cuts in pay and benefits contribute to the sharp decline in real earnings, which have fallen in the United States by more than 17 percent since peaking in the late 1960s.[76] Evidence also shows a very clear trade-off between wage and profit increases, implying that much of the current reduction in wages may have benefited profit margins.[77] While an economy clearly benefits from high productivity, the economic benefits of lower wages or even higher profits at the expense of wages are less clear.[78]

If collective bargaining reached maturity in the 1970s, then it is at present suffering from osteoporosis. To be sure, unions and management in many cases, such as in the auto industry, still use collective bargaining to fashion new and innovative solutions to common problems. But for every one case of cooperation, there are several others where the relationship has broken down, where conflict has spilled over to new arenas, and where unions have been eliminated altogether. As a result, firms now must deal with morale problems associated with imposing concessions and find a new system to replace collective bargaining.

One of the most popular solutions to morale problems is to get rid of the old work force and hire new employees who have lower expectations. Two-tier employment systems with early retirement provisions are part of this trend; other options include closing old facilities and sometimes opening new ones in different areas or subcontracting the work. All of these strategies share similar outcomes: The employees who made concessions and whose morale has been hurt are replaced by those who did not.

Less certainty surrounds the issue of what will replace collective bargaining. Especially where the threat of union organizing is absent, firms may not continue to develop the elaborate personnel systems that once substituted for much of what unions offered. If small subcontractors take over work previously performed in large bargaining units, perhaps the personal relationships found in small shops will suffice. If not, legislation and court decisions may provide a new employment system with a legal basis. Such developments are already underway in areas like employment-at-will, parental leave, and so on.

Some of the adjustment costs associated with the decline of collective bargaining remain to be seen. The severity of the 1981 recession mitigated these costs by sharply lowering expectations and making most employees glad simply to have a job. But as the "baby boom" ends and labor markets tighten, greater attention to worker concerns about the terms and conditions of work as well as issues of fairness and process may prove necessary in order to recruit and retain an adequate labor force.

◆

Notes

1. Material in this section is drawn from Cappelli (1987).
2. Golden and Parker.
3. Northrup (1964).
4. Bendix.
5. Weiler.

6. See Argyris and Hackman and Oldham as examples of seminal arguments that helped form the basis for the behavioral model. It is important to note that the academic proponents of the behavioral model did not necessarily think of it as a nonunion model.

7. *Business Week.*

8. Although the purpose of this chapter is not to investigate the behavioral model, it is worth noting in passing that very few employers actually practice all its good aspects, and in the absence of unions, no mechanism exists to prevent even a model employer from backsliding on these programs. Further, conflicts over zero-sum issues, such as wages, remain and the behavioral model offers no incentive for management to give workers a voice on these issues.

9. As a practical example, many readers will remember in the years before 1978 that General Motors would announce its annual price increases, and Ford and Chrysler would immediately announce virtually identical increases.

10. See Freeman and Medoff, Ch. 3, for an account of changing union differentials.

11. Cappelli (1983).

12. Perry (1986).

13. Perry and Cappelli.

14. In industries where foreign costs are far below those in the United States, this effect did not always occur. In the steel industry, for example, some employee leaders argued that no level of labor cost cuts would save jobs and markets for U.S. producers. See Miles and Hoerr.

15. Perry, Kramer, and Schneider.

16. Northrup (1983).

17. Bureau of National Affairs, Inc. (1988), p. E-5.

18. Other reasons certainly account for the decline of strikes, especially the economic vulnerability of some firms where strikes would have put them out of business. This factor, however, should have declined as the economy improved.

19. See Freedman for a discussion of the survey and its basic results.

20. See Verma and Kochan for an example of this shift in capital and resources within one large conglomerate.

21. Fiorito, Lowman, and Nelson.

22. Cappelli and Chalykoff.

23. Cherry. The ability to maintain nonunion facilities was of course not unrelated to what many see as a decline in union efforts at organizing during the 1970s. Voos (1985) argues, for example, that union resources spent on organizing per unorganized employee declined by about 30% between 1953 and 1974.

24. Miscimarra.

25. Freiberg and Dickens.

26. Cappelli (1985b).

27. Cappelli (1985a).

28. See Freedman and Fulmer for further evidence about the decline of pattern bargaining.

29. Freeman and Kleiner.

30. Cappelli (1987).

31. Mitchell (1987).

32. Union wages cannot be held down forever, and at some point they have to start climbing at least at the market rate. There are some signs that the long-term, relative decline of union wages may be over as union increases exceeded those in the nonunion sector in the last quarter of 1987. The preceding information on wages came from *Current Wage Developments*, various dates.

33. Bureau of National Affairs, Inc. (1988), p. 49.

34. Where lump sums rather than bonuses are granted in lieu of a pay

increase, they are more likely to be included as part of the base. See Bureau of National Affairs, Inc. (1988), Appendix F, for a discussion.

35. Material in this section is based on Cappelli and Sherer.

36. Bureau of National Affairs, Inc. (1987).

37. Liggett.

38. These figures may not accurately reflect the incidence of such plans in the economy as a whole, however, since the data examine changes in contracts and therefore may miss two-tier provisions that continue. Bureau of National Affairs, Inc. (1988).

39. Towers, Perrin, Forster, and Crosby.

40. Bureau of National Affairs, Inc. (1988), p. 42.

41. Bureau of National Affairs, Inc. (1987).

42. Towers, Perrin, Forster, and Crosby.

43. Bureau of National Affairs, Inc. (1987).

44. Towers, Perrin, Forster, and Crosby.

45. Walsh.

46. Martin and Peterson.

47. Cappelli and Sherer.

48. Hay Management Associates.

49. Voos (1987) finds similar support among a survey of unionized employers.

50. Strauss.

51. U.S. Department of Labor.

52. Hay Management Associates.

53. Meyer.

54. This material is based on Cappelli and McKersie.

55. Cappelli (1983).

56. Broadening tasks associated with jobs may be more difficult to achieve in production operations, especially assembly lines, where specific tasks occupy workers more or less continually. Even here, gains are possible from substitutions for absent workers, temporary reallocation of workers where operations run at varying capacities, and so on. GM's Delco-Remy plant recently cut its assembly job classifications from 75 to one.

57. Research has yet to validate this argument, and some observers have posited that the need for consensus among team members may actually prolong decision making.

58. Katz, Kochan, and Gobielle.

59. Thacker and Fields.

60. Bureau of National Affairs, Inc. (1988), p. E-7.

61. Cappelli (1985a).

62. The difficulties in changing work rules are illustrated by the efforts of People Express to impose its flexible system of work rules on Frontier Airlines, which it had purchased. Even though the tasks performed were identical at Frontier, the problems of meshing these two systems were so severe that they helped push People to sell Frontier and eventually led to the downfall of People as well.

63. Cherry.

64. See Walton's discussion of "High Commitment" work systems for more detail on such horizontal and vertical changes.

65. Cappelli (1984).

66. Sockell (1985).

67. Bureau of National Affairs, Inc. (1985), p. 1. See also Levin for a critical assessment of ESOPs' effects on firms and employees.

68. See Ross.

69. In many cases, however, even increased corporate investment does not guarantee job security. In the tire industry, for example, some companies met their contractual obligation for new investment in plants but closed them anyway. Cappelli (1985).

70. See *Management Review* for a discussion.
71. See Sockell (1986) for a discussion.
72. Perry (1987).
73. See Kochan, McKersie, and Cappelli.
74. Becker.
75. See Kirkpatrick for examples.
76. The amount of decline depends partly on the measure chosen; per capita hourly earnings fell faster than weekly earnings. Family earnings have held roughly constant, thanks to the increase in two-career couples. See Belous for a discussion.
77. Abowd.
78. As Keynes made clear, underconsumption can be an important cause of macroeconomic instability. Nor do higher profits necessarily lead to increased investment—certainly not unless there is demand for the product.

◆

References

Abowd, J.M. 1987. "Collective Bargaining and the Division of the Value of the Enterprise." Working paper no. 218. Princeton, NJ: Princeton University, Industrial Relations Section.

Argyris, C. 1964. *Integrating the Individual and the Organization*. New York: Wiley.

Becker, B. In press. "Concession Bargaining: The Meaning of Union Gains." *Academy of Management Journal*.

Belous, R. 1985. "Changes in Real Earnings in the U.S." Washington, DC: Congressional Research Service.

Bendix, R. 1956. *Work and Authority in Industry*. New York: Wiley.

Business Week. 1981. "The New Industrial Relations." May 11: 85–98.

Bureau of National Affairs, Inc. 1987. "Two-Tier Wage Systems Still on the Rise." *Daily Labor Report* (February 14): B1–4.

_____. 1988. *Changing Pay Practices: New Developments in Employee Compensation*. Washington, DC: Bureau of National Affairs, Inc.

Cappelli, P. 1983. "Concession Bargaining and the National Economy." *Proceedings of the Industrial Relations Research Association's 35th Annual Meeting*. Madison, WI: Industrial Relations Research Association.

_____. 1985a. "Competitive Pressures and Labor Relations in the Airline Industry." *Industrial Relations* 24 (Fall): 316–338.

_____. 1985b. "Plant-Level Concession Bargaining." *Industrial and Labor Relations Review* 39 (October): 90–104.

_____. 1987. "Employees and Unions: New Tactics and Strategies." In *NYU 40th Annual Conference on Labor*. New York: Matthew Bender Co.

Cappelli, P., and J. Chalykoff. 1986. "The Effects of Management Industrial Relations Strategy: Results of a Recent Survey." *Proceedings of the Industrial Relations Research Association's 38th Annual Meeting*. Madison, WI: Industrial Relations Research Association.

Cappelli, P., and R.B. McKersie, 1987. "Management Strategy and the Redesign of Workrules." *Journal of Management Studies* (September) 24(5): 441–462.

Cappelli, P., and P.D. Sherer. 1990. "Assessing Attitudes under Two-Tier Pay Plans." *Industrial and Labor Relations Review* 43(2): 225–244.

Cherry, R. 1982. "The Development of General Motors' Team-Based Plants." In *The Innovative Organization: Productivity Programs in Action*, ed. R. Zager and M.P. Rosow. New York: Pergamon Press.

Fiorito, J., C. Lowman, and F.D. Nelson. 1987. "The Impact of Human Resource Policies on Union Organizing." *Industrial Relations* 26 (Spring): 113–126.

Freedman, A. 1985. "The New Look in Wage Policy and Employee Relations." New York: The Conference Board.

Freedman, A., and W.E. Fulmer. 1982. "Last Rites for Pattern Bargaining." *Harvard Business Review* 60 (March/April): 30–48.

Freeman, R.B., and M.M. Kleiner. 1990. "The Impact of New Unionization on Wages and Working Conditions." *Journal of Labor Economics* 8(1): 58–525.

Freeman, R.B., and J. Medoff. 1985. *What Do Unions Do?* Boston: Basic Books.

Freiberg, B.J., and W.T. Dickens. 1985. "The Impact of the Runaway Office on Union Certification Elections in Clerical Units." Working paper no. 1693. Cambridge, MA: NBER.

Golden, C.S., and V.D. Parker. 1955. *The Causes of Industrial Peace Under Collective Bargaining*. New York: Harper.

Hackman, J.R., and G.R. Oldham. 1976. "Motivation Through the Design of Work." *Organizational Behavior and Human Performance* 16 (Fall): 250–279.

Hay Management Associates. 1988. "Contingent Compensation Survey." Philadelphia: The Hay Group.

Katz, H.C., T.A. Kochan, and K.R. Gobielle. 1983. "Industrial Relations Performance, Economic Performance, and QWL Programs: An Interplant Analysis." *Industrial Relations and Labor Review* 37 (December): 47–69.

Keynes, J.M. 1965. "General Theory of Employment, Interest & Money." San Diego: Harcourt Brace Jovanovich.

Kirkpatrick, D. 1986. "What Givebacks Can Get You." *Fortune* (November 24): 60.

Kochan, T.A., R.B. McKersie, and P. Cappelli. 1984. "Strategic Choice and Industrial Relations Theory." *Industrial Relations* 23 (Winter): 16–39.

Levin, W.R. 1985. "The False Promise of Worker Capitalism: Congress and the Leveraged Employee Stock Ownership Plan." *Yale Law Journal* 1: 148–173.

Liggett, M.H. 1987. "The Two-Tiered Labor-Management Agreement and the Duty of Fair Representation." *Labor Law Journal* 4: 236–242.

Management Review. 1986. "Should Unions Have a Seat on the Board?" February: 56–59.

Martin, J.E., and M.M. Peterson. 1987. "Two-Tier Wage Structure: Implications for Equity Theory." *Academy of Management Journal* (June): 297–305.

Meyer, H.H. 1975. "The Pay for Performance Dilemma." *Organizational Dynamics* 3: 39–50.

Miles, G.L., and J. Hoerr. 1985. "Desperate Steelworkers." *Business Week* (December 30): 54–55.

Miscimarra, P.A. 1983. *The NLRB and Managerial Discretion: Plant Closings, Relocations, Subcontracting, and Automation.* Philadelphia: Industrial Research Unit.

Mitchell, D.J.B. 1987. "The Share Economy and Industrial Relations." *Industrial Relations* 26 (Winter): 1–17.

Northrup, H.R. 1964. *Boulwarism: The Labor Relations Policies of the General Electric Company: Their Implications for Public Policy and Management Action.* Ann Arbor, MI: University of Michigan, Bureau of Industrial Relations.

———. 1983. "The New Employee Relations Climate in Airlines." *Industrial and Labor Relations Review* 36 (January): 167–182.

Perry, C. 1986. *Deregulation and the Decline of the Unionized Trucking Industry.* Philadelphia: Industrial Research Unit.

———. 1987. *Corporate Campaigns.* Philadelphia: Industrial Research Unit.

Perry, C., and P. Cappelli. 1988. "Labor Relations in Telecommunications." Working paper. Philadelphia: Industrial Research Unit.

Perry, C., A.M. Kramer, and T.J. Schneider. 1982. *Operating During Strikes.* Philadelphia: Industrial Research Unit.

Ross, I. 1986. "Labor's Man on Wall Street." *Fortune* (December 22): 123.

Sockell, D. 1985. "Attitudes, Behavior, and Employee Ownership: Some Preliminary Data." *Industrial Relations* 24 (Winter): 130–138.

———. 1986. "The Scope of Mandatory Bargaining: A Critique and a Proposal." *Industrial and Labor Relations Review* 40 (October): 19–34.

Strauss, G. 1987. "Participatory and Gainsharing Systems: History and Hope." Working paper no. OBIR17. Berkeley, CA: University of California at Berkeley, School of Business.

Thacker, J.W., and M.W. Fields. 1987. "Union Involvement in Quality-of-Work-life Efforts: An Investigation." *Personnel Psychology* 40 (Spring): 97–111.

Towers, Perrin, Forster, and Crosby. "Survey of Company Experiences With Two-Tier Wage Plans." Washington, DC: Towers, Perrin, Forster, and Crosby.

U.S. Department of Labor, Bureau of Labor-Management Relations and Cooperative Programs. 1986. "Exploratory Investigations of Pay for Knowledge Systems." Washington, DC: Bureau of Labor-Management Relations.

Verma, A., and T.A. Kochan. 1984. "The Growth and Nature of the Nonunion Sector Within a Firm." In *Challenges and Choices Facing American Labor*, ed. T.A. Kochan. Cambridge, MA: MIT Press.

Voos, P.B. 1987. "Managerial Perceptions of the Economic Impact of Labor Relations Programs." *Industrial and Labor Relations Review* 40(2): 195–208.

————. 1987. "Managerial Perceptions of the Economic Impact of Labor Relations Programs." *Industrial and Labor Relations Review* 40 (2) (January): 195–205.

Walsh, D.J. 1988. "Accounting for the Two-Tier Explosion in the Airline Industry." *Industrial and Labor Relations Review* 42(1): 50–62.

Walton, R.E. 1985. "From Control to Commitment in the Workplace." *Harvard Business Review* (March/April): 76–84.

Weiler, P. 1983. "Promises to Keep: Securing Workers' Rights to Self-Organize Under the NLRB." *Harvard Law Review* (June): 1769–1827.

———— ♦ ————

$$\diamondsuit$$

4.7

Workplace Safety and Employee Health

Judy D. Olian

The range of responsibilities of managers of HR has undergone several dramatic changes over the last few years. One area in which changes are most evident is employee health, safety, and wellness management. In the workplace, the types, magnitude, and complexity of decisions related to health, safety, and wellness are unprecedented and continue to evolve.

This chapter addresses the key factors responsible for changes in managing workplace wellness issues. It describes practices and issues which exemplify these changes, relevant research evidence, laws, and court decisions. The chapter ends with a discussion of interventions that can improve worker health and workplace safety.

Present Trends

The rising managerial preoccupation with health issues has paralleled the sharp increase in health care costs in recent years. In 1986, the United States spent 11.1 percent of its gross national product (GNP) on health care,[1] compared to 6 percent of a far smaller GNP in 1965.[2] That means that over 11 cents per dollar spent in America is for some form of physician or hospital services, drugs, or other health care needs. The total health care bill for 1986 was approximately $500 billion, or about $1,926 per man, woman, and child in this country. Over the last 10 years, health care costs have risen at almost double the rate of inflation. In 1990, estimated health costs will amount to $750 billion annually or 12 percent of the GNP.[3]

All but 37 million Americans have some form of health insurance, primarily through their present or past place of employment. As a result, employers have been directly affected by the rising costs of health care. Between 1975 and 1987, an employer's dollar cost of health care delivery (life, death, hospital, surgical, medical, and major medical) more than tripled, from $582 to $1,985 (or from 5.2 percent of payroll to 9.7 percent). In contrast, the total cost of fringe benefit packages just doubled between 1975 and 1985, from $3984 to $8166 (or from 35.4 percent of payroll to 37.7 percent).[4]

However, the rising costs of benefits alone cannot explain the growing preoccupation with health and safety as a managerial issue. There are several other contributing factors. Consider the following illustrations:

A railroad engineer smokes a marijuana cigarette and shortly thereafter, the train which he is operating crashes into another train, causing sixteen deaths and almost 200 injuries among passengers of his train. As a result of the crash, both trains are derailed on a route used heavily by freight and passenger trains. It takes two days to clear the tracks.

An employee, who on occasion has sought company supported emotional counseling, is put on administrative leave until a sexual harassment suit brought against him is cleared up. Two days before the charge is scheduled for hearing, the employee enters the company headquarters with several weapons concealed in his clothing. He proceeds to open fire on any employees encountered in the hallway. About 20 are left dead or wounded.

During the early hours of the afternoon, a manager notices that one of his employees appears intoxicated. He questions the employee who freely admits to drinking several shots of liquor over lunch. The manager tells the employee to go home since company policy forbids working while under the influence of alcohol. The manager accompanies the employee to his parked car and, satisfied with the employee's repeated assurances that he can drive, urges the employee to go straight home, rest up, and return to work the next day. A short while later the manager learns that the employee was involved in a serious car accident in which the driver of the other car was killed.

Several maintenance engineers in a pharmaceutical plant are unaware of pressure building up in the pipes transmitting a particularly potent chemical. The pipes burst, causing a massive fire in the plant. The burning chemical creates a lethal cloud that spreads for several miles around the plant's perimeter. Hundreds of people die and many hundreds more are injured from the burning heat and from the toxic effects of the chemical cloud.

An employee with a history of alcohol problems is the master of an oil super tanker. The tanker runs into a reef creating a large tear in its hull. Ten million gallons of crude oil flood the waters which house some of the most fertile breeding grounds for fish and wildlife. Many of the fish and wildlife die and breeding patterns are affected for years to come. Local fishing communities lose their primary economic livelihood.

In each of these cases, the employer is a partner—though often unwilling and indirect—to a horrible tragedy because of certain actions taken (or avoided) by company representatives. From a moral and ethical standpoint, such involvement is likely to be extremely troubling to an employer. The legal ramifications and the potential for extremely costly liability suits will also haunt the employers years after these incidents. Finally, the publicity surrounding such events may fundamentally change how consumers, shareholders, lenders, potential applicants, and employees perceive the company and what it stands for.

These are hypothetical illustrations of extreme crises. When such crises happen, managers must deal with an ever-expanding set of issues associated—directly and indirectly—with the mental and physical well-being of their work force. Beyond cost, trauma, and liability reasons, managers are increasingly involved in health and safety-related decisions because of federal, state, and local statutory requirements directly affecting activities in these areas.

Employees also see the workplace as a major contributor to their physical and psychological well-being over the short and long term. As a result, they are concerned about the strategies chosen for managing workplace health and safety issues, seek to participate in decisions related to workplace wellness, and demand safe and healthy work processes and practices as a working condition. In short, managing work safety and health has emerged in the last decade as a major and complex part of managers' jobs.

Impetus for Workplace Health and Safety Programs

Several contextual and organizational factors have played an important part in increasing managers' direct involvement in worker health, safety, and wellness policies and programs. In turn, these practices can have significant effects on key organizational outcomes. Figure 1 describes the key factors driving managerial implementation of health- and safety-related interventions. We discuss these factors in the next section.

External Conditions

A number of contextual features have contributed to the salience of workplace health and safety management issues. In some cases, the external factors *drive* organizational health and safety-related decisions as part of a general societal trend toward greater health and safety consciousness. In other cases, contextual factors like laws and regulations *result* from organizational practices or shortfalls in managing health and safety.

Societal Concerns

The Bureau of Labor Statistics (BLS) estimates that in 1984, 5.75 million workers experienced work-related deaths or disabling injuries in establishments with more than 11 employees.[5] The National Institute of Occupational Health projects that about 10 million people will be injured each year in work-related incidents, a figure representing 7 percent of the total labor force. Each workday, a worker is injured every 1.5 seconds and a fatality occurs every 12 minutes.[6] In addition, approximately 390,000 occupational illnesses and 100,000 fatalities are caused each year by diseases linked to workplace conditions.[7] The BLS estimates that 98 percent of lost workdays are due to work-related injuries while the remaining 2 percent are due to illnesses.

The opportunity or indirect costs of occupational injuries and illnesses also are very large. For the entire American work force, the total number of lost workdays due to injuries is between 60 to 70 million annually.[8] This loss is the annual productivity equivalent of about 280,000 full-time workers. Estimates of the direct and indirect costs of work injuries vary, depending on the value placed

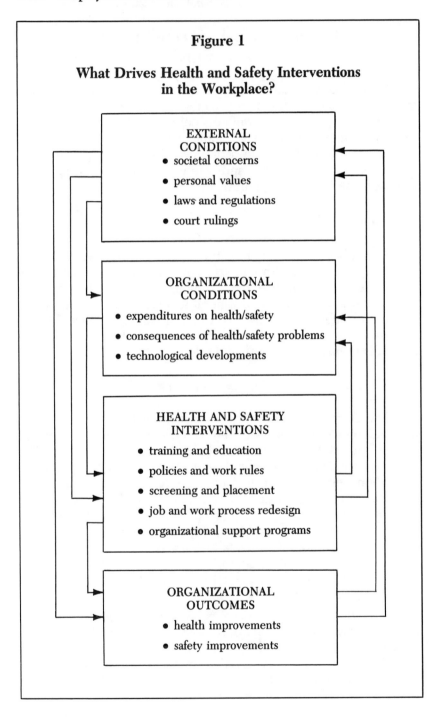

Figure 1

What Drives Health and Safety Interventions in the Workplace?

EXTERNAL
CONDITIONS
- societal concerns
- personal values
- laws and regulations
- court rulings

ORGANIZATIONAL
CONDITIONS
- expenditures on health/safety
- consequences of health/safety problems
- technological developments

HEALTH AND SAFETY
INTERVENTIONS
- training and education
- policies and work rules
- screening and placement
- job and work process redesign
- organizational support programs

ORGANIZATIONAL
OUTCOMES
- health improvements
- safety improvements

on human life and the weight assigned to indirect effects of work-place behaviors and reactions. The Occupational Safety and Health Administration places a value of $3.5 million on each life saved through safety measures.[9] This value considerably exceeds the $200,000 to $500,000 figure generally used by economists and other government agencies like the National Highway Traffic Safety Administration or the Consumer Product Safety Commission.[10] The average cost to an employer of a lost workday due to injury was $14,000 in 1978. Cumulating this expense across the total economy, the National Safety Council estimated that in 1984, the cost of work injuries was $33 billion.[11]

The consequences of shortfalls in safety and health manage-ment often spread beyond the workplace to members of the commu-nity at large. Cases in point are the Union Carbide tragedy in Bhopal, India with over 2,000 fatalities; the potential for community devastation as a result of Three Mile Island; the Chase, Maryland train crash which killed 16 passengers and injured close to 200; and the Exxon Valdez oil spill which caused wildlife devastation and the loss of community livelihoods.

These figures and incidents clearly illustrate the significant impact workplace safety and health practices can have on the quality of life of each member of the affected community. Public actions have resulted from concerns about the morality of certain practices, extensive publicity surrounding these incidents and issues, and the large direct and opportunity costs of mismanagement of health and safety in the workplace. In light of such concerns, communities have become increasingly vocal in their attempts to monitor and mini-mize the potential for work-related injuries, illnesses, and fatalities, and to inflict penalties on employers who fail to act responsibly. At least in part, managers' increased involvement in safety and well-ness management policies and practices reflects the public interest in these issues.

Employee Values

Attitudes toward health and wellness have changed. The baby boom generation because of its size, age, and earning power has a disproportionate influence on social trends. Baby boomers, some-times known as the "yuppie generation," have shaped social attitudes toward a greater preoccupation with wellness and preven-tive health. Undoubtedly, the persuasive evidence linking life-styles and life expectancies has encouraged this thinking.

As a result, Americans are paying much more attention to what they eat, how they exercise, and what they breathe. Since most Americans spend close to half their waking hours at work, concerns about healthy habits and life-styles have permeated the work environment. In fact, many employees see their employer as a key ally in preventing ill health, extending life expectancies, and improving the quality of their lives. Conveniently, many employers share parallel interests in preventive health care because of moral obligations to their employees and because of the productivity returns and savings in health-care and replacement costs.

Companies have responded to changes in employee values by offering a variety of wellness programs. Many of these benefits are available on company premises. Almost two-thirds of American workplaces with 50 or more employees have some health promotion activities, including smoking cessation programs, alcohol and drug education, weight reduction, blood pressure, nutrition and diet control, stress management, and exercise. [12]

Another manifestation of the changing personal values of American workers is their increasing assertiveness in achieving and maintaining safe work environments and practices. Consider the following illustrations:

- 82 percent of the 150,000 collective bargaining agreements in the United States contained some reference to health and safety, [13] up from 65 percent in 1971. [14]

- In 1988, 48 percent of contracts referred to the creation of joint labor-management safety committees, up from 31 percent in 1971. [15]

- The Supreme Court endorsed workers' rights to walk off the job and suffer no adverse employment actions if, in the employee's opinion, the conditions of work were imminently hazardous. [16]

- The right to access information about health and safety issues is steadily expanding, e.g., information about hazardous products in the workplace, workplace safety records, and personal medical records.

Managers' involvement in safety and wellness issues has derived in part from the changing values and demands of their employees. The presumption is that workplaces characterized by a high level of health and safety consciousness will have a relative advantage in attracting and retaining valued employees. This advantage has become especially important given the current and projected labor shortages in many segments of the economy.

Federal, State, and Local Statutes

Various pieces of legislation have an impact on managers' decisions in the areas of safety and health management. Six areas of statutory regulation are particularly relevant.

The Occupational Safety and Health Act (OSHA). OSHA imposes on employers a general requirement for safe working conditions. It also strives to achieve safe working practices through establishing equipment standards and permissible levels of substances, heat, or noise in the work environment.

While OSHA is typically administered at the federal level, it allows states to establish health and safety monitoring programs, as long as these programs are at least as effective as the federally administered program. As of 1984, 23 states plus the Virgin Islands and Puerto Rico had received federal approval to run their own occupational safety and health programs.[17]

The federal and state programs cover most private-sector employees in the United States. For a small number of occupational groups, safety and health is regulated by some other agency. For example, coal miners are protected through the Mine Safety and Health Act, while safety standards for certain railroad employees are enforced by the Federal Railroad Administration.

The Vocational Rehabilitation Act. A second major health regulatory requirement is the Vocational Rehabilitation Act, which covers employers with federal contracts worth in excess of $2,500. The law protects individuals with bona fide handicaps against employment discrimination, as long as they are capable of performing the job. Such individuals are entitled to reasonable accommodation in the workplace in terms of its physical layout, equipment, and the work procedures and practices. Virtually all states afford handicapped persons similar protections.

Since its passage, the federal law has protected employees with a variety of syndromes, including paraplegics, former alcohol and drug abusers, rehabilitated mental patients, and individuals with sight and hearing impairments. More recently, the Supreme Court found that the Vocational Rehabilitation Act covered individuals with contagious diseases that cannot be spread through casual contact in the workplace.[18] While the disease in this case was tuberculosis, many observers view the ruling as precedent setting. In particular, employees who have contracted Acquired Immune Deficiency Syndrome (AIDS) appear likely to receive protection under the federal Vocational Rehabilitation Act. Over half of the states have indirectly extended handicapped protections to persons with AIDS through judicial or regulatory interpretations. Five states (Florida, Iowa, Missouri, Rhode Island, and Washington) have explicitly named AIDS as a protected handicap under the state law.[19]

Hazard Communication Regulations. A third category of regulations affecting workplace health and safety concerns notification about potential work hazards. In August 1987, the Occupational Safety and Health Administration issued a comprehensive hazard communication standard covering almost every employer in the country. Under the standard, a warning label must appear on each container that includes any amount of about 2,300 hazardous substances. About 34 million workers in almost 4 million establishments now have this "right-to-know."[20] Workers must also be trained to use substances safely. The hazards communication standard largely preempts state and local right-to-know laws. As of 1983, 16 states and several cities had passed right-to-know laws, some of them quite stringent.[21]

Proposed legislation now before the House (HR 3067) and Senate (S582) would impose even greater communication requirements on employers. The High Risk Notification and Prevention Act would require employers to notify employees working with dangerous chemicals and other substances that they face a high risk of cancer and other diseases. The legislation establishes the Department of Health and Human Services as executor of the act. Employers would be required, also, to provide medical monitoring programs for these employees. Passage of the act could potentially require employers to write individual letters to some 100,000 to 300,000 employees annually.

Drug Testing Laws. Drug testing legislation is the most recent entrant into the health and safety regulatory arena. In the aftermath of the report of the President's Commission on Crime, President Reagan issued Executive Order 12564 in 1986, mandating drug testing for over 1.1 million federal workers. In accordance with this order, various government agencies have issued regulations requiring the random testing of selected agency employees. The agencies include the Departments of Agriculture, Defense, Transportation, Customs, Health and Human Services, Justice, Interior, the Immigration and Naturalization Service, and the Executive Office of the President. The Department of Transportation guidelines also require random testing of commercial operators of trucks and buses. Unions representing employee groups have challenged these regulations and, in a number of cases, they have been somewhat successful in obtaining at least temporary injunctions against the drug testing procedures.[22] In addition, the Anti-Drug Abuse Act of 1988 requires government contractors to comply with "drug free workplace" rules.[23] Seven provisions are specified including the requirements to establish clear work rules and penalties associated with drug abuse, to set up drug awareness programs and rehabilitation services, and to notify the government of every employee convicted of drug use.

At the state level, as of August 1989, at least 14 states (California, Connecticut, Iowa, Louisiana, Maine, Maryland, Minnesota, Montana, Nebraska, North Carolina, Oregon, Rhode Island, Utah, and Vermont) have passed statutes prescribing certain conditions under which drug testing is permissible.[24] Among the conditions specified in the various statutes are privacy, confidentiality, and chain of custody protections; requirements for state certified laboratories and confirmatory testing; and limitations on required submission to a drug test.

Consumer and Environmental Protection Standards. A final class of regulations affecting health and safety management practices extend beyond the workplace in their intended scope of protections. They are directed toward preserving the environment, the community, and consumers from potential hazards of business negligence. Based on the authorization provided in nine key pieces of environmental legislation, the Environmental Protection Agency (EPA) has responsibility in six areas of pollution: air, water, solid waste, toxic substances, radiation, and noise. In concert with state and local governments, EPA specifies standards of permissible levels in each of these areas and monitors compliance. The Food and Drug Administration was established to protect the public against unsafe drugs and medical devices and to regulate hazards in foods and cosmetics. Safety standards and hazard notification for consumer products are set and monitored by the Consumer Protection Agency.

All these regulations impose costs on employers. For example, the recently implemented hazard communication standard is estimated to cost employers $687 million in its first year and more than $200 million annually thereafter.[25] Opponents of the High Risk Notification and Prevention bill estimate that its price tag for businesses would total up to $6 billion a year,[26] or $33 to $50 per employee.[27] Pollution controls to abate toxic substance pollution amount to $40 billion annually.[28] From a more macro-perspective, one study found that environmental costs had lowered growth by 1.8 percent between 1967 and 1975.[29] About one quarter of that figure, or 0.42 percent was attributable to various types of health and safety regulation. However, it is unclear whether this estimate reflects the potential savings of health improvements as a result of regulation.

Regulatory bodies at various levels are focusing attention on an expanding number of safety, health, and wellness issues. By involving themselves directly in managing health and safety, managers—as pragmatists—are responding proactively to the realities of regulatory oversight.

Court Rulings

A number of recent court decisions have illustrated the significance of workplace health and safety management practices. These court decisions reflect diverse issues, including employer liability for safety violations, employee privacy rights, employment actions concerning communicable diseases, drug testing policies, worker compensation awards, and rights of smokers versus nonsmokers.

Employer Liability. In terms of employer liability, a case in Illinois illustrates the extent to which managers can be held liable for their safety management practices. Three corporate officers of a film recovery plant—the president, the plant manager, and a foreman—were found guilty of first-degree murder as well as 14 counts of reckless misconduct for the death of an employee exposed to toxic levels of liquid cyanide. The judge held that the corporate officers were fully aware of the hazardous working conditions, yet chose to withhold the information from employees and to correct nothing in the workplace. As such, the defendants were held individually responsible for the murder of an employee. This case marks the first time members of the corporate chain of command were found individually liable for physical harms or deaths suffered by employees. In the past, corporate structure provided a protective shield against such charges since a firm could disburse insurance payments or name itself, and not individual managers, as defendant in cases. In this case, *Illinois v. Film Recovery Systems*, each defendant received a 25 year sentence and a fine of $10,000. The case was remanded for a new trial by the Illinois Supreme Court.[30]

Drug Testing. The scope of employee privacy rights is also evolving through decisions rendered in a number of court cases. The Fourth Amendment of the Constitution protects all citizens against unreasonable search and seizures, provides a right to be left alone, and prohibits invasive activities by the government without justification. The privacy issue comes up when government agencies propose workplace drug tests or other types of medical examinations. While not entirely consistent with each other, most appellate courts have concurred that mandatory urinalysis of public employees violates the intent of the Fourth Amendment; that is, urinalysis constitutes a search into the individual's private life. However, most cases before the courts today present the dilemma of choosing the government's compelling interest in the search versus the individual's legitimate expectation of privacy.

The 1988 term of the Supreme Court rendered two decisions on drug testing issues. In one case, the justices affirmed the government's right to require mandatory drug tests of all railroad employees involved in certain accidents.[31] While drug tests did infringe upon individuals' privacy rights in the absence of particularized suspicion, the Court deemed the government's interest as compelling. In the second case, the Court ruled that a mandatory drug test required of customs agents seeking promotion was justifiable under selected job conditions.[32] The majority decision allowed drug tests of agents in the front lines of drug interdiction and of agents carrying firearms. While the decision compromised individual privacy rights, the government's compelling interest, given the nature of agents' jobs, outweighed individuals' expectations of privacy. A decision regarding drug tests of agents handling classified materials was remanded to the lower court.

Far fewer court rulings have been rendered regarding private-sector drug testing. While inconsistencies across decisions are evident, the 1988 Supreme Court decision in *Conrail v. Railway Executives Association*[33] suggested that introduction of drug testing into a workplace constitutes a minor dispute if the action is justifiable within the context of the parties' collective bargaining agreement. A minor dispute in the railroad industry is subject to mandatory and binding arbitration before the National Railway Adjustment Board and does not require collective bargaining between the parties. To the extent that Conrail v. RLEA might generalize to other cases, this ruling suggests employers can introduce unilaterally nonfrivolous drug testing programs without going through the collective bargaining process, even when a contract is in effect.

Even outside the protective structure of union-management relations, the courts have been willing to impose restrictions on drug testing programs. For example, in the first decision against private sector pre-employment drug testing, the Matthew Bender Publishing Company was enjoined from testing applicants for drugs because the policy violated California's constitutional right to privacy.[34]

Another aspect of drug tests that may render them vulnerable to legal challenge is their potential adverse impact on minority group members. Some highly controversial evidence suggests that melanin, a pigment more frequently found in dark-skinned rather than light-skinned individuals, breaks down into small elements that react, in tests, similar to marijuana components.[35] If this finding is accurate, drug tests could yield higher rates of positive results for certain minority groups—regardless of drug intake—because of an inherent validity problem in the tests.

Certain minority groups also have higher proportions of drug abusers and as a result, these minorities may test positive for drugs at a greater frequency than other groups. For example, in *New York City Transit Authority v. Beazer*,[36] defense attorneys showed that 62 to 65 percent of all rehabilitating heroine users were black or Hispanic. Under the Civil Rights Act and the Uniform Guidelines on Employment Testing, employment tests that create a differential impact on protected groups must serve a compelling business necessity and have job-related validity. Except in potentially hazardous job situations where business necessity prevails over all other factors, drug tests do not satisfy the validity requirement. No data to date establish a consistent relationship between levels of chemical traces in urine samples and levels of performance impairment. Too many individual differences and contextual factors contaminate the relationship. Thus, drug testing programs could be attacked—potentially successfully—by protected groups within the framework of the Civil Rights Act and *prima facie* arguments of disparate impact.

Other Privacy Issues. Substance abuse is not the only health matter raising concerns over privacy. In *Bratt v. IBM*,[37] the U.S. Court of Appeals in Boston held in favor of an employee who claimed his privacy rights were compromised when a few managerial employees were told of his emotional problems. The judges felt that this revelation of a "private fact" was not justified by the employer's business interests.

Judges have already made some decisions influencing employer behaviors toward individuals with communicable diseases. As indicated in the earlier discussion of the *Arline* decision, employees with a communicable disease that cannot be transmitted via casual contact are considered handicapped, with all the employment protections associated with that legal status. Legal observers feel that *Arline* generalizes to employees who have contracted the AIDS virus, whose disease symptoms are not severe enough to prevent them from working. *Arline* has certain implications for employment practices. For example, employees with AIDS are protected in their right to keep their jobs regardless of co-worker preferences, employer concerns over health costs, or minor work accommodations needed by the employee because of the illness. It also suggests that the practice of using AIDS antibody test results for employment decisions is not legally defensible.[38] Even if such tests are not prohibited by the relevant state or local authorities, the implications of *Arline* appear to bar exclusionary decisions based on future probabilities of illness.

Workers' Compensation. Recent trends in workers' compensation awards are changing health and safety management practices. Stress-related awards now account for nearly 14 percent of occupational disease claims, up from less than 5 percent just 8 years ago.[39] Workers' compensation is now routinely offered to employees who lose jobs and suffer emotional distress following the event. Workers' compensation also has been awarded in cases of occupational disease linked to toxic exposure,[40] and for certain adverse physiological reactions, such as eye strain, to VDTs.

Smoking in the workplace forms a final area in which court decisions have impacted the health and safety imperatives of managers. A Washington court ruled recently that an employee can sue her employer for negligence for failure to provide a healthy work environment free of tobacco smoke.[41] In earlier cases, a smoke-sensitive employee was awarded unemployment compensation benefits after voluntarily quitting a job because smoke at work adversely affected her health;[42] another smoke-sensitive person successfully sued for damages for being terminated as soon as she attempted to enforce the state Clean Indoor Air Act;[43] and yet another smoke-sensitive employee was awarded workers' compensation for "flu-like" symptoms suffered when surrounded by smokers on her job.[44]

These illustrations point to numerous health- and safety-related areas in which court decisions have favored employees, sometimes at great personal and financial costs to employers. Since the trend toward litigating health and safety questions is expected to continue, managers will find it difficult to divorce themselves from these issues.

Organizational Conditions

Up to this point, the discussion has focused on contextual factors mandating or encouraging managerial involvement in health and safety management. In addition to these factors, organizations have more immediate reasons to explain their concern for workers' health and safety. Several financial and technological features of organizations have a direct impact on the level of managerial involvement in health and safety.

Safety Expenditures

Employers make large expenditures to prevent workplace disease and injury. Some employer efforts in this direction are mandatory, while others are voluntary. The Business Roundtable did a study of 48 companies making up over 25 percent of the manufacturing sector in the United States.[45] In 1977, these companies had $26 billion in capital expenditures and almost $17 billion in after tax profits. In relation to those figures, the cost of providing safe working conditions as required by six regulatory agencies was $2.7 billion or almost 16 percent of after-tax profits. McGraw-Hill surveyed the capital expenditures of businesses between 1970 and 1981 and found that $43 billion was spent on safety issues.[46]

Cost estimates are also available for specific safety initiatives implemented by or proposed for industry. For example, the cost of implementing the vinyl chloride standard promulgated by OSHA is estimated at $250 million.[47] The estimated cost of engineering controls to limit industrial noise levels to 85 decibels is $19.4 billion, while using personal protective gear would be substantially cheaper at $2.4 billion.[48] The estimated effect of OSHA's cotton dust standard is $2 billion according to industry representatives versus $656.5 million using OSHA's figures.[49]

Owners of businesses must assure that no health hazards or toxins spread from the workplace into the broader environment. The Council on Environmental Quality estimated the combined capital, operating, and maintenance costs to industry of regulations designed to control various sources and consequences of environmental pollution.[50] In 1979, the cost to American businesses was $36.9 billion, while in 1988, pollution abatement expenditures were estimated at $69 billion (in 1979 dollars).

Health-Care Delivery Costs

Beyond assuring safe and healthy work environments, most employers also spend substantial amounts on the delivery of health care and benefits to their employees and, sometimes, to ex-employees and retirees. Figure 2 shows the rise in health care costs against changes in the consumer price index (CPI) between 1981 and 1986.

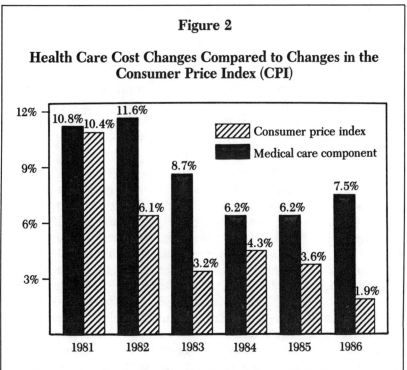

Figure 2

Health Care Cost Changes Compared to Changes in the Consumer Price Index (CPI)

Consumer price index

Medical care component

Source: Reprinted from *Monthly Labor Review*, U.S. Department of Labor, Bureau of Labor Statistics, 110, no. 2, February 1987, p. 79.

Figures for 1987 reflect that health care costs represent 46 percent of corporate operating profits, compared to 9 percent of corporate operating profits in 1965. Several reasons explain the inflation in health care costs. Doctors' fees, which make up 20 percent of total medical costs, are expected to continue increasing at a rate far greater than the changing CPI.[52] Malpractice insurance rate hikes also will keep adding to employers' medical bills. Scientific and technological advances have increased the cost of treating a given illness because of the vast range of options now available to physicians. Another factor adding to an employer's cost of providing health care is the price of prescription drugs, which increased an average of 9 percent in 1986 (versus a 1.9 percent rise in the CPI).

Employer expenditures have escalated for yet another reason. The range of health care services now offered to employees is unprecedented. Table 1 presents a list of the most commonly covered health care items in establishments employing at least 250 workers for 1982 and 1985. The data indicate that in firms of this size, most employees have access to a wide variety and increasing number of employer-subsidized health care benefits. Employers also are increasingly likely to cover nontraditional health care items, thus explaining some of the increase in health care costs. For example, Prudential Insurance Co. estimates that five years ago, reimbursable mental health claims, including drug and alcohol abuse cases, accounted for 8 percent of its claims. These claims now account for 20 percent of Prudential's medical claim coverage, making mental health services the fastest growing component of Prudential's medical reimbursement plan.[53]

The increasing breadth of health benefits is partly due to the growing number of work-related syndromes. For example, employers (and their insurers) routinely compensate employees, ex-employees, or their survivors for the psychological and physical consequences of work-related stress. The National Council on Compensation Insurance notes that stress accounts for nearly 14 percent of occupational disease claims, up from less than 5 percent in 1979.[54] A recent twist on the stress syndrome is "technostress," the adverse physical and psychological reactions experienced by users of VDTs. Individuals experiencing technostress have been awarded workers' compensation and temporary disability benefits.[55] Other syndromes now covered through workplace health benefits are the cumulative effects of workplace toxins, or chronic and terminal diseases for which new treatments and technologies are available.

Table 1

Percentage of Employees Receiving Benefits in Medium and Large Establishments, 1982 and 1985*

Benefit	1982	1985	Change
Accident/sickness insurance	51	52	+1
Noncontributory accident sickness insurance	41	43	+2
Long term disability	43	48	+5
Noncontributory longterm disability	33	38	+5
Health insurance	97	96	−1
Noncontributory health insurance	71	61	−10
Hospital/surgical	97	96	−1
Mental health care	96	95	−1
Private duty nursing	91	91	0
Dental	66	73	+7
Extended care facility	60	64	+4
Home health care	NA	54	NA
Vision	21	34	+13
In-house infirmary	NA	46	NA
Sick leave	67	67	0

*Excludes firms with fewer than 250 employees.

Sources: Adapted from *Statistical Abstract of the United States 1984*, 104th Edition, Table No. 722, p. 437; *Statistical Abstract of the United States 1987*, 107th Edition, Table No. 687, p. 406, Washington, D.C.: U.S. Department of Commerce, Bureau of the Census.

The rising number of employee assistance programs (EAPs) exemplifies the trend toward an expansion of employer-provided health benefits. EAPs typically offer a wide variety of preventive, counseling, and rehabilitation services. Today, over one quarter of the work force participates in at least 5000 employer-supported EAPs.[56] The increasing popularity of EAPs also reflects their presumed cost effectiveness. Proponents claim that every dollar an employer spends on an EAP is more than justified by the return in employee health and performance improvements. For example, Control Data Corporation reported a $4 to $6 return for every $1 spent on EAP services and the U.S. Postal Service estimates a savings of $5 per $1 allocated to its EAP.[58]

Health care management is reflected in the bottom line. In 1986, Chrysler announced that its car models cost $275 more because of health care benefits for employees while Safeway Stores reported that health care costs over the last two years exceeded their after-tax profits.[59] By the same token, cost savings due to improvements in worker health and safety also affect the bottom line and can add to the competitive advantage of the employer. These bottom-line implications prove very persuasive to managers and promote direct managerial involvement in strategic and practical decisions on health and safety matters.

Consequences of Health and Safety Problems

Workplace wellness and safety practices can have very significant effects on important organizational outcomes. The following discussion examines some of the evidence favoring employer interventions to address health matters.

Drug and Alcohol Abuse. Relative to nonabusers, a drug-dependent employee will have, on average, 4 times as many accidents, 2.5 times as many absences, 4 times the probability of filing a workers' compensation claim, and 3 times as many health claims.[60]

Drug abuse entails other, less quantifiable adverse consequences. Experts agree that drug-dependent employees are more likely than others to have strained co-worker relations, engage in theft of company and co-worker property to support their habit, and increasingly slide into irresponsible behavior and poor decision-making patterns as work takes a back seat to drug use.[61] Estimates suggest that chemically dependent workers function at 66 percent of their work potential. However, many of these estimates of drug abuse consequences are provided by the deliverers of drug treatment programs, not employers.[62]

Similar negative organizational consequences are associated with alcohol abuse. Average annual health care costs in families with an alcoholic member are higher than in families with no alcoholic present—$207 versus $107 per person, respectively.[63] In any given year, an employee with alcohol problems is likely to have:

- 3.8 to 8.3 more incidents of absenteeism than normal,

- 2 to 3 times the number of industrial accidents,

- 2 to 4 times as many on-the-job injuries, and

- 4 to 6 times the number of injuries off the job.[64]

Preventive Health Care. Encouraging workers to engage in safe and healthy lifestyles and to take preventive health measures has an impact on organizational indices. For example:

- Persons who are not regular exercisers (at least 1.5 miles vigorous walking 4 times a week) have 114 percent more health claims, 30 percent more inpatient days, and 41 percent more health claims over $5,000 than regular exercisers.

- People who weigh more than 30 percent above their ideal weight have 11 percent more health claims, 45 percent more inpatient days, and 48 percent more health claims over $5,000 than persons who are less than 20 percent over their ideal weight.

- People who wear safety belts less than 25 percent of the time have about 113 percent of the health claims of those who wear safety belts at least 75 percent of the time, and average 54 percent more hospital inpatient days.

- People with high blood pressure have 11 percent more health claims, 16 percent more inpatient days, and 68 percent more claims over $5,000 than those with normal blood pressure levels.

- Heavy smokers (one or more packs a day) have 118 percent more health claims and 25 percent more inpatient hospital stays than nonsmokers.[65]

Smoking. Related to smoking consequences in the workplace, the Department of Health and Human Services estimates that smoking accounts for 19 percent of all lost workdays, while the surgeon general reports a 35 to 45 percent higher than normal level of absenteeism among smokers.[66] Estimates of time lost on the job due to the act of smoking (hunting for cigarettes, lighting up, puffing) vary from a low of 8 minutes a day[67] to 15 to 30 minutes per hour.[68] The high estimate was provided by a general contractor in Seattle, Washington who had to fire a dry wall craftsman who lost up to 30 minutes each hour to his smoking habit.[69]

The American Council on Life Insurance estimates that each smoker adds $500 a year to an employer's cleaning and replacement bill and forces an air conditioning system to produce the equivalent of $3,000 in extra output. The Merle Norman Cosmetics Co. figured savings of $13,500 in cleaning fees the first year it banned smoking at employee workstations. ARCO calculated losses of $3 million in annual replacement costs for the 32 (out of 39,000) employees who die each year from smoking.[70] While precise figures are lacking, productivity costs undoubtedly result from strained working relationships when smokers' and non-smokers' interests clash, or when smokers suffer from withdrawal while adapting to nonsmoking policies in the workplace. Nonsmoking policies and incentives can benefit everyone. Employee health improvements translate into preferred rate discounts for the company, which can cut 10 to 15 percent off health insurance premiums. There are statutes on the books in at least 23 states on the issue of smoking in the workplace.[71]

AIDS. Organizational policies and behaviors towards workers with AIDS can have significant consequences on managers and employees. Managers often deal with worker reactions when a member of the work team has AIDS or is HIV positive (i.e., is an AIDS carrier but has no disease symptoms). While fears of contagion are unjustified given current medical knowledge, co-worker emotions and behaviors might still be affected. For example, temporary productivity declines might occur and some employees might refuse to cooperate with the AIDS patient, unless managers give workers the medical facts, address their concerns, and articulate unequivocal performance expectations. In addition, members of the work group might experience stress because of their emotional involvement in their co-worker's illness. Stress lowers immune systems, thereby increasing the probability of illness.[72] Firms' accommodation of the work needs of employees with AIDS also might have organizational consequences. Such accommodation is likely to include flexible work scheduling, and increased use of health benefits, personal, and sick leave.

In summary, in addition to direct health care costs, a wide variety of organizational outcomes can be affected by the health and safety-related behaviors of employees, and by the managerial, educational, and incentive programs designed to promote wellness reactions and behaviors.

Technological Developments

Innovations in a variety of scientific areas have had a direct impact on several health and safety management issues. Video display terminals (VDTs), semiconductors, chemicals, as well as medical technology pose potential problems in controlling health-care costs.

VDTs. More than 28 million VDTs are now in use in the U.S. workplace.[73] The projection is that by 1990, at least 60 million VDTs will be in use,[74] with 40 to 50 percent of the American work force turning to computer terminals on a daily basis.[75] This new technology raises concerns about its impact on the wellness of users. For example, over half the users of VDTs complain of a variety of syndromes including eye strain, blurred vision, repetitive motion disease, and muscular pains in the shoulder, back or neck.[76] Sixteen states are contemplating legislation related to video display terminals.[77] Concerns also are voiced over the apparent rate of pregnancy problems and miscarriages among female VDT operators.[78] Nevertheless, the Council on Scientific Affairs of the American Medical Association reviewed available evidence and concluded that clusters of birth defects among VDT users are explainable as chance occurrences or as heritable syndromes, and that there is no causal evidence linking these syndromes to VDT usage.[79]

Semiconductors. Another new technology that may have troublesome health side effects is the semiconductor production process involving acids and gases. Consider the following figures:

- According to the California workers' compensation statistics, 46.7 percent of the occupational disease claims made by semiconductor industry employees between 1980 and 1984 were for toxic exposure. In other industries, the proportion of disease claims for toxic exposure was 21 percent.

- Although maintenance and production workers combined constitute only 33.5 percent of the work force, they accounted for over 60 percent of the disease and injury claims.

- Semiconductor workers had three times the rate of occupational illness compared to those employed in general manufacturing—1.3 versus 0.4 per 100 workers, respectively.[80]

Various compounds used in the semiconductor production process are suspected of causing adverse health outcomes. For example, photoresists may lead to birth defects and reproductive problems; organic solvents such as trichloroethylene can be absorbed by breathing and through the skin and could potentially damage every body organ; and excessive radiation often causes various cancers.[81]

In a semiconductor manufacturing plant, Digital Equipment Corporation discovered a 39 percent miscarriage rate among women on the semiconductor production line, versus 18 percent in the rest of the plant. The national rate of miscarriages is between 10 and 20 percent.[82] In addition, statistically higher incidents of nausea, headaches, and rashes were reported among semiconductor producers relative to other plant workers. Digital encouraged any pregnant women involved in semiconductor production to transfer to other jobs in the company. AT & T identified 15 pregnant women among the 4,000 plant employees producing semiconductor chips. All 15 women transferred out of the plants with equal pay and seniority. Intel and Texas Instruments have adopted similar practices.[83]

Chemical Hazards. Scientific developments also have stimulated the proliferation of chemicals in the work environment and as part of the production process. The Occupational Safety and Health Administration estimates that 575,000 hazardous chemical products are now used in U.S. factories.[84] Some of these products are undeniably linked to illnesses. For example, William Winpisinger, president of the International Association of Machinists and Aerospace Engineers, cited these statistics:

- 3 million workers exposed to benzene run a 5 times greater than normal risk of leukemia.

- 2.5 million workers exposed to asbestos run a 5 times greater than normal risk of lung cancer.

- 1.5 million workers exposed to nickel run a 10 times greater than normal risk of lung cancer.

- 1.5 million workers exposed to arsenic run a 2–5 times greater than normal risk of lung cancer.[85]

The Office of Technology Assessment (OTA) has listed 29 chemical agents which produce consistent cancer effects.[86] Neurological disorders have been linked to 21 chemical agents, and skin disorders are associated with 24 occupational substances.[87] Using research estimates, OTA concluded that occupational exposure to chemical agents causes about 5 percent (or 20,000) of the annual cancer deaths in the United States, with asbestos alone accounting for 1 to 3 percent.[88] The National Cancer Institute goes a lot higher, attributing at least 20 percent of U.S. annual cancer deaths to workplace chemical exposure.[89]

Medical Advances. Scientific developments have also changed direct expenditures on health care. The range of medical diagnostic procedures and treatments has gone up considerably in the last decade because of scientific developments and technological break-throughs. As the number of diagnostic and treatment options grows, the cost per treatment increases. In many cases, these diagnostic procedures and treatments help cure disease sufferers who can then return to work at fully productive levels. In other cases the treatments prolong lives without rendering a cure to the disease. Although in some instances questions are raised about the morality of prolonging the lives—and suffering—of the terminally ill, in most cases medical innovations add to the quality of life of affected individuals. They also translate into significantly greater health care costs for employers. For example, a decade ago a doctor might have prescribed pills for a headache. Now, CAT scans costing between $300 to $350 per scan are often recommended to diagnose the same symptoms. Health care costs for individuals with AIDS usually amount to $140,000 over the course of the illness, though home-based health care options can lower the cost. Drug treatments using AZT add an extra cost of $10,000 to $14,000 annually.

Technological developments also offer the promise of delivering health and safety improvements in the workplace. A decade ago, cost-effective and accurate drug testing technologies were not available for mass screening purposes. Today, screening tests (like EMIT) take less than a minute at a cost below $5, yielding fairly high levels of accuracy. The drug screening industry now stands at over $1 billion annually, compared to $100,000 in 1985.[90] Genetic screening for disease and exposure susceptibilities will soon be a reality as scientists continue to link genetic markers with a wide array of behavioral and disease syndromes, and as advances in the technology of genetic testing allows cost-effective mass screening.[91] Despite the difficult ethical issues raised, genetic screening offers the potential of reducing the incidence of workplace disease.

Technological developments have created unforeseen health and safety challenges for managers. However, scientific advances also offer new and sometimes promising opportunities to improve workers' health and safety. In both cases, managers are involved in responding to the health and safety challenges and opportunities brought on by these technological developments.

Present Issues in Wellness and Safety

A number of contextual and organizational factors have come together, encouraging managers to participate actively and creatively in workplace safety and health issues. While numerous moral, economic, legal, and managerial dilemmas must be confronted, the following issues highlight some of the key dilemmas managers confront and the variables relevant to their decisions.

Workplace Smoking

About 26 percent of the American adult population smokes, down from 38 percent about 30 years ago. The remaining 74 percent of the adult population have become increasingly militant in protecting their rights for smoke-free air. Clashes between smokers and nonsmokers occur more and more frequently.

Things have come to a head since the Surgeon General's 1986 report on passive inhalation, the publication of which coincided with a National Science Foundation report. These reports made clear that smokers affect the health of nonsmokers. For example:

- Children of smokers suffer more bronchitis, pneumonia, and other respiratory illnesses than children whose parents do not smoke.[92]

- Spouses of smokers have a 25 percent greater risk of getting lung cancer than spouses of nonsmokers.[93]

- Exposure to a two-pack-a-day smoker is equivalent to smoking three cigarettes a day on one's own.[94]

- The health damage to nonsmokers through passive inhalation is one-fifth what it is for those who smoke.[95]

- Between 500 to 5,000 additional people die each year from passive inhalation of others' smoke.[96]

Workplace Smoking Policies

These facts help to fan an already smoldering movement to limit smoking in the workplace. The increasing popularity of state and local statutes limiting the freedom to smoke in public, and sometimes at work, has provided employers with added impetus to develop restrictive smoking policies.

A 1987 survey by the Bureau of National Affairs and the American Society for Personnel Administration found that 54 percent of 623 responding companies had instituted policies restricting smoking, compared to 36 percent in 1986.[97] This finding represents a more than 50 percent increase in company smoking policies over the course of just one year. An additional 4 percent of the responding companies planned to institute a policy in 1987 or 1988, and 21 percent had a policy under consideration.

Among the companies with smoking policies, the survey found that:

- 12 percent banned smoking everywhere, up from 6 percent in 1986

- 51 percent prohibited smoking in open work areas, up from 41 percent in 1986

- 9 percent allowed employees to designate their own areas as non-smoking, up from 2 percent a year before.

In the 6,800 federal government buildings, the General Services Administration has restricted smoking to designated areas. Fourteen states and 200 localities have also passed statutes that influence smoking practices in private firms.[98]

A small but growing number of companies are extending smoking prohibitions beyond the workplace. In some cases, pre-employment physicals are used to reject individuals identified as smokers. USG Acoustical Products, a company with 1500 to 2000 employees, instituted a "quit smoking or quit working" policy requiring employees to abstain from smoking at work *and* at home.[99] After paying for employees to go through stop-smoking clinics, the company planned to monitor the policy through pulmonary function tests that measure lung capacity. Company policy states that employees are fired if tests show they are still smoking after a one-week grace period.

Some experts characterize the smoking habit as a nicotine addiction, every bit as habit-forming as drugs or alcohol. A veritable industry has arisen to help smokers quit, to the tune of $100 million a year.[100] Kicking the habit is very difficult, even excruciating, just like any other addiction. The relapse rate among those who try to quit smoking is similar to that of heroin users; few who attempt to quit smoking make it through their first year of abstinence. The failure rate of smoking cessation programs is as high as 80 to 85 percent, perhaps because medical experts consider nicotine addiction much harder to break than dependency on alcohol.[101] Employers contemplating institution of no-smoking policies should be prepared to deal with some anxieties from smokers who question their ability to kick a long-term habit.

Legal Considerations

Employees who smoke are feeling increasingly cramped. An unresolved issue is whether smokers can use the courts in their battle to preserve the right to smoke. Most legal experts are skeptical about employees' innate right to smoke.[102] However, legal avenues possibly available to smokers include collective bargaining and equal employment laws.

Employers instituting smoking restrictions in a unionized workplace are probably under the duty to bargain, because changes in smoking policies constitute a change in working conditions. The duty to bargain is particularly relevant where no local or state laws require employers to institute such policies. This responsibility may end up placing unions in the difficult situation of challenging changes in working conditions such as smoking bans, despite the health benefits associated with such policies. It is likely that some unions will decline involvement in the issue, especially if the majority of the bargaining unit is non-smokers.

Equal employment laws may offer greater promise to smokers. Though being a smoker is not a protected characteristic (unless smoking is considered an addiction and, therefore, a protected handicap), protected groups could have different rates of smokers. Almost 47 percent of black males 25 to 34 years old are smokers, while the rate of smoking among all white men is 29.5 percent.[103] The rate of smoking among women—23.5 percent—is lower than the 29.5 percent of men who smoke.[104] In theory, if adverse employment actions differentially affect protected groups as a result of differences in their smoking rates, equal employment laws might offer the means to challenge no-smoking policies in the workplace.

A final issue is the perceived equity of a no-smoking policy. Half of all blue-collar workers smoke, a rate double that of white-collar employees.[105] As a result, smoking restrictions have a much greater impact on lower-level employees than on a firm's executives. While some groups may welcome the forced incentive to quit smoking, others might have greater difficulty adjusting and might see the policy as yet another right management has "inflicted" on lower-level employees.

Despite these potential difficulties, most companies apparently have few qualms about instituting a policy that has direct and measurable effects on the health of *everyone* in the workplace, smokers and nonsmokers. In fact, no other managerial practice could have such a uniformly positive effect on the wellness of employees. In addition, an organization will likely experience lower health care, absenteeism, and replacement costs as a no-smoking policy reaps its benefits over the long term.

Substance Abuse

Alcohol and drug abuse are said to cost American businesses $90 billion annually in productivity losses, absenteeism and tardiness, increased health care claims, accidents, liabilities, and replacement costs.[106] The costs of alcohol abuse are about 2.5 times the amount for chemical dependency. About 10 percent of the work force may have an alcohol problem, while 3 to 5 percent are thought to be drug abusers.[107]

The workplace is one of the primary arenas attempting to address the drug and alcohol crisis. Employers' concerns extend to any adverse effects attributable to alcohol and drug abuse, regardless of whether the drug or alcohol intake occurs during or after work hours.

Workplace Substance Abuse Policies

Answers to the question "How should we monitor substance abuse?" are many and varied. According to some experts, the best strategy is to rely on observable signs of performance impairment, intoxication, or unusual employee behaviors. Organizations typically expect supervisors or managers to deal with the immediate problem of an intoxicated or drugged employee, implement any disciplinary procedures, and verify the condition, as required by company policy. In many instances, the manager or supervisor immediately refers the employee to the appropriate support and rehabilitation services.

Some experts feel that reacting to a manifested behavioral problem may cause undue delay, since an employee abuses substances for at least five years before the problem becomes evident on the job.[108] In the interim, others in the workplace or community may have been endangered or hurt. Advocates of this thinking favor closer monitoring to prevent the development of an abuse pattern in the first place.

Drug and alcohol screening is one way of addressing these concerns. Employers often institute monitoring programs at the pre-employment screening phase and/or at random intervals during employment. Indeed, assuring health and safety is the reason most often cited by companies for instituting a drug testing program.[109] A 1985 American Society of Personnel Administration survey indicated that 13 percent of all companies screened applicants for excessive alcohol ingestion,[110] while other surveys show 25 percent tested applicants for illegal drug traces.[111] A recent survey of the Fortune 1000 companies suggests that such testing has increased significantly over the last two years.[112] Among the 378 responding companies, 24 percent prescreened applicants for alcohol traces above a minimum cutoff and 49 percent prescreened for illegal drug presence. Some of the responding companies monitored the behavior of their current employees through random testing—4 percent of the respondents tested for alcohol and over 10 percent did random employee drug testing.[113]

Legal Issues

Such monitoring approaches provide information about individual behaviors and life-styles as they occur within, as well as outside of, the workplace. Consequently, concerns have been raised over violations of individuals' privacy rights. In addition, alcohol or drug tests are more invasive than traditional employment inquiries since they require people to produce body fluids (that is, urine or blood samples), sometimes in very uncomfortable situations. Such concerns set the stage for the ongoing debate over whether drug and alcohol tests violate constitutional guarantees against invasions of privacy and unreasonable search and seizure (for public employees). Court rulings on the legality of drug test practices and proposals in state legislatures for statutes to monitor test policies and practices continue to address these issues.

AIDS in the Workplace

Managers are increasingly involved in developing policies to address the needs of, and co-workers' reactions to, employees who have AIDS. By 1988, the number of confirmed AIDS cases in the U.S. had reached 53,382;[114] that number is expected to reach 270,000 by 1991.[115] Depending on the estimate used, anywhere from 1.5 million[116] to 3 million[117] Americans test positive for the HIV antibody for AIDS.

Testing positive for the antibody does not mean that the individual currently has symptoms, although recent experience suggests that the vast majority testing positive will develop the disease and probably die sometime within 8 to 10 years.[118] Testing positive to the antibody does mean, however, that the individual can transmit the disease to another, not yet infected individual. All available medical evidence clearly indicates that such transmission cannot occur through casual contact. The AIDS virus is transmitted only if the carrier's virus directly enters the bloodstream of another individual. The most common routes of AIDS transmission are blood transfusions using infected blood, reuse of contaminated hypodermic needles by drug users, and sexual intercourse.

This evidence serves to appease most rational concerns about transmission of AIDS in the workplace. However, it does nothing to allay irrational fears of contagion among individuals who are unclear on how the disease is transmitted. This educational need is one aspect of the disease that managers must address. Another concern involves the many pragmatic and emotional issues raised when an employee contracts AIDS. These scenarios are becoming increasingly common in many work settings. A recent American Society for Personnel Administration (ASPA) survey indicated that 33 percent of the 273 responding companies had employees with AIDS, compared to 9 percent just 2 years before.[119]

Workplace AIDS Policies

The AIDS epidemic poses several employment policy issues for managers. First, is it their business and/or in their interest to know whether an individual is HIV positive, before any disease symptoms become evident? This issue seems to have been resolved by the Supreme Court's ruling in *Arline*. Since persons with AIDS are likely to qualify as handicapped as a result of the decision, their job status is protected provided their health disability does not prevent fulfillment of job duties, with "reasonable accommodation."

Reasonable Accommodation. How far reasonable accommodation should go is the crux of the dilemma for employers. Several guidelines for interpreting the reasonable accommodation requirement can be inferred from recommendations made by the courts:

- If employees pose a significant risk of infecting co-workers with the contagious disease, they will not be considered "otherwise qualified" to do the job unless the reasonable accommodation can remove the risk.

- Under reasonable accommodation, an employer cannot be expected to suffer undue financial or administrative burdens, or to change the fundamental nature of the business practices.

- Reasonable accommodation does not require employers to generate a job on which the afflicted individual is capable of working. However should such a job become vacant, the diseased person cannot be excluded from consideration.[120]

Based on the above court rulings, HIV testing is not advisable since individuals are protected in their employment rights until severely disabled by the disease. At that point, the performance impairment will be obvious without any need to rely on test information. Ethical standards would also preclude exclusionary actions directed at persons who test HIV positive.

Co-Workers' Rights. A second question concerns the rights of co-workers, if any, to decide whether and how they want to work with an AIDS sufferer. While employees have a right to refuse work assignments when there is a recognized hazard in the workplace (see discussion in text in this chapter at note 16), AIDS does not pose any hazard to co-workers. However, the scientific impossibility of infection through casual contact does not solve the practical and emotional problems encountered in the workplace. Managers still must educate co-workers on the facts regarding AIDS and be consistent in communicating and enforcing work expectations and rules for AIDS sufferers and their co-workers.

Benefits Policies. A third issue pertains to the management and benefit policies toward AIDS victims. To date, many companies appear to prefer dealing with AIDS cases on an *ad hoc* basis. One report indicates that only 18 percent of 378 responding Fortune 1000 companies have written AIDS policies.[121] The ASPA survey cited earlier reported an increase in AIDS policies from 3 to 8.5 percent between 1985 to 1987. Since the Fortune 1000 sample consists of much larger companies than those surveyed by ASPA, the higher figure among the Fortune 1000 sample may reflect the greater propensity among larger corporations to formalize AIDS policies. Among the companies without written policies, 89 percent provide benefits to AIDS victims as part of the general benefit structure.[122] Benefits offered include long-term disability (82.7 percent), short-term disability (78.6 percent), and leave of absence (79.8 percent); other provisions include continued benefits (82.5

percent), paid leave (80 percent), unpaid leave (68 percent), and continued employment (65 percent).

Among companies with written policies, the ASPA survey showed that 81.8 percent of the companies continue the employment of AIDS sufferers, 77.3 percent continue provision of benefits, 50 percent provide paid leave, 36.4 percent allow unpaid leave, and 18.2 percent arrange part-time employment. At least in the ASPA sample of 273 companies, the trend seems to be to treat AIDS like any other illness at least in terms of benefit policies. An alternative interpretation of the data is that a significant minority of companies withdraw generally available protections from AIDS sufferers. This interpretation is supported by data from a telephone survey of 100 of the Fortune 1000, in which 3 of the companies said they would fire an employee with AIDS, 25 might do so, 67 would not, and 5 refused to answer the question.[123] Such practices are potentially challengable under the Employee Retirement Income Security Act (ERISA) which prohibits discharge or discrimination against employees for purposes of interfering with their right to claim benefits under an employee benefit plan.[124] The definition of benefit plan is broad, including any health, life or disability insurance programs.

Benefit policies are only one dimension of management behaviors toward AIDS. Another dimension concerns educational programs and management reactions. The ASPA survey provided some insight into these issues. Four companies (or 1.5 percent of the respondents) said they would isolate employees with AIDS. On the positive side, 38 percent of the respondents were implementing some form of AIDS education program for their employees.

Disparate Impact. A final important issue for managers concerns the impact of AIDS-related employment policies and decisions on identifiable groups such as gay men or minorities. Both of these groups have been especially hard hit by the disease. To date, 65 percent of the AIDS cases have been among homosexual or bisexual men.[125] The disease is expected to increase among heterosexual men and women and by 1990, about 9 percent of the cases of AIDS will be among heterosexuals.[126] In addition, black men or black women account for 24 percent of AIDS cases—roughly twice the proportion of blacks in the general population—because of the greater propensity of intravenous drug use in these groups.[127] Hispanics constitute another 15 percent of AIDS cases so that the two groups (Blacks and Hispanics) together account for 39 percent of AIDS cases. Half the female AIDS victims are black; a black woman is 13 times more likely to contract AIDS than a white woman.

These grim statistics show very clearly that AIDS is not distributed equally across all groups in the population. Adverse work-related decisions taken against AIDS sufferers will have a disproportionate effect on identifiable groups. In addition to receiving protection as handicapped persons, individuals with AIDS who are members of protected minorities can probably rely on Title VII of the Civil Rights Act to challenge employment practices which yield disparate impact. Some state or local statutes explicitly prohibit discrimination against AIDS victims (e.g., California, Florida, Massachusetts, Denver, and Austin) or protect individuals against discrimination on the basis of sexual preferences (e.g., the District of Columbia).

The publicity surrounding AIDS has sometimes obscured the facts concerning the disease and how it is spread. In certain unfortunate cases, this lack of education has ended up severely victimizing persons who already have AIDS. Laws alone cannot assure fair and humane dealings with employees who suffer from AIDS. Managers can set the tone for behaviors and attitudes in the workplace, via explicit policies and through their own behaviors toward AIDS sufferers.

Workplace Exposure

Developments in technologies and work processes have introduced a variety of new products and materials into the workplace. Scientists are now discovering that some of these new, as well as established, materials and products may endanger workers who use them or who are exposed to them.

Some of these proven or presumed hazards have been mentioned earlier, such as chemical toxins, gases used in the production of semiconductors, and radiation from VDTs. While in certain cases, scientific investigations can alleviate health concerns, in other cases, research demonstrates the potential for adverse health consequences.

Adverse health consequences as a result of workplace exposure fall into the following main types: (1) immediately manifested injuries or illnesses following exposure or use of dangerous equipment; (2) illness symptoms manifested in the worker after a long latency period; (3) damage (immediate or latent) affecting only the reproductive capabilities of exposed employees; (4) adverse consequences to a fetus but not to the pregnant worker exposed to the hazard source.

Policies to Minimize Exposure

Each type of adverse health consequence poses a variety of managerial challenges. The most obvious management problem is introduced by the first category of health hazards, since something must be done—immediately—to control the source causing the illnesses or injuries. Engineering controls, personal protection equipment, job or work process redesign, material substitution, training and education, or—at the extreme—shutting down the work process, are possible managerial responses to this type of hazard.

The second category poses an additional challenge since in certain situations, nobody is aware of any health hazard. By the time the danger becomes known, 10 or 20 years may have passed and exposed employees may have moved on in their careers. Under such circumstances, pinpointing the source of the illness can prove difficult because it is usually no longer present in its original form and/or level. Additional problems arise in attempting to track down individuals exposed to the hazard many years before, piecing together their level of exposure at the time, and controlling many other factors that may have affected their health during the intervening period. All these factors obscuring the causal relationship between the hazardous substance and disease explain why only the most obvious sources of latent disease, such as asbestos, are identified and acted on. It also allows manufacturers or employers to contest liability suits on the grounds that causal responsibility is almost impossible to establish with certainty given such long latency periods and numerous confounding factors that hamper detection of relationships between exposure and disease.

The third category of health hazards affects the reproductive capabilities of men and women exposed in the workplace. For example, DBCP, a pesticide, severely depresses sperm production and prevents men from fathering children.[128] Exposure to lead may damage women's ability to conceive or to carry a fetus to term. Several options are available to managers in this instance. Workers planning to reproduce (both men and women) can be transferred temporarily out of the worksite, as long as short term removal eliminates the effects of exposure. This strategy can minimize the risk of lead exposure, for example, where temporary removal successfully lowers lead levels in employees' blood.[129]

Temporary removal is a feasible solution only if the level of exposure in the workplace is safe for all except those planning to have children. For example, dinoseb, a pesticide recently banned by the EPA, damages the reproductive capabilities of both men and women. However, because the product can cause other health problems like cataracts and poisoning, selective removal of just those with child-bearing intentions is not sufficient. Selective removal policies also work only for pregnancies that are planned. To address the problem of unplanned pregnancies, some companies have gone to the extreme of requiring women—but inexplicably, not men—to present proof of infertility before being eligible to work around reproductive hazards. This kind of policy induced several women working for American Cyanamid to undergo voluntary sterilization in order to qualify for certain high-paying jobs.

Concern for the potential reproductive hazards of a chemical or workplace practice has traditionally been directed selectively toward women. Since many chemical products (such as kepone, DBCP, and lead) pose reproductive hazards for *both* men and women, selective implementation of protective removal policies is seen by some as an alternative form of sex discrimination. Indeed, the American Cyanamid reproductive protection policy was challenged under Title VII on grounds of sex discrimination.

A final category of workplace hazards affect a fetus but not the pregnant mother. Such products are labelled teratogens. Dupont Corporation considers seven chemicals potentially toxic to the fetus at levels otherwise safe for adults. Based on this potential hazard, a number of companies have instituted "fetal protection" policies including 15 of the Fortune 500. Among this group are Exxon, General Motors, Dupont, B.F. Goodrich, and Olin.[130] Fetal protection policies reflect a concern for the vulnerability of the fetus and the fetus' inability to protect its own interests should they be contrary to those of its mother.

Fetal protection policies are very controversial. Critics see such policies as excessively paternalistic and presumptuous in assuming that a corporation can better protect fetal rights than the mother of the fetus. To such observers, fetal protection policies are a proxy for sex discrimination. In support, they claim that the rate of birth defects has remained stable around 7 percent of live births, despite an increasing number of women working with environmental and chemical agents. This evidence appears to contradict the purported link between birth defects and workplace exposure of the mother, thus negating the justification for fetal protection policies. Instead, corporations should invest in policies and practices resulting in a safer workplace for everyone, women *and* men, these critics argue.

These arguments aside, the federal government appears to endorse nondiscriminatory remedies for potential fetal hazards. For example, OSHA standards for lead and ethylene oxide mention fetal protection as goals. The lead standard specifies medical removal protection with full pay for up to 18 months, if the worker's lead blood level exceeds a trigger point. The EPA is proposing a federal radiation standard which limits fetal exposure to 10 percent of adult levels. If the policy is approved, OSHA is expected to require 18 months (or thereabouts) of full compensation for pregnant women excluded from jobs, similar to the protections offered under the lead standard.

In summary, different types of exposure hazards and health consequences require a variety of management actions. In some instances, managers are challenged with the burden of addressing the needs and rights of present employees as well as those of workers' progeny.

Managerial Interventions

Given the external and organizational factors inducing managerial involvement in workplace health and safety, policies and practices to address these concerns have multiplied in recent years. The following discussion surveys some responses with which industry has experimented, the problems these practices address, and the pros and cons of each approach.

Training and Education

A variety of training and education approaches have been introduced into worksites to improve safety and health records. These programs cover a broad spectrum of health and safety issues, as the following illustrations demonstrate.

Stress Reduction

The St. Paul Companies, a large U.S. insurance company, recently introduced a technostress intervention program to teach VDT users relaxation techniques, workstation organization, and health awareness, including the need for regular eye checkups. The company reported significantly lowered technostress levels following the program. [131]

Other types of programs aim at reducing more general job stress. Most stress management approaches begin with a stress audit designed to identify sources of tension in an employee's life. Some programs teach employees biofeedback, the Oriental art of tai chi, or humor strategies to help them unwind, while others use job design interventions to provide employees with greater control over what they do. Some companies use computer programs to reduce stress caused by "terminal boredom." One program developed by a Michigan firm, called Chuckle Pops, allows users to call up a series of jokes while they work.

While many companies spend resources on stress reduction strategies, the cost-effectiveness of these investments remains uncertain. Although most firms believe in the favorable productivity effects of such programs, a Department of Health and Human Services survey of 1700 companies found only 4.2 percent reported reduced health care costs as a result of stress reduction programs. [132] This low figure may be partially attributable to the tremendous variety in training philosophies and stress reduction approaches used in these programs.

Accident Prevention

Another area of training focuses on preventing work-related accidents. Such training is crucial, especially in the early periods of employment. The accident rate for an employee's first month on the job is substantially higher than the rate for the total subsequent duration of employment, [133] indicating that safety training must occur as soon as an employee is hired. Training successes in safety practices have been reported in a variety of industries including mining, [134] manufacturing of heavy machinery, and the painting and allied trades. [135] A number of training programs designed to enhance safety rely on operant conditioning procedures. [136]

Substance Abuse

Substance abuse is another area in which training and education are crucial to workplace wellness. Training usually focuses on educating managers and workers to spot behaviors that signal abuse. Education also helps managers react to substance abusers and provides them with information on appropriate support resources and referral strategies. Such training and education forms a critical element of any substance abuse rehabilitation program or EAP.[137]

In some cases, substance abuse education is delivered through information booklets rather than live presentations. For example, the Dallas Chapter of the Associated General Contractors (AGC) of America puts out three booklets:

- *AGC Drug Abuse Booklet.* This publication describes several drug screening strategies: pre-employment, random/annual, post-accident, and supervisor-suspected drug usage. The book also offers advice on such topics as educating employees, establishing overall company policies, conducting undercover investigations, and selecting contraband detection service organizations.

- *Employee Handbook on Drug and Alcohol Awareness.* Using a question and answer format, the booklet offers information on various drugs, the effects of drugs on users, and drug-related terminology and slang.

- *Drug Information Guide.* This guide lists common drugs with their street names and physical symptoms, and identifies the dangers these drugs pose.[138]

Managers share the view that drug education is an important element of effective anti-drug abuse interventions. One survey asked managers about successful elements of substance abuse programs.[139] Supervisory training to recognize employee drug abuse problems and information campaigns to increase employee awareness of drug testing were perceived as important components of successful programs.

AIDS Awareness

Training and education also play a critical role in developing an informed and humane response to cases of AIDS in the workplace.

Several companies have comprehensive strategies for dealing with AIDS including education, support programs, company and community task forces, and the provision of financial and social services.

A prime example is the San Francisco based Levi Strauss company. The commitment to a comprehensive and humane AIDS program shows up in the heavy involvement of Levi Strauss' chief executive Robert Haas in all aspects of the program. The company started its first education effort in 1982, by videotaping two nationally known physicians while they presented information and answered employee questions about AIDS. The videotape was then made available to all other company employees. Another facet of Levis Strauss' program educates managers who want to discuss AIDS with their staff regarding medical information about the disease, the emotional impact on co-workers, and sources of counseling and support for victims. The company publishes a regular newsletter called *Health and Lifestyles* which includes updated information on AIDS, and organizes lunchtime lectures on the subject.

Levi Strauss has also collaborated with a number of other San Francisco based corporations, such as BankAmerica, Wells Fargo, AT & T, and Chevron, to develop a comprehensive AIDS education program. The package, which is available to any employer in the country, includes an informational videotape called "An Epidemic of Fear: AIDS in the Workplace," an educational leaflet for employees, a resource manual for corporate policy makers suggesting strategies for developing AIDS policies and procedures, and a loose-leaf manual for managers on their role in dealing with employees who have AIDS and their co-workers.

The philosophy at Levi Strauss is that education is the most effective tool against prejudice, discrimination, and unproductive responses to cases of AIDS. Apparently employees share this view: "If a fellow employee is diagnosed and comes back (they're) accepted . . . and the educational program is a key reason why that's true," according to one employee of Levi Strauss.[140]

In summary, training and education interventions have addressed a wide variety of safety and wellness areas. Such interventions prove effective in providing employees with the requisite information to perform their jobs safely, to live healthy life-styles, and to evaluate health and wellness issues. In some cases, these programs also succeed in achieving behavioral changes that improve safety and wellness behaviors on and off the job.

Management Policies and Work Rules

Corporate policies and administrative procedures establish a framework of expectations and standards governing health and safety issues in the workplace. Policies and procedures serve to clarify corporate values, goals, expectations, and rules about employee health and safety, assure equity in distributing services and benefits, protect the job and privacy rights of affected individuals, and facilitate information exchange and dissemination among all segments of an organization. Especially relevant in this case are policies regarding safety and hazards in the workplace, substance abuse, and AIDS.

Safety Awareness

Management policies can create either a culture which emphasizes safety and health as an uncompromised goal for the workplace or one which implicitly tolerates unsafe products, chemicals, or procedures. Policies of the first type can take a variety of forms. As an illustration, consider the elements of Dupont's safety policies and procedures:

- Dupont's management holds all levels of management and employees responsible for safety on the job. Among other things, this requirement includes considering managers' safety records in promotion decisions.

- An environmental quality committee exists at the senior corporate level. The committee meets weekly and oversees four subcommittees, including one on occupational safety and health.

- Each plant has a central safety committee composed of plant staff managers, as well as safety and medical personnel. The committees meet at least once a month.

- Each plant has safety subcommittees which report to the central safety committee. These subcommittees comprise first-level supervisors and line employees, and are the focal point for line involvement in safety policy.

- Employees are encouraged to respond to safety hazards immediately. About 95 percent of all safety hazards are corrected on the line, without any involvement of safety subcommittees.

In addition to establishing clear policy statements and procedural mechanisms, some organizations design incentive schemes, award and competition programs, or rebate arrangements which provide employees with financial inducements to engage in safe behaviors. Apparently, clear management policies and a strong commitment to safety pay off. At least two studies have found lower accident rates in firms in which management is committed to and involved in safety policy and implementation.[141]

Substance Abuse

Many, although by no means all, companies choose to articulate the corporate philosophy for dealing with substance abuse in a policy statement. A recent survey of Fortune 1000 companies presently testing for drug presence found that 93 percent of respondents had a written policy while 5 percent did not.[142] Among companies that did not test for drugs, an American Management Association survey reported that 25 percent had a written substance abuse policy, 46 percent did not, and 24 percent were in the process of writing one.

Most experts agree that a corporate policy on substance abuse should be put in writing and disseminated to all employees, regardless of whether the company engages in alcohol or drug testing.[143] Gary Flowers, vice president for industrial relations at Daniel International (one of the country's largest construction firms), says that a written corporate policy has the advantages of letting employees know up front what to expect and of protecting the company if an employee takes legal action. A good policy deals with management reactions to substance abusers and the abusers' job and rehabilitation rights, if any. Both current employees and job applicants should receive copies of the policy. Constant reinforcement of the policy should occur through informal meetings and information booklets. Organizations which offer EAP facilities should guarantee confidentiality protections and encourage employees to seek help voluntarily.

As an example, the alcohol and drug policy at Philips Industries Inc. includes the following key elements:

- A cover letter from the company founder explaining the reasons for and philosophy underlying the policy

- A statement of the policy's purpose and scope

- Guidelines concerning pre-employment testing, voluntary testing, testing for reasonable cause, random or surprise testing, and testing on hazardous jobs

- Plant rules regarding possession, distribution, sale, or consumption of drugs or alcohol

- Disciplinary procedures and job rights

- Opportunities for voluntary rehabilitation and confidentiality guarantees

- Guidelines for managers dealing with suspected substance abusers

- Voluntary signature form for expression of support for a "Drug Free Philips Industries Inc."

AIDS Education

AIDS is another area in which management policies and structures help clarify expectations, establish rules, and facilitate information flow. The Levi Strauss AIDS program, which is generally regarded as a model for corporations, was announced and launched by the company's chief executive officer. The CEO has maintained high involvement in the program and has led efforts to get other San Francisco businesses to follow suit. The company established policies on benefits, rights, and support systems available to employees who have AIDS, and, in conjunction with a strong educational program for all employees, issued a clear statement that prejudicial behaviors toward persons with AIDS are not medically justified and will not be tolerated. In addition, an interdepartmental committee provides ongoing advice to the company on AIDS-related issues. Employees with AIDS, their coworkers, and managers seem to respond very favorably to the policies.[144]

Wellness Promotion

Finally, managerial policies can promote safety and wellness through designing incentive or reward programs that encourage such behaviors. Some organizations offer cost reimbursement incentives or "wellness rebates" to employees who do not exceed a certain level of benefit usage during any given year. Examples of such programs include the following:

- Speedcall Corporation gives a $7 weekly bonus to non-smokers.

- During a five-month period, Atco Properties paid $100 to each employee per pound lost, $500 for not smoking, and $500 for routinely walking up the stairs.

- Employees of Scherer Lumber Company collect a $300 bonus at the end of a year in which they have missed no more than three sick days.

- Hospital Corporation of America adds 24 cents to employees' paychecks each time they run or walk a mile, bike four miles, or swim a quarter of a mile.[145]

In addition to expected improvements in the health of their employees, each of the companies considers these incentive programs an effective health cost containment strategy.

In summary, management policies and procedures can significantly affect workplace safety and health by providing a clear message regarding a company's expected standards of behavior for employees. Policies also can add teeth to these expectations by specifying positive and negative reinforcers. Effective administrative procedures can achieve wide dissemination of the policies and involvement of all employees in policy implementation.

Safety Controls

A variety of safety control policies can attenuate the adverse consequences of unsafe and unhealthy workplace practices. Safety experts talk of three primary areas in which controls can be introduced: (1) at the hazardous source, (2) in the methods of transmitting the hazard, and (3) around the worker.

Source Controls

Improving safety and health at the source focuses on designing controls that prevent a hazard from reaching workers. Such controls include minimizing exposure to a hazardous source or substituting a less dangerous product for the hazardous material. For example, until the mid-1970s, workers were exposed to a carcinogen—vinyl chloride monomer (VCM)—every time they cleaned a VC reactor. To reduce this hazard, manufacturers developed a coating solution for the interior walls of the reactor system which dramatically reduced the need for cleaning. In addition, a mounted nozzle was installed inside the reactor to contain chemical leakage. These design changes dramatically reduced worker exposure and as a secondary benefit, significantly increased productivity.

Another example of control at the source is the substitution of asbestos with other, less toxic but equally effective insulating agents. A recent example of substitution at the source is the voluntary withdrawal of chlorofluorocarbons (CFCs) from the production process of foam plastic food containers (such as cups, plates, or egg cartons) by the 15 largest product manufacturers.[147] CFCs are nontoxic in the lower atmosphere, yet when they reach the stratosphere 25 miles above earth, they decompose and deplete the protective ozone layer. The manufacturers plan to switch to HCFC-22, a much less harmful product, and DuPont, the world's largest producer of CFCs, plans to achieve the changeover by the early part of next century. While the primary objective of this substitution is the long-term "health of the planet," health effects will also benefit workers directly involved in the product substitution. Most industrial hygiene experts believe that control at the source is the most effective means of preventing worker illnesses and injuries.[148]

Transmission Prevention

A second approach requires controlling the channels which can disperse a hazard. Such controls rely primarily on methods which isolate a hazardous material from contact with workers or prevent a toxic material from spreading through the air and/or settling in the air. Isolation of a toxin usually is achieved through enclosure of an operation to prevent fumes from escaping into the atmosphere, as in enclosed, ventilated blasting booths in foundries. Sometimes automation, robotization, and/or geographic distancing of operations is an effective means of removing a toxin from contact with the work group. For example, automobiles are spray painted and welded by robots to prevent human contact with paint solvent and welding fumes. Other manufacturers store extremely hazardous materials in remote, inaccessible areas to prevent human contact and to minimize the adverse consequences of accidental leakages.

Controlling the transmission of hazardous substances sometimes means stopping the hazard from mixing in the air. For example, silica dust must be wetted to prevent this dangerous substance from becoming airborne. Local exhaust systems (similar to kitchen-range hoods) are extremely important in minimizing worker exposure to carcinogens. Such local ventilation systems are used in aluminum reduction operations, spray paint booths, automobile garages, and foundries. More general ventilation systems dilute the air of toxic particles by maintaining a continual flow of fresh air through the worksite. Since many buildings have ventilation systems that recycle air, employers need to assure that recycled air is clean, free of toxins or smoke fumes. This safety need has prompted development of newer recyling systems, which clean the air of impurities before it reenters the system.

Employee Efforts

A third category of controls focuses on workers. In particular, employees are trained in safe work practices such as keeping hazardous areas tightly sealed off or vacuuming up silica dust regularly to prevent accumulation. Certain administrative procedures also can reduce hazardous exposure, such as routinely rotating workers assigned to dangerous areas or cleaning hazardous worksites on weekends, when the area is absent of workers.

Personal protection equipment provides another way of controlling hazards at the employee level. Workers wear gas masks, dust masks, hearing protectors, gloves, hard hats, helmets, protective goggles, footwear with reinforced toes as protections against various hazards and toxins. While personal protective equipment has occasionally failed to prevent illness or injury to workers, the Bureau of Labor Statistics has concluded that such equipment generally serves a protective function.[149] The degree of protection rendered depends largely on the design of the equipment, its quality, and the consistency of its use.

General Considerations

In many cases, federal regulations determine the nature of health and safety controls mandated for the worksite. However, where some latitude exists, experts offer the following hierarchy of controls. The hierarchy goes from most to least effective in controlling hazards and their negative health consequences.

- Eliminate the hazard from the machine, method, material, or plant structure.
- Control the hazard by enclosing or guarding it at its source.

- Train personnel to be aware of the hazard and to follow safe procedures to avoid it.

- Prescribe personal protection equipment for personnel to shield them against the hazard.[150]

Note that this hierarchy places personal protection equipment at the bottom of the list of preferred options. Since the effectiveness of such equipment depends on proper and consistent human use, it is inherently unreliable. On the other hand, engineering controls can be perfected and implemented into the work setting on a permanent basis. They also can often combat several exposure routes, while personal protection equipment typically can contain only one type of hazard. The efficacy of engineering controls can be monitored quite easily, and they do not create a burden on employees or hinder productivity. None of these features apply to personal protection equipment. In short, the most effective safety and hazard protection relies on technological developments that eliminate a hazard or control it at its source.

Screening and Placement Policies

Managers can also control health and safety by capitalizing on individual differences among applicants and employees. Managers may find such information useful if systematic relationships exist between measures of individual differences and susceptibility to illness or injury. The following discussion considers several dimensions along which personal information about applicants or employees might be collected: genetic, medical history, substance abuse behaviors, and personality characteristics.

Genetic Information

Genetic features of employees may affect employee behaviors and health in at least two ways. First, employees may differ in their susceptibility to disease if exposed to certain toxins or working conditions, depending on their genetic dispositions. Second, individuals may have varying probabilities of acquiring a disease, regardless of working conditions, as a function of genetic characteristics.

Susceptibility to Environmental Toxins. Regarding the first category of genetic syndromes, medical science is uncovering more and more links between possession (or absence) of a certain genetic trait and susceptibility to disease under particular exposure or working conditions. For example, G-6-PD (glucose-6-phosphate dehydrogenase) deficiency is an enzyme shortage caused by a biochemical genetic condition connected with the red blood cell. A deficiency in this enzyme hampers the process through which glucose is oxidized. As a result, employees with this genetic deficiency may suffer hemolytic anemia when they work with industrial chemicals like dye intermediates, amino compounds, copper, and arsine. Individuals with a deficiency in thalassemia—which affects the rate of hemoglobin synthesis—may be more vulnerable to the toxic effects of lead or benzene exposure.[151] Employees with alpha-1-antitrypsin deficiency could have greater sensitivity to asbestos or cotton dust exposure because of their predisposition toward lung disease.[152]

Generalized Susceptibility. A second and growing category of genetic developments links genetic syndromes to disease susceptibility, regardless of interactions with environmental agents. For example, a genetic defect on the 11th chromosome prevents removal of cholesterol from artery linings, thus increasing the likelihood of heart disease in people with this marker.[153] Increased probabilities of Huntington's disease, Alzheimer's disease, and colon cancer have been systematically associated with certain genetic characteristics. Genetic markers can even predict some personality dispositions, such as manic depression,[154] shyness or gregariousness,[155] and perhaps some forms of antisocial behavior like alcoholism or criminality.[156]

Beyond linking genetic syndromes to disease or behavioral outcomes, scientists now have fairly accurate diagnostic tests for a number of these genetic syndromes. About 100 genetic diseases can be identified through biochemical markers, and even more accurate tests which directly "probe" DNA material are available for some 15 genetic diseases. The DNA probes are about 90 percent accurate in predicting disease.[157]

Ethical and Legal Concerns. These developments have opened the potential for a whole new age in employment screening. In theory, employers can now identify individuals with higher probabilities of illness. Such identification can occur many years in advance of the onset of disease symptoms, at a point in employees' lives when they are perfectly healthy. However, fundamental moral and ethical issues confront employers in the face of this new technology, especially if scientific knowledge continues to expand at the present rate.[158] On the one hand, employers could exercise selective placement policies to protect workers against exposure to work situations that raise their probability of subsequent disease or psychological maladjustment. These policies could serve a preventive health care function, depending on how organizations handle the exclusionary decisions and protect worker rights. On the other hand, employers might use genetic test information for exclusionary purposes, denying employment opportunities and benefits because of a risk that at some point employees might become ill and be a burden on the employer. In other words, genetic tests offer significant potential benefits and costs, depending on their uses, or, as *The Economist* editorialized, these tests are "marvelous, so long as people are not denied jobs and insurance just because of their genes."[159]

Another troublesome aspect of genetic tests is that genetic markers do not appear evenly across the population. Since ethnic and racial groups vary systematically along genetic lines, employment decisions based on genetic information will end up creating subgroup inequality. For example, 7 to 13 percent of American blacks carry the sickle cell trait, while sickle cell anemia is almost nonexistent among other American racial groups.[160] A recent study of army recruits published in the *New England Journal of Medicine* suggested a link between the sickle cell trait and sudden death if carriers of the trait engage in extremely vigorous activities such as physical exercise.[161] While the *Journal* editorial emphasized that the results do not justify discrimination by employers or insurance companies against carriers of the sickle cell trait, the study illustrates the possibility that use of genetic information could have disproportionate effects on certain racial or ethnic subgroups.

In summary, genetic screening could have healthful effects in the workplace if used in ways that are fair, moral, protective of applicant and employee rights, and scientifically defensible. Few employers presently engage in such practices because of the many unresolved ethical, practical and scientific issues.[162] Yet, with the potential of a "total gene screen" within 10 to 15 years,[163] managers will likely have to consider genetic testing more seriously as they strive for a healthy and safe workplace.

Medical History

Another preventive strategy managers might use is to screen out individuals who are prone to illness or injury, provided the predisposing conditions do not qualify as protected handicaps. This screening typically involves examining applicants' medical history and present medical condition for illnesses, diseases, accidents, or unhealthy life-styles that pose a current health risk or might be predictive of health problems at a later point in time. Over 80 percent of medium-sized companies (250 to 500 employees) and virtually all large companies (over 500 employees) ask applicants to complete a preemployment medical questionnaire.[164] Physical exams are also required by almost 50 percent of medium-sized firms and 83 percent of large companies.[165]

Some common checks take place as part of a medical screening. They typically include a general evaluation of applicants' pulmonary, cardiovascular, and musculoskeletal systems; some blood work; skin, eye, ear, nose and throat conditions; height and weight; personal and family health history; and health-related habits including exercise, smoking, and drug and alcohol use. This information sometimes steers organizational gatekeepers away from hiring individuals who are poor health risks. The information also serves as a baseline to monitor employee health for any adverse consequences from job exposure.

Since medical screening does not rely on protected characteristics of applicants, employers are not required to reveal the specific medical reasons for rejecting a job candidate. As a result, it is hard to know which medical factors most frequently affect hiring decisions. Nevertheless, one investigator has found a couple of examples in which employers used medical factors to reduce occupational illnesses, albeit in a highly questionable way.[166] In one case, only men older than 50 were hired in a job which involved exposure to a carcinogen, so that by the time cancer became evident, the men would be dying of old age anyhow. Another illustration occurred in a steel plant where only deaf people were hired for jobs in areas with extremely high noise levels.

The railway industry routinely uses back X-rays to screen out individuals who show signs of lower back problems. Between 20 to 25 percent of all personal injury claims in the railroad industry are for back injuries. On average, each of the claims in 1981 was settled for $125,000 to $150,000. However, since lower back X-rays are poor predictors of subsequent back injuries and injury claims, many individuals are rejected from employment for no valid reason. Nevertheless, the railroad industry believes in the utility of such screening because even a small number of valid rejection decisions can save railway companies thousands of dollars.[167]

Medical screening for current or predicted health risks that are not protected handicaps is one, albeit problematic, strategy used by managers to reduce the present and future incidence of occupational illnesses. However, medical screening appears justifiable only where idiosyncracies of individuals significantly increase their odds of coming down with occupational illnesses relative to the average worker. Such screening should not be a substitute for increasing the health and safety of the workplace as a general goal. Additionally, employment policies using medical information should strive to accommodate those with less favorable medical records in jobs that do not expose them to health risks.

Substance Abuse Behaviors

Managers have two primary reasons to consider testing for substance abuse as a health and safety management strategy. First, testing will help pinpoint present alcohol and drug abusers among job applicants. A second reason for testing is deterrence, especially if the testing is directed toward employees and occurs on a fairly regular basis. The assumptions are that such testing will pass legal muster if challenged, and that the fear of being caught convinces even the occasional abuser to "go cold turkey."

Applicant Screening. Testing job applicants for substance abuse assumes that past behavior is the best predictor of future behavior or, said simply, someone who abuses alcohol or drugs now is likely to abuse them again.

Almost 47 percent of responding Fortune 1000 companies test applicants for illegal drugs.[168] It should be noted, however, that companies reporting that they test applicants rarely, if ever, test all applicants. Typically, only applicants for a few selected job categories will be tested. Among those companies that test, 66 percent reject applicants with positive results for illegal drugs. Regarding alcohol, about 15 percent of the companies test job applicants and 44 percent reject applicants with a single confirmed positive test result exceeding a particular cutoff point.[169] For example, IBM rejected 15 percent of applicants to positions in its San Jose, Calif. facility after urinalysis indicated they tested positive for drugs.[170] As a rule, 12 to 20 percent of jobs applicants are rejected because they test positive for drugs.[171] The only sizable predictive validity study to date provides weak though systematic evidence of higher rates of absenteeism and involuntary terminations among applicants testing positive for illegal drugs relative to applicants testing negative.[172]

Employee Screening. Managers considering substance abuse screening as a means of enhancing employee health and safety face some tough choices. A first consideration is the legality of the practices. Screening job applicants for substance abuse is more likely to pass legal muster than tests of current employees since, in general, employment laws provide less protection to applicants. Test practices are more likely to withstand challenges if an employer follows proper administrative procedures, obtains applicant consent, and assures privacy, and if the vacancy in question has some hazard associated with it. The bottom line, however, is that the jury is still out on the legality of drug testing for many types of job categories.

The claim that screening for substance abuse promotes health and safety because such tests deter abuse generates even more controversy. Proponents of drug testing programs point to a decline in the number of employees testing positive once a testing program has been implemented for a while. For example, naval personnel have been screened three times each year since 1982. At the beginning of the testing program, 37 percent of the sailors in junior grades tested positive for drugs. After two years of testing and drug education, the number testing positive dropped down to 4 percent.[173] In the eyes of naval officers, the testing program has been extremely successful in discouraging substance abuse. Such case studies, however, do not justify statements about the direct effects of drug tests on abuse or on workplace health and safety.

Beyond questions of causality, several writers point to costs in terms of employee morale and trust if screening occurs randomly, especially on jobs with no apparent hazard.[174] Instead, employee education, peer monitoring systems, rehabilitation, and counseling support services may offer more effective deterrent tools. According to this philosophy, drug screening in non-hazardous jobs should take place only when employees' behaviors suggest that they are under the influence of drugs or alcohol, and/or after a serious worksite accident has occurred.

These qualms aside, the trend points very clearly toward an increase in testing for substance abuse. Managers who choose to implement screening for health and safety purposes should consider testing as just one component of a comprehensive health and safety program.

Personality Characteristics

Selection strategies also may impact worksite health and safety by screening applicants for personality attributes associated with an increased likelihood of accident or disease involvement. However, empirical evidence linking personality factors and health and safety outcomes is weak for the most part.

For a long while, the concept of "accident proneness" enjoyed some popularity. The idea posited that accident rates are distributed unequally across populations of workers and that a handful of employees account for most accidents. Accordingly, if accident-prone employees could be screened out of jobs or remedially trained, most accidents would not occur. A Bureau of National Affairs survey indicated that the idea of accident-prone individuals is widely held among businesses.[175] Of those surveyed, 65 percent of the companies sought to identify accident-prone individuals as a safety management strategy.

These beliefs aside, the evidence suggests that personality factors alone do not predict accident frequency. The only individual characteristics consistently predictive of accident involvement are age and experience; older and more experienced employees have fewer accidents.[176]

Certain personality factors, however, may increase the likelihood of suffering illnesses while at work. A lot of recent publicity has focused on Type A and Type B personality profiles. According to the originators of this typology,[177] Type A individuals are competitive, multiphasic, achievement-oriented individuals who are impatient, easily aroused and often angry or belligerent. Type B individuals are lacking in such features. Type A individuals thrive in high-pressure environments while Type B persons react adversely under similar conditions. Aside from behavioral tendencies, Type As also have a higher risk of coronary heart disease.[178] Some evidence suggests that the increased risk of heart disease associated with a Type A personality exceeds the risk associated with age, smoking, and increased blood pressure.[179]

This evidence places managers in something of a "Catch 22" situation. On the one hand, it would be desirable to minimize the number of individuals hired who have a higher risk of disease such as coronary illnesses. However, certain high-pressure jobs are ideally suited to the Type A person. Unless an organization redesigns itself so that no job is stressful, a firm must hire some Type As for best fit to the jobs. Together with a better fit to stressful job demands, however, the organization has acquired a greater health risk in the Type A person.

Nevertheless, based on available evidence, selection decisions using personality dimensions as predictors will have limited effects on health and safety outcomes in the workplace. Organizations will improve health and safety outcomes to a much greater extent if their selection decisions take into account medical and life-style data about applicants.

Job and Work Process Redesign

Although few organizations use job and work process redesign to enhance safety and wellness in the workplace, this approach deserves serious consideration for a number of reasons. Several antecedents of accidents and illnesses such as fatigue, boredom, inattentiveness, stress, repetitive motions, and isolation can be alleviated through changes in job and work processes.

Many facets of a job can be altered to minimize sources of stress. The number of managers to whom a person reports, number of hours worked, degree of autonomy, and workload level all have impact on the stress levels experienced by workers.[180] Differences among individual needs and dispositions probably moderate this relationship; for example, Type As may need more autonomy than Type Bs.[181] However, employees in general experience less stress if given the opportunity to exercise greater control over their work responsibilities and processes.[182] Job control can be enhanced by delegating more responsibilities to individuals, providing authority over larger aspects of a job, physically separating employees from supervisors, monitoring performance on a fixed schedule or by project rather than using unscheduled or constant monitoring. Another strategy for reducing stress is to design work groups that act as social buffers to stress in the environment.[183] Some employees may need a balance between inclusion in group processes for social buffering purposes, while still retaining a level of autonomy over job duties and responsibilities.

Fatigue, inattentiveness, and boredom are significant predictors of accidents.[184] Variety can be introduced into the workflow via job rotation, job enlargement and enrichment, scheduled work breaks, and exercise periods. Such changes can contribute to a reduction in accident rates. However, something of a contradiction is suggested by one study in which coal mine operators working in isolation and, presumably, with fewer distractions experienced fewer accidents than did integrated work teams.[185] The possible tradeoff between higher health and safety costs and the benefits of group processes in the workplace cannot be dismissed.

Finally, the use of ergonomic principles in equipment and facility designs can alleviate several debilitating physical and psychological work effects. Organizations have applied ergonomic principles in designing furniture, equipment, lighting, space arrangements, and work flow practices for areas where VDTs are used. Repetitive motion disease, a syndrome common to VDT operators which afflicts as much as four percent of the work force can be mitigated by introducing ergonomically designed equipment, frequent work flow breaks, job rotations and increases in job variety.[186]

In summary, while job and work-flow redesign is typically implemented for reasons other than worker health and safety, such changes offer the potential for substantial improvements in safety and wellness. These work process and content adjustments frequently are more cost effective than other safety and health enhancement strategies, especially when psychological and behavioral results of job redesign are tallied in with the positive effects on health and safety.

Organizational Support Programs

Organizations invest resources in a number of different employee support structures that promote safety and health. Employer assistance programs (EAPs), health promotion programs, and integrated healthcare providers serve as examples of these increasingly popular health promotion structures.

Employee Assistance Programs—EAPs

EAPs act as umbrella structures that deliver a variety of health-related services. The most common EAP services are employee assessment, referral, and counseling for problems of substance abuse or mental health; education and training of supervisors and employees in various aspects of problem identification and benefit usage; and provision of support to employees and managers throughout the process of counseling and rehabilitation.

A precise estimate of the number of EAPs presently in operation proves difficult to obtain. Roughly 5,000 to 10,000 companies have EAPs, although most programs are concentrated among the country's largest corporations.[187] About a quarter of the work force is covered by an EAP.[188] Fortune 1000 corporations that test employees for alcohol or drugs, one survey found that 94 percent of responding firms provided company-supported rehabilitation (usually through EAPs) for employees testing above a positive trigger for alcohol. Eighty three percent provided similar benefits for employees testing positive for illegal drugs.[189]

Although EAPs can encompass a variety of programs, they typically fall into one of two categories:

- In-house programs, which use an EAP staff employed exclusively by the corporation or by the union. One study reported that 33 percent of the EAPs were of this type.[190]

- Outside contractors, in which EAP providers deliver services to the company on a contract basis. EAP deliverers are usually spread throughout the community, and often service a number of corporate clients. An outside contractor typically charges around $15 to $25 per employee per year.[191] As of 1985, an estimated 62 percent of EAPs were of this type.

A hybrid of these two options also is sometimes possible. For example, a corporation may use in-house specialists to develop an EAP policy, oversee the program, and evaluate its effectiveness, while hiring an outside contractor to deliver the EAP services.[193]

By providing EAP services, employers purportedly recover $3 to $5 for every $1 invested.[194] These returns on investment occur, supposedly, because EAPs: (1) facilitate early recognition, intervention, and resolution of employees' personal problems; (2) reduce the cases of tardiness and absenteeism due to such problems; (3) enable retention of skilled employees who might otherwise be lost because of emotional or health problems; (4) increase productivity by freeing employees of personal problems so that they can work to their full capacity; (5) reduce accident rates caused by substance abuse or emotional problems; and (6) improve employee morale as a result of all of the above.[195]

Consider the case of a recovering alcoholic. Inpatient treatment for a substance abuser adds up to an average of $10,000 to

$12,000. A six-month EAP rehabilitation program usually costs much less at about $2,500 per employee.[196] While such anecdotal examples abound, EAP proponents can produce little hard evidence to substantiate their claims of cost effectiveness and treatment success rates. Nevertheless, because the principle of EAPs makes sense and the problem of substance abuse increasingly preoccupies managers, the popularity of EAPs is expected to grow. Federal requirements for a "drug free workplace," which include mandated rehabilitation services, also seem likely to increase the prevalence of EAPs.

Health Promotion Programs

Organizations are increasingly expanding the range of wellness benefits in order to improve the general level of employee health. Health promotion programs (HPPs) are predicated on the substantial evidence linking life-styles to such work-related behaviors as productivity, tardiness, absenteeism, mental and physical health, accident rates, life expectancies, health claim submission rates, hospitalization rates, and employee replacement costs. Accordingly, it makes good sense to help employees develop healthy living habits. It also shows corporate responsiveness to the changing tastes among employees. Many employees view HPPs as an important fringe benefit for joining and staying with an employer.

On the basis of a 1987 survey, the Office of Disease Prevention and Health Promotion, part of the Department of Health and Human Services, concluded that 66 percent of employers in the U.S. now offer at least one health promotion activity.[197]

Programs mentioned in the survey include the following:

- smoking control programs (35.6 percent of the respondents)
- health risk appraisals (29.5 percent of the respondents)
- stress management (26.6 percent of the respondents)
- exercise/physical fitness (22.1 percent of the respondents)
- off-the-job accident prevention (19.8 percent of the respondents)
- nutrition education (16.8 percent of the respondents)
- high blood pressure control (16.5 percent of the respondents)
- weight control (14.7 percent of the respondents)

HPPs differ from EAPs in concept, although certain activities or components of the programs may overlap. One analysis differentiates HPPs from EAPs as shown in Table 2.

Some companies are offering idiosyncratic health promotion activities.[198] For example, the U.S. Health Care Systems distributes 300 apples a day to its employees, all of whom work in smoke-free facilities. Another case includes Marriott Hotel, which conducts a poolside morning aerobic class to reduce the incidence of pulled muscles among the maintenance staff.

Although many employees seek out the various health promotion activities available through their employer, this health consciousness is by no means true of all workers. As a case in point, Principal Financial Group, located in downtown Des Moines, offers regular aerobic classes and operates an onsite fitness center. Of the 4,400 employees at its Des Moines office, about 500 register for aerobic classes at any point in time while 200 to 300 use the fitness center regularly. Without support programs that educate people about the merits of fitness and wellness, "the fit get fitter but the non-fit don't get help," according to Richard Keelor, Chief Executive Officer of Health Designs International.[199]

Table 2

HPPs vs. EAPs

HPPs	EAPs
☐ Offer strictly voluntary services	☐ Use coercion and threat of job loss as stimuli for seeking assistance
☐ Deal with healthy employees	☐ Deal with employees who have personal problems
☐ Target all employees and often deal with employees in groups	☐ Focus on individual employees
☐ Concentrate on alcohol and drug abuse education as well as other life-style topics	☐ Address the diagnosis and treatment of alcohol and drug-addicted employees
☐ Emphasize health	☐ Stress job performance.

Source: Adapted from D.A. Masi. *Designing Employee Assistance Programs.* New York: AMACOM, copyright © 1984, citing R. Behrens.

One review of literature on HPPs found few scientifically rigorous studies addressing their effectiveness.[200] As a result, some analysts feel it is premature to conclude that such programs have systematic health effects, promising as they appear. Nevertheless, anecdotal evidence supports proponents' claims. For example, AT & T Communications has implemented a pilot HPP which, according to its designers, has had a significant effect on employee health and corporate healthcare expenditures. AT & T's Total Life Concept programs emphasize stress management, weight control, interpersonal relations, and physical fitness. Following the programs, participants' blood pressure and cholesterol levels dropped, their lower back pain declined, their weight dropped an average of 10 pounds, and half quit smoking. If the pilot program maintains its level of success over the next 10 years, AT & T projects savings of $72 million just from reduced heart attacks and $15 million from lowered cancer rates.

According to Kenneth P. Shapiro, Hay/Huggins president and Chief Executive Officer, "HPPs are today considered in the benefits mainstream. They are perceived as an obligation, like life insurance. As such, they will continue to increase [because] corporations are more socially aware and more productivity oriented."

Integrated Healthcare Providers

Integrated health care is designed to reduce employers' direct expenditures on health care. These programs also may improve worker health if they encourage preventive health care and deliver higher-quality professional expertise through integrated medical facilities. Health maintenance organizations (HMOs) and preferred provider organizations (PPOs) are two integrated approaches, in which organizations contract with coordinated (often group) deliverers of physician and hospital services for a reduced fee. A benefit survey conducted for the Council of Employee Benefits suggests that such healthcare approaches will be much more popular by 1995.[201] Fifty-seven percent of the companies indicated that they expect to use HMOs in 1995 (up from 16 percent now using HMOs) and 83 percent expect to use PPOs (up from the present 3 percent). Although attractive from a cost standpoint, it is unclear, yet, whether integrated healthcare approaches result in health improvements.

Conclusions

Health and safety management in the workplace has become a juggling act in which often conflicting interests and rights must be weighed. Although both employers and employees share the goal of healthful and safe working conditions, in some other areas their interests do not necessarily converge. The rights of employees to privacy, fair treatment, and a healthy and safe work environment must coexist with employers' interests in cost-effective work procedures, productivity, and reasonable healthcare costs. For example, organizations sometimes must implement new technologies or products in order to remain profitable. Some innovations improve the health and safety of the work environment, while others introduce the potential for hazard. At what point does the hazardous potential become so significant that it cannot be ignored, no matter how attractive the returns from the innovation?

To compound these dilemmas, even when a balance is struck, it is wavering and passing. Changing values, technological and scientific knowledge, economic conditions, statutory requirements, and judicial interpretations work against a lasting status quo in health and safety policies, procedures, and practices. Managers must be willing to evaluate a variety of strategies to improve health and safety while constantly striving to lower the costs of achieving that goal.

Several of the management practices discussed in this chapter can improve workplace health and safety as well as lower the costs of deficiencies in these areas. Strategies include HR activities (such as screening and placement, training and job redesign), industrial engineering interventions (that is, various forms of safety controls), executive practices (corporate policy articulation), and organizational support mechanisms (EAPs, HPPs, and integrated health care). None of these approaches, alone, is a panacea. However, taken together, these management activities create an organizational culture in which employee safety and health is seen by everyone as key to the bottom line.

◆

Notes

1. *Washington Post Health.*
2. McMahon.
3. Kiesler and Morton.

4. U.S. Chamber of Commerce (1976, 1986); A. Foster Higgins & Co.

5. Bureau of Labor Statistics (1984).
6. Ibid.
7. Office of Technology Assessment.
8. Ibid.
9. Bureau of National Affairs, Inc. (1985).
10. Greer.
11. National Safety Council (1985).
12. *Employee Benefit News* (1987c), p. 17.
13. Goldsmith and Kerr.
14. Bureau of National Affairs, Inc. (1989).
15. Bureau of National Affairs, Inc. (1989).
16. *Whirlpool Corp. v. Marshall*, 445 U.S. (1980).
17. Office of Technology Assessment.
18. *School Bd. of Nassau County v. Arline*, 480 U.S. 273, 43 FEP 81 (1987).
19. Hurd (1989).
20. *Baltimore Sun.*
21. Buchholz.
22. See, e.g., *National Treasury Employees Union v. Lyng*, 88-2515 and 88-2668 (concerning the Department of Agriculture's random testing program). See also *Owner-Operators Independent Drivers Ass'n of Am. v. Burnley*, C 884547 MHP (injunction issued against the Department of Transportation's testing rule).
23. *Congressional Record.*
24. Hurd (1988); Dodge.
25. *Baltimore Sun.*
26. *Washington Post* (1988b).
27. *Washington Post* (1986b).
28. Greer.
29. Denison.
30. Bureau of National Affairs, Inc. (1990); *Labor Law Journal.*
31. *Skinner v. Railway Labor Executives' Ass'n*, 489 U.S.——, 130 LRRM 2857 (1989).
32. *National Treasury Employees Union v. Von Raab*, 489 U.S. ——, 2 IER Cases 192 (1987).
33. 491 U.S. ——, 131 LRRM 2601 (1989).
34. *Employment Testing* (1988b).
35. Hanson.
36. 440 U.S. 568, 19 FEP 149 (1979).
37. 785 F.2d 352 (1st Cir. 1986).
38. Olian (1988).
39. Poe.
40. Office of Technology Assessment.
41. *McCarthy v. Washington*, Department of Social and Health Services, 46 Washington App. 125, 1986.
42. *Meyer v. C.P. Clare and Co. et al.*, Industrial Commission of Idaho, DOE 615-78, 1978.
43. *Andersen v. Anoka County Welfare Board et al.*, U.S.D.C. Minn., 4th Division, Civil No. 4-79-269, March 26, 1981.
44. *Batchelor v. Fresno County, California*, 1982.
45. Arthur Andersen.
46. National Association of Manufacturers.
47. Northrup, Rowan, and Perry.
48. Morral.
49. Greer.
50. Council on Environmental Quality.
51. *Newsweek* (1989).
52. *Wall Street Journal* (1987b).
53. Ibid.
54. Poe.
55. Jones and Wuebker.
56. *Washington Post* (1988a); Masi.
57. *Employee Benefit News* (1988).
58. Donkin.
59. Hellman.
60. *Washington Post* (1986d).
61. Bureau of National Affairs, Inc. (1986).
62. Ibid.
63. Bureau of National Affairs, Inc. (1986).
64. *Washington Post* (1986d).
65. *Employee Benefit News* (1987a), p. 20.
66. Gruenfeld.

67. Kristien.
68. Weiss.
69. Cascio.
70. Gruenfeld.
71. Lorber and Kirk.
72. Rodin and Salovey.
73. Bureau of National Affairs, Inc. (1987).
74. Rossignol, Morse, Summers, and Pagnotto.
75. Jones and Wuebker.
76. Ibid.
77. Lorber and Kirk.
78. Brooks.
79. Council on Scientific Affairs.
80. Harper.
81. Ibid.
82. *Wall Street Journal* (1986c).
83. *Wall Street Journal* (1987a).
84. *Washington Post* (1987e).
85. *Washington Post* (1986b).
86. Office of Technology Assessment.
87. Office of Technology Assessment.
88. Office of Technology Assessment, based on estimates from Peto and Schneiderman.
89. National Cancer Institute.
90. Rothstein (1989).
91. Olian (1984).
92. *Time* (1988).
93. Ibid.
94. Russell.
95. Wynder and Stellman.
96. Ibid.
97. *Washington Post* (1987g).
98. Ibid.
99. *Washington Post* (1987a).
100. *Time* (1988).
101. Gruenfeld.
102. Ibid.
103. *Washington Post* (1987e).
104. Ibid.
105. *Time* (1988).
106. *Washington Post* (1986d).
107. American Management Association.
108. Masi.
109. *Employment Testing* (1988a).
110. Cited in Bureau of National Affairs, Inc. (1986), p. 2.
111. *Time* (1986).
112. Guthrie and Olian.
113. Ibid.
114. *Newsweek* (1988a).
115. *Newsweek* (1986b), p. 68.
116. Centers for Disease Control.
117. Masters, Johnson, and Kolodny.
118. Lui, Darrow, and Rutherford.
119. *Resource*.
120. Lorber and Kirk.
121. Guthrie and Olian.
122. American Society for Personnel Administration.
123. *Washington Post* (1987d).
124. Banta.
125. *Wall Street Journal* (1987c).
126. *Newsweek* (1986c).
127. Hamil.
128. Office of Technology Assessment.
129. Ibid.
130. *Harvard Business Review*.
131. Jones and Wuebker.
132. *Newsweek* (1988b).
133. Siskind.
134. Fiedler et al.
135. Office of Technology Assessment.
136. Komaki and Jensen.
137. Masi.
138. Bureau of National Affairs, Inc. (1986).
139. Gomez-Mejia and Balkin.
140. *New York Times*.
141. Simonds; Smith, Cohen, Cohen, and Cleveland.
142. Guthrie and Olian.
143. Bensinger.
144. *Employee Relations and Human Resources Bulletin*.
145. McMahon.
146. This section draws heavily on Office of Technology Assessment.
147. *Washington Post* (1988d).
148. Office of Technology Assessment.
149. Bureau of Labor Statistics (1980).

150. National Safety Council (1980).
151. Rothstein (1984).
152. *Science.*
153. *Wall Street Journal* (1986a).
154. *Washington Post* (1987b).
155. *Washington Post* (1988c)
156. *Wall Street Journal* (1986b).
157. *Washington Post* (1986a).
158. Olian (1984).
159. Cited in *Washington Post* (1986c).
160. Rothstein (1984).
161. Cited in *Washington Post* (1987f).
162. Olian (1984).
163. Hunt.
164. U.S. Department of Health, Education, and Welfare.
165. Ibid.
166. Rothstein (1984).
167. Ibid.
168. Guthrie and Olian.
169. Ibid.
170. Howe.
171. *Wall Street Journal* (1985).
172. U.S. Postal Service.
173. Howe.
174. See, e.g., Lundberg.
175. Bureau of National Affairs, Inc. (1977).

176. Root.
177. Rosenman, et al.
178. Wright.
179. National Institutes of Health.
180. Spector, Dwyer, and Jex.
181. Frankenhaeuser.
182. Ibid.
183. Cohen and Wills.
184. Office of Technology Assessment.
185. Goodman and Garber.
186. *Business Week.*
187. Bureau of National Affairs (1986).
188. *Washington Post* (1988a).
189. Guthrie and Olian.
190. Levine.
191. *Washington Post* (1988a).
192. Levine.
193. Masi.
194. *Washington Post* (1988a).
195. Levine.
196. *Washington Post* (1988a).
197. *Employee Benefit News* (1987b).
198. McMahon.
199. *Employee Benefit News* (1987a), p. 20.
200. Terborg.
201. *Employee Benefit News* (1987b), p. 38.

◆

References

A. Foster Higgins & Co. 1988. *Foster Higgins Health Care Benefits Survey 1987.*

American Management Association. 1987. "Drug Abuse—The Workplace Issues." AMA Membership Publication.

American Society for Personnel Administration. 1987. "Few Companies Have Policies to Cover Employees With AIDS." *Resource* 6 (12) (October): 1.

Arthur Andersen & Co. 1979. "Cost of Government Regulation Study for the Business Roundtable." Executive Summary (March).

Baltimore Sun. 1987. August 20: A-1, A-11.

Banta, W.F. 1988. *AIDS in the Workplace.* Lexington, MA: D.C. Heath.

Behrens, R. 1983. "The Distinction Between Health Promotion Programs and Employee Assistance Programs." Lecture to U.S. Department of Health and Human Services EAP administrators in Employee Counseling Services Units Directors' Workshops, Washington, DC, February 14. Cited in Masi.

Bensinger, P. 1986. In *Drugs in the Workplace: What Lies Ahead?* Washington, DC: Bureau of National Affairs, Inc., pp. 126–128.

Brooks, G.E. 1986. "VDTs and Health Risks: What Unions Are Doing." *Personnel* (July): 59–64.

Buchholz, R.A. 1988. *Public Policy Issues for Management.* Englewood Cliffs, NJ: Prentice-Hall.

Bureau of Labor Statistics. 1980. *Accidents Involving Head Injuries.* U.S. Department of Labor, Report No. 6-5. Washington, DC: U.S. Government Printing Office.

————. 1984. "Occupational Injuries and Illnesses in the U.S. by Industry." Washington, DC: U.S. Department of Labor, p. 1.

Bureau of National Affairs, Inc. 1971. *Basic Patterns in Union Contracts*, 7th ed. Washington, DC: BNA Books.

————. 1977. *Safety Policies and the Impact of OSHA.* Personnel Policy Forum Survey No. 117. Washington, DC: Bureau of National Affairs, Inc.

————. 1985. *Occupational Safety and Health Reports* 15 (16) (September 19): 3.

————. 1986. *Alcohol and Drugs in the Workplace: Costs, Controls, and Controversies.* Washington, DC: Bureau of National Affairs, Inc.

————. 1987. *Daily Labor Report* (August 3): A-2.

————. 1989. *Basic Patterns in Union Contracts*, 12th ed. Washington, DC: BNA Books.

————. 1990. Daily Labor Report (April 9):A-6.

Business Week. 1989. "An Invisible Workplace Hazard Gets Harder to Ignore." (January 30): 92–93.

Cascio, W.F. 1987. *Costing Human Resources—The Financial Impact of Behavior in Organizations*, 2nd ed. Belmont, CA: Kent Publishing Co.

Cohen, S. and T.A. Wills. 1985. "Stress, Social Support, and the Buffering Hypothesis." *Psychological Bulletin* 98: 310–357.

Congressional Record. 1988. October 21: Part 2, pp. H 11146–47.

Council on Environmental Quality. 1980. "Environmental Quality 1980." Washington, DC: Council on Environmental Quality, p. 394.

Council on Scientific Affairs. 1987. "Health Effects of Video Display Terminals." *Journal of the American Medical Association (JAMA)* 257 (11) (March 20): 1508–1512.

Denison, E.F. 1979. "Accounting for Slower Economic Growth." Washington, DC: the Brookings Institute.

Dodge, G.E. 1989. "A Patchwork of Laws: States and Localities Regulate Employer Drug Testing Programs." *Employment Testing* 3(13): 447–451, 454.

Donkin, R. 1989. "What EAPs Are Doing to Rescue Addicted Workers." *Business and Health* 7(3) (March): 21–25.

Employee Benefits News. 1987a. "Exercise Leading to Better Health Habits by Employees." November/December: 20.

_____. 1987b. "Survey: More Benefits, Greater Diversity by 1995." November/December: 38.

_____. 1987c. "Wellness Programs Show Healthy Returns." November/December: 17.

_____. 1988. "Impacting the Bottom Line." February: 20.

Employee Relations and Human Resources Bulletin. 1978; "AIDS: How Levi Strauss Copes." January 21: 1.

Employment Testing. 1988a. "Drug Abuse as a Workplace Issue." Vol. 2 (5) (January 15): 151.

_____. 1988b. "Judge Halts Drug Testing of Job Applicants." Vol. 2 (12) (August 1): 254.

Fiedler, F.E., et al. 1984. "Improving Mine Productivity and Safety Through Management Training and Organizational Development: A Comparative Study." *Basic and Applied Social Psychology* 5 (1): 1–18.

Frankenhaeuser, M. 1986. "A Psychological Framework for Research on Human Stress and Coping." In *Dynamics of Stress*, ed. M.H. Appley and R. Trumbell. New York: Plenum.

Goldsmith, F. and L. Kerr. 1982. *Occupational Safety and Health: The Prevention and Control of Work-Related Hazards.* New York: Human Sciences Press.

Gomez-Mejia, L.R., and D.B. Balkin. 1987. "Dimensions and Characteristics of Personnel Manager Perceptions of Effective Drug Testing Programs." *Personnel Psychology* 40: 745–763.

Goodman, P.S. and S. Garber. 1988. "Absenteeism and Accidents in a Dangerous Environment: Empirical Analysis of Underground Coal Mines." *Journal of Applied Psychology* 73(1): 81–86.

Greer, D.F. 1983. *Business, Government, and Society.* New York, NY: MacMillan Publishing Co.

Gruenfeld, E.F. 1986. "Smoking, Drugs, and the Healthy Employee." *ILR Report* 23(2) (Spring): 9–17.

Guthrie, J.P., and J.D. Olian. 1989. "Survey of the Fortune 1000 Physiological Testing Practices." Paper presented at The Society for Industrial and Organizational Psychology, Boston.

Hamil, P. 1988. "Breaking the Silence: A Letter to a Black Friend." *Esquire* (March): 91–102.

Hanson, D.J. 1986. "Drug Abuse Testing Programs Gaining Acceptance in Workplace." *Chemical & Engineering News* (64) (June 2): 7–14.

Harper, S. 1986. "Unknown Variables: Assessing Risk in the Semiconductor Industry." *Occupational Health and Safety* (October): 28–38.

Harvard Business Review. 1986. "Protecting Pregnant Workers." May-June: 26–30.

Hellman, S. 1987. "A Method For Determining the Effectiveness of a Corporation's Healthcare Cost Containment Efforts." Employee Benefits Journal (Sept.): 27–32.

Howe, C.L. 1985. "Getting Straight Again." Datamation (31)(3)(16) (Aug. 15): 32–38.

Hunt, M. 1986. "The Total Gene Screen." New York Times (January 19): 33.

Hurd, S. 1988. "States Adopt Comprehensive Drug Testing Laws." Employment Testing 2 (14) (September 1): 263–267.

———. 1989. "States Pass AIDS-Related Laws." Employment Testing 3 (1 & 2): 351–353.

Jones, J.W. and L.J. Wuebker. 1985. "Combating the New Generation of Workers' Compensation Claims." Risk Management (December): 44–46.

Kiesler, C.A. and T.L. Morton. 1988. "Psychology and Public Policy in the Health Care Revolution." American Psychologist 43 (12): 993–1003.

Komaki, J.L. and M. Jensen. 1984. "Within-Group Designs: An Alternative to Traditional Control-Group Designs." In Health and Industry, eds. M.F. Dataldo and T.J. Coates. New York: Wiley.

Kristien, M.M. 1980. "How Much Can a Business Expect to Earn from Smoking Cessation?" Paper presented at the Connecticut Lung Association conference "Smoking in the Workplace," New Haven, CN.

Labor Law Journal. 1988. "Murder in the Workplace." 39(4) (April): 220–231.

Levine, H.S. 1985. "Consensus on . . . Employee Assistance Programs." Personnel 62 (April): 14–19.

Lorber, L.Z. and R.J. Kirk. 1987. Fear Itself: A Legal and Personnel Analysis of Drug Testing, AIDS, Secondary Smoke, and VDTs. Alexandria, VA: ASPA Foundation.

Lui, K.J., W.W. Darrow, and G.W. Rutherford III. 1988. "A Model-Based Estimate of the Mean Incubation Period for AIDS in Homosexual Men." Science 3 (240) (June): 1333–1335.

Lundberg, G.D. 1988. "Is Random Mandatory Drug Testing Needed?" Washington Post Health (April 19): 8.

Masi, D.A. 1984. Designing Employee Assistance Programs. New York: American Management Association.

Masters, W.H., V.E. Johnson, and R.C. Kolodny. 1988. Crisis: Heterosexual Behavior in the Age of AIDS. New York: Grove Press.

McMahon, P.Q. "Labor-Management Health Care Cost Containment: Present and Future Challenges to Cooperative Problem Solving." Employee Benefits Journal (June): 14–19.

Morral, J.F. 1979. "Exposure to Occupational Noise." In Benefit-Cost Analysis of Social Regulation. Washington, DC: American Enterprise Institute.

National Association of Manufacturers. 1985. "Reform of Occupational Safety and Health Act of 1970." Analysis and Background Report, Washington, DC, September 11, p. 5.

National Cancer Institute. 1978. "Estimates of the Fraction of Cancer in the United States Related to Occupational Factors, National Institute of Environmental Health Sciences." Paper prepared for/by the National Institute for Occupational Safety and Health, Washington, DC, September 15.

National Institute of Health, Review Panel on Coronary Prone Behavior and Coronary Heart Disease. 1981. "Coronary-Prone Behavior and Coronary Heart Disease: A Critical Review." *Circulation* 63: 1199–1215.

National Safety Council. 1985. "Accident Facts." Washington, DC, p. 2.

_____. *Accident Prevention Manual for Industrial Operations: Engineering and Technology*, 8th ed. F.E. McElroy (ed.) Chicago.

New York Times. 1987. "Levi's Broad AIDS Program." Business sec., March 12: 1.

Newsweek. 1986a. "Can You Pass the Job Test." May 5: 46–54.

_____. 1986b. "Spreading Alarm About AIDS." June 12: 68.

_____. 1986c. "Future Shock: The AIDS Epidemic." November 24: 30–47.

_____. 1988a. "The AIDs Threat: Who's at Risk?" March 14: 42.

_____. 1988b. "Stress on the Job." April 25: 40–45.

_____. 1989. "Biting the Insurance Bullet." August 28: 46.

Northrup, H.R., R.L. Rowan, and C.R. Perry. 1978. "The Impact of OSHA." Paper prepared for the Philadelphia Industrial Research Unit, University of Pennsylvania, pp. 291–418.

Office of Technology Assessment, Congress of the United States, 1985. *Preventing Illness and Injury in the Workplace*. Washington, DC: U.S. Government Printing Office.

Olian, J.D. 1984. "Genetic Screening for Employment Purposes." *Personnel Psychology* 37: 423–438.

_____. 1988. "AIDS Testing for Employment Purposes: Facts and Controversies." *Journal of Business and Psychology* 3(2): 135–153.

Peto, R. and M. Schneiderman. 1981. *Quantification of Occupational Cancer: Bambury Report 9*. Cold Spring Harbor, NY: Cold Spring Harbor Laboratory.

Poe, R. 1987. "A Challenge to Supervisors: Coping with Employee Stress." *Across the Board Midway Airline Magazine* (May): 67–69.

Resource. 1987. "Few Companies Have Policies to Cover Employees With AIDS." October: 1–2.

Rodin, J. and P. Salovey. 1989. "Health Psychology." In *Annual Review of Psychology* 40: 533–579.

Root, N. 1981. "Inquiries at Work Are Fewer Among Older Employees." *Monthly Labor Review* 104(3): 30–34.

Rosenman, R.H., M. Friedman, R. Strauss, M. Wurm, R. Kositchek, W. Hahn, and N.T. Wertthessen. 1964. "A Predictive Study of Coronary Heart Disease." *Journal of American Medical Association* 189: 15–22.

Rossignol, A.M., E.P. Morse, V.M. Summers, and L.D. Pagnotto. 1987. "Video Display Terminal Use and Reported Health Symptoms Among Massachusetts Clerical Workers." *Journal of Occupational Medicine* 29 (2): 112–118.

Rothstein, M. 1984. *Medical Screening of Workers*. Washington, DC: BNA Books.

———. 1989. "Medical Screening and Employment Law: A Note of Caution and Some Observations." *Employment Testing* 3(6) (May 1): 363–370.

Russell, C. 1984. "Exposure to Smoke Affects Health." *Washington Post* (November 4): A-2.

Science. 1986. "Genetic Screening Raises Questions for Employees and Insurers." vol. 232, April 18: 317–319.

Simonds, R.H. 1973. "OSHA Compliance: 'Safety Is Good Business.'" *Personnel* 50(4) (July-August): 30–38.

Siskind, F. 1982. "Another Look at the Link Between Work Inquiries and Job Experience." *Monthly Labor Review* 105(2): 38–41.

Smith, M.J., H.H. Cohen, A. Cohen, and R.J. Cleveland. 1978. "Characteristics of Successful Safety Programs." *Journal of Safety Research* 10: 5–15.

Spector, P.E., D.J. Dwyer, and S.M. Jex. 1988. "Relation of Job Stressors to Affective, Health and Performance Outcomes: A Comparison of Multiple Data Sources." *Journal of Applied Psychology* 73(1): 11–19.

Terborg, J.R. 1986. "Health Promotion at the Worksite: A Research Challenge for Personnel and Human Resources Management." In *Research in Personnel and Human Resources Management*, vol. 4, eds. K. Rowlands and G. Ferris. Greenwich, Ct: JAI Press Inc.

Time. 1986. "Battling the Enemy Within." March 17: 52–61.

———. 1988. "Butt Out—The War Over Smoking." April 18: 64–75.

U.S. Bureau of the Census. 1983. *Statistical Abstract of the United States 1984*, 104th ed. Washington, DC: U.S. Government Printing Office.

———. 1986. *Statistical Abstract of the United States 1987*, 107th ed. Washington, DC: U.S. Government Printing Office.

U.S. Chamber of Commerce. 1977. *Employee Benefits, 1976*. Washington, DC: Government Printing Office.

———. 1987. *Employee Benefits, 1986*. Washington, DC: Government Printing Office.

U.S. Department of Health, Education, and Welfare. 1977. *National Occupational Hazard Survey*, vol. 3. Washington, DC: U.S. Government Printing Office.

U.S. Postal Service. 1989. *An Empirical Evaluation of Preemployment Drug Testing in the United States Postal Service*. Interim report. Washington, DC: Office of Selection and Evaluation.

Wall Street Journal. 1985. August 8:

———. 1986a. February 6: 1, 16.

———. 1986b. February 12: 1, 24.

———. 1986c. November 26.

———. 1987a. January 14.

———. 1987b. September 29: 41.

———. 1987c. November 13: 1.

Washington Post. 1986a. July 7.

———. 1986b. July 13: 64.

———. 1986c. July 24: A-24.

———. 1986d. September 21: D-1, D-4.

———. 1987a. January 21: A-7.

———. 1987b. February 26: A-1.

———. 1987c. August 20: A-21.

———. 1987d. August 27: F-1, F-4.

———. 1987e. September 18.

———. 1987f. September 24: A3.

———. 1987g. December 9: F1, F4.

———. 1988a. Business section. January 11: 30.

———. 1988b. March 24: A7.

———. 1988c. April 11: A-10.

———. 1988d. "Makers of Foam Containers Pledge to Stop Using CFCs: Substitute Is Less Damaging to Ozone Layer." April 13: A-10.

———. 1988e. April 25.

Washington Post Health. 1989. February 14: 5.

Weiss, W.L. 1980. "Impove Productivity Overnight. *The Collegiate Forum*: 2.

Wright, L. 1988. "The Type-A Behavior Pattern and Coronary Artery Disease." *American Psychologist* 43(1) (January): 2–14.

Wynder, E.L. and S.D. Stellman. 1987. "Comparative Epidemiology of Tobacco-Related Cancers." *Cancer Research* 37: 4608–4622.

Author Index

Authors appearing in this Index appear in the Notes and References at the end of each chapter. The individual authors of the chapters appear here also. Anyone referenced in the body of the text will appear in the Subject Index.

A. Foster Higgins & Co.   4–276n,
      4–279
Abbasi, S.M.   4–122
Adodeely, J.   4–174n, 4–176
Abowd, J.M.   4–28n, 4–40n, 4–41,
      4–214n, 4–214
Abraham, K.G.   4–20n, 4–22
AFL-CIO   4–174n, 4–176
Ahern, R.W   4–78n, 4–78
Alchian, A.A.   4–40n, 4–41
Allen, S.G.   4–33n, 4–40n, 4–41n,
      4–41
American Management
      Association   4–278n, 4–279
American Society for Personnel
      Administration   4–278n,
      4–279
Anderson, J.C.   4–176n, 4–176
Apcar, L.   4–174n, 4–176
Argyris, C.   4–212n, 4–214
Arthur Andersen & Co.   4–277n,
      4–279
Axelrod, J.   4–120n, 4–126

Balkin, D.B.   4–278n, 4–281
Baltimore Sun   4–277n, 4–279
Banta, W.F.   4–278n, 4–279
Barkin, S.   4–174n, 4–176
Barnes, T.J.   4–121n, 4–122n, 4–123
Barron, J.M.   4–40n, 4–41
Bartel, A.   4–33n, 4–41n, 4–41
Becker, B.E.   4–28n, 4–40n, 4–41,
      4–214n, 4–214
Bedikian, M.A.   4–118n, 4–123
Behrens, R.   4–274n, 4–279
Bell, D.   4–174n, 4–176
Belous, R.   4–214n, 4–214
Bendix, R.   4–211n, 4–214
Bensinger, P.   4–278n, 4–280
Bernstein, J.   4–175n, 4–176

Bethel, T.   4–175n, 4–176
Bills, R.D.   4–120n, 4–123
Bishop, J.   4–40n, 4–41
Block, R.N.   4–40n, 4–42, 4–176n,
      4–176
Boudreau, J.   4–120n, 4–121n, 4–125
Bouillon, M.   4–33n, 4–41n, 4–42
Bradshaw, D.A.   4–122n, 4–123
Brealey, R.   4–40n, 4–41
Briggs, S.   4–20n, 4–21
Brooks, G.E.   4–278n, 4–280
Brown, C.   4–33n, 4–40n, 4–41
Brown, R.B.   4–174n, 4–179
Buchholz, R.A.   4–277n, 4–280
Bullock, R.J.   4–78n, 4–78
Bunn, G.   4–118n, 4–119n, 4–125
Bureau of Labor Statistics   4–233n,
      4–277n, 4–278n, 4–280
Bureau of National Affairs,
      Inc.   4–119n, 4–120n,
      4–121n, 4–123, 4–175n,
      4–176n, 4–177, 4–212n,
      4–213n, 4–214, 4–277n,
      4–278n, 4– 279n, 4–280
Bureau of the Census   4–284
Business Week   4–77n, 4–78, 4–120n,
      4–121n, 4–122n, 4–123,
      4–212, 4–214, 4–279n, 4–280
Busman, G.   4–176n, 4–176

Campbell, J.P.   4–41n, 4–41
Campbell, R.J.   4–41n, 4–41
Cappelli, Peter   4–77n, 4–78,
      4–180—4–217, 4–211n,
      4–212n, 4– 213n, 4–214n,
      4–214, 4–215, 4–216
Caras, H.S.   4–118n, 4–123
Cascio, Wayne F.   4–278n, 4–280
Cecere, M.S.   4–119n, 4–120n,
      4–124

Centers for Disease Control 4–278n
Chalykoff, J. 4–176n, 4–178, 4–212n,
        4–214
Chamber of Commerce,
        U.S. 4–276n, 4–284
Chamberlain, N.W. 4–20n, 4–21
Cherry, R. 4–212n, 4–213n, 4–215
Clark, K.B. 4–33n, 4–40n, 4–41n,
        4–41
Cleveland, R.J. 4–278n, 4–284
Cohen, A. 4–278n, 4–284
Cohen, H.H. 4–278n, 4–284
Cohen, S. 4–279n, 4–280
Congressional Record 4–277n, 4–280
Cook, R.W. 4–122
Cook, S.H. 4–121n, 4–124
Cooke, W.N. 4–77n, 4–78, 4–175n,
        4–176n, 4–177, 4–179
Coulson, C. 4–20n, 4–21
Council on Environmental
        Quality 4–277n, 4–280
Council on Scientific Affairs 4–278n,
        4–280
Craft, J.A. 4–175n, 4–177
Cullen, D.E. 4–20n, 4–21
Cummings, T.C. 4–78n, 4–78

Darrow, W.W. 4–278n, 4–282
Deacon, L.V.W. 4–122n, 4–123
Deane, W.B. 4–118n, 4–125
Deitz, P.O. 4–78n, 4–79
Delaney, J.T. 4–21n, 4–22, 4–175n,
        4–177
DeMaria, A.T. 4–175n, 4–177
Demsetz, H. 4–40n, 4–41
DeNisi, A.S. 4–176n, 4–179
Denison, E.F. 4–277n, 4–280
Diaz, E.M. 4–118n, 4–124
Dickens, W.T. 4–20n, 4–21, 4–176n,
        4–177, 4–212n, 4–215
Dodge, G.E. 4–277n, 4–280
Doeringer, P.B. 4–20n, 4–21
Donkin, R. 4–277n, 4–280
Dreher, G.F. 4–40n, 4–42
Dressler, J.B. 4–121n, 4–124
Drexler, J.A. 4–77n, 4–78n, 4–80
Duffy, J. 4–119n, 4–120n, 4–121n,
        4–124
Dulles, F.R. 4–20n, 4–21
Dunkelberg, W.C. 4–40n, 4–41

Dunlop, J.T. 4–174n, 4–177
Dwyer, D.J. 4–279n, 4–284
Dyer, L.D. 4–9n, 4–11n, 4–77n,
        4–78n, 4–78, 4–79, 4–175n,
        4–177

Edwards, H.T. 4–119n, 4–124
Ehrenberg, R.G. 4–33n, 4–40n,
        4–41, 4–42, 4–78n, 4–79
Eischen, Dana Edward 4–82–4–133
Elkouri, F. and E.A. 4–118n,
        4–119n, 4–120n, 4–121n,
        4–122n, 4–124
Employee Benefit News 4–277n,
        4–279n, 4–280, 4–281
*Employee Relations and Human
        Resources Bulletin* 4–278n,
        4–281
Employment Testing 4–277n,
        4–278n, 4–281
Etzioni, A. 4–20n, 4–21
Ewing, D.W. 4–118n, 4–124
Extejt, M. 4–175n, 4–177

Federal Mediation and Conciliation
        Service 4–40n, 4–42
Fein, M. 4–78n, 4–79
Fiedler, F.E. 4–278n, 4–281
Fields, M.W. 4–213n, 4–216
Finner, W. 4–121n, 4–122n, 4–124
Finney, M.I. 4–122
Fiorito, J. 4–176n, 4–177, 4–178,
        4–212n, 4–215
Flanagan, S.M. 4–119n, 4–124
Flores, J. 4–122
Florey, P. 4–118n, 4–124
Fossum, John A. 4–1–4–22,
        4–118n, 4–120n, 4–124
Foulkes, F. 4–20n, 4–175n, 4–177
Frankenhaeuser, M. 4–279n, 4–281
Fraser, C.R.P. 4–77n, 4–80
Freedman, A. 4–40n, 4–174n,
        4–177, 4–206n, 4–212n,
        4–215
Freeman, R.B. 4–40n, 4–41n, 4–42,
        4–212n, 4–215
Freiberg, B.J. 4–212n, 4–215
Friedman, J.M. 4–119n, 4–124
Friedman, M. 4–283
Frost, C.F. 4–78n, 4–80

Fukami, C.V.   4-77n, 4-79
Fulmer, W.E.   4-212n, 4-215

Gagala, K.   4-175n, 4-177
Garber, S.   4-279n, 4-281
Gautschii, F.H., III   4-175n, 4-177
General Accounting Office   4-78n,
   4-81
Gershenfeld, W.J.   4-41n, 4-42,
   4-78n, 4-79
Getman, J.   4-175n, 4-176n, 4-178
Gilkey, R.   4-122
Glendenning, C.   4-21n, 4-21
Gobeille, K.R.   4-28n, 4-40n, 4-42,
   4-213n, 4-215
Goddard, R.W.   4-121n, 4-122n,
   4-124
Goldberg, S.B.   4-175n, 4-176n,
   4-178
Golden, C.S.   4-211n, 4-215
Goldsmith, F.   4-277n, 4-281
Gomez-Mejia, L.R.   4-278n, 4-281
Goodman, P.S.   4-77n, 4-78n, 4-79,
   4-279n, 4-281
Gordon, M.E.   4-41n, 4-42, 4-175n,
   4-178
Gorman, E.J., III   4-120n, 4-126
Green, R.M.   4-120n, 4-122
Greer, C.   4-176n, 4-177
Greer, D.F.   4-277n, 4-281
Grenig, J.   4-20n, 4-21
Grier, K.B.   4-21n, 4-21
Gross, B.   4-119n, 4-120n, 4-121n,
   4-124
Grossman, D.   4-21n, 4-21
Gruenfeld, E.F.   4-277n, 4-278n,
   4-281
Gulas, A.M.   4-118n, 4-124
Guthrie, J.P.   4-278n, 4-279n, 4-281

Hackman, J.R.   4-212n, 4-215
Hahn, W.   4-283
Hamil, P.   4-278n, 4-281
Hammer, R.   4-174n, 4-176
Hanlon, M.   4-77n, 4-80
Hanson, D.J.   4-277n, 4-281
Harper, S.   4-278n, 4-281
Harvard Business Review   4-278n,
   4-282

Hay Managememnt
   Associates   4-213n, 4-215
Health, Education, and Welfare
   Department   4-279n, 4-284
Health and Human Services
   Department   4-120n, 4-126
Healy, J.   4-77n, 4-79
Heilbroner, R.L.   4-20n, 4-21
Hellman, S.   4-277n, 4-281
Heneman, H.G., III   4-9n, 4-11n,
   4-20n, 4-21
Herman, E.E.   4-118n, 4-124
Herman, J.B.   4-175n, 4-176n,
   4-178
Hirsch, B.T.   4-40n, 4-42
Hoerr, J.   4-212n, 4-216
Holder, G.   4-175n, 4-177
Hollman, K.W.   4-122
Holloway, W.J.   4-119n, 4-120n,
   4-121n, 4-122n
Holzer, H.J.   4-33n, 4-40n, 4-42
Holzhauer, J.D.   4-119n, 4-124
Howard, B.B.   4-78n, 4-79
Howe, C.L.   4-279n, 4-282
Hoyer, D.T.   4-78n, 4-79
Hughes, C.   4-175n, 4-178
Hunt, J.C.   4-176n, 4-178
Hunt, M.   4-279n, 4-282
Hurd, S.   4-277n, 4-282
Hutchins, D.   4-120n, 4-121n, 4-124
Huxley, C.   4-174n, 4-178

Ichniowski, C.   4-28n, 4-40n, 4-42
Irwin, Richard D.   4-122

Jacoby, S.M.   4-20n, 4-21, 4-122n,
   4-125
Jensen, M.   4-278n, 4-282
Jex, S.M.   4-279n, 4-284
Johnson, V.E.   4-278n, 4-282
Johnson, W.A.   4-41n, 4-42
Jones, J.W.   4-277n, 4-278n, 4-282

Katz, H.C.   4-21n, 4-21, 4-28n,
   4-40n, 4-42, 4-77n, 4-78n,
   4-79, 4-80, 4-174n, 4-175n,
   4-178, 4-213n, 4-215
Kerr, L.   4-277n, 4-281
Kettler, D.   4-174n, 4-178
Keynes, J.M   4-214n, 4-215

Kiesler, C.A.   4–276n, 4–282
Kilgour, J.   4–175n, 4–178
Kirk, R.J.   4–120n, 4–125, 4–278n, 4–282
Kirkpatrick, D.   4–214n, 4–215
Klein, J.A.   4–77n, 4–79
Kleiner, Morris M.   4–23—4–43, 4–25n, 4–28n, 4–33n, 4–40n, 4– 41n, 4–42, 4–43, 4–212n
Klug, M.   4–122
Kochan, T.A.   4–21n, 4–21, 4–28n, 4–40n, 4–42, 4–77n, 4–78n, 4–78, 4–79, 4–80, 4–174n, 4–175n, 4–176n, 4–178, 4–212n, 4–213n, 4–214n, 4–215, 4–216
Koepp, S.   4–120n, 4–125
Kolodny, R.C.   4–278n, 4–282
Komaki, J.A.   4–278n, 4–282
Korando, K.J.   4–121n, 4–125
Kositchek, R.   4–283
Koys, D.J.   4–20n, 4–21
Kramer, A.M.   4–212n, 4–216
Kristien, M.M.   4–278n, 4–282
Kuhn, A.   4–118n, 4–124

Labor Department   4–78n, 4–81, 4–177, 4–213n, 4–216, 4–233n
Labor Law Journal   4–277n, 4–282
Larker, D.   4–33n, 4–41n, 4–43
Larson, E.   4–77n, 4–79
Lawler, E.E., III   4–41n, 4–43, 4–77n, 4–78n, 4–78, 4–80
Lawler, John J.   4–134—4–179, 4–175n, 4–176n, 4–178, 4–179
Ledford, G.E., Jr.   4–78n, 4–80
Ledvinka, J.   4–119n, 4–120n, 4–121n, 4–122n, 4–125
Leech, M.J.   4–119n, 4–120n, 4–121n, 4–122n, 4–124
Leonard, J.S.   4–20n, 4–21
Leone, R.D.   4–77n, 4–80
Levin, W.R.   4–213n, 4–215
Levine, H.S.   4–279n, 4–282
Lewicki, R.J.   4–122
Lewin, D.   4–25n
Liggett, M.H.   4–213n, 4–215
Linde, H.A.   4–118n, 4–119n, 4–125

Lipsky, D.B.   4–77n, 4–78n, 4–78, 4–79
Litterer, J.A.   4–122
Locke, E.A.   4–78n, 4–80
Lorber, L.Z.   4–120n, 4–125, 4–278n, 4–282
Lovell, M.R., Jr.   4–77n, 4–80
Lowman, C.   4–176n, 4–177, 4–212n, 4–215
Lui, K.J.   4–278n, 4–282
Lundberg, G.D.   4–279n, 4–282

Majerus, R.E.   4–77n, 4–80
Management Review   4–214n, 4–215
Maranto, C.   4–176n
Martin, J.E.   4–213n, 4–216
Marx, G.T.   4–121n, 4–125
Masi, D.A.   4–274n, 4–277n, 4–278n, 4–279n, 4–282
Masters, M.F.   4–21n, 4–22
Masters, W.H.   4–278n, 4–282
Mauer, G.W.   4–122
Maye, W.T.   4–77n, 4–80
Mazadoorian, H.N.   4–123
McClenahen, J.S.   4–121n, 4–125
McDonald, C.   4–175n, 4–178
McGuiness, K.C.   4–147n, 4–174n, 4–178
McKelvey, J.T.   4–119n, 4–125
McKersie, R.B.   4–21n, 4–21, 4–77n, 4–78n, 4–79, 4–80, 4–81, 4–174n, 4–175n, 4–176n, 4–178, 4–213n, 4–214n, 4–215
McLean, R.A.   4–40n, 4–42
McMahon, P.Q.   4–276n, 4–278n, 4–279n, 4–282
McOmber, R.A.   4–122n, 4–125
Medoff, J.L.   4–20n, 4–22, 4–33n, 4–40n, 4–41, 4–42, 4–212n, 4–215
Meyer, H.H.   4–213n, 4–216
Meyers, M.S.   4–175n, 4–178
Miles, G.L.   4–212n, 4–216
Milkovich, G.T.   4–33n, 4–40n, 4–42, 4–78n, 4–79, 4–120n, 4–121n, 4–125
Millhauser, M.   4–123
Mills, D.Q.   4–77n, 4–80
Minton, J.W.   4–118n, 4–124

Mintzberg, H.   4–175n, 4–178
Miscimarra, P.A.   4–212n, 4–216
Mitchell, D.J.B.   4–78n, 4–80,
    4–212n, 4–216
Mobley, W.H.   4–176n, 4–179
Molleston, J.L.   4–176n, 4–179
Molloy, E.S.   4–78n, 4–78
Morral, J.F.   4–277n, 4–282
Morse, E.P.   4–278n, 4–284
Morton, T.L.   4–276n, 4–282
Mowday, R.T.   4–77n, 4–80
Munger, M.C.   4–21n, 4–21
Mur, R.   4–123
Murrey, J.H., Jr.   4–122
Myers, S.   4–40n, 4–41

Nadler, D.A.   4–77n, 4–80
National Association of
    Manufacturers   4–277n,
    4–282
National Cancer Institute, 4–278n,
    4–283
National Institutes of Health   4–279n,
    4–283
National Safety Council   4–277n,
    4–279n, 4–283
Nelson, F.D.   4–176n, 4–177,
    4–212n, 4–215
Neumann, G.   4–28n, 4–40n, 4–43
New York Stock Exchange   4–78n,
    4–80
New York Times   4–174n, 4–278n,
    4–283
Newsweek   4–277n, 4–278n, 4–283
Nickelsburg, G.   4–28n, 4–40n,
    4–41n, 4–43
Nobile, R.J.   4–121n, 4–125
Norris, J.A.   4–147n, 4–178
Northrup, H.R.   4–211n, 4–212n,
    4–216, 4–277n, 4–283
Nurick, A.J.   4–175n, 4–178

O'Dell, D.   4–78n, 4–80
Oldman, G.R.   4–212n, 4–215
Olian, Judy D.   4–218—4–285,
    4–277n, 4–278n, 4–279n,
    4–281, 4–283
Olson, C.A.   4–28n, 4–40n, 4–41
O'Reilly, C., III   4–176n, 4–176
Osterman, P.   4–40n, 4–43

Pagnotto, L.D.   4–278n, 4–284
Palmer, G.M.   4–121n, 4–122n,
    4–123
Parker, M.   4–77n, 4–80
Parker, V.D.   4–211n, 4–215
Pepe, S.P.   4–119n, 4–120n, 4–121n,
    4–124
Perry, C.R.   4–176n, 4–178, 4–212n,
    4–214n, 4–216, 4–277n,
    4–283
Peters, T.J.   4–40n, 4–43
Peterson, M.M.   4–213n, 4–216
Peto, R.   4–278n, 4–283
Phillips, P.   4–119n, 4–125
Pilarski, A.   4–28n, 4–40n, 4–41n,
    4–43
Piore, M.J.   4–20n, 4–21
Poe, R.   4–277n, 4–283
Ponak, A.M.   4–77n, 4–80
Porter, L.W.   4–77n, 4–80
Postal Service, U.S.   4–279n, 4–284
Poulin, G.J.   4–77n, 4–80
Premack, S.L.   4–176n, 4–176
Prentice, R.A.   4–121n, 4–122n,
    4–125
Prentice Hall/American Society for
    Personnel Administration
    (ASPA)   4–121n, 4–125
Prosten, R.   4–174n, 4–179

Rayback, J.G.   4–20n, 4–22
Redeker, J.R.   4–122n, 4–125
Reed, T.   4–176n, 4–179
Reibstein, L.   4–120n, 4–123
Reibstein, R.J.   4–120n, 4–122
Resource   4–278n, 4–283
Robbins, L.P.   4–118n, 4–125
Rodin, J.   4–278n, 4–283
Roomkin, M.   4–40n, 4–42
Root, N.   4–279n, 4–283
Rosen, P.B.   4–119n, 4–120n, 4–124
Rosen, S.   4–20n, 4–22
Rosenman, R.H.   4–279n, 4–283
Ross, I.   4–213n, 4–216
Rossignol, A.M.   4–278n, 4–284
Rothstein, M.A.   4–120n, 4–121n,
    4–125, 4–126, 4–278n,
    4–279n, 4–284
Rowan, R.L.   4–277n, 4–283
Rowe, M.P.   4–118n, 4–126

Ruback, R.   4–28n, 4–40n, 4–43
Ruh, R.H.   4–78n, 4–79, 4–80
Russell, C.   4–278n, 4–284
Rutherford, G.W., III   4–278n,
       4–282

St. Antoine, T.J.   4–122n, 4–126
Salovey, P.   4–278n, 4–283
Salsburg, S.W.   4–40n, 4–42
Saltzman, G.M.   4–21n, 4–22
Sandler, A.   4–174n, 4–176
Sandver, M.H.   4–20n, 4–21
Saunders, D.M.   4–118n, 4–124
Schein, E.   4–20n, 4–22
Schlossberg, S.   4–174n, 4–175n,
       4–179
Schneider, T.J.   4–212n, 4–216
Schneiderman, M.   4–278n, 4–283
Schuster, Michael   4–44—4–81,
       4–77n, 4–78n, 4–80, 4–81
Schwab, D.P.   4–9n, 4–11n
Schweiger, D.M.   4–78n, 4–80
Science   4–279n, 4–284
Scott, J.   4–174n, 4–175n, 4–179
Seeber, R.L.   4–118n, 4–124,
       4–176n, 4–179
Sheflin, N.   4–136n, 4–137n, 4–174n,
       4–179
Sherer, P.D.   4–213n, 4–215
Sherizen, S.   4–121n, 4–125
Silver, M.   4–120n, 4–126
Simonds, R.H.   4–278n, 4–284
Siskind, F.   4–278n, 4–284
Slaughter, J.   4–77n, 4–80
Smith, M.J.   4–278n, 4–284
Sockell, D.   4–175n, 4–177, 4–213n,
       4–214n, 4–216
Spector, P.E.   4–279n, 4–284
Spencer, D.   4–40n, 4–43
Stagner, R.   4–77n, 4–81
Staudohar, P.D.   4–123
Steers, R.M.   4–77n, 4–80, 4–81
Stein, R.E.   4–120n, 4–126
Stellman, S.D.   4–278n, 4–285
Stratton, K.   4–174n, 4–179
Strauss, G.   4–213n, 4–216
Strauss, R.   4–283
Strickler, G.M.   4–119n, 4–124
Struthers, J.   4–174n, 4–178
Summers, C.W.   4–119n, 4–126
Summers, V.M.   4–278n, 4–284

Taft, P.   4–20n, 4–22
Talbott, Vern   4–77n
Taylor, B.J.   4–119n, 4–126
Technology Assessment, Office
       of   4–277n, 4–278n, 4–279n,
       4–283
Terborg, J.R.   4–279n, 4–284
Thacker, J.W.   4–213n, 4–216
Theilmann, J.   4–21n, 4–22
Thomas, S.   4–28n, 4–40n, 4–43
Time   4–278n, 4–284
Towers, Perrin, Forster, and
       Crosby   4–213n, 4–216
Troy, L.   4–136n, 4–137n, 4–174n,
       4–179
Twomey, D.P.   4–122

United States entries (see other part of
       name)

Vaughan, D.   4–120n, 4–126
Verma, A.   4–78n, 4–81, 4–175n,
       4–179, 4–212n, 4–216
Voos, P.B.   4–174n, 4–176n, 4–179,
       4–212n, 4–213n, 4–217

Wakely, J.H.   4–78n, 4–79
Walker, J.M.   4–176n, 4–179
Wall Street Journal   4–277n, 4–278n,
       4–279n, 4–284, 4–285
Wallace, R.L.   4–78n, 4–80
Walsh, D.J.   4–213n, 4–217
Walton, R.E.   4–77n, 4–78n, 4–81,
       4–213n, 4–217
Washington Post   4–277n, 4–278n,
       4–279n, 4–285
Washington Post Health   4–276n,
       4–285
Wasson, R.P., Jr.   4–123
Waterman, R.H.   4–40n, 4–43
Watts, G.E.   4–77n, 4–81
Weber, M.   4–28n, 4–40n, 4–42
Weiler, P.   4–174n, 4–179, 4–211n,
       4–217
Weimer, D.   4–119n, 4–126
Weiss, W.L.   4–278n, 4–285
Weitzman, M.   4–41n, 4–43
Wertthessen, N.T.   4–283
Wesman, Elizabeth C.   4–82—4–133
West, R.   4–176n, 4–178

White, J.K.   4–78n, 4–81
White, R.A.   4–176n, 4–178
Whitney, F.   4–119n, 4–126
Wilhite, A.   4–21n, 4–22
Williams, J.F.   4–120n, 4–126
Williams, R.   4–175n, 4–179
Wills, T.A.   4–279n, 4–280
Wilson, D.   4–175n, 4–178
Winslett, B.J.   4–121n, 4–122n, 4–125
Wright, L.   4–279n, 4–285

Wuebker, L.J.   4–277n, 4–278n, 4–282
Wurm, M.   4–283
Wynder, E.L.   4–278n, 4–285

Yoder, D.   4–20n, 4–22, 4–123
Youngblood, S.   4–176n, 4–179

Zalesny, M.   4–176n, 4–179
Zimmerman, M.B.   4–28n, 4–40n, 4–43

Subject Index

A

Access rights
employees, to health and safety
information 4–224
employees, to personnel
records 4–111—4–115
unions, to company
property 4–154
Accident prevention 4–254
Accident proneness 4–269
Acquired immune deficiency
syndrome (AIDS)
company policies
articulated 4–259
employment discrimination, 4–226,
4–231, 4–249—4–250
health care costs 4–241
incidence statistics 4–246—4–247
testing 4–103—4–105
workplace concerns 4–238,
4–247—4–248, 4–255—4–256
Administrative Procedure
Act 4–118n
Advisory Committee on
Labor–Management
Policy 4–56—4–57
Affirmative action 4–15
AFL-CIO 4–138—4–139, 4–163,
4–166
Age Discrimination in Employment
Act of 1967 (ADEA) 4–8,
4–15, 4–16, 4–90
Agriculture Department 4–227,
4–277n
Air traffic controllers 4–182
Airline industry
labor relations 4–48, 4–49
statutory coverage 4–6, 4–142
strike insurance plans 4–191
unionization obstacles 4–185,
4–187, 4–190
wage concessions/swaps 4–192,
4–197, 4–205, 4–207, 4–208
workrule changes 4–201—4–203,
4–213n

Alcohol abuse (*see* Drug and alcohol
abuse)
Alcohol testing (*see* Drug and alcohol
testing)
Allied Bendix Co. 4–87
*Amalgamated Ass'n of Street
Employees v.
Lockridge* 4–119n
Amalgamated Clothing and Textile
Workers Union
(ACTWU) 4–208
American Airlines 4–190, 4–197,
4–202
American Arbitration Association
(AAA) 4–84—4–85, 4–87
American Council on Life
Insurance 4–237
American Cyanamid 4–252
American Federation of Labor
(AFL) 4–4, 4–138
American Management
Association 4–258
American Medical Association
(AMA) 4–239
American Plan 4–4
American Productivity Center 4–68
American Society for Personnel
Administration (ASPA)
survey data 4–242, 4–246—
4–249
American Stock Exchange 4–29
*Andersen v. Anoka County Welfare
Bd.* 4–277n
Andrade v. City of Phoenix 4–121n
Anti-Drug Abuse Act of 1988 4–227
Antitrust laws 4–4
Arbitration 4–16, 4–31, 4–45, 4–84—
4–85, 4–87, 4–229
Arbitrators, 4–84, 4–87
ARCO 4–237—4–238
Areawide labor-management
committees 4–59—4–61
Arrest records 4–100—4–102
Associate union membership 4–19,
4–163

Associated General Contracters of
    America (AGA)   4-255
Associated Press   4-202
AT & T   4-240, 4-256, 4-275
Atco Properties   4-260
Attitude surveys   4-160, 4-165,
    4-188
At-will employment (*see*
    Employment–at–will)
Austin, Texas   4-250
Australia   4-17
Authorization cards   4-143—4-144
Auto industry   4-32, 4-211
    concession bargaining, union
        initiatives   4-207, 4-208
    labor-management
        cooperation   4-53, 4-59,
        4-70, 4-73
    structural economic
        changes   4-182, 4-184,
        4-194
    workplace safety and health   4-261
    workrule changes   4-202—4-204
Automation committees   4-45
Automation effects   4-47
Autonomous work teams   4-71—
    4-72, 4-201

B

B. F. Goodrich Co.   4-207, 4-252
Back pay awards   4-16, 4-94, 4-153,
    4-156
BankAmerica Corp.   4-256
Bar to election   4-149
Bargaining (*see* Collective bargaining)
Bargaining agreements (*see* Collective
    bargaining agreements)
Bargaining orders   4-151, 4-155
Bargaining unit
    transfer of work from   4-190
    unit determination
        questions   4-149, 4-171
    what constitutes   4-143
*Batchelor v. Fresno County,
    California*   4-277n
*Beck v. Communications Workers of
    America*   4-21n
Behavioral model of employee
    management   4-182—
    4-183, 4-188, 4-189
Best Foods Co.   4-204

Beverly Enterprises   4-209
Bill of Rights   4-111
Bonham, Thomas   4-82
Borg-Warner Co.   4-87, 4-204
Boulwarism   4-181, 4-182
Bowen v. U.S. Postal Serv.   4-119n
Boycotts   4-154, 4-166, 4-208
Bratt v. IBM   4-230—4-231
Bribery   4-154
Bumping   4-202
Burch v. A & G Associates   4-120n
Burdeau v. McDowell   4-121n
Bureau of Cooperative Labor-
    Management
    Programs   4-46
Bureau of Labor Statistics
    (BLS)   4-135, 4-187,
    4-193—4-195, 4-221, 4-262
Bureau of National Affairs
    (BNA)   4-135, 4-195,
    4-203, 4-242, 4-269
Burlington Northern Railroad   4-188
Bush administration   4-57
Business Roundtable   4-232

C

Calculative employment
    relationship   4-14
California   4-227, 4-230, 4-239,
    4-250
Campbell Soup Co.   4-209
Canada   4-19, 4-53, 4-134
Captive audience speeches   4-159,
    4-164
Carter administration   4-57
Certification elections (*see*
    Representation elections)
Chemical hazards   4-238, 4-240,
    4-251—4-253
Chevron Corp.   4-256
Child care assistance   4-198
Child labor   4-3
Chlorofluorocarbons   4-261
Chrysler Corp.   4-17, 4-208, 4-212n,
    4-236
Chuckle Pops program   4-254
Civil Rights Act of 1964, Title
    VII   4-8, 4-15, 4-90, 4-100,
    4-230, 4-250
Civil rights issues (*see* Employment
    discrimination)

Civil Service Commission 4–91
Civil Service Reform Act of 1978, Title
        VII   4–7, 4–91, 4–142
Clean Indoor Air Act   4–231
Cleveland Bd. of Educ. v.
        Loudermill   4–118n
Coal mining industry
    labor-management
            cooperation   4–45, 4–59
    pattern bargaining   4–191, 4–192
    workplace safety   4–225, 4–271
Code of Professional Responsibility for
        Arbitrators of Labor-
        Management Disputes   4–84
Coercive employment
        relationship   4–14
Coke (justice)   4–82
Collective bargaining   4–180—4–217
    bargaining environment
            changes   4–180—4–186
    bargaining orders   4–151, 4–155
    duty and subjects   4–5, 4–9, 4–11,
            4–16—4–17, 4–97, 4–208
    impact on industrial
            performance   4–30—4–31,
            4–209—4–211
    labor-management cooperation
            reconciled with   4–74—4–75
    management tactics   4–186—4–190
    settlement changes   4–193—4–205
    statutory framework   4–5
    structural changes   4–190—4–193
    union initiatives   4–205, 4–207—
            4–209
Collective bargaining
        agreements   4–11
    AIDS and genetic testing
            provision   4–105
    drug and alcohol testing
            provision   4–97
    due process provision   4–83—4–84
    as election bar   4–149
    health and safety provisions   4–224
    smoking restriction
            provisions   4–244
Color-based discrimination   4–8,
        4–16
Columbia Graduate School of
        Business   4–39
Common situs picketing   4–49, 4–57

Communication programs   4–187—
        4–189
Communications industry   4–53,
        4–70, 4–184
Company unions   4–4, 4–154
Compelled self-publication   4–115
Compensation (*see* Wage entries)
Compensatory damages   4–92
Competition   4–47, 4–52, 4–140—
        4–141, 4–183—4–185
Concession bargaining (*see* Wage
        concessions)
Conference Board surveys   4–139,
        4–168, 4–189, 4–191, 4–205
Congress of Industrial Organizations
        (CIO)   4–136, 4–138
Connecticut   4–112, 4–227
Conrail v. Railway Executives
        Ass'n   4–229
Consent elections   4–146, 4–148,
        4–151, 4–165
Constitutional issues (*see* Due process;
        Privacy rights)
Construction industry   4–58, 4–162,
        4–190
Construction Industry Stabilization
        Committee   4–57
Consultants   4–158—4–159, 4–166,
        4–171—4–172
Consumer boycotts   4–166, 4–208
Consumer Product Safety
        Commission   4–223
Consumer Protection Agency   4–227
Consumer protection
        standards   4–227—4–228
Contextual control tactics   4–159—
        4–160, 4–162, 4–163,
        4–165—4–166, 4–171
Continental Airlines   4–190
Contracts
    bargaining (*see* Collective
            bargaining agreements)
    employment   4–12—4–14, 4–16,
            4–117
Control Data Corp.   4–235
Control environment   4–54
Copper industry   4–199
Corporate campaigns   4–166, 4–167,
        4–208—4–209

Cost-of-living adjustments
    (COLAs)   4–194—4–195
Cost of Living Council   4–57
Cotton dust standard, OSHA   4–232
Council of Employee Benefits   4–275
Council on Environmental
    Quality   4–233
Council on Scientific Affairs,
    AMA   4–239
Credit bureau reports   4–111
Criminal records   4–100—4–102
Current Population Survey
    (CPS)   4–135
Customs Service   4–227, 4–229

D

Damage awards   4–16, 4–92
Dana Corp.   4–207
Daniel International Co.   4–258
Decertification elections (see
    Representation elections)
Defamation suits   4–114—4–115
Defense Department   4–227
Delaware   4–17—4–18
Denver, Colorado   4–250
Deregulation   4–48, 4–185, 4–192
Detroit Edison Co. v. NLRB   4–111
Deunionization (see Unionization)
DiCosala v. Boy Scouts of
    Am.   4–120n
Digital Equipment Corp.   4–201,
    4–239—4–240
Direct action tactics   4–160—4–161,
    4–167
Directed elections   4–148, 4–151
Discipline and discharge
    arbitrary or retaliatory   4–16, 4–91,
        4–92
    due process   4–115—4–117
    lifestyle preferences   4–106—4–107
    off-duty smoking   4–106
    off-duty substance abuse   4–98
    refusal to take polygraph test   4–95
    for union activity   4–153, 4–156
Discrimination, employment (see
    Employment discrimination)
Discrimination, by unions   4–93—
    4–94

Disease Prevention and Health
    Promotion, Office of,
    HHS   4–273
Disloyalty   4–92
Displaced workers   4–58—4–59
Distribution of literature   4–154,
    4–164
District of Columbia   4–250
Domestic nonunion
    competition   4–47, 4–140—
    4–141, 4–184—4–185
Double-breasted operations   4–162,
    4–190, 4–207, 4–209
Dronenburg v. Zech   4–121n
Drug Abuse Protection and Treatment
    Act of 1972   4–121n
Drug and alcohol abuse
    monitoring concerns   4–245—
        4–246
    rehabilitation programs   4–271—
        4–273
    training and education   4–255
    workplace costs   4–236, 4–245
    written company policy   4–258—
        4–259
Drug and alcohol testing
    company implementation   4–245—
        4–246, 4–267—4–268
    costs   4–241
    due process   4–96—4–100,
        4–229—4–230, 4–246
    statutory framework   4–226—4–227
Due process (see also Privacy rights)
    discipline and discharge   4–115—
        4–117
    legal basis   4–82—4–84, 4–118
    statutory entitlement   4–89—4–94
    union/nonunion grievance
        procedures   4–84—4–89
Dunlop, John T.   4–57
DuPont Corp.   4–252, 4–257, 4–261
Duty of fair representation   4–93—
    4–94, 4–196

E

E.I. du Pont de Nemours & Co. v.
    Finklea   4–121n
Earnings decline   4–210
Eastern Airlines   4–49, 4–205

Economic theories of
        employment   4–7
Economist, The   4–265
Education and training
        programs   4–37, 4–253–
        4–256
Efficiency wages   4–35
Elections (*see* Representation
        elections)
Electrical companies   4–54
Electrical contracting industry   4–45
Employee assistance programs
        (EAPs)   4–4, 4–235, 4–255,
        4–258, 4–271—4–274
Employee associations   4–4
Employee benefits   4–197—4–198,
        4–219, 4–248—4–249
Employee compensation (*see* Wage
        entries)
Employee health and safety (*see*
        Occupational safety and
        health)
Employee participation programs
    gainsharing and profit–sharing plans
        as   4–63—4–69
    as labor-management
        cooperation   4–45, 4–48,
        4–69—4–70, 4–76
    management attitudes   4–53—4–54
    productivity effects   4–37—4–38
Employee Polygraph Protection Act of
        1988   4–95
Employee referrals   4–33—4–34
Employee relations (*see also* Labor
        relations)
    definition   4–11—4–12
    emergence and evolution   4–1,
        4–3—4–5, 4–20
Employee Retirement Income
        Security Act (ERISA)   4–249
Employee rights (*see also* Due
        process; Privacy rights)
    NLRA Sec. 7 rights   4–142—4–143
Employee searches   4–108—4–109
Employee stock ownership plans
        (ESOPs)   4–18, 4–207
Employee surveillance   4–109—
        4–110, 4–154, 4–165
Employee training programs   4–37

Employer associations   4–191—4–192
Employer liability   4–228—4–229
Employment
    definition and parameters   4–5, 4–7
    economic theories   4–7, 4–9
    future scenarios   4–19—4–20
    historical evolution   4–1—4–5
Employment and Earnings
        (CPS)   4–135
Employment-at-will   4–211
    employee vulnerability   4–92
    legal standing   4–3, 4–12
    limitations   4–12—4–16, 4–117
Employment contracts   4–12—4–14,
        4–16, 4–117
Employment discrimination
    AIDS victims   4–103—4–105,
        4–226, 4–231, 4–246—4–250
    alcoholics and drug addicts   4–97—
        4–98
    company rules   4–107
    employment tests   4–100
    drug testing   4–230
    genetic tests   4–103, 4–263—4–265
    laws and regulations   4–8—4–9,
        4–15—4–16, 4–90, 4–225—
        4–226
    reproduction and fetal protection
        policies   4–252
    smoking restrictions   4–244
    societal changes   4–14—4–15
    for union activity   4–153, 4–156
Employment relationship (*see* Labor
        relations)
Employment testing   4–100
Engineering controls   4–251, 4–263,
        4–276
Enterprise unions   4–193
Environmental Protection Agency
        (EPA)   4–227, 4–253
Environmental protection
        standards   4–227—4–228
Equal Employment Opportunity Act
        of 1972   4–91
Equal Employment Opportunity
        Commission (EEOC)   4–8,
        4–9, 4–90, 4–91
Equal Pay Act of 1963   4–9, 4–91
Ergonomic design principles   4–271

Ethylene oxide standard,
        OSHA   4–253
Europe   4–17, 4–134
Excelsior lists   4–150
Exclusive representation   4–134,
        4–143
Executive compensation   4–37
Executive Office of the
        President   4–227
Executive Order 11246   4–8
Executive Order 12564   4–98, 4–226
Exxon Corp.   4–252
Exxon Valdez oil spill   4–223

F

Facility–level labor-management
        cooperation   4–61—4–63,
        4–76
Fair Credit Reporting Act   4–111
Fair dismissal   4–117
Fair Labor Standards Act
        (FLSA)   4–16, 4–91
Fair representation duty   4–93—
        4–94, 4–196
Federal Aviation
        Administration   4–98
Federal Bureau of
        Investigation   4–101—4–102
Federal Contract Compliance
        Programs, Office of
        (OFCCP)   4–8
Federal contractors   4–8, 4–225,
        4–227
*Federal Employees for Non–Smokers
        Rights*   4–121n
Federal employment (*see* Public
        sector employment)
Federal Labor Relations
        Authority   4–7, 4–142
Federal Mediation and Conciliation
        Service (FMCS)   4–7, 4–60,
        4–61, 4–85, 4–87
Federal Mine Safety Act of
        1969   4–10—4–11
Federal Mine Safety and Health
        Review Commission   4–10
Federal Railroad
        Administration   4–98, 4–225
Fetal protection policies   4–252—
        4–253

Fifth Amendment   4–89, 4–107
Finnegan v. Leu   4–119n
*Fleisher v. City of Signal
        Hill*   4–121n
Florida   4–226, 4–250
Flowers, Gary   4–258
Food and Drug
        Administration   4–227
Ford, Henry   4–3
Ford administration   4–57
Ford Motor Co.   4–47, 4–212n
Foreign competition   4–46, 4–47,
        4–140—4–141, 4–183—4–184
Fourteenth Amendment   4–8, 4–111
Fourth Amendment   4–94, 4–97,
        4–108, 4–229
Fraser, Douglas   4–57
Frontier Airlines   4–213n
Frye v. United States   4–119n

G

Gainsharing   4–45, 4–63—4–69,
        4–73, 4–76, 4–194, 4–199
Garment industry   4–45
General Accounting Office   4–68
General Electric Co.   4–87, 4–181
General Motors Corp. (GM)   4–189,
        4–201—4–204, 4–207,
        4–212n, 4–213n, 4–252
*General Motors Corp. v.
        Piskor*   4–121n
General Services
        Administration   4–243
Genetic testing   4–102—4–103,
        4–105, 4–241, 4–263—4–265
Germany   4–17
Gissel doctrine   4–146, 4–155
Golden parachutes   4–37
Government contractors   4–8, 4–225,
        4–227
Gregory v. Litton Indus.   4–120n
Grievance procedures   4–16, 4–74
    due process provision   4–83—4–84
    filing procedures   4–85
    grievance, what constitutes   4–84
    impact on industrial
        performance   4–31—4–32,
        4–39
    management-established   4–85—
        4–89, 4–127—4–128

Griggs v. Duke Power Co.   4–120n
Grooming standards   4–107

H

Haas, Robert   4–256
Handicap discrimination
    AIDS victims   4–103—4–104,
        4–226, 4–231, 4–247—4–248,
        4–250
    alcoholism and drug
        addiction   4–97—4–98
    smokers   4–244
    statutory coverage   4–8, 4–90,
        4–225—4–226
Harvard Business School   4–29
Hay/Huggins Co.   4–275
Hazard communication
        regulations   4–226, 4–227
Health and Human Services
        Department (HHS)   4–226,
        4–227, 4–237, 4–254, 4–273
Health and safety (*see* Occupational
        safety and health)
Health care industry   4–58, 4–174n
Health Designs International   4–274
Health insurance   4–198, 4–219
Health maintenance organizations
        (HMOs)   4–275
High Risk Notification and Prevention
        Act   4–226, 4–228
Hiring practices   4–32—4–34, 4–202,
        4–263—4–270
Hollywood Ceramics doctrine   4–155
Homosexuality   4–107
Hospital Corporation of
        America   4–260
Hot-cargo agreements   4–175n
Hotel industry   4–45
Human resource management
        (HRM)   4–7, 4–19
    behavioral model of employee
        management   4–182—4–183
    effect on industrial performance (*see*
        Productivity and
        profitability)
    health and safety
        management   4–276
    unionization and   4–155—4–156,
        4–168, 4–172—4–173
Hunter v. Port Authority   4–120n

I

IBM Corp.   4–267
Illinois   4–60
Illinois v. Film Recovery
        Systems   4–229
Immigration effects   4–15
Immigration and Naturalization
        Service   4–227
Implied employment
        contracts   4–13—4–14,
        4–16, 4–117
Improshare Plan   4–63, 4–65, 4–68,
        4–69
Independent contractors   4–149
India   4–223
Industrial performance measures (*see*
        Productivity and
        profitability)
Industrial Revolution   4–2—4–3,
        4–20
Industrial Workers of the World
        (Wobblies)   4–3
Influence tactics   4–159, 4–162,
        4–164—4–166, 4–169—4–171
Information access   4–111—4–114
Information disclosure   4–114—4–115
Information-sharing
        programs   4–37—4–38
Information technology   4–1
In-plant strategies   4–167
Insurance benefits   4–197—4–198
Interest on back pay awards   4–156
Interference with elections   4–151—
        4–152
Interior Department   4–227
Internal organizing programs   4–167
Interrogation   4–154, 4–165
Interunion cooperation   4–166
Investigatory reports   4–113
Iowa   4–226, 4–227

J

J. P. Stevens Co.   4–166, 4–208
Japanese competition   4–184
Job description changes   4–201—
        4–202
Job redesign   4–45, 4–71—4–72,
        4–251, 4–270—4–271
Job security provisions   4–207
Job sharing   4–202

Johnson, Lyndon B.   4–56—4–57
"Just cause" discharge
        standard   4–16, 4–92,
        4–116, 4–117, 4–153
"Just in Time" strategy   4–71
Justice Department   4–227

K

Kaiser Aluminum   4–199
Keelor, Richard   4–274
Kennedy, John F.   4–56
Kentucky   4–59
Kirkland, Lane   4–138, 4–141
Knowledge, skills, abilities
        (KSAs)   4–5

L

Labor costs   4–23, 4–35
Labor Department   4–7, 4–199
Labor force
    demographic changes   4–14—4–15,
        4–20, 4–48, 4–140
    unionization rate   4–134
Labor-management advisory
        committees   4–56—4–58
Labor-management
        committees   4–61, 4–62
Labor-management
        cooperation   4–44—4–81
    areawide formats   4–59—4–61
    assessment and outlook   4–72—
        4–77
    current stimuli for   4–46—4–48
    definition and model   4–49—4–56
    employee involvement   4–69—
        4–70
    facility level   4–61—4–63
    gainsharing and profit
        sharing   4–63—4–69
    historical development   4–44—
        4–46
    industry level   4–58—4–59
    information–sharing
        programs   4–37—4–38
    national level   4–56—4–58
    national versus workplace
        trends   4–48—4–49
    quality of work life   4–71—4–72
Labor-Management Cooperation Act
        of 1978   4–60

Labor Management Relations
        Act   4–6, 4–7
Labor-management Relationships by
        Objectives (RBOs)
        program   4–61—4–62
Labor Management Reporting and
        Disclosure Act
        (LMRDA)   4–89
Labor markets   4–12—4–13, 4–141
Labor relations (see also Collective
        bargaining; Unionization)
    current concerns   4–14—4–19
    future prospects   4–19—4–20
    historical development   4–1—4–5
    definition   4–9, 4–11, 4–12
    laws and regulations   4–6—4–7,
        4–89—4–90
    legislative reform defeated   4–49
    positive, as deunionization
        strategy   4–161—4–162,
        4–168
Labor relations consultants   4–158—
        4–159, 4–166, 4–171—4–172
Landrum-Griffin Act of 1959   4–6,
        4–7, 4–89
Layoffs   4–186, 4–202, 4–207
Lead standard, OSHA   4–253
Levi Strauss Co.   4–256, 4–259
Lewis v. Equitable Assurance Soc'y of
        the U.S.   4–122n
Lifestyle preferences   4–106
Literature distribution   4–154, 4–164
Lockouts   4–187
Longshore industry   4–45, 4–59,
        4–185
Louisiana   4–227
Louisiana-Pacific Co.   4–209
LTV steel   4–205
Luddism   4–2, 4–20
Lump-sum payments   4–194, 4–195,
        4–199

M

Machinists union   4–53, 4–191
Maine   4–227
Manufacturing industries   4–184,
        4–193
Maritime industry   4–57, 4–58
Marriott Hotel   4–274
Maryland   4–223, 4–227

Massachusetts   4–250
Master contracts   4–191
Matthew Bender Publishing
    Co.   4–230
*McCarthy v. Washington Dep't of
    Social and Health
    Serv.*   4–277n
McClelland hearings   4–181
McGraw-Hill   4–232
Meany, George   4–138
Meat packing industry   4–45, 4–59,
    4–192
Mechanical Contractors
    Association   4–201
Medical advances   4–238, 4–240—
    4–241
Medical records   4–113, 4–265—
    4–267
Meech v. Hillhaven West, Inc.   4–20n
Merit pay   4–36, 4–200
Merle Norman Cosmetics Co.   4–237
*Metropolitan Edison v.
    NLRB*   4–119n
Meyer v. C.P. Clare & Co.   4–277n
Midland Nat'l Life Ins.   4–155,
    4–175n
Military records   4–100—4–102
Military service   4–107
Mine Safety and Health Act   4–225
Mine Safety and Health
    Administration   4–10
Minimum wage legislation   4–49
Minnesota   4–227
Minority workers   4–15, 4–140
Misrepresentation of facts   4–155
Missouri   4–226
Mohawk Valley Formula   4–4
Monitoring tactics   4–160, 4–163,
    4–165, 4–166, 4–171
Montana   4–16, 4–227
Motion picture industry   4–201

N

National Academy of
    Arbitrators   4–84
National Board of Adjustment   4–6
National Cancer Institute   4–240
National Center for Productivity and
    Quality of Work Life   4–46

National Commission for Industrial
    Peace   4–47
National Commission on
    Productivity   4–57
National Council on Compensation
    Insurance   4–234
National Highway Traffic Safety
    Administration   4–223
National Institute for Occupational
    Safety and Health   4–10,
    4–221
National Labor Relations Act (NLRA)
    coverage and exclusions   4–141—
        4–142, 4–148—4–149
    due process considerations   4–89—
        4–90
    Sec. 7, employee rights   4–142—
        4–143
    Sec. 8, unfair labor
        practices   4–152—4–155
    Sec. 8(a)(5), employer duty to
        bargain   4–97
    union recognition   4–143—4–144
National Labor Relations Board
    (NLRB)
    election procedures (*see*
        Representation elections)
    establishment and purpose   4–5,
        4–6
    jurisdiction   4–93, 4–148—4–149
    membership and
        procedures   4–152
    policy positions   4–97, 4–141,
        4–190
    regional offices   4–174n
*National Labor Relations Board
    (NLRB)*
    Detroit Edison Co. v.   4–111
    v. Gissel Packing Co.   4–174n
    v. Jones & Laughlin Corp.   4–119n
    Metropolitan Edison v.   4–119n
    v. Pfizer, Inc.   4–121n
    *Salt River Valley Water Users Ass'n
        v.*   4–121n
    Wallace Corp. v.   4–119n
National Mediation Board   4–6, 4–85
National origin discrimination   4–8,
    4–16
National Railway Adjustment
    Board   4–229

National Safety Council   4–223
National Science Foundation   4–242
National Treasury Employees Union
    v. Lyng   4–277n
    v. Von Raab   4–277n
Natural resources industry   4–54
Nebraska   4–227
New England Journal of
        Medicine   4–265
New York   4–59, 4–60
New York City Transit Authority v.
        Beazer   4–230
New York Stock Exchange   4–29,
    4–68
Newspaper Writers Guild   4–202
Nixon administration   4–57
Noise standard, OSHA   4–232
Nonunionized companies
    competition from   4–47, 4–140—
        4–141, 4–184—4–185
    deunionization strategies   4–161—
        4–162
    development of nonunion
        capacity   4–189—4–190
    unionization strategies   4–163
No-raiding agreements   4–167
Normative employment
        relationship   4–14
Norris–LaGuardia Act of 1932   4–6
North Carolina   4–227
Nuclear power industry   4–47
Nursing homes   4–209

O

Occupational safety and
        health   4–218—4–285
    AIDS (*see* Acquired immune
        deficiency syndrome)
    death and injury statistics   4–221
    health care costs   4–218—4–219,
        4–233—4–236
    impetus for managerial
        concern   4–218—4–220,
        4–222, 4–232—4–241, 4–276
    job and work process
        redesign   4–270—4–271
    management policies and work
        rules   4–257—4–260
    organizational support
        programs   4–271—4–275

preventive health care   4–237
safety committees   4–45, 4–61,
    4–76, 4–224
safety controls   4–260—4–263
safety expenditures   4–232—4–233
screening and placement
    policies   4–263—4–270
smoking (*see* Smoking)
societal concerns   4–221, 4–223—
    4–225
statutory and judicial
    framework   4–10—4–11,
    4–91, 4–225—4–232
substance abuse (*see* Drug and
    alcohol abuse)
training and education   4–253—
    4–256
workplace exposure   4–240,
    4–250—4–253
Occupational Safety and Health Act of
        1970 (OSHA)   4–61
    coverage and administration   4–10,
        4–225
    provisions   4–16, 4–91, 4–96,
        4–105
Occupational Safety and Health
        Administration
        (OSHA)   4–223, 4–240
    on genetic testing   4–103
    industrial standards   4–226, 4–232,
        4–253
    statutory mandate   4–10
Occupational Safety and Health
        Review Commission   4–10
Off-duty behavior   4–98, 4–106—
    4–107
Ohio   4–59, 4–60
Olin Corp.   4–252
Ombudsmen   4–87—4–88
Omnibus Crime Control and Safe
        Streets Act of 1968   4–121n
Open–door policies   4–86, 4–164
Oregon   4–227
Organizational commitment   4–4,
    4–54—4–55
Oscar Meyer & Co. v. Evans   4–119n
Overcapacity   4–47
Overseas competition   4–47, 4–140—
    4–141, 4–183—4–184
Owen, Robert   4–2—4–3

*Owner-Operators Independent
    Drivers Ass'n of Am. v.
    Burnley* 4-277n
Ozone layer depletion 4-261

P

Paper mills studies 4-32
Parental leave 4-198, 4-211
Part-time employment 4-202
Past practice 4-153
Pattern bargaining 4-190—4-193
Patton v. J.C. Penney Co. 4-106,
    4-121n
Pay Board 4-47
Pay-for-knowledge systems 4-71,
    4-72, 4-199, 4-205
Pay issues (*see* Wage entries)
*Payne v. Western & A.R.R.
    Co.* 4-20n
Peer/management review
    committees 4-86—4-87
Peer review committees 4-86—4-87
Pennsylvania 4-60
Pensions 4-36
People Express Airlines 4-213n
Performance measures (*see also*
    Productivity and
    profitability) 4-24
Personal protective
    equipment 4-251, 4-262,
    4-263
Personality screening 4-269—4-270
Personnel management 4-4
Personnel records, access 4-111—
    4-115
Petermann v. Teamsters 4-119n
Phelps-Dodge Co. 4-209
Philips Industries, Inc. 4-258—
    4-259
Picketing 4-49, 4-57, 4-154
*Pierce v. Ortho Pharmaceutical
    Corp.* 4-119n
*Pine River State Bank v.
    Mettille* 4-122n
Placement policies 4-202
Plant closings and relocations 4-49,
    4-167, 4-207
Plastic food containers 4-261
Plumber and pipefitter unions 4-201
Police officers 4-106—4-107

Political action committees
    (PACs) 4-18—4-19
Polls and surveys 4-160, 4-165,
    4-188
Polygraph testing 4-95—4-96
Positive labor relations 4-161—
    4-162, 4-164, 4-167, 4-168
Postal Service, U.S. 4-235
Postal workers 4-6, 4-196
Preferred provider organizations
    (PPOs) 4-275
Presidential Labor-Management
    Committee 4-57
Presidential labor-management
    committees 4-45, 4-56—
    4-58
President's Commission on
    Crime 4-226
Principle Financial Group 4-274
Privacy Act of 1974 4-111, 4-112
Privacy Protection Study
    Commission 4-112
Privacy rights 4-94—4-110
  access to personnel
      records 4-111—4-115
  AIDS testing 4-103—4-105
  communicable diseases 4-225—
      4-226, 4-231
  criminal records 4-100—4-102
  drug and alcohol testing 4-96—
      4-100, 4-227, 4-229—4-230,
      4-245—4-246
  emotional problems 4-230—4-231
  employee searches 4-108—4-109
  employee surveillance 4-109—
      4-110, 4-154
  employment tests 4-100
  genetic testing 4-102—4-103,
      4-263—4-265
  military records 4-102
  polygraph testing 4-95—4-96
  smoking policies 4-105—4-106
  social relationships and lifestyle
      preferences 4-106—4-107
  typical concerns 4-94—4-95
Probationary periods 4-32
Production standards 4-202—4-203
Productivity and profitability 4-23—
    4-43

Productivity and profitability—*Contd.*
  collective bargaining
      effects   4–30—4–31
  compensation practices
      effect   4–34—4–37
  employee participation program
      effects   4–69—4–70
  employee productivity
      profile   4–13—4–14
  future HR research
      requirements   4–38—4–39
  grievance procedure
      effects   4–31—4–32
  HR polices affecting,
      overview   4–24—4–25,
      4–39—4–40
  information-sharing program
      effects   4–37—4–38
  limitations of current HRM
      studies   4–23, 4–25—4–26
  performance-based pay plans
      effect   4–63—4–69, 4–199—
      4–200
  as performance measure   4–23—
      4–24
  productivity committees   4–45
  QWL program effects   4–71—4–72
  recruitment and screening practices
      effect   4–32—4–34
  strike effects   4–29—4–30
  training program effects   4–37
  turnover rates relationship   4–34
  unionization impact   4–26—4–29,
      4–38—4–39
Productivity sharing
      (gainsharing)   4–45, 4–63—
      4–69, 4–73, 4–76, 4–194,
      4–199
Profit sharing   4–35—4–36, 4–63—
      4–64, 4–67—4–69, 4–194,
      4–199
Prudential Insurance Co.   4–234
Pruitt v. Pavelin   4–120n
Psychological employment
      contracts   4–14
Public Employment Relations
      Board   4–93
Public policy   4–16, 4–117

Public sector employment
  displaced worker issues   4–59
  drug and alcohol testing   4–97—
      4–99, 4–226—4–227, 4–229
  due process rights   4–89—4–94
  employee searches   4–108
  off-duty behavior   4–106—4–107
  polygraph testing   4–95—4–96
  privacy laws   4–111
  smoking restrictions   4–243
  statutory coverage   4–7, 4–8, 4–142
  unionization activity and
      rate   4–18, 4–141
  unionization impact on
      productivity   4–27
Puerto Rico   4–225
Punitive damages   4–16, 4–92

Q

Quality circles   4–45, 4–47, 4–162
Quality of work life (QWL)
      projects   4–182
  assessment   4–72—4–73, 4–201
  elements and focus   4–71—4–72
  as labor-management
      cooperation   4–45, 4–50,
      4–76
  union attitudes   4–53

R

Racial discrimination   4–8, 4–15,
      4–16
Radiation standard   4–253
Raiding   4–167
Railroad industry
  drug testing   4–229—4–230
  health and safety   4–225, 4–266
  statutory coverage   4–6, 4–15,
      4–142
  unionization obstacles   4–185,
      4–190—4–192
  workrule changes   4–202
Railway Labor Act of 1926   4–6,
      4–15, 4–142
Reagan administration   4–135
  drug testing mandated by   4–98,
      4–226
  firing of striking air traffic
      controllers   4–182

labor relations attitude   4–48,
4–57, 4–141
polygraph legislation   4–95
Reasonable accommodation
requirement   4–90, 4–104,
4–225, 4–247—4–248
Recession effects   4–186
Recruitment and screening
practices   4–32—4–34,
4–202, 4–263—4–270
Reinstatement remedy   4–153
Relationships by Objectives (RBOs)
program   4–61—4–62
Religious discrimination   4–8, 4–16,
4–90
Remedies
for breach of fair representation
duty   4–94
for election interference   4–146,
4–151—4–152
for wrongful discharge   4–16
Repetitive motion disease   4–271
Representation elections
campaign strategies   4–163—
4–166, 4–168—4–172
HRM implications   4–155—4–156
interference   4–151—4–155
procedures   4–146—4–152
types of   4–146, 4–148
for union certification or
decertification   4–144—
4–146
Reproduction and fetal protection
policies   4–251—4–253
Restatement (Second) of
Torts   4–122n
Retail food industry   4–58, 4–196
Retail industry   4–54
Retaliatory discharge   4–16, 4–91,
4–92
Retirement policies   4–15
Rhode Island   4–226, 4–227
Right-to-know laws   4–91, 4–226
Right-to-work laws   4–142, 4–143
Risk aversion   4–9
Robotics   4–47
Rohm and Haas Co.   4–202
Rubber industry   4–184
Rucker Plan   4–63, 4–65, 4–69

S

Safety and health (see Occupational
safety and health)
Safeway Stores   4–236
St. Paul Companies   4–254
Salary issuses (see Wage entries)
Salt River Valley Water Users Ass'n v.
NLRB   4–121n
Scanlon, Joseph   4–64
Scanlon Plan   4–63, 4–64, 4–67—
4–69
School Board of Nassau County v.
Arline   4–103, 4–231, 4–247,
4–277n
Scherer Lumber Co.   4–260
Scientific management   4–4
Search policies   4–108—4–109
Self-esteem   4–171
Self-managed work teams   4–20, 4–72
Semiconductor production   4–238,
4–239
Seniority   4–202
Sex discrimination   4–8, 4–16, 4–252
Shah v. American Synthetic Rubber
Corp.   4–122n
Shamrock Holdings, Inc. v. Polaroid
Corp.   4–21n
Shapiro, Kenneth P.   4–275
Shawgo v. Spradlin   4–121n
Shimp v. New Jersey Bell Tel.
Co.   4–120n
Shopping Kart Food Mkts.   4–175n
Skill-based pay systems   4–199
Skinner v. Railway Labor Executives'
Ass'n   4–277n
Smoking
company policies, legal
concerns   4–105—4–106,
4–244—4–245
company policies
implemented   4–242—
4–243
effect on nonsmokers'
health   4–242
workers' compensation
issues   4–231—4–232
workplace costs   4–237—4–238
Social relationships   4–106—4–107
Social secretaries   4–4

Solicitation of union
        membership   4-154
Source controls   4-260—4-263
Speedcall Corp.   4-260
State laws
    anti-takeover statutes   4-17—4-18
    employment-at-will
            restrictions   4-16
    right-to-know laws   4-226
    right-to-work laws   4-142, 4-143
Steel industry   4-205
    bargaining structure   4-191
    labor-management
            cooperation   4-45, 4-70,
            4-73
    strikes   4-56
    structural economic
            changes   4-182, 4-184,
            4-212n
Steele v. Louisville & Nashville
        R.R.   4-119n
Steelworkers union   4-186, 4-187,
        4-207
Steelworkers v. Marshall   4-120n
Stipulated elections   4-148, 4-151
Stock ownership plans   4-18, 4-207
Stress syndrome   4-234, 4-254
Strike insurance   4-191
Striker replacements   4-187
Strikes
    arbitration in lieu of   4-84
    to compel recognition   4-154
    impact on industrial
            performance   4-28, 4-29
    management responses   4-187
    steel industry   4-56
Substance abuse (see Drug and alcohol
        abuse)
Supervisors
    monitoring of union
            activities   4-156, 4-160,
            4-165
    NLRA exclusion   4-149
    position elimination   4-201—4-202
    substance abuse training   4-255
Surgeon General smoking
        report   4-242
Surveillance   4-109—4-110, 4-154,
        4-165

Surveys and polls   4-160, 4-165,
        4-188
Sweden   4-17

T

Taft–Hartley Act of 1947   4-6, 4-89,
        4-141, 4-142, 4-150
Takeover statutes   4-17—4-18
Tasks, duties, responsibilities
        (TDRs)   4-5
Taylor, Frederick   4-4
Teamsters union   4-207
Technological change   4-47, 4-58—
        4-59
Technology Assessment, Office
        of   4-240
Technostress   4-234, 4-254
Telecommunications industry   4-185,
        4-199
Tennessee   4-15
Teratogens   4-252
Thorne v. City of El
        Segundo   4-121n
Three Mile Island   4-223
Tire industry   4-189, 4-213n
Tort of bad faith dealing   4-117
Toyota Motor Co.   4-204
Trade unions (see Union entries)
Training and education
        programs   4-37, 4-251,
        4-253—4-256
Trans World Airlines v.
        Hardison   4-119n
Transfer of bargaining unit
        work   4-190
Transfer of employees   4-202
Transportation Department (DOT)
    drug testing   4-227, 4-277n
    urine custody control form   4-99,
            4-129—4-133
Transportation industry   4-20, 4-184,
        4-185, 4-190
Trucking industry   4-48, 4-185,
        4-190—4-192, 4-207, 4-209
Truth tests   4-95
TRW Co.   4-201, 4-204
Turnover rates, impact on industrial
        performance   4-34

Two-tier wage and benefit
   programs   4-31, 4-190,
   4-194, 4-195

U

Unemployment insurance   4-186
Unfair labor practices   4-4
   breach of fair representation
      duty   4-93
   deunionization strategies   4-167
   election interference   4-146,
      4-151—4-155
   statutory coverage   4-89, 4-153
*Uniform Guidelines for Employee
   Selection Procedures*   4-100
Uniform Guidelines on Employment
   Testing   4-230
Union Carbide Co.   4-223
Union consultants   4-158—4-159
Union dues   4-19
Union insignia   4-154
Union-management cooperation (*see*
   Labor–management
   cooperation)
Union recognition   4-135, 4-143—
   4-146, 4-161, 4-208
Union-security clauses   4-142
Unionization   4-134—4-179
   associate membership   4-19, 4-163
   bargaining position (*see* Collective
      bargaining)
   employer opposition   4-49,
      4-139—4-140, 4-180—4-182
   exclusive representation
      right   4-134, 4-143
   foreign countries'
      experiences   4-17
   future prospects   4-19—4-20
   growth and decline   4-17, 4-134—
      4-141
   historical development   4-2—4-4
   HRM implications   4-172—4-173
   impact on industrial
      performance   4-26—4-32,
      4-38—4-39
   management tactics to
      undermine   4-182—4-183,
      4-186—4-190
   organizing efforts   4-138—4-139

   political activities of unions   4-18—
      4-19
   public support decline   4-181—
      4-182
   representation elections   4-146—
      4-156
   research findings   4-167—4-172
   statutory framework   4-5—4-7,
      4-141—4-143
   union recognition   4-143—4-146
   unionization and deunionization
      strategies   4-157—4-167
   women and minority groups   4-15
Unit for bargaining (*see* Bargaining
   unit)
United Airlines   4-207
United Auto Workers (UAW)   4-186,
   4-202, 4-203, 4-207
United Food and Commercial
   Workers Union   4-192
United States
   v. Alexander   4-119n
   v. Westinghouse   4-121n
United Transport Union   4-202
Urinalysis tests   4-99, 4-229—4-230
   DOT control form   4-129—4-133
U.S. Health Care Systems   4-274
USG Acoustical Products   4-243
USX Corp.   4-187
Utah   4-227
Utilities industry   4-54

V

Vaca v. Sipes   4-119n
Vendor certification   4-47
Ventilation systems   4-261—4-262
Vermont   4-227
Veterans Readjustment Act of
   1974   4-8—4-9
Veterans Reemployment Act of
   1976   4-91
Video display terminals
   (VDTs)   4-231, 4-234,
   4-238, 4-239, 4-254, 4-271
Vinyl chloride monomer   4-260
Vinyl chloride standard,
   OSHA   4-232
Virgin Islands, U.S.   4-225

Vocational Rehabilitation Act of
   1973   4–8, 4–90, 4–98,
   4–103, 4–225—4–226
Voluntary recognition   4–143—
   4–144, 4–161
Voter eligibility challenges   4–150—
   4–151

W

Wage concessions
   alternative pay
      arrangements   4–194,
      4–195, 4–205—4–207
   COLAs elimination   4–194—4–195
   decentralized bargaining
      effects   4–190—4–193
   decline in real earnings   4–210
   decline in union wage
      gains   4–193—4–194
   effects   4–30—4–31, 4–209—4–210
   evaluation   4–194
   management demand   4–49, 4–190
   performance–based pay
      plans   4–63—4–69, 4–199—
      4–200
   two–tier wage plans   4–31, 4–190,
      4–194, 4–195
Wage differentials   4–185
Wage practices
   impact on industrial
      performance   4–23, 4–34—
      4–37
   unionization effects   4–26—4–29,
      4–38—4–39, 4–160, 4–162
Wage–price controls   4–57

Wagner Act of 1935   4–6, 4–15, 4–89,
   4–141, 4–150
Wallace Corp. v. NLRB   4–119n
Washington (state)   4–226, 4–231,
   4–237
Watkins v. U.S. Army   4–121n
*Weiner v. McGraw–Hill,
   Inc.*   4–122n
Wells Fargo Co.   4–256
*Whirlpool Corp. v.
   Marshall*   4–119n, 4–277n
Whistleblowers' protection   4–16,
   4–92—4–93, 4–117
Winpisinger, William   4–240
Women
   in labor force   4–14, 4–15, 4–140
   reproduction and fetal protection
      policies   4–251—4–253
Work force (*see* Labor force)
Work redesign   4–45, 4–71—4–72,
   4–251, 4–270—4–271
Workers' compensation   4–231—
   4–232
Workplace safety (*see* Occupational
   safety and health)
Workrule changes   4–183, 4–200—
   4–205
Wrongful discharge   4–16, 4–117

X

Xerox Corp.   4–202

Y

Young workers   4–140